LINGUISTIC RIVALRIES

OXFORD STUDIES IN THE ANTHROPOLOGY OF LANGUAGE

Series editor
Laura M. Ahearn, *Rutgers University*

This series is devoted to works from a wide array of scholarly traditions that treat linguistic practices as forms of social action.

Editorial Board
Alessandro Duranti, *University of California at Los Angeles*
Paul B. Garrett, *Temple University*
Justin Richland, *The University of Chicago*

Thank You for Dying for Our Country: Commemorative Texts and Performances in Jerusalem
Chaim Noy

Singular and Plural: Ideologies of Linguistic Authority in 21st Century Catalonia
Kathryn A. Woolard

Linguistic Rivalries: Tamil Migrants and Anglo-Franco Conflicts
Sonia N. Das

LINGUISTIC RIVALRIES

Tamil Migrants and Anglo-Franco Conflicts

Sonia N. Das

OXFORD
UNIVERSITY PRESS

OXFORD
UNIVERSITY PRESS

Oxford University Press is a department of the University of Oxford. It furthers the University's objective of excellence in research, scholarship, and education by publishing worldwide. Oxford is a registered trade mark of Oxford University Press in the UK and certain other countries.

Published in the United States of America by Oxford University Press
198 Madison Avenue, New York, NY 10016, United States of America.

Library of Congress Cataloging-in-Publication Data
Names: Das, Sonia N., author.
Title: Linguistic rivalries : Tamil migrants and Anglo-Franco conflicts / Sonia N. Das.
Description: Oxford ; New York : Oxford University Press, [2016] |
Series: Oxford studies in the anthropology of language | Includes bibliographical references and index.
Identifiers: LCCN 2015039130| ISBN 9780190461782 (pbk. : alk. paper) |
ISBN 9780190461775 (hardcover : alk. paper) | ISBN 9780190461799 (ebook) |
ISBN 9780190461805 (online content)
Subjects: LCSH: Tamil language—Social aspects—Canada—Montreal. |
Tamil diaspora—Social aspects—Canada—Montreal. | Anthropological linguistics—Canada—Montreal. | Sociolinguistics—Canada—Montreal. |
Languages in contact—Canada—Montreal. | Tamil language—Usage.
Classification: LCC PL4751 .D325 2016 | DDC 306.442948110714/28—dc23
LC record available at http://lccn.loc.gov/2015039130

To the memories of
Simonne and Aswini

CONTENTS

LIST OF FIGURES

LIST OF TABLES

PREFACE

The idea to conduct research on the heritage language education of Tamil migrants in Montréal, Québec came to me in 2000 when I was teaching physics and chemistry at a high school in Baton Rouge, Louisiana. My principal and I bonded over our mutual experiences growing up as French-speaking minorities in the United States. She, a Cajun (*Acadien*) and native French speaker from Lafayette, explained to me that from 1915 to 1968, the State Board of Education had banned the use of French in public schools and punished students like herself who spoke it in the playgrounds. This reminded me of a college friend, the daughter of Indian immigrants, who once told me that she had been punished for speaking English at the playground of her French-medium school in Montréal. I did not enforce such a policy with my ESL students, recent Vietnamese immigrants who, coincidentally, professed to have French-educated family members of their own. I often wondered if their migration to Louisiana was influenced by Vietnam's French colonial history, even though nowadays most people of Cajun and Creole ancestry in Baton Rouge speak a Louisiana variety of English, including African American English, and not French. My students referred to me as the fast-speaking Yankee by comparison.

Federal desegregation laws required that every few months I keep track of the number of black and nonblack students (that is, Vietnamese and white) in my classroom. This practice reinforced stark lines of racial allegiance at the high school. Of all the teachers, I alone did not exclusively self-identify as white or black and would sit on either side of the racially divided assembly hall during faculty meetings. Casual conversations and observations at the school suggested that language conflicts, although less overtly discussed, further exacerbated racial and ethnic tensions. One year, a fellow South Asian teacher with a doctorate degree in biology lost her job because, according to the math teachers, students had complained about her thick Indian accent. Once again, I recalled the outrage expressed by immigrant parents who were obliged to send their children to French-medium public schools in Montréal and wondered how racial and ethnic tensions there instead complicated language conflicts. After finishing my two-year teaching contract, I enrolled in the doctoral program in linguistic anthropology at the University of Michigan to pursue a dissertation on the topic and learn more about these issues.

An animated conversation at a roundtable discussion session at the Tamil Studies Conference in May 2010 later inspired the theme for this book, "linguistic rivalry." Held each year at the University of Toronto to showcase new research, literature, and art produced by or about Tamils, the conference also presented scholarly works relevant to the Tamil diaspora. Flying in from Vancouver where I had just finished a two-year postdoctoral teaching fellowship at the University of British Columbia, and eager for feedback from an audience that promised to be mostly Canadian Tamils and fellow Tamil scholars, I was also nervous that my theoretical framework, which drew comparisons between the Tamil scholarship of French and British officials in colonial India and the Tamil heritage language education programs of francophone Montréal and anglophone Toronto, would be met with skepticism. I felt out of my realm, having only recently begun to put together ideas based on my analysis of the colonial archives in Aix-en-Provence and connecting these with findings from my ethnographic research in Montréal. After staying up all night revising the paper, early the next morning before my session began, on a whim I inserted the phrase "linguistic rivalry" to lend the presentation some drama. It worked. Afterward, a local Tamil Canadian news team asked to conduct an interview with me comparing Tamils in Montréal and Toronto, and audience members who had grown up in Paris, London, and elsewhere in Europe informed me of the different language conflicts over there. The premise that linguistic rivalries could and did grow to encapsulate competitions and debates between other communities, cities, and societies appealed to the crowd.

I ultimately settled on this title to emphasize the important role that Anglo-Franco conflicts have played and continue to play in influencing Sri Lankan and Indian Tamil migration decisions and language learning practices. My first task in writing this book was to weave together the different strands of Québécois, Indian, and Sri Lankan linguistic nationalisms into a single narrative that captured their commonalities, yet also highlighted the particularities of how Anglo-Franco conflicts have influenced local language politics. I then incorporated archival evidence from my postdoctoral research on mid-nineteenth-century printing in Tamil to compare French, British, and South Asian roles in codifying the language. Kept largely intact from my dissertation are autobiographical sections written in 2007. I wrote the rest of the book in the summer of 2014 in a small cubicle at Bobst Library at New York University (NYU) and, while working on revisions in Paris, presented four chapters at the *École des Hautes Études en Sciences Sociales* in June 2015.

Yet before this, I consulted with my uncle, *mon oncle* Jacques Lévesque, who was a separatist even before the *Parti québécois* was formed in 1968, to discuss the book from his point of view. Seated on a covered swing in his backyard in Blainville, Québec with several bottles of beer in hand, Jacques spoke proudly of his militant involvement in the separatist movement (*mouvement indépendantiste*) since 1965. He made me aware of the progressive ideology central to Québécois separatism, including its advocacy for gay rights, feminism, and tolerance, just as he spoke with regret of its shortcomings with regard to the integration of ethnic and racial minorities. Pointing out coincidences in both of our stories, he revealed that in the 1950s, he and the rest of my mother's family resided in the heart of what is now a Sri Lankan Tamil neighborhood. They even worshipped at the same church, Église Sainte-Thérèse-de-l'Enfant-Jésus, that Father Joseph first attempted to purchase with my assistance, and attended the school, École-Saint-Vincent-Ferrier, located next door to the mission house where the Father now lives. Jacques concluded by lamenting that the recent "ghettoization" of these neighborhoods has made it difficult for other Québécois folk to interact with Tamils and, just as importantly, for Tamils to interact with other Québécois folk. I did not disagree with his statement, yet in recalling the racism that I have witnessed in Montréal, did not share in his tacit blame.

We adjourned to the den to watch an acclaimed documentary from the series *1001 Vies* produced by Radio-Canada, called *L'empreinte* (*The Footprint*) (ISCA 2015), exploring the repercussions of Native and French Canadian contact on the evolution of Québécois liberalism, including the collective denial that white Québécois society maintains toward its significant Native ancestry. Mentioning that my aunt, Diane, had recently traced our family's genealogy on both the paternal and maternal sides, Lévesque and Lavoie, to France, he replied that this record represents only our white ancestors. He told me that, like many others in her generation, my grandmother did her best to erase her Amerindian heritage, defiantly informing her children, "Je suis pas une sauvagiste!" The documentary explains that the term "*sauvage*" (savage) in the seventeenth and eighteenth centuries referred in a neutral fashion to the Native lifestyles adopted by French Canadian woodsmen. Yet by the nineteenth and twentieth centuries, racist connotations of cultural backwardness, intellectual inferiority, and dark-skinned-ness prevailed. The documentary concludes that all Québécois would need to face the repressed memories of their own *métissage* in order to recount a new chapter of Québec's history and better chart the future course of a nation.

My ambitions in writing this book are similarly inclined. Writing against convention, I seek to narrate Québec's contemporary history and society by featuring Tamil migrants as the protagonists and, in addition, by illustrating the contours of Tamil belonging from the vantage point of Québec's diasporic settlements.

Many voices have been necessarily excluded in this book, which highlights how Anglo-Franco conflicts have fashioned Tamil-speaking worlds yet mentions little of other alliances or contact zones that may have been equally influential. My hope is that these omissions, contingent upon the use of ethnographic methods that are partial and grounded, will invite future retellings and revisions.

ACKNOWLEDGMENTS

There are so many people to thank for helping me research and write this book. First and foremost are the men, women, and children (who must remain nameless) who graciously invited me to visit their homes, temples, churches, and schools and who openly shared their life experiences in Montréal with me. This includes the board members of the Thiru Murugan Temple, chaplain and priests of the Our Lady of Deliverance mission, student leaders of Concordia University Tamil Mantram (CUTAM) and Québec Tamil Association, members of the Religious Studies Department at Université du Québec à Montréal (UQAM), the Trudel family, Mark Bradley, and the Port of Montreal. I also owe my gratitude to the English Montreal School Board and the teachers and principal of "Parker" Elementary School for supporting my research. To Deirdre Meintel and Patricia Lamarre of the Université de Montréal, I convey my thanks for offering me a working space at their center. I also benefitted from the assistance of many Tamil teachers, tutors, and translators along the way, including K. Karunakaran at the University of Michigan, S. Bharathy at the American Institute for Indian Studies in Madurai, R. A. Krishnan, M. Balasubramanian, S. V. Mahadevan, and R. Subramanian. The National Science Foundation Doctoral Dissertation Improvement Award, the Canadian Studies Graduate Student Research Grant, and the Rackham Humanities Fellowship funded this research.

During my graduate school years, I was most fortunate to have Judith Irvine as my dissertation advisor. No one could open my mind and give me the tools to think as she did, without actually telling me what to think, because to do so would take away the thrill of the adventure. Her reputation as an eminent scholar is well known, but it is her gentle, almost imperceptible nudges to help me consider other angles to an issue or theory or story that make her an incredible teacher, who could, with a single comment, give birth to an idea that I would chew on for years or, when needed and with great empathy, relieve the pressure I impose on myself. I am also deeply grateful for the advising, mentorship, and friendship of Barbra Meek, who shared with me her knowledge of heritage languages and Canada, her analytical prowess when it comes to linguistic detail, her lab space, and her experiences as a woman of color in the academy. The exhilaration of brainstorming sessions with Andrew Shryock, who always left me with clearer insights into human behavior as only he could, was matched by the generosity of Thomas Trautmann, who shared archival sources and encouraged me to investigate the link between Lord Durham's writings about race and language in British and French Canada and policies emerging from British and French India at around the same time. Due to the patient counsel and critical feedback of these four dissertation committee members, I finished my dissertation in due time and was soon gainfully employed.

Other faculty members of the University of Michigan who provided feedback on articles and conference papers or wrote letters of reference over the years include Sharad Chari, Jennifer Dickinson, Gillian Feeley-Harnik, Janet Hart, Jarrod Hayes, Matt Hull, Webb Keane, Bruce Mannheim, Lesley Milroy, Jennifer Robertson, and Sally Thomason. I am also grateful to the Center for South Asian Studies for providing me with academic year and summer funding through the Foreign Language and Area Studies Fellowships Program (FLAS) to learn Tamil. Friends and colleagues who proofread drafts, took notes at my defense, and supported me in writing the dissertation are Laura Brown, Nishaant Choksi, Christina Davis, Emanuela Grama, Britt Halvorson, Erika Hoffmann-Dilloway, Alexandra Mao, Laurie Marx, Robin Nelson, Xochitl Ruiz, Sherina Feliciano-Santos, Howard Tsai, Vanessa Will, and Jennifer Yim. I am also grateful to former colleagues at the Department of Anthropology at the University of British Columbia, including John Barker, Patrick Moore, Vinay Kamat, Alexia Bloch, Peter Johansen, Sonja Luerhmann, and Jennifer Shannon, for broadening my knowledge of anthropology and inspiring me to transform the dissertation into a more engaged ethnography.

In New York City, a new circle of linguistic and cultural anthropology colleagues has nourished me with their expertise and moral support during the book-writing process, opening my eyes once again to the rich diversity of perspectives in the discipline. The reinvention of my book was enriched by discussions with my senior colleague, Bambi Schieffelin, who in asking new and interesting research questions could also locate exactly the right books, articles, films, and media clippings needed to answer them. In addition to Bambi's trove of knowledge about language, I have been enriched by the work and feedback of linguistic anthropologists at NYLAWG (New York Linguistic Anthropology Working Group) and sociolinguists at the Department of Linguistics at NYU. My writing has also improved by witnessing the prowess of my anthropology colleagues at NYU in this regard, including Bruce Grant, who explained to me the nuts and bolts of academic publishing and whose careful editing of my entire manuscript gave me the confidence to assert a more emphatic and polished voice; Tejaswini

Ganti, who taught me to appreciate the value of a well-constructed argument and who shares with me a passion for South Asian language politics; Fred Myers and Jane Anderson for their last-minute feedback on the readability of the manuscript; and Noelle Stout and Aisha Khan, who gave general advice about publishing. The meticulous copyediting of Grace Gu and Schuyler Marquez and indexing by Nathan Madson also testify to the impressive writing skills of our doctoral students.

Sharing my work with anthropologists, sociologists, linguists, and historians in the fields of South Asian, Canadian, and French studies has been enormously constructive. I would like to thank Dennis McGilvray and Kira Hall at the University of Colorado-Boulder, the late Bernard Bate at Yale NUS College, Francis Zimmermann, Michel de Fornel, Caterina Guenzi, and Jean-Luc Chevillard at the École des Hautes Études en Sciences Sociales, Monica Heller at the University of Toronto, Michelle Daveluy at Laval Université, and Chris Kirkey and the CONNECT program at SUNY Plattsburgh. I have also benefitted from the opportunity to present my work at multiple Michicagoan Linguistic Anthropology conferences, American Anthropological Association meetings, conferences on South Asia at the University of Wisconsin-Madison, Tamil Studies conferences, and invited talks at California State University Long Beach, City University of New York, Université Laval, Yale University, University of Colorado-Boulder, and Michigan State University.

Many family members contributed to my research in unique ways. My great-aunt Gertrude Champagne, with whom I shared an apartment in the summer of 2002, and her daughter Andrée helped me to get my bearings during my first foray into the field. When I returned in the fall of 2004, I stayed a month with my aunt Diane Lévesque who, along with her son, Manuel Bisson, her daughter, Magali Bisson, and Magali's daughter, Anaël, became my family away from home. I also regularly visited the homes of my late aunt Rita Allaire and her late partner, Claude Chapleau, my uncle and aunt Guy and Danielle Lévesque, and my cousin Martin Allaire and his wife Manon for their candid views on Québec politics. None were as forthcoming as my aunt Francine and uncle Jacques Lévesque, though. A special thanks to my brother, Joel Das, and his wife, Susan, for giving me the family deal on their old car, allowing me to drive back and forth between Michigan, Québec, and New Jersey for years. I am profoundly grateful for the love and support of my parents, Suzanne and Asish Das, who bore with me as I labored over the dissertation and the book and never once questioned my resolve to finish. I want to thank Nasim Yaqoob for her loving care of my son, my husband, Pierre-Alex Vachon, for understanding the creative process better than anyone I know, and my two children.

I save my final praises for my series editor, Laura Ahearn, my editor, Hallie Stebbins, my project manager, Prabhu Chinnasamy, and Mela Sarkar and another anonymous reviewer, whose incisive comments, helpful suggestions, and timely feedback greatly facilitated the revision process. I also appreciate the feedback of previous editors who have worked with me on publishing related material, including Paul Manning, Alexandra Jaffe, Donald Donham, Alexandre Duchêne, and Michelle Daveluy. Portions of chapters 1, 3, and 4 appear in the *Journal of Linguistic Anthropology* (2008) 18(1): 1–23, *Studies in Ethnicity and Nationalism* (2008) 8(2): 230–247, *American Ethnologist* (2011) 38(4): 774–789, and *Anthropologie et Sociétés* (2015) 39(2): 153–172.

NOTES ON TRANSLITERATION AND ORTHOGRAPHY

Since phonetic detail is important in accounting for Tamil variation, I have chosen to represent sounds using the format of the University of Madras Lexicon. Long vowels (ā, ē, ī, ō, ū) are contrasted with short vowels, and alveolar (ṟ, ṉ), retroflex (ṭ, ṇ, ḷ, ḻ), palatal (ñ), and velar (ṅ) consonants are distinguished by using diacritic marks. Dental sounds (t, n, l, r) do not have diacritics. Following Tamil custom, voiced sounds (b, d, j, g) are usually graphically represented as voiceless sounds (p, t, c, and k), which are always voiced after nasals. The fricative sounds (s, ch) are represented here as (c, cc). Personal names do not feature diacritics, yet the names of deities and castes do. "Tamil" is spelled without diacritics. All Indian terms are pluralized in the way that English words are usually pluralized (by adding "s" at the end of the word). Words from other Indian languages are written without diacritics and by using the most common Anglicized spelling. Sounds specific to spoken Tamil, such as [ɛ], are represented using the International Phonetic Alphabet (IPA). Below are common sounds in Tamil that are not phonemic in English:

Madras Lexicon	**IPA**
ṅ	[ŋ]
ṇ	[ɳ]
ṉ	[n̺]
n	[n]
cc	[tʃ]
ḻ	[ɻ]
ḷ	[ɭ]
l	[l]
ṟ	[r]
r	[ɾ̺]
ṭ	[ʈ]
t	[t̪]
c	[s]

I use my own orthographic conventions for representing nonstandard varieties of Québécois French since there is no one agreed-upon standard. Also, I have devised transcription conventions, through the use of underlining, boldfacing, over score, and italics, to differentiate words or morphemes belonging to standard or nonstandard Québécois French, International French, literary Tamil, colloquial Indian Tamil, and colloquial Jaffna Tamil contained within a single conversation, narrative, or text. See the footnotes for a key of the specific conventions used in each segment. I italicize foreign words the first time that they appear in the text. Unless English spelling is legally required, Montréal and Québec are spelled according to the French system. Dr. K. Karunakaran, Dr. S. V. Mahadevan, and Mr. R. Subramanian assisted me with Tamil translations. All French translations are my own and have been proofread by Pierre-Alex Vachon.

LINGUISTIC RIVALRIES

1 INTRODUCTION

"Viens, pō, thanks!" a teenage altar boy named Arun says in French, Tamil, and English as we leave the Tamil Catholic mission in Montréal, Québec to visit a church in Ottawa, Ontario, where our driver, a Sri Lankan priest, is officiating at mass the next day to raise funds for tsunami victims in South Asia. The phrase's grammatical structure is loosely modeled on the Tamil expression, "poyiṭṭu vaṟēn," which literally means, "I am going and coming back," but is commonly used as a farewell. Arun, after hearing about my research during the car ride over and learning that I am keen to hear someone his age use French, Tamil, and English in the same sentence, proudly informs me that this expression is quickly catching on with his Sri Lankan friends back home. Speaking three languages is a valuable resource in defeating stereotypes about the disloyalties of Tamil Canadian youth, and Arun aims to be outspoken in dispelling these myths.

Arun represents the new face of ethnic and racial minority youth in Montréal who, after years of public and private schooling in three languages, effortlessly alternates between French, Tamil, and English in ways that confound less verbally agile youth, adults, and elders who might expect him to be incompetent in at least one of these languages. Since 2004 when I began my research in Montréal, a city considered to have the most trilingual speakers in North America, I have sought—sometimes successfully but more often fruitlessly—to find examples of French, Tamil, and English being mixed in similarly creative ways by the children of Tamil-speaking immigrants from India and refugees from Sri Lanka growing up in Canada.[1] While I had correctly assumed that they would draw on all three languages (and sometimes use multiple varieties of each) to assert their social identities, resist racialization, and display provocative moral and political stances as does Arun in rejecting assumptions of his monolingualism, I did not realize how competing values and norms of linguistic purism associated with three distinct nationalist movements, Québécois French, Sri Lankan Tamil, and Indian Tamil, would deter the uninhibited mixing of multiple languages across the different domains of Montréal's Tamil diaspora. Even Arun confesses that he rarely mixes French with Tamil. Trilingualism, indeed.

Have ideological rivalries among nationalists pursuing different social and political agendas established clear preferences and dis-preferences among Tamil speakers about which linguistic codes to combine and how to combine them? If so, then what do parents, teachers, community elders, and government officials instruct children and youth about the "right ways" to speak and write in Tamil, French, and English for engaging in social and political life at home and abroad, and how do children and youth respond to these prescriptions? How do other residents of Montréal, who are known to be hyper-vigilant about language change, regard Tamil speakers who code-switch and code-mix in these languages?[2] These questions run through my mind as I seek to understand how nationalist movements promoting linguistic purism contribute to diasporic initiatives to preserve or revitalize Tamil, a popular heritage language in Montréal.

In Canada, "heritage languages," also known as *langues d'origine* in French, are commonly understood to be languages spoken and sometimes written by aboriginal peoples, immigrants, and their descendants that, in return, define them as "ethnolinguistic minorities." Upon immigrating to Montréal, Tamil speakers who study in English or French are viewed as conveying public support for federalists or separatists in their respective efforts to integrate into larger Canadian or Québécois publics. Furthermore, depending on their nationality, Tamil speakers may be expected to profess loyalty to Dravidian politicians in Tamil Nadu, India or *Tamil Eelam*[3] separatists in Jaffna, Sri Lanka. Immigrants and refugees manage these multiple allegiances to competing anglophone and francophone, and Indian and Sri Lankan Tamil regimes by appearing to keep certain languages separate while surreptitiously mixing together unmarked linguistic resources. Since politicians and leaders are not familiar with all spoken and written varieties of French, Tamil, and English, and many instances of code-mixing in daily conversation and writing go undetected, the circumscribed audibility and visibility of these multilingual activities enable Tamil speakers to appear exclusively invested in nation-building projects when they are, in actuality, engaged in diverse world-building ventures as well.

This book weaves together anthropological accounts of diaspora, nation, and empire to explore and analyze the multifaceted processes of globalization characterizing the migration and social integration experiences of Tamil-speaking immigrants and refugees from India and Sri Lanka to Montréal, Québec in the late twentieth and early twenty-first centuries. I argue that Anglo-Franco rivalries have been a constant force shaping Tamil language politics, from the colonial period in South Asia to the contemporary period in the diaspora, driving competition and collaboration between different ethnonational, caste, and religious communities in ways that have inordinately influenced the codification and standardization of Tamil. To elucidate the exact nature and outcome of this rivalry in the *longue durée*, I draw on broadly comparative methods.

I begin by investigating whether diasporic values and goals associated with teaching Tamil as a heritage language to Indian and Sri Lankan children in Québec reinforce or, alternatively, contest provincial norms and strategies associated with state-sponsored efforts to teach French and English as civic languages to immigrants in public schools. Among my first inquiries is how parents choose among competing Tamil heritage language programs and between different French-medium public schools, English-medium private schools, and French immersion programs in English-medium public schools, and to what extent municipal, provincial, national, and international policies impact their funding structures and language curricula. Also, to explore how ideological conflicts between Canadian federalists and Québécois nationalists, and between Indian and Sri Lankan Tamil nationalists inform mundane pedagogical decisions in the classroom, I then ascertain whether heritage language teachers use Tamil or Roman script to write in standard or regionally inflected varieties of Tamil, French, and English, and whether they stigmatize the use of "foreign" English, Hindi, and Sanskrit words or permit borrowing, code-switching, and code-mixing in ordinary conversations, and for what reasons.

I also delve into the roots of the Anglo-Franco rivalry and its impact on Tamil migration and educational practices by examining archival evidence from 150 years ago. In French-controlled Pondicherry, there was a small-scale printing press run by Catholic missionaries publishing bilingual dictionaries and grammar handbooks in French and Tamil for local and overseas distribution that competed in output with Protestant missionaries and British officers working for the Madras Presidency, which instead published philological texts and literary translations in English and Tamil. Originally designed for teaching Tamil to the French officers of the *sipahi*, or Indian cavalry soldiers fighting on behalf of France against other European imperial powers, these bilingual books were later used in vernacular schools and then shipped away to Parisian libraries before eventually making their way to the colonial archives in Aix-en-Provence, France. In 1863, the governor of French Guiana also ordered a shipment of bilingual Tamil-French books to be possibly given as end-of-year prizes to the children of Tamil-speaking indentured laborers attending plantation schools there. I argue that these rival publication and distribution networks for Tamil books, translated into either French or English, contributed to debates about typography, orthography, and metalinguistic labels that became entangled with competing French and British imperialist discourses about race and citizenship popular at that time. Although most Tamil speakers living in Montréal are the descendants of English-speaking subjects from India and Sri Lanka, a few families from Pondicherry still retain this legacy of French imperialism in their political allegiances and communicative practices.

Subsequent to the Norman Conquest of Britain in 1066, protracted continental wars and colonial expansionary projects in Africa, North America, and Asia pitted England against France and engendered the mythology of an enduring Anglo-Franco rivalry (Grillo 1989). Arguably, this mythology has been kept most alive today in the Canadian province of Québec, where, despite eighteenth-century battles for territory and natural resources conclusively ending in an British Protestant victory, unmitigated feelings of persecution among the majority French Catholic population have persisted. Twentieth- and twenty-first-century politicians have since reframed this imperial narrative of conquest as one of ongoing struggle between separatists seeking Québec's sovereignty as a "distinct society" composed of mostly French speakers (Carens 1995), and federalists striving to unify Canada through legal precedents established by the Act of Confederation of 1867. The coexistence of two sociolinguistically differentiated institutional domains—French and English—in the city of Montréal attests to the delicate balance of power shared between francophone and anglophone elites, each promising a different pathway to citizenship for "allophone" residents (that is, speakers of languages other than French and English) who immerse themselves entirely in French- *or* English-speaking worlds.

Yet in 1977, legislation enforcing French as Québec's sole official language, partly drafted in retaliation of federalist policies promoting the virtues of Canadian multiculturalism, obligated for the first time immigrant parents to enroll their children in French-medium public schools. This law outraged ethnic minority leaders who perceived the lack of school choice as an unacceptable threat to their civil liberties. To win back the loyalty of ethnic minority voters, Québec's Ministry of Education increased funding for heritage language instruction in public schools and community organizations in 1978. Over the following decades, minority parents who were originally suspicious of the motives of this government-funded program became among its most enthusiastic supporters and eagerly petitioned their local school board officials to offer additional courses in heritage languages such as Vietnamese, Arabic, Haitian Kreyòl, and Tamil.

Tamil heritage language programs vary in their pedagogical approaches and political agendas, depending on how much funding they receive from provincial and transnational sources. Yet a principal contrast exists between Sri Lankan leaders, who initially collaborated with Québécois government officials to write a curriculum to preserve "literary Tamil" as their heritage language, and Indian leaders, who in modernizing "colloquial Tamil" have instead developed a curriculum on their own. As a rule, Indian and Sri Lankan children do not attend the same Tamil schools. In fact, despite speaking Tamil and sharing similar religious and cultural traditions, these ethnonational subgroups live, work, study, and worship in relative segregation from one another.[4] Therefore, in contrast to the ethnonationally mixed churches, temples, schools, and businesses that one commonly finds in neighborhoods in Toronto and Paris, estranged social relations between Indian and Sri Lankan Tamils are more the norm in Montréal.[5]

Probing into Québec's language politics partly elucidates this antagonism. Given the importance attached to language in asserting Québec's provincial identity, residents are first and foremost categorized by the government, media, and general public according to their linguistic affiliations and only secondly according to other social distinctions. This classificatory logic suggests that speakers of the same minority language belong to the same "ethnolinguistic community"; hence, French-speaking Québécois commonly refer to both Indian and Sri Lankan speakers of Tamil as "tamouls."[6] Among themselves, Tamil speakers also pay painstaking attention to differences of caste, class, regional origin, religion, and political ideology. Indian elites especially object to being included in the same ethnic group as less elite Sri Lankans without having their caste and class differences also acknowledged. Tamil leaders, by couching their identity claims primarily within a discourse of "ethnolinguistic community" familiar to the general Québécois public, have instead created the fiction of a linguistic rivalry by suggesting that grammatical and stylistic contrasts between written and spoken varieties of Tamil are representative of Sri Lankans' and Indians' intransigent moral and cultural differences. Heritage language schools reinforce these sociolinguistic distinctions by teaching a literary style of Tamil to Sri Lankan children and different colloquial styles to Indian children, who grow up believing that Indians speak "Spoken Tamil" and Sri Lankans speak "Written Tamil" as their respective heritage languages.

Nowhere else in the Tamil diaspora have researchers encountered this belief. In fact, only in Montréal does a sociolinguistic division of labor enable cosmopolitan, upwardly mobile Indians to enhance their prestige by modernizing colloquial styles of Tamil and, at the same time, Sri Lankan refugees, who seek to preserve the purity and classical provenance of literary Tamil, to assert their unparalleled cultural authenticity. Also, by declaring that their heritage languages are grammatically distinct, Indians and Sri Lankans can effectively claim separate ethnolinguistic identities and pursue divergent strategies of social and geographic mobility. Where social status is the objective, therefore, linguistic maneuvering is the means. Sri Lankan children attending French-medium public schools bring these ethnolinguistic contrasts into even sharper relief by incorporating into their communicative repertoires nonstandard varieties of Québécois French learnt through informal peer networks. Upon hearing Sri Lankan youth speak in an unaccented style of Québécois French, the public readily acknowledges them as belonging to Montréal's ethnically diverse *francophonie*. Yet Indian children who attend English-medium schools and learn standard Québécois French remain essentially anglophones in the public's eye.

Transnational politics further drive the ethnolinguistic differentiation of Indian and Sri Lankan Tamils. Although the provincial government fully funds heritage language classes offered in public schools, most children in Montréal learn to read and write in Tamil in community schools primarily funded by transnational organizations. Among Sri Lankans, the World Tamil Movement (WTM) is a valuable organizational partner that funnels large sums of money and resources into Tamil heritage language schools around the world. These investments have given rise to a small-scale heritage language industry headquartered in Canada that produces textbooks and other pedagogical materials written in literary Tamil for global distribution and consumption. In the eastern Canadian market encompassing the cities of Toronto, Montréal, and Ottawa, publishers of pedagogical materials link up with local merchants to furnish children and teachers with storybooks, dictionaries, and CD-ROMs tailored to diverse Western audiences. Translators, interpreters, and tutors working in French, English, and Tamil also seek to publicize their services through online business directories. From the perspective of the Canadian government, these heritage language industries add value to federal and provincial economies by branding Toronto, Montréal, and Ottawa as cosmopolitan cities attractive to foreign business investors and highly skilled and semiskilled immigrants.

Studying heritage language industries also provides insights into how minority languages are made to link up, through semiotic processes, with stereotypical speaker roles, stances, and activities (Agha 2005b).[7] By referring to "semiotic processes," I specifically draw from the Peircean paradigm of "semeiotics" to identify and analyze interpretative acts that naturalize causal chains and essentialist claims (Peirce 1955). Similar to other heritage industries involving communicative resources (Boudreau and White 2004; Jackson and Ramírez 2009; Kockelman 2006), heritage language industries operate by essentializing language codes and social identities through standardization. By erasing the dynamic nature of language and identity formation as a social and cultural practice, this process constructs a more simplistic view of language as a repository of tradition and cultural knowledge. Moreover, strategies involving the "allocation of resources, the coordination of production, and the distribution of goods and services" (Irvine 1989:249) that transform verbal practices, discursive skills, and linguistic codes into economic resources also serve to legitimate a local "sociolinguistic" division of labor. In Montréal, this division of labor empowers Indian and Sri Lankan leaders to construct alternative "regimes of value," defined as the "hierarchical organization of the values adhering to . . . objects" (Myers 2004:10), from inferred qualities of prestige, purity, or authenticity that are believed to be intrinsic to the grammatical forms and stylistic conventions of two distinct heritage languages: colloquial and literary Tamil.[8]

With a vast literary history spanning more than two thousand years and diverse verbal repertoires spanning multiple continents, Tamil represents a particularly rich semiotic resource for constructing alternative regimes of value. Since precolonial times, Tamil literary pandits have described written varieties of "literary Tamil" as older and purer than the vernacular varieties of "colloquial Tamil" spoken in everyday life, primarily because literary Tamil is believed to be modeled on the poetry and prose of a South Indian classical literature written during the Sangam period (ca. 100 B.C.E. to C.E. 300).[9] Colonial philologists and modern sociolinguists have reinforced this belief in the antiquity of written Tamil by categorizing the language as a *diglossic* code with functionally differentiated High and Low varieties. According to this typology, purist styles of "literary Tamil" or "Written Tamil" (*ceṉtamiḻ* or *eḻututtamiḻ*) spoken in oratorical and ritual contexts and used for writing poetry and literature have withstood the vagaries of time better than impure styles of "colloquial Tamil" or "Spoken Tamil" (*koṭun tamiḻ* or *pēccu tamiḻ*), which comprise a diverse set of regional varieties evolving through time with informal, everyday use (Annamalai and Steever 1998; Britto 1986; Pillai 1965). In 2004, the Indian government officially declared Tamil a "classical language" on the basis of its ancient literary tradition. Celebrating this news, linguists from India, France, Germany, and the United States petitioned UNESCO to establish a central library for storing rare collections of palm-leaf and paper manuscripts written in classical Tamil (UNESCO n.d.b).[10] This global collaboration underscores how Indians in South Asia and among the diaspora no longer regard classical Tamil as a living, spoken language. Yet Sri Lankans residing in South Asia and the diaspora express a different perspective; they praise speakers originally from the province of Jaffna (which includes most Sri Lankan refugees in Montréal) for retaining traces of "classical" morphology and lexicon in their everyday speech and preserving the purity of this "older" style of Tamil in Montréal.

So far, few scholars have heeded historical connections between literary production and educational initiatives in precolonial and colonial South Asia and contemporary North America. This book occasionally draws on archival evidence to explore this connection by highlighting points of convergence and divergence between colonial policies and practices in French and British India and contemporary Québec. By clarifying the causes, mechanisms, and consequences of contact between French, Tamil, and English across varying sociohistorical contexts, I aim to reveal the enduring potency of linguistic rivalries and their impact on more or less consequential matters pertaining to Tamil and Canadian societies. This book also demonstrates, through the different vantage points and writing styles of historical, ethnographic, and linguistic analysis, that multilingual practices in Montréal's Tamil diaspora are everyday actions taken to construct divergent pathways of social and geographic mobility and alternative narratives of global modernity. Interlaced throughout the book are also autobiographical vignettes shedding further light on the affective dimensions of growing up in Montréal, post-1977. Altogether, this account of Anglo-Franco conflicts and Tamil migration traverses several centuries and multiple continents to illustrate the power of commonsensical beliefs and assertions about language to construct social worlds.

An Origin Story

As a child born of a French Canadian mother and Indian father in Montréal in 1977 at the dawn of a new nationalist era, my own family's experiences of social and geographic mobility partly inspired this project. On the evening of October 30, 1995 at the beginning of my freshman year of college in California, I watched the news to learn of the results of a referendum occurring in my mother's home province. Nineteen years after citizens had elected Québec's first separatist party, the *Parti québécois* (PQ), to power on the promise that its leader, René Lévesque, would secure the province's independence from Canada, and eighteen years after the PQ had passed its most stringent law to date enforcing the official use of French in public and commercial sectors, I stood witness to the latest act in an unfolding nationalist drama focused on the question of Québec becoming an independent country. Waiting impatiently for the results, my mind wandered from how my *Québécois de souche* (that is, ethnic French Canadian) relatives, who are distant cousins of René Lévesque himself and some bona fide members of the PQ, had voted earlier that day, to whether the referendum would spark another massive wave of emigration from Montréal like the one in which my family and my father's Indian friends had participated following the 1980 referendum. When I heard the unbelievable news—49.42 percent of Québec's residents had voted "yes" for secession and 50.58 percent, "no"—I stopped to reflect on my own ambivalent reaction. Was I hoping for the separatists to win or lose? Even now I cannot say.

For many people, myself included, the 1995 referendum was a perplexing time as we tried to make sense of our social identities and political allegiances. Shortly afterward, this shared confusion turned into anger and embarrassment when Premier Jacques Parizeau, in his concession speech, blamed the referendum's defeat on "wealthy elites" and "ethnic minorities":

> My friends. It didn't work this time, but not by a great deal. And it was successful in one sense of the word. Look, let's stop talking about the francophones of Québec. Let's talk about *us*: 60% of *us* voted in favor. And we fought a good battle and we did manage to clearly show what we wanted. And we only failed by a tiny margin, some tens of thousands . . . I would like for it to have gone through . . . We were so close to having our own country. Well, it's just put off for a short while. Not for a long time. Not for a long time. We won't wait another 15 years this year. Oh no . . . It's true, it's true that we have been defeated, but basically by what? By money and by the ethnic vote.[11] (CBC Digital Archive n.d.)

Parizeau's statements shocked the public, dismayed many of his supporters, and opened new rifts among family members and communities divided by politics. Ironically, during his campaign, Parizeau had sought to unify the Québécois public under the principles of civic nationalism. Yet the explicit *nous* (us) in his speech, which refers only to those French speakers who voted in favor of the "sovereignist" movement, betrays an implicit ethnolinguistic nationalist agenda.

Noticeable changes in Québec's social and political landscape ensued after the 1995 referendum. First, Parizeau was forced to relinquish his seat as the head of the PQ in response to a fierce political backlash criticizing his views as xenophobic and anti-Semitic for scapegoating residents living in ridings with predominantly ethnic and racial minority or Jewish voters.[12] Also, from 2003 to 2012, the federalist *Parti liberal* (PLQ) repeatedly defeated the PQ in provincial elections and prevented the occurrence of any new referendums.[13] Predictably, many ethnic minorities who had voted against Québec's independence emigrated to live elsewhere in North America. Left behind were less affluent or geographically mobile ethnic minorities and immigrants who remained invested in the province's future, regardless of their actual voting records, and sought to build their permanent homes in the politically divided city of Montréal.

Among my extended family, only my eldest aunt, a proud federalist, and my mother, an American expatriate, continued to self-identify as French Canadians after the referendum. Overnight, the rest paid tribute to unfulfilled dreams of nationhood by calling himself or herself *Québécois* or *Québécoise*. My immediate family had joined the bandwagon of other anglophiles relocating to the United States in the 1970s and 1980s, even though as a mixed-race and bilingual family we were slightly atypical in this regard. By "bilingual," I mean that members of my family speak different languages with one another, depending on our kinship roles. Since birth, my brother and I have spoken to my mother only in French (or more specifically, in a Québécois variety of nonstandard French, sometimes known as *joual* or *français populaire* and commonly associated with working-class Montrealers). We speak to our father and with each other in English, just as my parents communicate with one another in this language, although we all speak to my mother's relatives in French. My brother and I never learned to speak Bengali well and only acquired passive competence in this language by hearing it spoken often between my father and his Bengali friends. Since my parents believed that children should not learn more than two languages at one time and my mother would not speak to us in English, Bengali was neglected. Raised as a linguistic purist (even though her spoken language would be considered far from pure by international standards), my mother assiduously corrected our grammatical mistakes (especially errors with gendered nouns) and spoke menacingly of the fate that would befall us if we were to mix French with English. Only after marrying a Québécois man did I learn how to code-mix in French and English, though still now I feel pangs of guilt each time I do so and hear my mother's voice in the back of my mind saying, "You will forget your French!"

My father convinced our family to move to the United States after the first referendum in 1980 partly because he did not want my brother and me to attend public schools in French and grow up as francophones. Instead, we settled in a New Jersey suburb of Philadelphia where many of his former college classmates from West Bengal lived. My mother enrolled in English as a Second Language classes at the community center with the wives of other immigrant men from our apartment complex. Even though she had learned English at her Catholic school in Montréal and spoke it well enough with my father, she could not function at full capacity in a monolingual English world. My father, on the other hand, spoke English well after having studied at an English-medium university in India and worked for Canadian and American engineering firms. While living in Montréal, my father also enrolled in government-funded French classes for immigrants and practiced speaking French with his brother-in-law, a foreman, who taught him to swear like a native joual speaker. Mercilessly, I used to tease my parents that my mother speaks English with an Indian accent and my father, French, with a working-class, Québécois accent.

Both my mother and father's families spent most of the twentieth century migrating between countryside and metropolis and learning new languages in the process. My maternal grandfather was from a small agricultural farm in the village of St-Pacôme, a tiny municipality in the logging county of Kamouraska in eastern Québec. As a young man he laid tracks for the Canadian Pacific Railway and traveled extensively throughout the region. One day, upon arriving at the small fishing village of Petite-Rivière-St-François on the opposite bank of the St. Lawrence River in Charlevoix, he met my maternal grandmother and slipped her a ten-dollar bill. She was impressed enough to marry him and, soon after, they left the region to settle in the city of Joliet and later in Montréal, joining other French Canadians of the post-WWI generation who abandoned their traditional peasant occupations for wage labor and city life. My grandfather worked as a carpenter and my grandmother as a seamstress, raising six children in a working-class, French-speaking neighborhood in Montréal. Eventually, they bought land and built a house in the suburb of Île Bizard. Neither grandparent had much education; they both spoke joual and knew next to no English (all my grandfather could say in English was "sugar"). My aunts and uncles attended French Catholic schools taught by nuns, and some later learned English in the workplace. Yet my mother, who was a transcriptionist at a French-medium hospital when she met my father, spoke little English. Apparently, a dictionary greatly facilitated their courtship.

My father comes from a middle-class Hindu family in the West Bengal town of Malda situated along the international border of India and Bangladesh. Although the District of Malda was divided at the time of Partition in 1947, when my paternal grandfather was growing up, his natal village on the Bangladeshi side was still considered part of British India. Despite being the penniless son of a low-caste artisan who died when he was only six, my grandfather was well versed in English, Bengali, and Sanskrit poetry and literature, having won academic scholarships and paying the rest of his way through grade school, university, and law school by tutoring a cousin adopted by a wealthy landowning family. My grandmother came from a village on the Indian side of Murshidabad District, where she completed a few years of primary school before getting married. In the 1930s, my grandparents moved to Malda Town, where my grandfather could practice law. There they joined a communal movement in which fellow *jāti* or sub-caste members adopted the non-Bengali and higher-caste *Vaishya* surname of Agarwal to escape prejudice targeted against lower-caste *Sudras*. During Partition in 1947, my grandfather, then the district attorney of Malda Town, exchanged his house in Bangladesh for a similarly sized one in India. All eleven children were raised and educated in Bengali-medium public schools. Most of my aunts and uncles completed their higher education studies in engineering, law, or arts in Malda and Calcutta colleges, where they learned English to varying extents. In 1965, after my grandfather was diagnosed with terminal cancer, my father accepted a job at a civil engineering firm in Calgary and left India with the intention to send remittances to support his mother and siblings. Living in Calgary two years before the Canadian government repealed its anti-Asian immigration policy, my father recollects being one of the first Indians in this city. After Calgary he moved to Vancouver, Winnipeg, and Philadelphia before settling in Montréal, where he married my mother in 1973. At first, the Canadian government denied my father a visa to remain in the country since he already had an American green card; yet the Minister of Immigration finally granted him a personal exception due to his engineering skills.

Reflecting on my family's genealogy, I often ponder the consequences of these language and migration choices on my own opportunities for social and geographic mobility. How would my life have turned out differently if we had stayed in Montréal after the 1980 referendum? Would my brother and I have attended English-medium private schools like other middle-class immigrant kids did at that time or gone to French-medium public schools like the rest of my mother's family? Would I have learned to speak, read, and write in Bengali at a government-funded heritage language school? Would I self-identify as francophone, anglophone, allophone, or something else entirely? Would I code-switch in French, English, and my heritage language, as many youth of the post-1977 generation do? Would I speak in standard or nonstandard Québécois French at home? Would I have voted no or yes for Québec's independence in 1995?

Montréal's Tamil Diaspora

In the 2000s, when the referendum had become a less politically sensitive topic, researchers began to take interest in multilingualism in Montréal from the point of view of its diasporic communities. In popular usage, the term "diaspora" refers to communities of dispersed peoples and the neighborhoods where they settle. Political scientist William Safran (1991) offers a more specific definition by stating that diasporas are comprised of immigrants and their descendants who share a common history or collective memory of an actual or mythological homeland to which they aspire to return, due to discrimination and persecution experienced in the host society.[14] Not all immigrants belong to diasporas, and not all diasporas construct their identities similarly. Drawing on historical and ethnographic evidence, anthropologist Engseng Ho (2006) further differentiates between the temporal and spatial scales of "new" diasporas—spaces of contraction where the politics of cultural and linguistic purity and "long-distance nationalism" play out in rapid time—and "old" diasporas—spaces of expansion where practices of mobility and creolization unfold over longer time-scales. Brian Axel (2004), a historical anthropologist who rejects the idea that diasporas are static and bounded communities since this conception stems from spatialized thinking about "culture" endemic to colonial and postcolonial theory, instead argues for regarding the "context of diaspora" formation as a "process productive of disparate temporalities (anteriorities, presents, futurities), displacements, and subjects" (27). Patrick Eisenlohr (2006) similarly describes the process of "diasporization" as involving ongoing reinterpretations of history and geography through narrative and other communicative practices. Drawing on these various insights,

I distinguish between the Indian and Sri Lankan Tamil diasporas of Montréal; each of these disaporas, although internally differentiated, orients itself to an imagined homeland in South Asia and relies on shared strategies of social and geographic mobility to navigate local and transnational rivalries of imperial and nationalist legacies.

Nineteenth-century colonial India, firmly under British rule except for small French and Portuguese territories located along the coastline, gave birth to the science of philology, now called historical linguistics, which endeavored to prove the divergent origins of Dravidians and Aryans as rival races and civilizations (Trautmann 1997, 2006). Nearing the time of Independence in 1947, Dravidian nationalists in Tamil-speaking South India used this research to lambaste the rumored federal imposition of Hindi, an Indo-Aryan language, as akin to a second Indo-Aryan invasion. They further argued that instating Hindi as the country's sole official language would threaten the values of democratic pluralism enshrined in India's linguistically demarcated provinces. In 1967, the federal government succumbed to threats of secession from Tamil Nadu and agreed to recognize the majority languages of all Indian provinces. Furthermore, the government allowed English to serve as a co-official language along with Hindi. These legislative moves ended talks of secession in Tamil Nadu yet could not reverse the decades of stigma attached to high-caste Tamil Brahmins, historically portrayed by Dravidian nationalists as the Indo-Aryan purveyors of a Sanskritized language and religion in the south. In the late nineteenth century and through the 1950s and 60s at the height of the Dravidian nationalist movement, Tamil Brahmins migrated en masse to Indian cities outside of Tamil Nadu (such as Bangalore, Mumbai, and Delhi) and abroad to avoid altering their linguistic and religious habits and adapting to the dominant nationalist ethos of Dravidian politicians. Today, Tamil Brahmins from all over the world commemorate their families' urban and cosmopolitan migration histories as part of a "middle-class caste" legacy (Fuller and Narasimhan 2008, 2014).

Race and ethnic relations in colonial Ceylon, successively governed by the Portuguese, Dutch, and British, were instead forged by growing socioeconomic inequalities between a rural Sinhalese-speaking Buddhist majority and a powerful Tamil-speaking Hindu and Catholic minority centered in Jaffna and Colombo. Although Tamils had disproportionately benefitted from colonial British patronage before Independence in 1948 due to their privileged access to English missionary schools, after the British recommended that the postcolonial Parliament be based on numerical rather than communal representation, this irrevocably changed the country's balance of power. A newly elected Sinhalese-Buddhist-majority Parliament imposed quotas restricting the number of desirable government jobs and university seats granted to Tamils and instituted Sinhala as Sri Lanka's sole official language. These policies, which ensured fewer English-educated Tamil students and fewer government services in Tamil, instigated a separatist movement to create an "Eelam" state in the Jaffna homeland of northeastern Sri Lanka, where Tamils are the historical majority. In 1983, civil war broke out between the government's army and the paramilitary forces of the Liberation Tigers of Tamil Eelam (LTTE) after a violent anti-Tamil pogrom in Colombo led to many civilian deaths. Both sides endorsed Orientalist narratives about the racial and linguistic purity of Sinhalese and Dravidian civilizations to assert their sovereignty claims. This took a heavy toll on an entire generation of children once brought up to speak both Sinhala and Tamil and who could no longer acquire knowledge of the other language due to educational policies favoring monolingual schooling. Language shift was most pronounced among Sinhalese living in the south and Tamils in the north, where a decline in English-medium schooling also negatively impacted oral proficiency in this prestige language.

In 1967, English-dominant urban elites were among the first cohorts of Tamil speakers to settle in Montréal, after the Canadian government eliminated discriminatory restrictions on Asian immigrants that dated back to a head tax imposed in 1885 and quotas imposed in 1923 (Haque 2012). Many Brahmins emigrated from large cities in Tamil Nadu, such as Chennai, Coimbatore, and Madurai, and elsewhere in India, such as New Delhi, Bangalore, and Mumbai; a few Sri Lankan Tamils also emigrated from Colombo (Statistics Canada 1991a, 1991b). Trained as engineers, doctors, and scientists, these educated, well-to-do, high-caste professionals purchased single-family homes in middle-class or affluent neighborhoods and suburbs of Montréal, where they enrolled their children in English-medium public and private schools before sending them to universities elsewhere in Canada and the United States. Among this cohort, only two to three thousand remained in Montréal after the election of 1976 and the passage of Bill 101 in 1977, due to concerns that working in French-dominant businesses or sending their future children to French schools would jeopardize their family's social and geographic mobility.

During Sri Lanka's civil war from 1983 to 2009, Sri Lankan Tamil immigration to Canada vastly outpaced Indian Tamil immigration, which by then had slowed to a trickle. Instead of high- and middle-caste and upper-middle-class families arriving from Colombo and Chennai, immigrants and refugees from Jaffna and rural regions in the island's northeast predominated. Many of these refugees belonged to lower castes and had experienced dire losses in wealth and status in wartime Sri Lanka due to the government's restrictions on higher education and interruptions in post-secondary education. Many also lacked adequate speaking knowledge of English or French to qualify as federal skilled workers and struggled upon arrival to validate their university accreditations. Countless men and women once respectably employed as teachers and engineers in prewar Sri Lanka became mechanics, factory workers, and convenience store managers in Montréal. Newcomers will usually join their relatives in overcrowded apartments in lower-income neighborhoods, where they can remain for several months until they learn how to navigate the asylum process and save money to move elsewhere. Some aspire to purchase homes in middle-class neighborhoods, whereas others dream of returning home to Jaffna after the war.

Despite such hardships, between twenty and thirty thousand Sri Lankan Tamil refugees currently reside in Montréal.[15] Overall, the global diaspora regards the Canadian government's record in granting asylum to applicants of minority race, religion, and political views in a positive light, especially compared to American, Australian, and European statistics (Cheran 2000, 2007).[16] Canadian law professes to "offer refugee protection to people in Canada who fear persecution and are unwilling or unable to return to their home country" (Citizenship and Immigration Canada n.d.). Judges in federal courts generally sympathize with the well-rehearsed narrative that Sri Lanka's Sinhalese-Buddhist-dominant government has persecuted Tamil citizens. Other asylum seekers accuse the LTTE of kidnapping child soldiers and extorting money from civilians. Since many Canadians regard the LTTE as terrorists, this narrative also proves convincing. In the 1990s, 90 percent of Sri Lankan Tamil applicants received political asylum in Canada (International Crisis Group 2010).

Toronto's Sri Lankan Tamil population, which at two hundred to three hundred thousand is ten times larger than Montréal's, is indisputably the largest in the global diaspora. Toronto is also presumably the LTTE's diasporic headquarters, with Montréal acting as an important auxiliary office. Given the choice, most refugees would prefer to settle in the "Little Jaffna" neighborhoods of Scarborough and Mississauga in metropolitan Toronto than in Montréal's smaller and poorer "Little Jaffna" neighborhoods in Côte-des-Neiges, Parc-Extension, and Dollard-des-Ormeaux. For one, children in Toronto are free to attend English-medium schools, whereas in Montréal they must attend French-medium schools and comply with pro-francophone policies. Despite these preferences, however, less affluent and politically well-positioned refugees often have no choice but to join their sponsoring relatives who are already established in Montréal. When in 1991 the Québec government instituted a new law favoring the admission of immigrants from French-speaking countries, South Asian applicants who could demonstrate an affinity for assimilating into francophone society or learning French also increased their likelihood of being admitted to Québec.

Indian Tamils have consistently supported anglophone and federalist causes since they immigrated to Canada beginning the 1960s. Accounting for Sri Lankans' political allegiances is more complicated because the members of a multigenerational family may have conflicting political affiliations and speak in standard or nonstandard styles of French (including European, African, Caribbean, and Canadian varieties) learnt through different educational and social networks. Sometimes, French varieties and code-mixing practices that are stigmatized as lacking prestige elsewhere are viewed by residents as being more "authentic" than speaking a purist French and Tamil or Standard English. These contestations fuel heated discussions about what constitutes "good" or "bad" speech and highlight the public's growing awareness of arbitrary linguistic standards.

Hyperawareness of arbitrary linguistic standards also extends to adult community leaders who design and implement curricula to teach heritage languages to children growing up in Montréal. Since choosing a medium of instruction is tantamount to endorsing a standard language, leaders carefully base this decision on consensus or precedent. All schools in South Asia teach in literary Tamil (*e̱lututtami̱l*), a standardized and codified language written in Tamil script that is described as being stylistically and morphosyntactically similar to classical Tamil; that is, literary Tamil shares some vocabulary, as well as similar verb endings and word order, with classical Tamil. Colloquial Tamil (*peccutami̱l*)—what people speak in everyday life—is more difficult to represent graphically because it lacks Tamil characters for certain sounds (Annamalai 2007; Schiffman 1998). No standardized pedagogical materials exist for teaching colloquial Tamil in South Asian schools. Yet in Montréal, where community leaders have divided the labor of preserving the literary language and modernizing the colloquial language by encouraging Sri Lankans to teach in "Written Tamil" and Indians to teach in "Spoken Tamil," teachers have developed two distinct curricula, each with its own codified standard and different script system, that collectively characterize Written Tamil and Spoken Tamil as two grammatically distinct heritage languages with their own unique qualities—old vs. modern, authentic vs. elite, and pure vs. impure.

Such ideas about linguistic prestige, antiquity, and purity are examples of language ideologies, discussed widely in the anthropological literature (Kroskrity 2000; Schieffelin et al. 1998; Silverstein 1979). Linguistic anthropologist Judith Irvine defines these as "the cultural (or subcultural) system of ideas about social and linguistic relationships together with their loading of moral and political interests" (1989:255) to emphasize that language ideologies often serve the agendas of elites by concealing how comments about the nature of language are also evaluations of speakers' and writers' attributes and activities (see also Irvine and Gal 2000; Woolard 1998; Woolard and Schieffelin 1994).[17] Whether they are explicitly asserted or implicitly immanent through cultural practices and worldviews, language ideologies are always formed through semiotic processes and naturalized by historical narratives, institutional practices, and state policies.

In Montréal's Tamil diaspora, several language ideologies mediate the economic valuation and social valorization of heritage languages as both commodity and emblematic good. In reality, literary Tamil is not a direct descendant of classical Tamil, just as certain regional varieties of colloquial Tamil are neither more nor less pure or modern than literary Tamil. What colonial scholars and some modern sociolinguists have labeled as literary (or "Written Tamil") and colloquial (or "Spoken Tamil") have always exhibited signs of contact with other languages—principally Sanskrit and Hindi, but also increasingly English (Annamalai 2011). Whose moral and political interests do the simplifying and erasing of these complex histories of language contact serve? What analytic tools do linguists and anthropologists have at their disposal to recontextualize this language change in non-essentialist terms? If, as Terry Eagleton suggests, "the study of ideology is among other things an inquiry into the ways in which people may come to invest in their own unhappiness" (1991:xiii), then perhaps analyzing the language ideologies pertaining to Tamil heritage language education in Montréal will elucidate some of these high-stakes struggles between elites and non-elites over contested social, political, and moral values.

Language Contact and Issues of Scale

Narratives about contact offer explanations and, at times, admonishments for the human-created forces of impurity or corruption threatening vulnerable or endangered languages. Or alternatively, they celebrate language mixing as a means to liberate endangered languages and their speech communities from decline and hardship. Even though such narratives may appear to be logically opposed to one another, they collectively participate in a unitary "moral narrative of modernity" (Keane 2007). Modernist narratives, which include assorted stories and intuitions about the inevitability and universality of human liberation and historical progress, first circulated through the intertwined projects of Protestantism, print capitalism, and European colonialism and then spread globally from the sixteenth through the nineteenth century (Appadurai 1996; Berman 1982; Eisenstein 1983; Habermas 1981; Harvey 1990). This discursive regime posited a fundamental contrast between society and nature upon which finer-grained oppositions between the modern (that is, rational, scientific, urban, avant-garde, literate West) and the premodern (that is, tradition-bound, provincial, oral non-West) were then rationalized, despite the existence of many proliferating hybridities (including those produced in contexts of language contact) defying this hegemonic order (Bauman and Briggs 2003; Comaroff and Comaroff 1993; Gilroy 1993; Latour 1993).

Irvine (2004) further suggests that oppositional versions of modernist narratives commonly appear as dyadic pairs in the conversations of policymakers, language activists, and academics. For example, technocratic talk about the inevitability of scientific progress justifies proposals for internationalist policies designed to preserve cultural and linguistic traditions and heritage (Duchêne 2008; Kirshenblatt-Gimblett 2004; Schmitt 2008). Chief among dialogically constructed dyads are also stories about modernization that posit a radical break between the present and past, juxtaposed with those positing a break between the present and future, that is, stories about globalization (Tsing 2000). In fact, cultural anthropologists Jean Comaroff and John Comaroff argue that the condition of modernity itself generates transformations that "have made the very idea of 'the global' thinkable in the first place" (1993:xiii). Across diverse projects of global modernity, similar images and tropes that celebrate a liberated world order of networks and circulatory flows often rationalize or prescribe communication in a futurist world as moving predictably toward greater uniformity for some people, and greater fragmentation for others (Blommaert 2010; Gal 2012; Heller and Duchêne 2012). Since narratives of contact between the languages of migrants, indigenous peoples, and settlers are no exception to this rule (Eisenlohr 2006; Faudree 2013; Makihara and Schieffelin 2007; Meek 2010; Silverstein 1996), there is a particular need for historiographers and ethnographers to collectively "disentangle the dialectics of continuity and change that characterize all social milieus" (Comaroff and Comaroff 1993:xiv) through discourse analysis.

Heritage language programs ranging from Hindi schools in Mauritius (Eisenlohr 2006), Yiddish schools in New York City (Fader 2009), and Tamil schools in Montréal (Das 2008, 2011) specifically contribute to projects of global modernity by producing homogenizing discourses that essentialize languages as emblems of cultural heritage on the verge of extinction or renewal. Indian and Sri Lankan Tamil schools in Montréal additionally promote narratives of language contact that underscore the two diasporas' alternative visions of global modernity. One such narrative highlights the globalist project of Indian Tamils to reenact the transcontinental scale of their imagined homeland, "Tamilagam," through acts of leisurely travel and commercial venture. Late nineteenth and early twentieth-century Tamil nationalists first popularized the use of this cartographic topography, which encompasses South India and Sri Lanka and sometimes includes Tamil diasporas in Southeast Asia and abroad, to promote the idea of a cosmopolitan yet primordial Dravidian civilization resisting the encroachment of Hindi and yet welcoming of other prestigious foreign languages (Ramaswamy 1997). Latching onto this idea, socially and geographically mobile Indians in Montréal have founded a community organization named "Tamilagam" to publicize their own transnational experiences, cosmopolitan aspirations, and prestigious multilingual practices. Sri Lankan Tamils instead subscribe to a globalist mission articulated by the WTM, which raises funds to elicit international awareness of the plight of Sri Lankan Tamil refugees and, simultaneously, to replicate the ancient language of Jaffna in Canada and secure the sovereignty of the Tamil Eelam state in northeastern Sri Lanka. Incidentally, both Indian and Sri Lankan globalist narratives conjure similar ideological distinctions between the linguistic qualities of modernity and tradition. These ideas were first popularized by eighteenth- and nineteenth-century European scholars, including French and British rivals, printing separate grammars and dictionaries of colloquial and literary Tamil.

Montréal's heritage language programs, especially the publicly funded ones, also popularize migration narratives depicting speakers of minority languages as the mediators of Anglo-Franco conflicts in Québec. The implicit mission of these educational programs is thus to guarantee the loyalty of heritage language speakers in reproducing Québec as a majority anglophone or francophone society. From the perspective of Tamil leaders, however, divisive Canadian politics potentially threaten the long-term profitability of the heritage language industries in which they are financially and politically invested. Increasingly, minority children who feel pressured to integrate into either anglophone or francophone society are responding like Arun by code-mixing in innovative ways that challenge the essentialist logic of heritage language programs, especially those endorsing norms of linguistic purity and promoting identification within a single ethnolinguistic community. Ethnic minority leaders also worry that the government may soon replace popular heritage language programs with new initiatives to teach "international languages." Notably, proposals to fund the provincial-wide instruction of Spanish and Arabic over, say, Tamil and Tagalog directly correlate the geopolitical value of a minority language with its number of speakers worldwide. These technocratic discourses expose the hierarchical scaling of heritage languages, ranging from ones esteemed to be fully international, such as Spanish, to those only diasporic in scale, such as Tamil.

Scale-making projects of a global order employ various metrics to quantify and qualify indices of social and linguistic change.[18] Among these, cartographic metrics plot geographically precise points of latitude and longitude and project three-dimensional grids onto municipal, provincial, national, and international territories to show isomorphic differences in *degree* from "local" to "global." Temporal metrics instead parse time into units of *duration*, such as decades, centuries, eons, and radiocarbon half-lives, or qualities of *durability*, such as classical, timeless, modern, and evolving, to construct alternative genealogies of human activity. In both cases, one can feasibly "scale up" or "scale down" these metrics to alter their basic spatial or temporal dimensions while maintaining an invariant ratio between the coordinates. Sociolinguist Jan Blommaert's (2007) discussion of "sociolinguistic scale" illustrates this principle of scalability. Elaborating on linguistic anthropologist Michael Silverstein's (2003) concept of the "indexical order," Blommaert explains how processes of typification concomitantly change the value of communicative resources in accordance with users' shifts in social and geographic mobility.

However, when transformations in social mobility and political regime introduce new metric standards, one begins to notice the "contested and ideological nature of scale" (Friedman and Das 2013). For example, sociolinguists Crispin Thurlow and Adam Jaworski (2010) expose how criteria constituting the "international" and "high-speed" dimensions of hyper-elite travel continuously move out of reach of most ordinary consumers who comprehend little of what these dimensions and velocities actually entail. Cultural anthropologist Anna Tsing (2000) similarly suggests that global "scale-making" projects of various institutional orders—environmental, legal, commercial, etc.—privilege the use of spatial and temporal metrics that disproportionately emphasize elite experiences in the historical and ethnographic record. To rectify these biases, one can attempt to combine the ethnographic and archival analysis of both elite and non-elite discourses of global modernities, such as those expressed by Indians and Sri Lankans in Montréal, to illuminate the specific sociohistorical circumstances under which competing metric standards can and do indeed challenge hegemonic globalist discourses.

Far from advocating for the greater use of quantitative methods in ethnography, therefore, I suggest paying attention to mathematical concepts and operations such as scale and scaling to disclose how people *interpret* complex semiotic processes to reproduce social hierarchies. As linguistic anthropologist Dell Hymes once noted, there is a longstanding ethnographic tradition that originally developed from a "branch of formal scientific inquiry" which draws inspiration from "qualitative and discrete mathematics, not statistics or experimental measurement" (1977:166). Rigorously comparative, these ethnographic methods seek to decipher patterns of functional contrast across linguistic elements by asking questions such as, "which changes of form have consequences for meaning [and] what choices of meaning lead to changes of form" (1997:174). To be exact, Hymes did not envision this relationship to be correlational but instead dialectic (Blommaert 2008; Silverstein 1985), a statement that gives us insights into the mystifying properties of scale.

Even though linguist and anthropologist Paul Friedrich (1991) argues that formal tropes such as scalar metaphors discursively resonate with the statistical properties of the world, it is perhaps more accurate to state that grammatical structures and everyday communicative practices objectify notions of time and space in ways that reinforce the dominance of certain scalar metaphors (Hill and Mannheim 1992:397). Why else would the fallacy that linguistic evidence is micro in scale and cultural evidence is macro persist even though the mutual patterning of language and culture in grammar, interaction, and ideology has been decisively proven (see Silverstein 1985)? Why else would studies of language contact overwhelmingly rely on the use of temporal metrics with fixed origins and regularized units of change to analyze how mixed codes or other languages evolve, even though such processes are rarely unidirectional or predictable? Why else would politicians and activists describe the grammatical and phonological forms of some languages as more mutable or durable than others, if not to deny coeval status to the speakers of "Othered" languages?

My questions echo those posed by Judith Irvine and fellow linguistic anthropologist Susan Gal, who identify three semiotic mechanisms—rhematization, fractal recursivity, and erasure—driving all processes of sociolinguistic differentiation (Irvine and Gal 2000).[19] What I add to this discussion is the ethnographic and historical investigation of how interlocutors make sense of and act upon what they perceive as the inevitable *directionality* of ethnolinguistic identification and language shift, the material *durability* of linguistic and other semiotic resources, and the auditory and perceptual *discreteness* of phonological and grammatical forms, in ways that authenticate global scale-building projects. When Indians and Sri Lankans debate how to differentiate between the grammar and phonology of colloquial and literary Tamil and combine these with French and English, they are also arguing about the *discreteness* and *durability* of standard and nonstandard linguistic forms used in the past, present, and imagined future among different societies. Many reputations and livelihoods are at stake in these contestations. Indian Tamil immigrants can showcase their "cosmopolitan" languages to enhance their upward mobility, and Sri Lankan Tamil refugees, dispossessed of their ancestral homes by a war and tsunami in Jaffna, can draw on the resources of their "primordialist" language to rebuild their homeland in the diaspora and, from there, launch a "global" critique of racism, war, and environmental devastation.

This book thus foregrounds diverse narratives of contact and experiences of global modernity arising out of the context of Montréal's Tamil diaspora to deepen our understanding of scale in three respects. First, I demystify scale as an ideological construct that, although privileging elite experiences, is also contestable by non-elites. Second, I discuss how the principle of scalability involves establishing metric standards that must at least appear to be based on regularized units of hierarchical value. Finally, I affirm that the hegemonic status of spatial scales like "global" or "local" and temporal scales like "modern" or "classical" is based on the near-ubiquitous use of scientific metrics such as chronological time or GIS coordinates, in addition to statistical "indicators" (Merry 2011), to analyze complex social problems of national and global governance. It is insufficient to measure, using statistical and mapping techniques, the hardships of migrants fleeing war, racism, and a global warming–induced tsunami, when by instead employing ethnographic and archival methods to identify metrics foundational to their global imaginaries, subtler nuances to these experiences can be revealed. For Tamils, these nuances point to rituals that instantiate the scope of human travel as a consubstantial and contiguous relationship to itinerant religious icons, and narratives that calculate the passage of time in terms of fateful serendipities, among other cultural practices.

Of Tides and Wars

International events of large-scale devastation abruptly marked the start and end of my research among Montréal's Tamil diaspora. Although I moved to Montréal in November 2004, my research did not begin in earnest until after the Indian Ocean tsunami struck on December 26, 2004. Remembered as one of the most destructive natural disasters in recorded history, this series of tidal waves temporarily linked together the misfortunes of Tamil speakers living in India and Sri Lanka with the coastal peoples of Southeast Asia and eastern Africa and prompted assurances of humanitarian assistance from governments and nongovernmental organizations (NGOs) worldwide. Among the most active mobilizers of international aid were Tamil NGOs familiar with rebuilding efforts in Sri Lanka after more than two decades of civil war. Able to exploit vast fundraising networks, they amassed resources and volunteers to help rehabilitate the tsunami-ravaged regions of South Asia.

Anusha Ondaatje, a journalist for the London-based online newspaper *Tamil Guardian*, specifically applauded the LTTE's humanitarian efforts when she wrote, "Sri Lanka's Tamil Tigers group is using its own funds to build homes for tsunami survivors in areas under its control, raising concern aid money still isn't reaching the parts of the island were [*sic*] it's needed most" (2005). Other online newspapers such as *Tamilnet.com, TamilCanadian.com*, and *TamilEelamNews.com*, which had openly supported the LTTE during the war, published similarly appreciative reports of the paramilitary group. Standing out among these is Tamilnet, described by cultural anthropologist Mark Whitaker as a "spectacularly successful indigenous cyberactivist site" that challenges the government's and the foreign presses' narrow and often biased coverage of Sri Lanka's ethnic conflict (2006:256). Founded in 1995 by expatriate engineers and computer scientists living in North America and Europe and then reorganized in 1996 into a Sri Lankan–based wire service by Dharmeratnam Sivaram, a former member of the People's Liberation Organization of Tamil Eelam and an esteemed newspaper columnist before he was killed in 2005, Tamilnet became "*de rigeur* reading" for all expatriates, government officials, and foreign news agencies, including BBC, Reuters, AP, and *The Hindu*, seeking first-hand journalistic reports of wartime and tsunami casualties and relief efforts.

Rumors soon circulated through these online newspapers that the Sri Lankan government, led by then-President Chandrika Kumaratunga, was obstructing aid from reaching hard-hit areas in northern and eastern Sri Lanka from where most refugees in Montréal and Toronto emigrated. Official reports published by the Task Force for Relief and Reconstruction confirmed that only $58 of $919 million US dollars collected in aid since December 2005 had safely reached the northern Tamil cities of Jaffna, Mullaitivu, and Kilinochchi. Upon hearing this news, Sri Lankan Tamils in Toronto and Montréal began donating their money directly to the Tamil Rehabilitation Organization (TRO), a transnational organization established in 1985 to build shelters for internally displaced war refugees. The TRO is affiliated with the *Eelam Tamil Association de Québec* and Canadian WTM, diasporic organizations that critics argue operate in disguise as civil branches of the LTTE. Although unclear exactly how TRO, WTM, and LTTE memberships overlap, most of the WTM-sponsored events that I personally attended in Montréal did indeed feature TRO fundraising booths with prominent LTTE flags.

After the assassination of Indian Prime Minister Rajiv Gandhi on May 21, 1991 near the city of Chennai in Tamil Nadu by a presumed Tamil Tiger female suicide bomber, the TRO and LTTE joined the Indian government's list of banned terrorist organizations. Banished from their original headquarters in Tamil Nadu, the TRO relocated to Jaffna, then epicenter of the Tamil Eelam separatist movement and LTTE military stronghold. Many politicians in Tamil Nadu remained sympathetic to the Eelam separatist movement, even though Gandhi's assassination further strained international relations between the two countries, already soured after the unsuccessful and unpopular intervention of the Indian Peace Keeping Force in Jaffna from 1987 to 1990. Although Indian Prime Ministers Indira and Rajiv Gandhi had initially supported the Tamil separatist cause in Jaffna at the urging of politicians in Tamil Nadu, both leaders abruptly changed course and pitted Indian soldiers, many later accused of rape and plunder, against the LTTE. Chief Ministers of Tamil Nadu belonging to one of two Tamil nationalist parties in power—Dravida Munnetra Kazhagam (DMK) and All India Anna Dravida Munnetra Kazhagam (AIADMK)—have had to tread a fine line between garnering sympathy for internally displaced Sri Lankan Tamils and running unpopular settlement camps for the nearly 80,000 refugees fleeing to Tamil Nadu (Daniel 1996). In 1992, with popular and political support for the LTTE in Tamil Nadu waning in the wake of Gandhi's assassination, 54,188 refugees were repatriated to Sri Lanka.

Before the tsunami, most Indians living in Montréal had avoided involving themselves in Sri Lankan politics, regardless of what their private feelings about the war might be. Muthu, president of the student organization Concordia University Tamil Mantram (CUTAM), alludes to this tense state of affairs when pointing out the exclusively Sri Lankan membership of CUTAM; Indian students instead join the Québec Tamil Association, also known as "Tamilagam," he tells me.[20] Some members of CUTAM and Tamilagam are on friendly terms and attend each other's social functions; yet, as one graduate student, Nita, explains to me, many Indian students shun Sri Lankan classmates whom they suspect of collaborating with the LTTE. Nita was living in Chennai at the time of the prime minister's assassination and remains deeply suspicious of the LTTE's presence in Montréal. Refusing numerous requests upon her arrival in the city to perform *bharatanatyam* (a classical South Indian dance) at WTM fundraising events, Nita now conceals her identity by calling herself Indian, never Tamil, in public.

The tsunami briefly brought together students from CUTAM and Tamilagam, who collectively raised $10,000 in humanitarian aid for victims in India and Sri Lanka. Mayor Gérald Tremblay formally congratulated these student leaders at a citywide memorial for tsunami victims held on January 15, 2005 (see Figure 1.1).

FIGURE 1.1 Tsunami memorial in Montréal, Québec.

Muthu invited me to attend the memorial as well as a private party held afterwards for high school and college student leaders at the Ganesh Party Palace in Ville St-Laurent. Entering the auditorium of *École Secondaire Marie-Anne* at 6:30 pm, I see many high-profile faces from the Canadian government on stage. After the welcome speech, volunteers raise the Tamil Eelam flag (featuring a roaring tiger with claw-bearing paws resting on two crossed bayonets and encircled by yellow bullets) and dramatically unfurl it with the aid of a carefully positioned fan. A moment of silence ensues as members of the audience stand up to honor the LTTE national anthem. Volunteers then raise the Canadian flag (without a fan) to the music of "O Canada." Lastly, Québec's flag goes up without anthem or fanfare.

The family next to me and I get out of our seats to join other people lining up to place flowers in front of a single burning candle onstage. In return we each receive a tea candle. Most people are dressed in blue—blue shirts, blue pants, blue saris, blue *salwar kameezes*, blue ribbons—in honor of the dead. After the procession, we watch a documentary of the tsunami's destruction in northeastern Sri Lanka. Never-before-seen images of dead bodies and decimated landscapes elicit tears and gasps from the audience. A teenage boy next to me says to his sister, "C'est dégueulasse!" (That's revolting!) I notice that code-mixing in French and English is common among young children, who nonetheless speak with their parents in Tamil. Officiating at the event is a middle-aged man who speaks exclusively in literary Tamil, followed by two college-aged girls who translate his speech into French and two college-aged boys who then translate this into English. Canadian politicians ceremoniously begin their speeches with *vaṇakkam* (greetings) and end with *nanṛi* (thank you) and code-switch between French and English when addressing the audience. After a brief interlude during which two bharatanatyam dancers interpretively reenact the tsunami tragedy, an elderly WTM leader invites audience members to individually come up on stage and receive a CD of Tamil poetry thanking them for their charitable contributions. Everyone earns a CD, even children. The ceremony concludes with poetry readings in literary Tamil by distinguished members of the Sri Lankan community.

Students at the afterparty also code-switch between English and Tamil, but never in English and French, or French and Tamil. When I walk around the restaurant to introduce myself, I observe that Indian students are clustered together at tables near the back of the reception hall and Sri Lankan students are sitting at tables near the front, each separately enjoying the spicy seafood buffet. After dinner, Nalini, a CUTAM officer, asks everyone to bring his or her chair together to form a circle on the dance floor. She first praises the shared commitment of Indian and Sri Lankan student leaders to helping tsunami victims. Then, acknowledging that many people at the party do not know each other well, she proposes an icebreaker. Nalini picks a name out of a hat and asks this person to choose between performing a silly task with a partner and answering a trivia question. One of the first trivia questions inquires about the Tamil word for "computer," stumping everyone until a recent emigrant from Jaffna, a young man who speaks little English, shouts the right answer: "kaṇakku iyantiram!" When my name is picked I choose the silly task, feeling shaky about my Tamil language trivia skills. Nalini instructs me to choose a partner from the circle and dance with him in a "Latin style." A moment of silence ensues as I contemplate my choice. Wishing to avoid dancing in public with a man, I ask Nalini to be my partner. She laughingly agrees and we swirl awkwardly around the dance floor for a minute.

I leave the party full of hope that my fieldwork will proceed just as smoothly as it has this night. In my mind, I am already planning group interviews to compare the language practices and identification strategies of Catholic, Protestant, Muslim, and Hindu students of Indian and Sri Lankan Tamil origin. I am particularly intrigued by what I perceive to be a competence gap between elementary school-aged children speaking mostly in French, high school and university students speaking mostly in English and Tamil, and adults speaking mostly in Tamil with one another. Because I know that many Indian children opt out of the public school system and Sri Lankan children must attend French-medium public schools due to their limited finances, I hypothesize that ethnonational distinctions will also map onto generational differences and Indians will increasingly favor English and Sri Lankans, French, with each passing generation.

Unfortunately, this party was the last time that I would socialize with such a diverse group of Tamil speakers. I was never able to establish contact with Protestant and Muslim community leaders. Also, less than two years later, relations between Indian and Sri Lankan Tamil leaders became strained once again as international rhetoric condemning the LTTE's war activities in Sri Lanka intensified. In April 2006, the newly instated Conservative Prime Minister of Canada, Stephen Harper, banned the LTTE as a terrorist organization and ordered the Royal Canadian Mounted Police to raid WTM offices in Montréal and Toronto (see Figure 1.2) to search for evidence of illegal LTTE fundraising activities (CBC 2006a, 2006b).[21] If caught, extortionists could face up to fourteen years in prison and donors ten. Canada was one of the last countries to join the international community in banning the LTTE. Rumors of deportation fueled paranoia, and my informants, previously open to discussing language issues with me, became reticent to say anything possibly construed as disloyal to the Canadian or Québec governments (Cheran 2007).

Moreover, fear of being labeled a "traitor" by the LTTE leadership, exacerbated by uncertainties over who exactly in one's social circle is LTTE or not, also

FIGURE 1.2 Former headquarters of the WTM in Côte-des-Neiges.

made it risky for my informants to speak about even the most mundane matters.[22] Cultural anthropologist Sharika Thiranagama analyzes this culture of anxiety in an insightful essay about the perils of participating in ethnographic research for Sri Lankan Tamil refugees. She recalls a moment of epiphany when her informant, a Toronto-based activist, likened her interview questions about his everyday life with those used by LTTE sympathizers to build an "archive of Tamil sociability" with which to accuse diasporic community members about their supposedly traitorous activities (2010:141). In my research, I follow the advice of a school board official in Montréal to not photograph or film any of my informants (especially children), exclusively use pseudonyms, and sometimes alter the basic details of life stories (and omit some stories altogether) to obscure individual identities. Never once during my interviews did I initiate or pursue conversations about the civil war in Sri Lanka.

Despite these precautionary measures, my research officially ended in May 2006 when war became imminent. In November 2005, Sri Lankans elected a new president, Mahinda Rajapakse, who promised an aggressive military solution to ending more than two decades of civil war, stalled without peaceful resolution since the internationally brokered ceasefire of 2001. Many Sri Lankan Tamils living in Montréal, who could visit their relatives in the LTTE-occupied province of Jaffna during the ceasefire, stopped immediately after the election, heeding the warning from LTTE military leader Velupillai Prabhakaran, who announced the onset of new hostilities during his internationally televised Martyr's Day speech on November 27, 2005. That afternoon as I am entering Rosemount High School, I observe several men working at the TRO booth in the lobby who are eyeing me cautiously as I pick up a tea candle at the entrance of the auditorium and take a seat. Following the ritual raising of the Canadian, Québécois, and Eelam flags, the officiating woman announces that a new song chosen as Eelam's national anthem has won first place in an international contest. Tamilnet reports that several hundred entries of poems were written in eighteen stanzas of literary, "immaculate Tamil . . . extolling the virtues of those who sacrificed their lives in [the] Tamil struggle, celebrat[ing] the unique qualities of exclusiveness and resourcefulness of the Tamil Homeland, and manifest[ing] the resoluteness, dedication and the aspirations of the Tamil People for freedom and dignity" (Tamilnet 2005). After a documentary film displays sorrowful images of women wailing and weeping as they place garlands on the graves of fallen heroes, Prabhakaran delivers his long-awaited speech: war is coming. By the following summer, the Sri Lankan army had invaded eastern Sri Lanka and, three years later, eviscerated the entire LTTE-controlled northeast. Prabhakaran was proclaimed dead, and rumors that the Sri Lankan army had killed more than a hundred thousand Tamils and the LTTE had used civilians as human shields spread without confirmation due to Rajapakse's policy forbidding journalists and human rights watch groups from monitoring wartime activities.

In the spring and summer of 2009, Canadian Tamils in Toronto, Ottawa, and Montréal organized massive street protests condemning Rajapakse's military offensive, but to no avail. Canadian public opinion had already turned decidedly against the LTTE. Regardless of the stigma attached to the LTTE in Canada, however, civilians still prefer to immigrate to this country above most others, even though entry is becoming increasingly difficult for applicants who are legally immobilized elsewhere. From 2004 to 2009, numerous peace pilgrimages held in succession in North America, Europe, and finally South Asia featured peripatetic statues of the Virgin Mary displaying a greater range of travel than Sri Lankan refugees, who must adopt creative strategies to remain globally connected in a post-terror world. In August 2010, five hundred or so undocumented Sri Lankan Tamil men, women, and children stowed aboard a Japanese-owned commercial cargo ship docked at the port of Vancouver, where police seeking to verify their lack of affiliation with the LTTE held them in custody for weeks. As a postdoctoral fellow at the University of British Columbia at the time, I overheard my colleagues animatedly discussing the possible outcome of this case as a litmus test that would either confirm or deny Canada's internationally acclaimed reputation as a society welcoming of all immigrants and, especially, refugees.

Yet given the Canadian media's frequently negative coverage of Sri Lankan Tamil gangs and Harper's recent attacks on the WTM and LTTE, in writing this book I have been more attuned to the likelihood that my informants' activities and narratives might be interpreted as unlawful or disloyal to Canadian, Québécois, and Tamil readerships.[23] I recall my initial confusion when a friend offhandedly commented to me, after hearing about my research on Tamil heritage language education, that "tamouls" are widely considered to be thugs and terrorists in Canada. She did not distinguish between Indians and Sri Lankans and I did not ask for clarification. Puzzling over this statement, nevertheless, helped me to better understand the context of Tamil ethnic and social relations in Montréal. I realized that, although Indians might feel sympathy for the plight of Sri Lankan refugees and kinship with their nationalist cause, none would welcome racist labels such as "terrorist" and "thug" jeopardizing their own career and personal ambitions, whether based in Québec or abroad. Unfortunately, for Sri Lankan refugee youth such as Arun who all too frequently encounter racist stereotypes, their feelings of alienation cannot be mitigated by unrealistic dreams of foreign travel or returning to an embattled homeland. Rather, depicting the Indian heritage language as "Spoken Tamil" and Sri Lankan as "Written Tamil," or code-mixing in French, Tamil, and English, are some of the modest ways by which he and other Tamil speakers in Montréal demonstrate their agency and dare to imagine what their social histories and life trajectories can be like on their own terms.

2 PURISM ACROSS THE SEAS

On a bitterly cold January afternoon, Muthu, student president of CUTAM (the Sri Lankan organization Concordia University Tamil Mantram) puts me in contact with Hemanth, student leader of Tamilagam (the Indian organization). Muthu and Hemanth had first met and become friends as fellow students attending Concordia University's master's degree program in engineering. That day, I arrange to visit Hemanth at a small office in the university student center on Boulevard de Maisonneuve, where we chat about his childhood growing up in Chennai, his experiences living in Montréal, and, most of all, his abiding love of cricket. An avid player in Chennai, Hemanth joined an intramural cricket team immediately upon arriving in Montréal. In addition to a few Indians like himself, most of his other teammates are Sri Lankans who speak with one another exclusively in Tamil. Given what Muthu has previously told me about the social and linguistic segregation of Indian and Sri Lankan Tamils in Montréal, I am surprised to learn of his team's mixed membership. Is cricket the exception to the rule, or should we instead conclude that an ideology of language purism only *promotes* ethnonational segregation among Tamils while neglecting to *enforce* this norm in everyday life?

Hemanth explains how he eventually came to "move with" his Sri Lankan teammates upon discovering common interests, despite initially maintaining his distance and speaking with them in English because he regarded their variety of Tamil to be utterly incomprehensible. Only later in the first season, when Hemanth had proven himself to be a valuable teammate and the Sri Lankan players invited him to after-game dinners and parties, did he become less reserved. "Once you know [them]," Hemanth emphasizes, "they are the best." He explains how, over time, he even developed an ear for discerning certain lexical and morphosyntactic distinctions in Indian and Sri Lankan regional varieties of Tamil and now speaks to his teammates mostly in Tamil.

> As far as language is concerned, yeah in the beginning it was a little bit difficult. The thing is, like, I had my Tamil language course . . . until 12th grade in India. I was in English-medium school. I had that one course that comes from all the way, from 1st grade through 12th grade. I was good in Tamil at that time. So I know the, what do you call them, the classical Tamil part, the literature, so if you know that thing, then it is easy to grasp the Sri Lankan Tamil. Because that's the platform. The classical Tamil is the platform and we diversified from that this way and they diversified from that in a different way, so if you put a link [in between them], this way you can really get at what they mean, except for a few words which you really don't know, but the other words are mostly derived from these words, but basically . . . whenever they speak I try to grasp from the classical . . . I try to equalize the words that they have in the classical and those with what they say. I try to come up with the oral distance.

He concludes that Sri Lankans speak the purer and more ancient language of both groups:

> Sri Lankan Tamil is very pure. It has not got polluted. I am coming from Chennai. It is the worst place to speak Tamil. Even people from South India, especially from Madurai, they will laugh at us. So I try to change myself when I speak to those people. Because it is very slang and colloquial language . . . so many dialects . . . When I first met Sri Lankans here, it is totally like I didn't even understand, they were laughing at me. So it is very different.

Hemanth's self-deprecating tone in referring to his own native variety of "Chennai Tamil" as slang and colloquial betrays a pervasive anxiety that many Indian Tamils shared with me about the deteriorating quality of their vernacular. Regionally dominant languages such as English, Hindi, and Telugu have heavily influenced "Chennai Tamil" through lexical borrowing and phonological interference (Annamalai 2011). Even though "language mixing" is considered to be the norm among many circles in Chennai, elsewhere in South India where a strong purist language ideology prevails, such as in Madurai, Chennai speakers are stigmatized as being less authentic speakers of Tamil.[1] Later, when I relay Hemanth's views about the impurity of his Indian Tamil speech to Muthu, he compares his friend's linguistic self-consciousness with how some Québécois French speakers feel about their preponderant use of "anglicisms" when conversing with speakers of Parisian French, globally considered to be the purer and more prestigious language.

Arjuna, another Indian player on Hemanth's cricket team who is also from Chennai and studies engineering at Concordia University, expresses a different point of view. When I ask him to reflect on the linguistic differences between spoken varieties of Tamil from India and Sri Lanka, he begins with the emphatic disclaimer: "Though I grew up in Chennai, though I speak Tamil as my mother tongue, I don't know Tamil officially. I don't know the nuances of the language." Notwithstanding, he promptly blames his own communication barrier with Sri Lankan Tamil teammates on what he describes as the phonological impurity of Sri Lankans' speech:

> I am friends with lot of Sri Lankan Tamils. Their Tamil is completely different. We cannot match their Tamil. Our way of speaking is different. Their way of speaking is completely different. One roommate of Hemanth, his name is Thileepan. I could not understand the way he spoke (*makes garbled noise*). Even now I ask him three times or something and only then I am able to understand. Already his language is a bit fast. Thileepan will say "valaipalam" instead of "vaḻaipaḻam." I ask him to repeat. Not only me. I think it is the case with many guys.

Thileepan, a doctoral student in computer systems engineering at McGill University who is originally from the Jaffna region of northern Sri Lanka, is Hemanth's roommate and best friend. Daily conversations with Thileepan have greatly enhanced Hemanth's facility in understanding Sri Lankan Tamil speech. Praising Thileepan's spoken Tamil, Hemanth recommends him to me as a potential tutor. Arjuna, on the other hand, reproaches Thileepan for collapsing the phonemic distinction between /ɻ/ and /l/ into one sound, [l]. Some speakers regard /ɻ/, found only in Dravidian languages and not Indo-European languages, as emblematic of "pure" Tamil. Unsure if Arjuna is aware that Sri Lankans generally perceive [ɻ] and [l] to be allophones of the same phoneme, /ɻ/, I wonder whether Arjuna is specifically chastising Thileepan for his sloppy speech or arguing that all Sri Lankans, as a rule, speak a less phonologically pure Tamil than do Indians.

After these conversations, I am curious to meet Thileepan for myself. Sharing an interest in exploring the city of Montréal by foot, we become fast friends and Thileepan agrees to tutor me in "Jaffna Tamil," the variety spoken by most Sri Lankans residing in Montréal. I had previously studied literary Tamil for two years at the University of Michigan under sociolinguist Dr. K. Karunakaran, a former faculty member of Annamalai University in Chennai. Later, I developed greater oral and written competence in Tamil by attending the American Institute of Indian Studies' summer intensive program in Madurai, India. Given my limited knowledge of Tamil regional variation when beginning our lessons, Thileepan deliberately modifies his speech to approximate my South Indian variety. I hardly notice this accommodation until he points out differences between my Indian and his Sri Lankan sentence constructions. Thileepan easily identifies these grammatical and lexical contrasts despite his lack of training in linguistics. When I mention this feat to him, he minimizes it by explaining that Sri Lankans are more familiar with Indian Tamil varieties primarily because Sri Lankans consume more films, television shows, and print media produced and published in Chennai than Indians consume media from Sri Lanka.

Reflecting on these and other interviews with Indian and Sri Lankan graduate students in Montréal, I realize that asymmetrical claims of mutual intelligibility and differential knowledge of sociolinguistic variation characterize how many Tamils perceive their interactions with one another.[2] Sociolinguist S. Suseendirajah (1970) attributes such asymmetries to primarily geographic factors. He argues that Jaffna Tamil is the most grammatically unique of all Tamil varieties due to the historical isolation of its speakers in northern Sri Lanka over many centuries. Sociolinguist R. Kalainathan (2000) adds that more than a millennium of contact between Jaffna Tamil and the neighboring Indo-Aryan language, Sinhala, has altered its phonological features. Gair and Suseendirarajah further proclaim, "Indians encountering it for the first time are likely to think that they are hearing some other Dravidian language such as Malayalam" (1998:171). Spoken in the western Indian province of Kerala, Malayalam is the closest "living relative" to Tamil, according to F.W. Ellis, who published the "Dravidian Proof" in 1816 positing proto-Tamil as the original Dravidian language. Through this scholarship, Ellis established an authoritative scale ranking the purity of modern Tamil, Malayalam, Kannada, and Telugu—all Dravidian languages—from greatest to least, based on their relatively increasingly degrees of phonological and grammatical interference from Sanskrit, the progenitor Indo-Aryan language (Trautmann 2006).

Even today this philological research predisposes Indians to quantitatively correlate cross-linguistic borrowing with linguistic impurity. Yet what is evident in Muthu's, Hemanth's, Arjuna's, and Thileepan's contentious evaluations of their languages' purity and mutual intelligibility is that these measurements also depend on different lexical, phonological, and grammatical criteria. In other words, competing ideological frameworks inform how Tamil vernaculars and other Dravidian languages are compared against an ancient (and imaginary) standard. Furthermore, the sociohistorical context in which such comparisons and contestations occur is significant. Immigrants and refugees ranking the purity of regional Tamil varieties in Montréal do so against the backdrop of Anglo-Franco conflicts in Québec and colonial South India, which were also influenced by religious and political rivalries. Disentangling these respective influences necessitates comparing how nationalist and imperial policies of linguistic purism in South Asia and Québec, from the medieval period through the present, have driven language standardization. Not surprisingly, in both mid-nineteenth-century Québec and South Asia, abiding ideologies about language purity were explicitly tied to theories of modernity, which instigated identity politics and nationalist movements in more or less virulent forms.

This chapter outlines the taxonomy of different colloquial and literary, spoken and written, and modern and classical languages used by Indian and Sri Lankan Tamils living, working, and studying in Montréal by chronicling the religious, nationalist, and other social movements shaping ideologies of language purism in present-day India, Sri Lanka, and Québec. As a historical overview, this chapter highlights two important points. First, there is no predictable correlation between a particular version of language purism and political or religious philosophy. Each movement exhibits manifold sources and outcomes with its own tensions and internal contradictions. Moreover, these tensions and contradictions underscore how narratives of modernity are fundamentally *heteroglossic*, a term used by Mikhail Bakhtin to refer to "a diversity of social speech types (sometimes even diversity of languages) and a diversity of individual voices, artistically organized" (1981:262). This chapter also foreshadows how multiple language purisms, whether popularized as prescriptions of *diglossia* in South Asia or as norms of *ethnolinguistic identification* in Québec, converge in the context of Montréal's Tamil diaspora to produce language ideologies about "spoken" and "written" heritage languages. Prior to this contact across the seas, however, one witnesses a dominant narrative of global modernity correlating material and social progress with linguistic change emerge and contend with another powerful narrative, which instead envisions language contact as engendering the signs of spiritual, moral, and racial decay.

Language Purism in South Asia

Classical and medieval attitudes of language purism, sociolinguist Francis Britto (1986) asserts, can be discerned in the early stylistic divergence of a literary Tamil standard used to write ancient texts for elites and temple inscriptions written instead in a vernacular style for the popular masses.[3] Beginning at around 200 B.C.E., literary *Sangams*, or informal associations of non-Brahmin bards and poets, congregated in the temple city of Madurai to solicit the patronage of local kings and compose secular-themed literature. Most poets came from South India, although a few literary allusions refer to poets arriving from the island of Sri Lanka during the period of Chola King Ellara's rule from the

Table 2.1 Classical and medieval South Indian dynasties

Pandyan	ca. 100 B.C.E. to C.E. 15th century	Based in Madurai and southern Tamil Nadu; invaded and ruled Sri Lanka in the 13th century
Chola	ca. 300 B.C.E. to C.E. 13th century; declined from C.E. 4th to 9th century	Based near the Kaveri River in northeastern Tamil Nadu; invaded and ruled Sri Lanka in the 10th and 11th centuries
Chera	ca. 200 B.C.E. to C.E. 12th century	Based in western Tamil Nadu and Kerala

second to first centuries B.C.E. (Kalainathan 2000) (see Table 2.1 for an overview of South Indian dynasties). Among the most renowned Sangam texts is the grammar book *Tolkāppiyam*, written sometime during or before the first century B.C.E. by an unknown yet celebrated writer known simply as Tolkappiyar. Tamil scholars describe the language of the *Tolkāppiyam* as modeled on the spoken vernacular of Madurai's ancient *literati* (Zvelebil 1995:705–706). Referring to this vernacular as *ce̱ntami̱ḻ* or pure Tamil, Tolkappiyar contrasts it with other varieties he calls *koṭun tamiḻ*, which literally means "crooked Tamil" but also refers to the speech of people living outside of Madurai and among the lower social classes. Medieval Tamil pandits (scholars of ancient Hindu texts) revering the classical writings of Sangam bards and poets as emblematic of an ancient wisdom, or *mutuvāy*, modeled their literary standard on ce̱ntamiḻ as well (Devaneyan 1966). The spoken language of Madurai elites thus became the written standard in Tamil literature from the fourth to the fourteenth century, a period coinciding with Pandyan and Chola dynastic rules in South India and, at times, also in Sri Lanka.

In the twelfth century, however, Tamil faced a new contender for the religious patronage of South Indian Brahmins, who regarded Sanskrit, the language of the Vedas, as more sacred. Over the centuries, Brahmins had gradually modified their spoken vernacular to incorporate more Sanskrit-derived lexicon and phonology and, in the process, created the caste dialect now referred to as "Sanskritized Tamil." Medieval Tamil pandits of middle-caste status viewed this borrowing from Sanskrit with great alarm and prescribed that loanwords assimilated into Tamil use only native Dravidian phonemes (Annamalai 2011). Simultaneously, the circulation of *bhakti* devotional literature written in a purist register of Tamil, which espoused anti-Brahminical and anti-Sanskrit views and promoted the ancient *Agamic* or ritual worship of Siva, gave momentum to a prominent philosophical movement known as *Shaiva Siddhanta* from the twelfth through the fourteenth century.[4] Extremely popular among the villages and towns of South India and especially of Sri Lanka, where non-Brahmin *Vellālas* were and still are the "dominant caste,"[5] Shaiva Siddhanta permitted non-Brahmins to worship without the assistance of Brahmin priests, as well as establish monasteries and write their own theological works in Tamil and Sanskrit.[6]

In addition to these cultural and religious flows across the narrow Gulf of Mannar that separates Sri Lanka and India (see Figure 2.1), migrants, merchants, and conquerors frequently traveling from South India to Jaffna during Pandyan and Chola dynastic rules helped to maintain fluid though politically contentious boundaries between both Tamil-speaking societies. South Indian kings saw Sri Lanka as a valuable asset in realizing their imperial ambitions and became periodic conquerors there. Although not concerned with language conquest per se, these dynasties further spread the use of Tamil in northeastern Sri Lanka. Later in the twentieth century when Sinhalese nationalists denounced the foreignness of Indian rulers, they insisted on the non-autochthon origins of Sri Lankan Tamils as speakers of the South Indian conquerors' language.

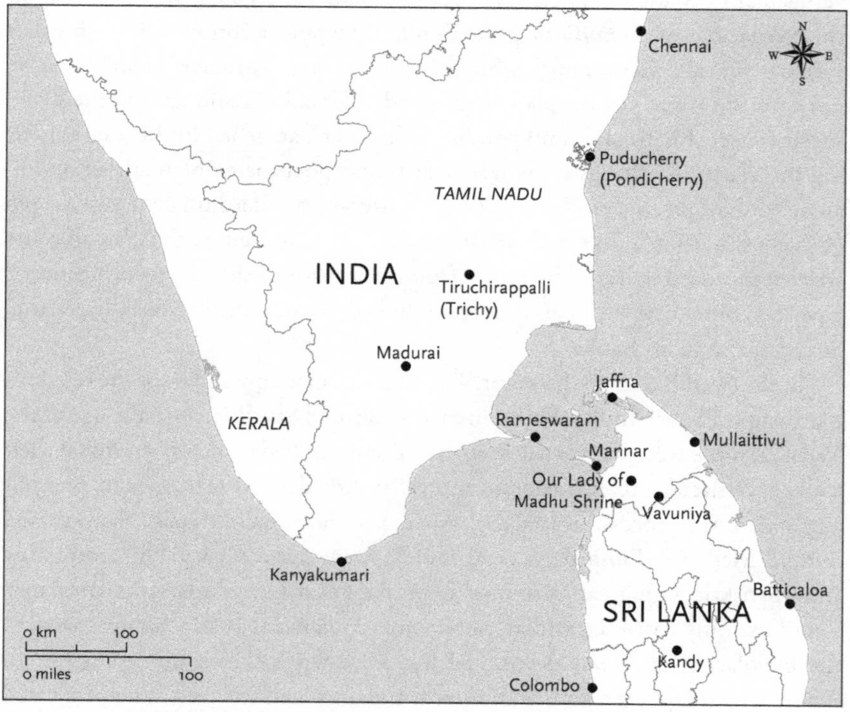

FIGURE 2.1 Map of Tamil-speaking regions in South India and Sri Lanka.

From the sixteenth through the nineteenth century, though, European incursions and colonial rule had stymied contact between Indian and Sri Lankan Tamils and fostered their cultural and political divergence. In spite of this isolation, mid-nineteenth-century scholarship jointly conducted by British, French, and high-caste Tamil pandits dramatically altered the aesthetic and pragmatic features of Tamil. When rising anti-colonial sentiment in the late nineteenth and early twentieth centuries once again brought Tamil nationalist leaders from India and Sri Lanka together in their collective mission to prove the antiquity of Dravidian civilizations in South Asia, this collaboration produced primordialist narratives that, Britto argues, challenge easy assumptions that "purity is generally associated with the Brahmins and high castes, and impurity with the untouchables and low castes" (1986:112). No longer ranking the purity of regional or caste varieties of Tamil based on their spatial distance from foreign Indo-Aryan languages, instead, temporal distance from the so-called pure, classical language became the defining metric. As the following sections explain, the resulting nationalist narratives depicted residents of Jaffna and Madurai as speaking the oldest and purest of Tamils and those in Chennai and Colombo, a more modern Tamil, by virtue of their vernaculars' hybrid features. Considered among the least pure was the language of Brahmins, the steadfast patrons of Sanskrit.

Colonial and Postcolonial India

After years of poring over ancient Sanskrit and Persian texts, in 1786 Welsh philologist Sir William Jones published a proof that would become famous for positing the existence of a proto-Indo-European language and explicating the structural foundation of most contemporary South Asian and European languages. At the time, Jones's proof also lent credence to scientific theories of comparative philology, which historian Thomas Trautmann describes as a regime of inquiry seeking "the elucidation of historical relations among language and their classification into families on the basis of the radiation, segmentary family tree model taken over from the Mosaic ethnology" (1997:131–132). For Jones's and all subsequent proofs of Indian languages, European philologists worked closely with Indian scholars to compile core word lists extracted from classical and medieval texts and compare these with modern languages' by following two Brahminical principles of language study. The first principle asserts "the Vyākaraṇa doctrine of the unity of all languages as corruptions of the eternal and incorruptible Sanskrit language," and the second classifies the "vocabularies of the modern languages of India into words of Sanskrit, foreign, and local (*deśya*) origin" (Trautmann 1997:136–137). By categorizing and hierarchically ranking the grammatical purity of Indian languages based on their calculated deviance from an imagined source language, that is, classical Sanskrit, this "science" reinforced folk beliefs that Indian vernaculars in possession of a classical literature are "pure" languages par excellence.

Upon establishing the parameters of Indo-Aryan, Dravidian, and other language families, nineteenth-century Indologists proposed theories of human evolution equating linguistic purity with racial purity. Friedrich Max Müller first named the *Arya* race after the speakers of Indo-Aryan languages. South Indian leaders later argued that the Indo-Aryan race had conquered the Dravidians, described as the indigenous inhabitants of prehistoric India, and expelled them to the south ca. 1500 B.C.E., before infiltrating and imposing their caste system there. Dravidians who integrated into the caste system became *Sudras*, or low-caste menial workers. Those who intermarried with Indo-Aryan settlers to join the ranks of higher-caste priests (*Brahmins*), kings (*Kshatriyas*), and merchants (*Vaishyas*) in South India, could not be racially pure Tamils, or so the theory posits.[7] With few Vaishya and Kshatriya caste groups in South India, the real racial and linguistic divide lies between the Brahmins and Sudras, and their vernacular languages.

Over the nineteenth century, European scholarly interest in Indian vernaculars grew as Britain's ascendant Liberal Party started challenging colonial language policies favoring the study of classical languages and instead argued that knowledge of Indian vernaculars would improve local governance. Already, the Charter of 1813 had permitted Christian proselytization in India and encouraged missionaries to learn Indian vernaculars for translating the Bible and other classical texts. The College of Fort William in Calcutta, established in 1804, followed by the Literary Society of Bombay in 1805 and the College of Fort St. George in Madras in 1812, taught to Indian and British functionaries classical Indian languages, such as Tamil, Telugu, and Sanskrit. Subsequent policies, such as Macaulay's Minute of 1835, the Dispatch of 1854, and the Hunter Commission of 1882, instead promoted the virtues of vernacular education, first among elites and then among non-elites. Ironically in South India, the first vernacular schools to be run by British and French colonial administrators were taught in literary Tamil, not colloquial Tamil.

This distinction between literary and colloquial Tamil partially overlaps with the *Tolkāppiyam*'s earlier categorization of three genres: *eḻututtamiḻ* (written Tamil), *mēṭai tamiḻ* (staged Tamil), and *pēccu tamiḻ* (spoken Tamil). Europeans added new functional distinctions—High and Low, literary and colloquial, and classical and modern—when in 1816, Sir Francis Ellis of Fort St. George in Madras published his proof of the Dravidian language family in a "note to the introduction" of Alexander Campbell's *Grammar of the Teloogoo Language* (Trautmann 2006). Following Jones's technique, Ellis's proof compared the core words of colloquial registers of Tamil, Malayalam, Telugu, and Kannada with those extracted from classical Sangam and other literary texts written in Tamil. The latter included poems and dictionaries written by the eighteenth-century Italian Jesuit missionary, Father Constantine Joseph Beschi, who, among other accomplishments, wrote the first bilingual grammar of *koṭun tamiḻ*, or colloquial Tamil, in Latin in 1728, receiving the title of *Viramamunivar*, "Father of Tamil Prose," for this and other works (Gaur 1968). Ellis, also inspired by Beschi's scholarship (which was itself inspired by the *Tolkappiyam*), interchangeably used such terms as "High Tamil" with *ce̱ntamiḻ* and "Low Tamil" with *koṭun tamiḻ* to conflate premodern and modern folk ideologies about functional, stylistic, and grammatical variation. Ellis concluded that "High" or literary Tamil is the oldest and purest of all Dravidian languages, based on its greater number of *deśya* or native lexicon compared to those of "Low" Tamil, Telugu, Malayalam, and Kannada, which are the purported descendants.

Before Ellis's work, British scholarship on Tamil lagged behind that of the French, who followed closely in the footsteps of celebrated Catholic (mostly Jesuit) Portuguese and Italian predecessors, such as Beschi, in sponsoring Tamil scholarship and the writing of grammars, dictionaries, religious exegeses, and classical reprints. During the eighteenth and nineteenth centuries, the best Tamil teachers lived in the French Indian colony of Pondicherry, where its press and metal types were said to be the envy of the British. During a routine raid in 1762, the British stole these types and invited a prized teacher and printer from Pondicherry to print books in Tamil and English at the newly founded Vepery Press in Madras in order to establish British preeminence in Tamil scholarship. From the point of view of the Governor of French India, more Tamil books translated into French (and Latin or French texts translated into Tamil) were needed to stem the tide of British and Anglican propaganda infiltrating their coastal territories from the surrounding British lands. These Anglo-Franco rivalries drove literary production in Tamil until the late nineteenth century, when Indians operating their own presses printed more and more anti-Christian and anti-colonial periodicals. By then, no one questioned the codified existence of the two languages, High and Low Tamil, also called literary and colloquial Tamil or Written and Spoken Tamil by both European and Indian printers.

Twentieth-century sociolinguists would later reinterpret these classifications one of two ways (see Table 2.2). Some would reconstruct a temporal narrative periodizing the use of classical Tamil from ca. 500 B.C.E. to C.E. 500, literary Tamil from ca. C.E. 600 to C.E. 1700, and modern Tamil from ca. C.E. 1800 to the present. Others would distinguish between the social functions of formal (i.e. "High") and informal (i.e. "Low") registers to argue for Tamil's diglossic nature, drawing on the work of sociolinguist Charles Ferguson (1959) and Joshua

Table 2.2 Taxonomy of Tamil linguistic variation in India

Modalities	"Spoken" Tamil (*pēccu tamiḻ*)	"Written" Tamil (*eḻuttu tamiḻ*)
Registers	"Colloquial" Tamil (*koṭun tamiḻ*)	"Literary" Tamil (*ilakkiya tamiḻ*)
Historical Periods	"Modern" Tamil (C.E. 1600–present)	"Classical" Tamil (300 B.C.E. –C.E. 700)
Social Attributes	"Vulgar" Tamil (*koccai tamiḻ*)	"Pure" Tamil (*ceṉtamiḻ*)

Fishman (1965), who define *diglossia* as functionally differentiated varieties of a language used by a single speech community. Although Ferguson insists that no one speaks the high variety because this would sound artificial, such has not been the case with Tamil. During the Sangam period, Madurai elites spoke the same ceṉtamiḻ variety used to write poetry. Even today, political and religious orators and media figures in South Asia deliver speeches in literary Tamil. Thus, even though nationalists may use "High Tamil" and "ceṉtamiḻ" interchangeably with "Written Tamil" and "literary Tamil," none of these labels refer exclusively to languages used for writing.

In 1925 when E. V. Ramasamy, an orator and leader affectionately known as Periyar or "respected one," founded the Self-Respect Movement, his intention was to restore the ancient Dravidian civilization of South India to its former, pristine glory by eradicating all caste inequalities. In addition to arguing that the "Sanskritized" Tamil spoken by Brahmins in South India is a sign of their racial miscegenation (Annamalai 2011), Ramasamy regarded the archaeological discovery of supposedly Dravidian inscriptions in the Bronze Age Indus Valley civilization of northwest India as proof of the Dravidian peoples' prehistoric habitation across the entire subcontinent.[8] As the prospect of India's independence became more certain in the 1930s and 1940s and new leaders and parties emerged, Dravidian nationalists increasingly shifted their attention away from caste issues to focus squarely on language. Referring to this phase of Tamil nationalism as "language devotion," historian Sumathi Ramaswamy discusses how politicians interchangeably deployed gendered images of Tamil as a mother goddess (*Tamiḻttāy*) and mother tongue (*tāymoḻi*) to cultivate sentiments of ethnolinguistic unity among the general populace. Replacing the premodern personification of Tamil as a king with powers "beyond the total comprehension and control of its human speakers," this image of Tamil as a goddess instead derives powers not "from the gods, but from the 'imagined' community of 'the people,' its speakers"

(Ramaswamy 1998:85–87; see also Anderson 1983).[9] Paradoxically, the "feminization of languages" and depiction of "mother tongues" as symbols of "pure and true [political] communities" (1997:17), Ramaswamy clarifies, also reinforced the "new patriarchy" of modern India in the early twentieth century (see also Chatterjee 1993).[10]

In Tamil Nadu, where the extent of religious veneration for Tamil as a mother tongue matches the public's disdain for Hindi as an invading language, rumors of Hindi being imposed as a compulsory school subject instigated riots in 1937. Ten years later a compromise policy was formulated; the resultant three-language formula required that all Indian schools teach Hindi, English, and a regional language.[11] Politicians from Tamil Nadu, rejecting Hindi instruction altogether, immediately threatened to secede from India. Succumbing to pressure from Dravidian political parties, in 1956 the Indian Parliament reorganized the boundaries of former British provinces and princely states into linguistic provinces based on census information gathered on "mother tongues."[12] The definition of mother tongue at that time, which was far from exact, led to many contentious border issues still unresolved today.[13] In the South, however, shared defiance of Hindi as a non-Dravidian language eclipsed minor conflicts along the border zones. Ultimately, the Official Language Acts of 1963 and 1967 recognized Hindi as India's official language yet allowed for the official use of English in non-Hindi-speaking provinces and granted provincial governments the authority to establish their own three-language formula for school instruction.[14] Political scientist James Manor (2001) credits these conciliatory language legislations with preventing further violence during postcolonial India's transition to democratic rule.

Although leaders no longer talk of secession, Dravidian political parties in Tamil Nadu still prescribe Tamil purism and discourage learning Hindi, especially within the academy, media, and government (Annamalai 1979; Pandian 1987; Subramanian 1999). For example, public figures are expected to write and speak in an oratorical style of literary Tamil to highlight the classical origins of a Tamil civilization (Bate 2009). Literacy campaigns, on the other hand, seek to modernize literary Tamil and make it more accessible as a "language of the people" (Ramaswamy 1993:701). Yet this process still involves "purifying" spelling and vocabulary to approximate classical Tamil, as well as "simplifying" syntax, phonology, and morphology to approximate colloquial Tamil (Annamalai 2007, 2011). Today, idiosyncratic choices about how to graphically represent colloquial Tamil in writing reveal new openness toward language mixing, especially among intellectuals and artists (Schiffman 1998). For example, innovations in literary realism enable novelists to convey populist voices by writing dialogue in colloquial Tamil and highlight characters' upward social mobility by having them speak in literary Tamil. Similarly, television and radio programming use regional varieties of Tamil and code-mix with English to cultivate populist appeal among diverse listening publics (Nakassis and Dean 2007). Previously, language mixing associated with Brahmins and urbanites had connoted racial impurity or cultural inauthenticity. Widespread changes in this attitude are perhaps due to the overall rising prosperity of Tamil Nadu, which has one of the highest literacy rates in India, or the unflinching stewardship of Dravidian nationalist parties toward the Tamil language over the last century. Ultimately, primordialist nationalist narratives that link material progress with linguistic decay no longer appeal to upwardly mobile Tamils living in cosmopolitan cities like Chennai or Delhi, where signs of urban progress are instead linked to language change and modernization.

Colonial and Postcolonial Sri Lanka

Across the Gulf of Mannar, precolonial Ceylon was divided into three regional polities—the Tamil kingdom of Jaffna in the north, the Sinhalese kingdom of Kandy in the center, and the Sinhalese kingdom of Kotte in the south—where caste and religious cleavages among Muslims, Catholics, Protestants, Hindus, and Buddhists, rather than linguistic or ethnic allegiances, organized community life. Piece by piece, these kingdoms gradually succumbed to Portuguese rule from 1517 to 1660, Dutch rule from 1660 to 1802, and British rule from 1802 to 1948. At first, the British renamed the three kingdoms the "Principal Nationalities" of Tamils, Kandyan Sinhalese, and Low Country Sinhalese. Yet in 1833, they created two linguistic administrative regions, a Tamil-speaking northeast out of the former Jaffna kingdom and a Sinhala-speaking southwest out of the former Kandyan and Kotte kingdoms (Arudpragasam 1996).[15] These ethnolinguistic classifications captured neither Ceylon's multiethnic and multilingual communities nor its history of collaboration among early nationalist leaders. For example, A. Canagaratnam (of Tamil origin) and G. K. W. Perera (of Sinhala origin) had led the *Swabhasha* movement of the 1920s and 1930s together by successfully appealing to the British government to guarantee universal education in both Tamil and Sinhala. As a result, Sri Lanka's literacy rate rose dramatically from 17 percent in 1881 to 65 percent in 1953 to reach the highest in South Asia.

Hoping to foster mistrust and deter future solidarity between Tamil and Sinhalese leaders, the British altered the country's balance of power by consolidating Kandyan Sinhalese and Low Country Sinhalese census categories into a single ethnolinguistic unit in 1881 and again in 1925. Sinhalese speakers, accounting for approximately three quarters of the total population, became the country's undisputed majority. Tamils, henceforth its minorities, were shown to have disproportionately benefitted from British patronage during the nineteenth and early twentieth centuries, when European missionaries built many bilingual English-Tamil schools in the northern region of Jaffna. Attended mostly by the children of the dominant Vellāla caste, Christian schools produced English-educated subjects who then claimed the best government jobs and seats in higher education. Once this practice was exposed, British favoritism of Jaffna Tamils aggravated tensions between Sri Lankan Tamil and Sinhalese nationalist leaders formerly working jointly for Ceylon's independence (Arasaratnam 1994).[16]

Tension turned into outright rivalry when the British-appointed Donoughmore Commission, charged with writing Sri Lanka's constitution, made the fateful decision to grant universal franchise to the electorate. The newly empowered Sinhalese-speaking rural masses, under the guidance of Sinhala-Buddhist nationalists recently elected to Parliament, voted as an ethnolinguistic block to promote the tenets of the Sinhala-Only Movement. Based on the nativist discourse that *Damilas*, described as an ancient race of Tamil speakers from South India, had conquered the original Sinhala-speaking inhabitants of Ceylon, this movement proposed that Sinhala be reinstated as the sole official language of Sri Lanka, replacing English as well in the process (Rajan 1995). Tamil nationalists countered that the Dravidian rulers of the ancient kingdom of Eelam in northeastern Sri Lanka were also indigenous to the island (Bose 1994; DeVotta 2004; Pfaffenberger 1994). Neither group admitted to Ceylon's cosmopolitan history of language mixing, migration, and intermarriage. Rather, attitudes of purism prevailed on both sides.

Once firmly in power, Sinhalese-Buddhist nationalists passed a series of discriminatory policies targeted at Sri Lankan Tamils through Parliament (Rajasingham-Senanayake 2001). First in the 1930s, the government relocated Sinhalese families to newly nationalized and irrigated lands in the northeast in order to erode the traditional dominance of the Vellālar Tamil agricultural caste (Peebles 1990).[17] Then in 1948, Sinhalese-Buddhist nationalists disenfranchised Ceylonese-born Upcountry Tamils, whose ancestors had emigrated from South India in the nineteenth and twentieth centuries to work on Ceylon's coffee, tea, and rubber plantations, by declaring them "foreign nationals" (Bass 2013; Peebles 2001). By 1956 when Sinhala became the sole official language of Ceylon,[18] most Tamils, who neither spoke nor wrote this language, could no longer aspire to work for the government. Affirmative action policies and government quotas in 1973 further restricted the number of students from Jaffna that could attend medical and engineering schools and also required them to score higher on entrance exams than Sinhalese applicants.[19] In five years time, Sri Lankan Tamil enrollment in universities had declined by 40 percent while Sinhalese enrollment had risen by 78 percent. The discontent of an entire generation of disenfranchised Sri Lankan Tamil youth would soon breed more drastic political and military action.

At first, Tamil leaders iterated their grievances through constitutional means (Bose 1994; Gopal 2000; Nesiah 2001; Sivarajah 1996). In 1973, the Tamil United Liberation Front (TULF) demanded that the Sri Lankan government recognize the sovereignty of the Tamil Eelam state in the northeast. Yet after the anti-Tamil pogrom in Colombo in 1983 led to nearly three thousand Tamil deaths at the hands of Sinhalese civilians, who were outraged by a prior assault on Sinhalese policemen and soldiers in Jaffna, most Sri Lankan Tamils rejected the possibility of constitutional reform and supported only the LTTE (Liberation Tigers of Tamil Eelam). The LTTE intermittently gained and lost territory in the east yet eventually established a fortified proxy government in Jaffna, from where it ruled for the next two and a half decades.

As the former seat of the medieval Tamil kingdom, Jaffna symbolizes the heart and soul of the Tamil Eelam nation. Some LTTE leaders are Vellālar Tamils from Jaffna who view Eelam as a "young woman . . . with her face in the Jaffna peninsula, the Tamil areas on the western and eastern coasts appear as her long, free-flowing hair" (Fuglerud 1999:167). Images of weeping mothers placing garlands on pictures of fallen LTTE soldiers televised around the world every year on Martyrs' Day (*Māvērer Nāl*) evoke familiar tropes of grieving mothers popular in Sangam poetry and help to constitute a LTTE cyclical calendar based on events celebrating an ancient Tamil militarism or "tiger-identity" (Schalk 1997:38). Also, the liberal use of adjectives such as *inimai* to describe the sweetness, sensuality, and delightfulness of Tamil, and *kannimai* to speak of the youthfulness, purity, and chasteness of Tamil Eelam in nationalist rhetoric resembles the gendered images of linguistic and moral purity also used by Dravidian nationalists in India (Fuglerud 1999).

Yet Eelam nationalism is not the same as Dravidian nationalism. For one, Sri Lankan elites living in Colombo in the late nineteenth century rejected the use of Indian *ceṉtamiḻ* as their literary standard on account of it being too outdated. With their own vernacular being perceived as riddled with English, Colombo elites instead turned to the vernacular spoken by the people of Jaffna, instead regarded as the purest and most ancient of Tamil languages. Strategic borrowings from *ceṉtamiḻ* conveyed "a kind of traditional sanction" to the literary standard of Sri Lanka (Kandiah 1978:68), and, through the "archaic features . . . that were lost in the course of its history in other countries," Jaffna Tamil gained an aura of antiquity (Kalainathan 2000:301). Though sharing the same literary standard, people living outside of Jaffna were depicted as speaking Tamil with varying degrees of impurity; that is, the Tamil varieties spoken in Muslim-dominant Batticaloa and Sinhalese-dominant Kandy were said to be corrupted by Arabic and Sinhala.[20] Sri Lankan Tamil nationalists thus ranked the purity of vernaculars spoken on the island to differentiate between regional and religious groups with varying levels of support for the LTTE. Yet they also emphasized the ethnolinguistic unity and territorial claims of all Tamil speakers living in Sri Lanka, including Hindus, Catholics, and Muslims of Tamil ethnicity, based on their shared use of literary Tamil. This strategy worked well as long as no one questioned the reality of Tamil diglossia as an ideology. This language ideology, jointly articulated through the efforts of British, French, and Indian scholars, was also evoked by Sri Lankan nationalists in the late nineteenth century.

Although the LTTE denounced the government's subcategorization of Jaffna, Upcountry, and Muslim Tamils into three separate speech communities as being a retaliatory strategy to fragment the territorial collectivity of Eelam, its own treatment of non-Jaffna Tamils was far from consistent. In the 1990s, the LTTE expelled Muslims from Jaffna in retribution for supporting rival political parties and, for the same reason, denied support to Upcountry Tamil leaders voicing constitutional grievances.[21] These mistakes proved costly for party loyalty. Exemplifying the backlash, former LTTE leader Colonel Karuna Amman, who established the opposition party *Makkaḷ Viṭuthalai Puḷikal* (TMVP) to represent eastern Tamils disenchanted by LTTE politics favoring Jaffna Tamils, helped the government to accelerate the LTTE's defeat in 2009 (Sumathy 2001).

In postwar Sri Lanka, where Sinhalese nationalism faces little deterrent and the government has banned public demonstrations of Tamil nationalism and war memorials, Sri Lankan Tamils are entering a new phase of vulnerability as provisional citizens in Sri Lanka and unwanted refugees abroad. Human rights activists warn that the increasingly hostile stances of conservative Western governments toward Sri Lankan Tamil refugees have emboldened the Sri Lankan government to ignore discrimination and abuse in their own country. Desperate and destitute refugees often pay smugglers hefty sums to make perilous oceanic journeys on shoddy boats, supposedly heading west but often marooning passengers on other continents (BBC 2014; Haviland 2013). Since 2009, only six hundred Sri Lankan Tamil refugees traveling by boat have safely reached Canada.[22] Returning to Sri Lanka can be just as grim for those facing police torture, social ostracism, and linguistic discrimination. Although recently, President Rajapakse has heralded the importance of educational policies promoting trilingualism in Sinhala, Tamil, and English to facilitate reconciliation and national unity (Davis 2014), it is impossible to predict what new linguistic rivalries and ideologies of language purism will emerge in the future, and whether these will continue to encourage the emigration of Sri Lankan Tamils overseas.

Summary: Purism across the Gulf of Mannar

From ancient to contemporary times, poets, missionaries, philologists, nationalists, and sociolinguists in India and Sri Lanka have collectively participated in legitimizing discourses that depict literary or poetic styles of Tamil as pure, classical, timeless, and ancient. These folk ideologies also reinforce modern-day diglossia taxonomies that distinguish between High and Low varieties of "Written" and "Spoken" Tamil in functionalist terms. The language ideology first solidified when rival British and French presses in the nineteenth century competed to control the production of Tamil grammars, dictionaries, Bibles, and classical reprints. Also crucial to the development of Tamil nationalisms have been ideas about "the antiquity (*to<u>n</u>mai*) and primordiality (*mu<u>n</u>mai*) of Tamil, as well as its uniqueness (*ta<u>n</u>imai*) and purity (*tūymai*)" (Ramaswamy 1997:39) that exploited poignant images of vulnerable mothers and virgins and powerful metaphors of endangered languages and civilizations to divergent effects in India and Sri Lanka. By granting provinces the right to establish their own language policies, India's postcolonial government effectively quelled a twentieth-century separatist movement in Tamil Nadu. Recent literacy campaigns and literary movements there now foster participatory democratic publics by hybridizing "High" and "Low" Tamil and condoning code-switching between regional Tamil varieties. This shift away from endorsing language purism reinforces a new liberal narrative of modernity linking indices of sociolinguistic change with material progress. Wartime Sri Lanka has instead validated the existence of a sovereign Eelam state by arguing for the territory's antiquity and its inhabitants' linguistic and racial purity. Despite their differences, both narratives have been sustained by religious, imperial, and nationalist rivalries that have instigated recent and reinforced existing waves of Tamil migration in and beyond South Asia.

Language Purism in Québec

Popular opinion credits Eugène-Étienne Taché, an eighteenth-century surveyor, civil engineer, and architect working for the Department of Crown Lands in British Canada, with coining Québec's official motto, "Je me souviens" (I remember), in a poem commemorating the British conquest of New France on the Plains of Abraham in Québec City in 1759. The official story suggests that Taché included this phrase in a poem alluding to the unforgettable hardships experienced by French colonists during and after the war. A less popular interpretation proposes that the motto was extracted from the longer phrase, "Je me souviens que né sous le lys, je croîs sous la rose" (Born under the lilies, I grow under the roses), memorializing the intertwined histories of British and French imperialism in Canada (Deschênes 2012). Both sources speak of an enduring Anglo-Franco rivalry shaping English Canadian and French Canadian destinies. However, only in the mid-nineteenth century did French Canadian nationalists begin to reinterpret earlier class and religious struggles shaping the country's history as racially and linguistically motivated and, consequently, prescribe policies of linguistic purism to alleviate moral anxieties about English, the Anglo-Saxon language, corrupting French. Connecting ideological assertions of language rights to claims of territorial and political sovereignty, French Canadian nationalists have since used these varied discourses to argue for their province's right to be legally recognized as a distinctly French-speaking society.

New France and British Canada

Explorers and merchants from France (primarily Île-de-France, Normandy, and Poitou) first arrived in Canada in the early sixteenth century and settled along the St. Lawrence River basin, where they established commercial relations with semi-nomadic Algonquin and sedentary horticulturalist Iroquois bands and tribes (collectively known as Amerindians) and created trading companies under charters granted by the French monarchy. After the Iroquois invaded the Huron and their Jesuit allies at Sainte-Marie-au-pays-des-Hurons in 1649, King Louis XIV exploited this period of social and political instability to proclaim New France a royal colony and encouraged new waves of French emigration to replace the Amerindian populations decimated by disease and war. By 1650, French Canadian woodsmen (*coureurs des bois*), ignoring native claims, had seized control of the lucrative North American fur trade, and French settlers (*habitants*) had built many small farming and fishing villages across the rural hinterland.

New France grew to encompass present-day Québec, Ontario, Acadia, Hudson's Bay, Newfoundland, and Louisiana, and stretched from the Canadian Rockies to Newfoundland and the Gulf of Mexico to the Hudson Bay. Overseeing New France was a king-appointed Governor General, who implemented the feudal laws and customs of the Ancien Régime, including a *seigneurial* (seignorial) system permitting the landowning aristocracy to collect tithes and services from the majority peasant population.[23] By the mid-eighteenth century, diverse Roman Catholic orders—Jesuits, Sulpicians, Ursulines, Franciscans, Congregation of Notre-Dame, and Hospital of Mercy of Jesus—had amassed a third of all *seigneuries* in New France, most of them close to the large cities of Montréal, Trois-Rivières, and Québec, where the clergy built churches, hospitals, and schools to serve the indigent and train priests from local bourgeois families to run their own smaller parish churches (Hamelin and Provencher 1997; Létourneau 2004).

Although rich in natural resources, New France generated little revenue for France through mercantile trade. After France's defeat in the War of the Spanish Succession in 1713, King Louis XIV willingly ceded French territories in Acadia and the Great Lakes to Britain. The Seven Years War (1756–1763), a terrestrial and naval conflict waged between the imperial rivals, France and Britain, and their European, American, and Indian allies, saw the loss of France's North American possessions, which went to the British after their army conquered Québec City in 1759 and Montréal in 1760. The Treaty of Paris, signed in 1763, officially designated Canada a British colony with a dual system of governance under French civil law and English criminal law. When the Québec Act of 1774 guaranteed freedom of religion and the right to hold office to Catholic settlers and restored seigneurial rights to landowning clergymen, this act ensured the Church's steadfast loyalty to the British for centuries to come.

Since most French intellectuals and business leaders had fled for France after the war, only the clergy possessed the moral authority to enforce civil order in the colony.[24] Although secretly collaborating with British and American merchants in ventures of industrial speculation, the clergy also cultivated a face of public virtue through their philanthropic investments in hospices, orphanages, hospitals, and schools. Historians John Dickinson and Brian Young (2000) describe the Catholic Church as espousing a "conservative national ideology" that denounced the vices of industrialism, capitalism, urban life, and English and instead praised the virtues of family, rural life, and French. Village priests famously denied communion to parishioners partaking in labor unions, friendly societies, taverns, secular entertainment, divorce, and premarital sex. Women, strictly prohibited from joining the workforce or using birth control, were expected to be fecund and teach their families to respect rural traditions and the Catholic sacraments.

Certainly, tensions between minority English-speaking Protestants and majority French-speaking Catholics existed in Canada, yet most conflicts in the early years of the British colony dealt with widespread discontent with the clergy's autocratic rule and the urban bourgeoisie's taxation policies. This discontent transcended religious, ethnic, and linguistic communities; in fact, working-class and rural English and French-speaking settlers collectively participated in two class-motivated rebellions in Lower Canada (present-day Québec) in 1837 and Upper Canada (present-day Ontario) in 1838 (see Figure 2.2). Concerned about the source of this colonial unrest, Queen Victoria commissioned John George Lambton, Earl of Durham, to investigate its social and economic causes. Durham published his final *Report on the Affairs of British North America* in February 1839, yet a segment appeared several months earlier in Canadian newspapers on October 9, 1838. Marcel-Pierre Hamel, the official translator of Durham at

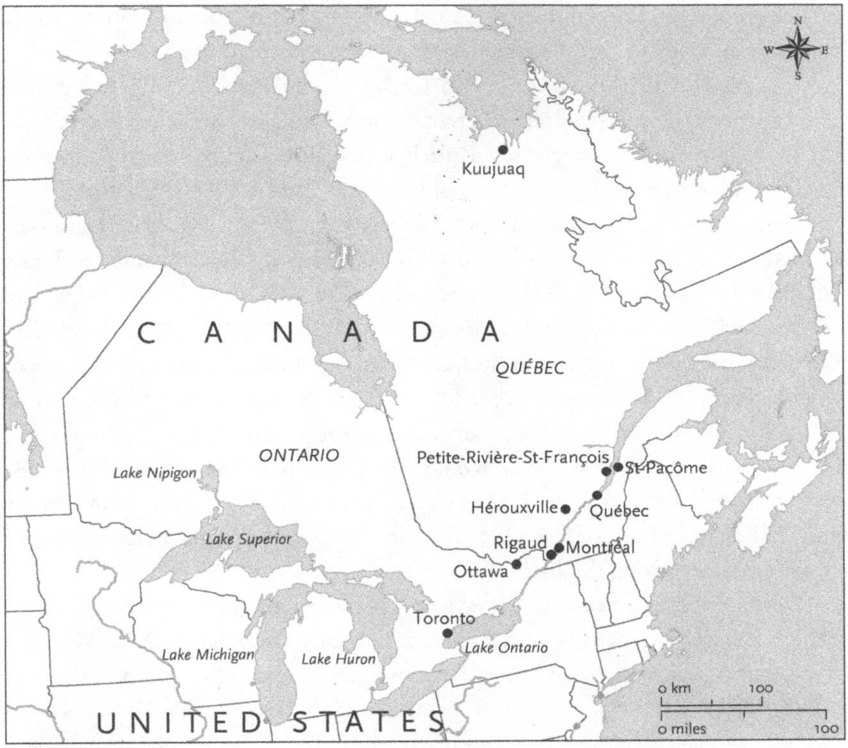

FIGURE 2.2 Map of the provinces of Québec and Ontario, Canada.

the *Société Historique de Montréal*, refers to this date as a "date mémorable dans l'histoire du Canada" (unforgettable date in Canadian history) because the report had first articulated the idea, now taken for granted by federalists and nationalists, that French Canada and English Canada are ethnically, linguistically, and racially distinct and adversarial civilizations (Hamel 1948:24).

Setting the tone early, Durham begins his report by contrasting the "glory of the English people" with the "petty jealousies of a small community" of French settlers who, in displaying animosity toward the "more noble and understanding nationality," were engaged in a "war against the Government" (Hamel 1948:24, 72). This conflict, Durham argues, arises out of a "mortal hatred" between two endemically hostile groups (also labeled as "races"), the French and English, living in Lower Canada (Hamel 1948:67–68). Hamel suggests that British Loyalists and Anglo-American business leaders based in Montréal deliberately misled Durham into thinking that racial tensions, rather than socioeconomic problems, had instigated the Patriot rebellion in Lower Canada. Perhaps, Hamel surmises, bourgeois elites hoped that Durham would use this story as ammunition to recommend unifying French-dominant Lower Canada and English-dominant Upper Canada to ensure an English-speaking majority in the reconstituted country.

Indeed, Durham did recommend to the Queen that unifying Lower and Upper Canadas would assimilate French Canadians into what he described as the more modern and progressive British society. Criticizing French Canadians for holding onto the "old prejudices, old customs, old laws" (Hamel 1948:81) of the Ancien Régime, Durham depicted Lower Canada as "an outdated and outmoded society in a new and progressive world" (Hamel 1948:82) and deridingly concluded, "There can hardly be conceived a nationality more destitute. They are a people with no history, and no literature" (Durham 1839 [2000]:288–299). Denying that French Canadian literature could ever achieve the same stature as English literature because, he argued, writers are limited by the ideas generated by their own community, Durham advanced the argument that the culturally and intellectually inferior Frenchmen would never govern as well as Englishmen. He recommended abolishing the French civil code and the seignorial system entirely and abdicating the rule of Canada to the natural leadership of the better-educated and more enterprising English.

Durham's writings exacerbated a deeply ingrained linguistic insecurity felt by French Canadians since the mid-eighteenth century (Bouchard 2008). Whereas the linguistically uniform, early settler population spoke a lower-class variety of *françoys* deemed to be pure by continental standards, after the French Revolution foreign travelers deplored the prevalence of anglicisms, such as calques, and English phonological interference heard in Canadian French to comment disdainfully on its grammatical and lexical divergence from the new Parisian standard. Efforts to redefine Canadian French as an "archaic" language resembling the vernacular of seventeenth-century France and eradicate anglicisms did not lessen this negativity. By the end of the nineteenth century, most French Canadians had internalized the belief that they spoke a devalued, non-modern, impure patois. Such sentiments of linguistic insecurity prevailed throughout the next century and peaked from 1940 to 1960 when, in 1956, the Third Congress on the French Language issued a statement declaring war on "limp lips" and journalists decried the "three great dangers [that] threaten the integrity of French in Canada: sloppy pronunciation, impoverished vocabulary, and anglicisms of all kind" (Laurence 1957, quoted in Bouchard 2008:186).

Durham's writings about Anglo-Franco rivalries in Canada also resonated with popular German Romanticist writings by Johann Gottfried Herder (ca. 1772) and Wilhelm von Humboldt (ca. 1836), which posited that language shapes worldview and expresses the essence of a folk-nation or *Volk* (Losonky 1999; Olender 1992). Anthropologist and sociolinguist Monica Heller (2011) writes that these continental political philosophies greatly influenced French

Canadian ethnic nationalism, especially after the mid-nineteenth century when the notion of "ethnolinguistic identity" became ubiquitous in Canadian political discourse. Prior to Durham's report, however, French Canadians had constructed their identities in more complex ways based on multiple religious, socioeconomic, occupational, regional, and linguistic affiliations. Fatefully, although French Canadian leaders had vociferously denounced Durham's Report for misrepresenting their culture and literature, they failed to reject the hypothesis that Anglo-Franco rivalries, and not other religious, class, or social conflicts, drive Canadian history.

Upon Durham's recommendation, Queen Victoria joined Lower and Upper Canada to create the administrative province of Canada through the Union Act of 1840. French became a judicially protected language several decades later in 1867, when the Act of Confederation also combined the provinces of Ontario, Québec, Nova Scotia, and New Brunswick to form the Dominion of Canada. Six years later, Manitoba, British Columbia, and Prince Edward Island joined the Canadian Confederation, which was recognized by the British government as a federal parliamentary democracy and constitutional monarchy in 1931. Despite this act of confederation, strong provincial identities prevailed, especially in Québec, where the movement for French Canadian language rights began in earnest and leaders grappled with the contentious work of incorporating minority voices and diverse ethnolinguistic communities into the provincial polity.

Twentieth-Century Québec

Once the Industrial Revolution had belatedly arrived in Québec in the late nineteenth century, the Catholic Church's condemnation of it could not prevent the dramatic restructuring of community and religious life that ensued in the following century (Handler 1988). Beginning with the interim war period, French Canadians left the countryside en masse to seek low-wage labor in Montréal, Trois-Rivières, and Québec City, where they first encountered suffragist organizations urging women to enter the salaried labor force and English-speaking European immigrants competing for the same jobs. Wealthy capitalists and poor immigrants soon became objects of anti-English sentiment among working-class French Canadians, who also resented the Church for prohibiting their participation in labor unions and anti-draft and suffrage rallies. When nationalist leaders in the 1960s and 1970s exposed the clergy's complicity with British rulers and English capitalists, this sparked a large-scale exodus from the Church and attendance at mass dropped precipitously from 88 percent of the population in 1965 to 46 percent in 1975 and 38 percent in 1985 (Langlois et al. 1990:352). The Catholic Church never recovered in Québec.

Secular institutions also gradually replaced confessional ones. When the *Ministère de l'Éducation* (MEQ) was created in 1964, it seized control of primary and secondary schools from the clergy and, in 1998, reorganized Catholic and Protestant school boards into French and English institutions (McNicoll 1993).[25] The government further nationalized public utilities and financial institutions in which Catholic clergymen were heavily invested. Women exercising their rights to vote, hold property, attend university, divorce, and practice birth control engendered a drop in the province's fertility rate from 3.9 children per household in 1955 to 1.5 children in 2007 (Marcil-Gratton and Lapierre-Adamcyk 1983), and commonplace civil unions and domestic partnerships challenged the normativity of marriage.[26] By the end of the twentieth century, French secularism, and no longer Catholicism, defined Québécois identity (Oakes and Warren 2007).

Hoping to forestall the growing separatist movement in Québec, Canadian Prime Minister Lester Pearson created in 1963 the Royal Commission on Bilingualism and Biculturalism to recommend federal policies validating the equal partnership of Canada's "two founding races" (Haque 2012). Québécois nationalist leaders warned the commission that they would oppose any policies relegating French Canadians to one "ethnic group(s) among many" (Milroy 2001:82). In 1969, based on the commission's recommendations, Pearson's successor, Prime Minister Pierre Trudeau, declared French and English the official languages of Canada (McNicoll 1993). Ethnic minority and aboriginal leaders immediately criticized this law for not recognizing the "multicultural" contributions of non-settler populations and English Canadians opposed it for diluting Canada's British identity (Abu-Laban and Gabriel 2002). In 1971, to mollify his critics, Trudeau implemented a new multicultural policy, subsumed under the legal framework of official bilingualism, requiring provincial governments to fund ethnic minority organizations and provide institutional resources for teaching English or French to immigrants. This time, Québécois nationalists and aboriginal leaders (Coon Come 1995) condemned the policy for violating federal treaties and agreements, and ethnic minority leaders berated Trudeau for not adequately addressing issues of racism.[27]

Québécois nationalists passed their own language legislation in retaliation (Lemco 1992). In 1974, the provincial government, headed by the *Parti liberal* (PLQ), signed into law Bill 22 declaring French to be Québec's sole official language.[28] Yet since Bill 22 could only prescribe and not enforce the use of French in the public sector, in 1977 the newly elected separatist political party, *Parti québécois* (PQ), passed a more exacting law, *Loi 101* (Bill 101), officially known as the Charter of the French Language. In addition to requiring immigrant children to henceforth attend French-medium public schools, Bill 101 also stipulated that all communication occurring in the contexts of the legislature, courts, and business, ranging from writing informal memos to formal correspondences and commercial signs, be conducted in French.[29] The PQ also followed through on its campaign promise to hold referendums to decide if Québec should secede from Canada, to which 40.44 percent of the population voted affirmatively in 1980 and 49.42 percent in 1995.

Alarmed by the especially close call in 1995, Prime Minister Jean Chrétien abolished the Department of Multiculturalism and, in its stead, created the Department of Canadian Heritage to brand and publicize federalist values of civic unity, social equity and integration, and neoliberalism. Montréal business leaders also pressured the Québec government to amend Bill 101 to permit the outdoor posting of multilingual commercial signs, as long as the writing in French text is most visible, whereas immigrant parents discovered legal loopholes they could exploit to enroll their children in English-medium public schools.[30] Despite these conspicuous acts of resistance, most residents of Montréal complied with Bill 101 and joined the growing ranks of multilingual speakers conversant in English, French, and a third or fourth language.[31]

With the official status of French assured, nationalists turned their attention to elevating its stature in Québec, where most people speak nonstandard registers sometimes referred to as joual. Originally associated with working-class speakers living in Montréal, the term joual, which perhaps comes from the mispronunciation of *cheval* (horse), carries with it the negative connotation of speaking uncouthly or sloppily like a horse.[32] Simply the inclusion of liturgical profanity may render someone's speech joual-like and, hence, morally depraved. An emerging consensus among public intellectuals asserts that many residents of Québec, and especially the Québécois de souche, speak a nonstandard variety of Québécois French at least some of the time: "Québec is still a joual-speaking society, regardless of what the Office of the French Language would have you believe" (Saletti 1998). Elites in Québec who aspire to speak International French will usually distance themselves from the nonstandard features of Québécois French, including diphthongs, lexical anglicisms, morphology, and syntax deviating from written French (Jobin 1987; Mougeon and Beniak 1994; Papen 1998), reinforcing stereotypes that depict Québécois French as grammatically impure and its speakers as uneducated (Bouchard 2008; Oakes and Warren 2007). Expressing his aggravation upon hearing Québécois actor Patrick Huard speak in nonstandard Québécois French at the Jutra Film Awards in 2005, French linguist Lionel Meney writes a scathing editorial in which he rhetorically asks, "Is it possible that one day at a gala in Quebec we can say something intelligent and funny without speaking joual?" and sarcastically concludes that TV5, the international francophone station, would need French subtitles to broadcast the ceremony (Meney 2005a). This comment underscores the popular perception that nonstandard

Québécois French may be acceptable as a spoken language, but definitely not as a written language.

Yet in the 1960s and 1970s, during a period of intellectual and social transformation known as the Quiet Revolution, writers, playwrights, journalists, and other intellectuals actually wrote in joual, recontextualized as the authentic language of a people freed from the dual domination of the Catholic Church and English-speaking capitalists. These literary works sought to elevate joual's status and encouraged readers to identify with it as a modern, national language, and not just as a patois (Denis 2008). Conveying its populist qualities, Jean-Paul Desbiens, who wrote *Les insolences du Frère Untel* (1960), compares joual to "rock and roll, hot dogs, fashionable parties, and automobile cruises" (Caouette 2003:D1). Well-known dramatist Michel Tremblay, who penned plays entirely in joual despite the lack of a codified orthography, provides a template for future writers to textually represent joual's phonological, lexical, and morphosyntactic features.[33] Other popular writers such as Pierre Vallières (1968) in his book entitled *Nègres Blancs d'Amérique* (1968), and Michelle Lalonde (1979) in her poem entitled "Speak White," highlighted the social history of joual as a language oppressed by capitalist elites.

A countervailing movement to standardize Québécois French in the 1980s and 1990s, led by International French–educated elites who selected their own "purified" vernacular modeled on the phonology and lexicon of Canadian French and the morphosyntactic features of International French, sought to enforce new communicative norms in radio, television, and literature.[34] These self-proclaimed "linguistic nationalists" or *aménagistes* justified using native varieties of Québécois French, rather than the foreign-sounding International French, as the written standard, by arguing that linguistic variation is normal in "colloquializing" francophone societies ranging from "Montréal to Dakar, and passing through Paris, Brussels, and Algiers," where "the oral language is increasingly imposing itself" on and changing literary conventions (Nadeau and Barlow 2007). In 2001, the *Office québécoise de la langue française* (Quebec Board of the French Language) endorsed the view that four hundred years of language contact have enriched Québécois French (Lévesque 2001). The Board asserts, "This Québécois French standard will be the French standard both written and spoken throughout *la francophonie*, with the same grammar and syntax but with an assortment of words used only in Québec" (Dutrisac 2008) and praises standard Québécois French for being a language equally in possession of the prestigious, literary qualities of a written language and the authentic, colloquial qualities of a regional vernacular.

When in 2005 the Board subsidized the writing of the *Dictionnaire general et normatif du français québécois* and proposed to implement it as the standard textbook for use throughout the public school system (Cajolet-Laganière and Martel

2005; Corbeil 2005), self-proclaimed "linguistic purists" responded indignantly by warning of Québec's impending "ghettoization" among *la francophonie*. Arguing that the government has a responsibility to preserve the sanctity of the national language, purists disparaged Québécois French not only as substandard and grammatically incorrect but also for corrupting written French (Meney 2004; Meney 2005b; Paquot 1992, 2001).[35] Another editorialist contended that immigration to Québec would be adversely affected, writing in an ironic tone: "A Moroccan or a Senegalese would say that he doesn't understand why, in order to become a Québécois, he must speak French poorly" (Courtemanche 2008). Claiming that Québécois students who fare poorly in tasks of French composition do so because they learn to write the way they speak, purists argued that this problem is exacerbated by the blurred boundaries of standard and nonstandard Québécois French.[36] Meney, author of the *Dictionnaire québécois-français* (2004), in which he characterizes the non-systematic nature of French grammatical variation in Québec, points to many similarities between standard and nonstandard Québécois French and rejects the premise that Québécois French differs from International French primarily due to lexical variation, which he describes as minor compared to the more substantive grammatical differences (Oakes and Warren 2007).

Yet the belief persists that in Québec, peppering one's speech with nonstandard Québécois French or joual lexicon is the best way to endow it with an almost subversive aura of cultural authenticity or historical antiquity, due to linguistic research tracing the origins of certain Québécois words to the patois of seventeenth-century France (Corbeil 2005; de Villers 2005). Linguists Leigh Oakes and Jane Warren (2007) weigh in by arguing that nonstandard Québécois French should be considered the native vernacular of the Québécois de souche and standard Québécois French the civic language (*langue d'usage publique*) of the entire province, drawing from the principles of both German Romanticism, which asserts that every ethnic group possesses its own vernacular, and French Republicanism, which argues that citizens must forget their ethnic and linguistic allegiances by adopting the same literary standard (Renan 1990). Both views also inform Québécois policies of *interculturalism*, which, in contrast to Canadian multiculturalism, stresses the importance of dialogue between ethnolinguistic communities as well as integration into the majority francophone society (Bouchard 2012; Bouchard and Taylor 2008; Heller 2011; Oakes and Warren 2007; White 2014). However, imperiling the values and goals of the interculturalist project are the ongoing struggles of non-elite monolingual Québécois de souche to learn a standardized French not usually spoken at home,[37] and "visible minorities"[38] to be fully recognized as Québécois, even if they by comparison command the use of standard Québécois French (Helly 1996, 2001).

On the other hand, efforts to scale up and standardize Québécois French have not diminished the prestige of English, still considered to be the preeminent language of science, business, and international affairs. What has changed is that fewer French Canadians are learning English on the job as they once did by accommodating monolingual English-speaking bosses or coworkers, who knew little French before Bill 101 made French the official language of the workplace (Heller 1988). Since no government-funded classes for learning English exist outside the school system and since most children in Québec attend French-medium public schools, without further conversational practice monolinguals do not easily acquire proficiency in English. Hearing bilingual youth, who transfer to English-medium universities to become more proficient in this language, code-switch and code-mix triggers alarmist discourses that depict English as corrupting French and Canadian multiculturalism as diluting Québécois culture.[39]

The target of this moral panic, Montréal, although officially the second largest francophone city in the world, is better described as a "contact community" (Silverstein 1996) situated at the historical crossroads of multiple waves of settlement, colonization, and immigration by Amerindian peoples, francophones, anglophones, and allophones (Piché 2002). Since British colonization, most immigrants settling in Montréal have arrived from English-speaking countries, such as England, Scotland, Ireland, and the United States, as well as southern and eastern Europe. When the federal government initiated a new point system to recruit immigrants based on their occupational skills, education, age, and language abilities in 1967 and eased restrictions on refugees in 1969 and kin in 1976, major source countries shifted to include Haiti, France, the United Kingdom, Italy, Vietnam, Portugal, Greece, and Poland (Indra 1980). West African and Middle Eastern immigration to Montréal also escalated after the Canada-Québec Accord of 1991 permitted Québec to prioritize French-speaking applicants (Singer 2009).[40] Today, interlocutors of diverse regional varieties of French (including French-lexifier creoles such as Haitian Kreyòl) regularly interact in Montréal where they can compare their vernaculars against one another and Québécois and International French standards (Dumas 1987). These comparisons inevitably engender competing scales based on the different values of grammatical purity, social prestige, or cultural authenticity attributed to French vernaculars or their speakers, who are also taken to be representative of specific racial, class, and ethnic groups.

Despite Montréal's importance as a commercial, industrial, and francophone hub, non-francophone immigrants and minorities often depart for other Canadian and American cities competing for their labor power, especially during periods of intense separatist fervor such as in the late 1970s and mid-1990s. For example, in 1957 there were 11.5 immigrants for every thousand inhabitants living in Québec, 7.8 in 1966, 2.1 in 1984, and 3.9 in 1988. Generally speaking, French-speaking immigrants are more invested in Québécois politics. Among the 70.2 percent of all immigrants who stayed in Québec in the 1980s, 97.2 percent of Franco-Mauritian immigrants remained in the province compared to 31.9 percent of Chinese immigrants. In the 1990s and 2000s when Asians comprised the largest immigrant groups, among these, speakers of Arabic, Tagalog, Chinese languages, and Indian languages (that is, Punjabi, Urdu, and Tamil) predominated (Statistics 2007). Whether new Asian immigrant cohorts, including Tamil speakers, will endorse or challenge the prevailing nationalist views about the importance of ethnolinguistic identification, or quell moral anxieties about the deteriorating quality of Québécois French and the menace of English, depends on where their loyalties lie.

Purism across the Seas

Comparing Québécois and Tamil nationalisms reveals how similar language ideologies about purity, authenticity, and identity have different political outcomes and social repercussions. The federal protection of provincial languages successfully ended a twentieth-century separatist movement in Tamil Nadu but not in Québec, where the perceived threat of English as an invading language remains strong today. Ironically, the government-sponsored standardization of Québécois French and the legislation of French language use in public space have exacerbated inequalities between monolingual (often French-speaking) non-elites and bilingual elites, while government-sponsored efforts to modernize Tamil Nadu's literary standard have fostered more participative publics among the lower castes and classes yet not obliged politicians to speak in a more accessible oratorical style. These incongruities expose the shortcomings of language policies.

Similar shortcomings are revealed in Sri Lanka, where entrenched political, cultural, and religious differences between Jaffna Tamils, Upcountry Tamils, and Muslims preclude them from forging a common ethnolinguistic identity, even if these groups share the same literary standard and similar vernaculars. Also, standard Québécois French, which functions as a civic language to unite minorities, immigrants, and the Québécois de souche, has neither dispelled fears among Québécois nationalists that Canadian multiculturalism is eroding Québec's cultural and linguistic authenticity, nor convinced ethnic and racial minorities that Québécois nationalism and interculturalism are genuinely inclusive. Finally, for as long as Dravidian political parties have held power in Tamil Nadu, Tamil Brahmins have been depicted as racially, linguistically, and religiously foreign; yet, these antagonist politics have not deterred them from emigrating elsewhere to re-establish their status and commemorate a legacy of language mixing. Refugees from Jaffna, who are forced to leave behind a homeland widely acclaimed for the purity of the Tamil language, must now celebrate this purism by continuing the work of language preservation abroad.

In addition to comparing the unpredictable outcomes of language policies, this historical overview has highlighted how religious and nationalist rivalries promoted the institutionalization of ideologies of linguistic purism in South Asia and Québec during a critical time period in the mid-nineteenth century when Anglo-Franco conflicts profoundly shaped modernist imaginaries about language and belonging. Effectively, the language ideologies that Tamil migrants carry with them and also encounter in Québec connect the North American and Indian peripheries of the British and French empires and, therefore, facilitate the replacement of older and more fluid notions of sociolinguistic variation with newer and more modern concepts, such as diglossia and ethnolinguistic identity, that render talk of linguistic rivalry politically expedient. The following chapter examines the migration narratives of Indian Tamil immigrants and Sri Lankan Tamil refugees in Montréal as they reminisce about their different language choices and strategies of ethnolinguistic identification and learn how to navigate the city's treacherous political terrain.

3 NARRATIVES OF A DIASPORA

I have a phobia. I have a phobia. Because, when I was a little girl, you see, that is when they started the war and I became ill along with the war, and then, since that time . . . yes, it was like a fear. When I was a little girl, whenever there was something that displeased me, I became ill. I was like that. It was like, I had . . . it was like, a fever . . . it was killing me there, all the time. It started with a fever and then at the end I would be on the floor. So, they could not continue to see me like this. It was then that they moved to India.[1]

—INTERVIEW WITH SELVAMANI, *April 19, 2005*

Immigrants and refugees tell stories tinged with nostalgia, relief, anticipation, and fear to memorialize personal and familial trajectories of leaving their homelands for a foreign country. Sometimes, as Selvamani, a refugee from Sri Lanka, reveals through her words, these stories can produce disfluencies due to the trauma of recollecting painful past experiences.[2] Migrants also recount experiences of moving from the countryside to the city, fleeing war and environmental destruction, and following nomadic routes within and across state boundaries. Even non-migrants imagine through stories what life might be like living abroad or being forced to remain at home. As with all genres, narratives about migration do not obey hard and fast rules to produce conventional speech events. Rather, storytelling practices create orienting frameworks to help audiences identify which communicative and poetic features render the past and future retellings of a narrative interpretable as a unified, distinct genre (Baker 2015). By transforming personal recollections of mobility and immobility into recognizable life stories, "interdiscursive processes" (Briggs and Bauman 1992) imbue migration narratives with the power to order collective experiences and organize biographical and social identities in more or less normative ways.

"Montreal Life Stories," an oral history project that memorializes the mass violence and displacement experiences of Cambodian, Haitian, Rwandan, and Holocaust-survivor Jewish refugees through life history interviews, art installations, digital storytelling, exhibitions, radio, and theater, further reminds us that migration narratives do not always have the capacity to render life histories or social identities sensible or even admissible as testimony (High 2014, 2015; see also Crapanzano 1996). Dialogically produced as open-ended interviews, this project, conducted between 2005 and 2012, sought to curate person-focused rather than event-centric tributes to the experiences of refugees and exiles in Montréal. Echoing the disciplinary view of linguistic anthropology, oral historian Steven High partially attributes the project's enormous success to the researchers' attention to the subjective and poetic dimensions of narrative form:

> Meaning and memory can be found not only in the words spoken but also in the form and structure of the oral narratives . . . People's relationships to their own stories—where they linger and what they skip over—helps us to understand the logic of what we are hearing. (2014:39)

Though not featured in this project, the recollections of Sri Lankan Tamil refugees have also given rise to a critically acclaimed literature coming out of Jaffna that, in addition to memorializing war, attempts to make sense of a life of peace in the "altered landscape" of the diaspora that has "meant new relationships, new perceptions, and a need to come to terms with the psychological trauma of violence" (Kanaganayakam 2007:124). Speaking to this literature and drawing from his own sociological research in Toronto, Rudramoorthy Cheran defines the Tamil diaspora as a "kind of imaginary that derives sustenance from nostalgia, pain and loss" and functions as "an engine of rebuilding" (2007:157). As a literary genre, Sri Lankan Tamil migration narratives display ambivalent sentiments that at once lament their people's banishment from the Jaffna homeland yet also appreciate new possibilities for renewal and transformation in the host societies. A source of inspiration to both Sri Lankans and Indians, this literature poignantly addresses themes of racism and displacement that resonate across diverse publics transnationally.

Similar to life history projects, the "new mobility paradigm" of diaspora and migration studies, by "imagin[ing] the world as being in constant motion" yet also subject to competing spatial and temporal realities, simultaneously seeks to account for both the experiences of immobility and its unique forms of exclusion (Salazar and Smart 2011). Anthropologists and historians studying the circulation of people, commodities, objects, ideas, diseases, and money have long argued that mobility and immobility are flip sides to globalization (Appadurai 1996), even though hegemonic narratives of modernity, by proposing a linear view of social progress and conflating "getting ahead" socioeconomically with "moving from place to place" geographically, tend to obscure this relationship. By assuming that migrants who move from the rural Global South to the urban Global North always benefit from the byproducts of industrial development and modernization, researchers neglect the creative capacity of immobility for social advancement and personal transformation. Analyzing narratives comparing the livelihoods of migrants and non-migrants living in Uriangato, Mexico, where discourses of social and geographic mobility are so tightly linked that people remaining behind have to work hard to disprove their doom to a less privileged fate, linguistic anthropologist Hilary Dick concludes, "Over time, working-class speakers learn to use migration discourse as a point of reference against which they measure their own lives, regardless of whether they migrate" (2010:281). By theorizing immobility as a potentiality rather than disability, mobility studies aim to deconstruct these progress narratives.

Studies of language contact also correlate the presumed unidirectionality of social and geographic mobility with developmental trajectories of self-identification and language learning, and historical trajectories of intergenerational language shift. The underlying premise here is that people will always self-identify with the languages they know best or in which they have acquired dominance over their life trajectories.[3] Seeking to disentangle these assumptions, linguistic anthropologist Kathryn Woolard (2011) conducted longitudinal research on urban migrants in Barcelona and found that, although still self-identifying as Castilian, teenagers switched from being dominant in Castilian to Catalan in adulthood because of marriage, motherhood, travel, and employment choices, attitudinal factors often overlooked by variationist sociolinguistic research that only factor "apparent time" correlations between synchronic linguistic variation and diachronic language change (see Labov 1963).[4] Woolard also criticizes developmental psychological models that envision childhood and adolescence as the sole "critical periods" for inculcating a linguistic habitus and instead highlights studies demonstrating the ongoing acquisition and socialization of linguistic and cultural competence across the lifespan (Fader 2009; Kulick and Schieffelin 2004) and the fluid identities of interlocutors as they move in and out of interactional spaces (Bucholtz and Hall 2005; Mendoza-Denton 2008).

In addition to contributing to the formation of multilingual repertoires, interaction is equally integral to the construction of migrant subjectivities over a person's lifetime. Linguistic anthropologist Stanton Wortham (2004) argues that pathways of identification gradually accrue vector-like dimensions through interactions repeatable at both micro and macro time scales. Yet a focus on interaction must not reduce the production format and participation roles of "acts of identity" to an exclusively speaker-focused perspective, linguistic anthropologists Adi Hastings and Paul Manning (2004) caution, recommending instead that narrative "acts of alterity" be studied as relational processes emergent through voicing and stance-taking. Literary theorist Mikhail Bakhtin (1981) earlier described the literary phenomenon known as "double-voicing" in which protagonists borrow the words of other characters of different social types. Similarly, Hastings and Manning write, "Speakers align themselves with respect to other interactants by *identifying* themselves with the features of exemplary figures, by adopting their 'voice,' for example" (2004:304). These exemplary figures become the stuff of stereotypes; whether or not they correspond with actual (that is, "authentic") social groups, they are still "real" in their narrative entailments.

Yet nationalists and other policymakers in Québec mistakenly presume that becoming multilingual is as straightforward as first migrating to the province, then assuming an ethnic and racial identity, and finally learning one of two dominant languages, French or English, in addition to maintaining one's heritage language. In competing for the loyalties of ethnic minorities and immigrants, Québécois leaders prescribe separate categories for heritage and civic language use and attempt to control how immigrants, refugees, and their descendants self-identify with these languages. Reflecting on the more complex construction of migrant subjectivities among Tamil speakers in Montréal further reminds me of Woolard's (1998) research in the comparable city of Barcelona, where she reveals "bivalency" to be a dominant modality of everyday multilingual communication. Bivalency is a concept that refers to the simultaneous membership of a linguistic element in two separate codes, which are presumed to be genealogically or functionally related to one another, usually in a hierarchical fashion. For example, certain words or morphemes can appear to be both etymologically Castilian, the national language of Spain, as well as Catalan, the language of Barcelona elites. Similarly in Montréal, there are words that may sound or look like both literary and colloquial Tamil, standard and nonstandard Québécois French, or French and English, in either their spoken or written form, depending on which linguistic resources are marked (depicted as special or abnormal in some way) or unmarked (that is, seen as ordinary or normal) by the surrounding discourse.

Bivalent forms and double-voiced utterances play a crucial role in the migration narratives of Tamil speakers featured in this chapter. Although varying substantially in semantic content, these narratives all use bivalent and double-voiced utterances to index how racist images and stereotypes of *tamouls* as "thugs" and "terrorists" inform Tamil youth's idiosyncratic self-identifications, language learning choices, and code-mixing and code-switching practices. Also, during my interviews and ethnographic encounters, I have witnessed these stereotypes being self-consciously contemplated and transformed into more positive images, including ones that juxtapose the "hyper-mobility" of Indian elites with the "immobile" yet imaginative life trajectories of Sri Lankan non-elites. Such "acts of alterity" disclose how the choice to speak standard and nonstandard varieties of French, Tamil, and English hinges not only on personal prospects for social and geographic mobility, but also on one's divided loyalty to anglophones and francophones.

Migration and Racism

Migration has historically brought both prosperity and hardship to Tamil speakers. Starting in the second century B.C.E., Vellālar farmers, *Karaiyar* fishermen, and *Chettiar* bankers and traders emigrated from South India to northeastern Sri Lanka and, over time, became the most affluent, dominant castes there. In the nineteenth and twentieth centuries, Chettiar bankers and traders from southern Tamil Nadu and northern Sri Lanka once again immigrated to Southeast Asia and eastern and southern Africa to join existing communities of prominent business leaders and merchant traders. Yet fortunes for Tamil migrants declined substantially during the colonial period, from 1830 to 1920, when lower-caste villagers recruited as indentured laborers through the *kangani* system worked on sugar and spice plantations in the former British colonies of South Africa, Mauritius, Fiji, Singapore, Guyana, Sri Lanka, and Trinidad, the former French colonies of Réunion, Martinique, French Guiana, and Guadeloupe, and the former Dutch colonies of Guyana and Sumatra, where they faced incredible hardships and discrimination. In some of these colonies, Tamil indentured laborers lived separately from upper-caste professionals and merchants of the same ethnicity. Even in India, *Dalits* fleeing drought-stricken and economically deprived rural Tamil Nadu in the 1940s for the urban slums of Delhi, Bombay, Calcutta, and Bangalore were socially ostracized by Tamil Brahmins with government posts, university positions, and more lucrative jobs (Charusheela 2007). Other elite travelers after Independence included the French citizens of Pondicherry, who voyaged back and forth between India, France, and its colonies to benefit from educational and job opportunities.

Among the present-day Tamil-speaking diasporas in North America, Europe, and Australia, Sri Lankans often encounter Indians of vastly higher class and caste backgrounds. With subsequent waves of asylum seekers arriving from progressively lower castes and lower socioeconomic statuses, these differences grow starker. Political scientist Christopher McDowell (1996) identifies two immigrant cohorts in Switzerland: lower-middle-class refugees from urban Sri Lanka who arrived between 1983 and 1991, and lower-caste, poorly educated refugees from the rural regions of Sri Lanka who arrived after the 1990s. Cultural anthropologists E. Valentine Daniel and Yuvaraj Thangaraj (1995) note similar trends in Britain, where different socioeconomic class and caste groups of Sri Lankans rent apartments in segregated residential neighborhoods. It is notable that even the most successful Sri Lankan Tamil immigrants in London prefer to remain financially solvent in order to liquefy their assets if given the chance to immigrate to Canada. As one of Daniel and Thangaraj's informants in London explains, "In Toronto and Montreal there are places called 'Little Jaffna.' That is enough of a Tamil nation for me. Wherever there are enough Tamils, there is a Tamil nation" (Daniel and Thangaraj 1995:175–176). Toronto, the preeminent city of business and commerce in Canada, attracts more upper-class and higher-caste refugees than does Montréal. Consequently, diasporic patterns of caste and class segregation and competition for migrant labor characterize social relations between these neighboring cities as well.

Muthu informally characterizes four generational cohorts in Montréal according to their substantive differences in linguistic competence and schooling. Members of the first cohort, first-generation immigrants aged forty and above, almost always speak in Tamil with one another and know very little English or French. The second group includes recent immigrants from Sri Lanka between the ages of fourteen and forty who attend college or high school, or work in Québec. They speak in Tamil with each other, but also know English to varying extents. The third group includes migrants arriving in Montréal as primary and secondary school students. This "first and a half" generation, who are mostly youth between the ages of six and twenty-five, speak in Tamil with their parents, though many cannot read or write it, and converse with their friends in French and English. Finally, the last group includes second-generation, Montréal-born children below the age of thirteen who will have completed their entire education in French or English. My observations confirm these categories, yet I would add to them the less publicly discussed caste distinctions between Indian Brahmins (who are speakers of "Sanskritized" Tamil), the dominant Vellālar and Karaiyar castes of Sri Lanka (who are speakers of a purified register of Jaffna Tamil), and other non-elite castes. Since the elite populations of India and Sri Lanka rarely come into contact except in the diaspora, Vellālar and Karaiyar Tamils from Jaffna find themselves in the unfamiliar position of being unable to assert their social and ritual dominance over the more affluent and higher-caste Tamil Brahmins from India, who instead find themselves struggling to prove their authenticity, yet this time to Jaffna Tamils. These estranged conditions feed into the ambient linguistic rivalries shaping migrant subjectivities in Montréal.

Based on anecdotal evidence and a comprehensive survey of media representations of Tamil speakers living in Montréal since 1977, I have analyzed the xenophobic and sometimes outright racist discourses impinging on the formation of Tamil-Canadian identities. My first inkling of a hostile attitude toward Tamil speakers came in the summer of 2002 at a dinner party during which I overheard a middle-aged Québécois de souche man, an employee of a large pharmaceutical company in an English-dominant West Island suburb, scornfully complain of his company's recent decision to hire a new Sri Lankan CEO, by stating emphatically, "Y'ont engagé un maudit Sri Lankais! Pourquoi pas un Canadien ou même un Américain? Ben non, il fallait engagé un Sri Lankais"[5] (They hired a damn Sri Lankan! Why not a Canadian or even an American? But no, they had to hire a Sri Lankan). I am struck by the audacity of this statement, inflected with nonstandard Québécois French syntax, phonology, and idioms (underlined in this order of appearance) and spoken in a high volume and pitch, which can be interpreted as embodying a populist voice that questions the suitability of a South Asian man heading a Canadian company. Whether this man is referring to a Sinhalese or Tamil person when speaking of a "Sri Lankan" is unclear. The Québécois media sometimes uses "Sri Lankan" and "Tamil" interchangeably when reporting news on so-called "terrorists" working for the Liberation Tigers of Tamil Eelam (LTTE), "thugs" in street gangs and criminal drug networks, and "illegal boat people" (Colpron 1988; Côte 2004; La Presse 2004; Laroche 1997; Pelchat 1991; Tasso 1986, 2004). Efforts by Tamil activists to challenge these images through public education campaigns showcasing the richness of Sri Lankan Tamil culture and the persecution of a people have little effect (Première Chaîne 2006).[6]

"Tamoul" has become a generic racial epithet. In a 2003 article published in *La Presse*, a French-medium newspaper popular with middle-class Québécois readers, the report reveals that "tamoul" is a racial slur equivalent to "animal," "camel rider," "fucking Arab," and "job stealer":

> Bahjat Muhtaseb, a hard working store clerk of Palestinian origin who had been promised the position of manager at the Maxi supermarket in Cote-des-Neiges, has often been insulted by his co-workers and threatened by one of them in particular. He was labeled a "Tamil," "animal," "camel rider," "fucking Arab," and "job stealer" by three colleagues, who were severely punished by their employer, Provigo Corporation. (Dugas 2003)

I visited this supermarket almost every day from January to May 2005 while residing in Côte-des-Neiges, a mixed residential and commercial neighborhood (*quartier*) with the largest ethnic Sri Lankan Tamil population in Montréal. It is hard to believe that the offending coworkers could have mistaken the Palestinian clerk as a Tamil in a store with so many Sri Lankan cashiers and clients. Since this case did not involve linguistic discrimination, however, it did not become high-profile news. The number of public references to language discrimination far eclipse those concerning racial discrimination, Sarkar et al. (2007) note, regardless of how deeply entangled are the aural and visual dimensions of language and race in constructing notions of citizenship in Québec.

This point became evident in 2006 and 2007 when Premier Jean Charest appointed a commission headed by sociologist and historian Gérard Bouchard and philosopher Charles Taylor to investigate attitudes of "intercultural" tolerance across the province and assemble a statement on which "reasonable accommodations" (*accommodements raisonnables*) Québec's public institutions and spaces should offer to its ethnic and religious minorities.[7] Also resulting from these conversations was a clearer articulation of Québec's "interculturalism" policy, which, in opposition to Canadian multiculturalism, strives to combat racism and discrimination while also promoting integration into the majority Québécois culture, explicitly defined by Bouchard as celebrating the norms and values of a francophone, secular, gender egalitarian, and democratic society (Bouchard 2012:29).[8] When candidates for provincial office in the *Parti liberal* (PLQ), *Parti québécois* (PQ), and newly formed *Action Démocratique du Québec* (ADQ) affirmed their commitment first to women's rights, second to secularism, and third to religious and cultural tolerance in a televised debate during the 2008 election, minority leaders criticized this stance-taking as scapegoating religious groups, also called "visible minorities," for threatening the province's liberal ideals. Yet these politicians soon shifted footing when the commission stopped in Hérouxville, a small rural town of 1,338 Québécois de souche inhabitants who presented them with a list of their limits to religious tolerance, explicitly targeting the head coverings and religious symbols associated with Muslims, Jews, and Sikhs (Girard 2007). Aghast community and business leaders from Montréal promptly condemned this so-called *code de vie* as racist and certainly not representative of urban outlooks.

A comedy sketch entitled "Hérouxtyville," televised on the popular end-of-year variety show "Bye Bye 2007," issued the most scathing critique. Growing up I have always associated the "Bye Bye" show with my family's *jour de l'an* (New Year's Day) party, when my aunts and uncles would dance and drink through the night and my cousins and I would watch the "Bye Bye" over delicious bowls of chocolate mousse. As the only Americans in the group, my brother and I never understood most of the show's popular culture references and would rely on our cousins to explain. Originally broadcast in 1968 though temporarily discontinued in 1998, the "Bye Bye" was revived by *Rock et Belles Oreilles*, a comedy duo, who produced two new shows in 2006 and 2007, after a long hiatus. The night before my family's party, I decide to watch "Bye Bye 2007" on my own. Though not understanding most of the skits, I am suddenly jarred out of my drowsy state when I hear someone mention the word "tamoul." Knowing that the "Bye Bye" always replays on New Year's Day, the following night I ask my cousin's wife, the hostess of the party, to record the show on a VHS tape so that I can transcribe the skit for my research.

The scene begins with a man (M) wearing a fez and long tunic and a woman (W) wearing a headscarf driving together in a car while singing the popular Québécois neo-folk song "Dégénération," by *Mes Aïeux*. Suddenly the car stalls. Discussing their options, the man and woman turn to speak to one another in what sounds like International French, using expressions such as "panne d'essence" and "p'tite merguez" and syntax such as "où sommes-nous?" revealing them to be elites, foreigners, or both, but certainly not people from rural Québec.[9]

W: Qu'est-ce qu'y a?
What's wrong?
M: *Panne d'essence.*
We ran out of gas.
W: Calme-toi *ma p'tite merguez.*
Don't worry, my little spicy sausage (pet name).
M: Mais, *où sommes-nous* exactement?
But where are we exactly?

Viewers see a sign that reads, "Bienvenue à Hérouxville, Population: Juste assez" (Welcome to Hérouxville. Population: Just enough). The voice-over narrator then announces in a deep voice, "Les films de peur vous présentent 'Hérouxtyville,' la p'tite ville intolérante" (We present to you the horror film "Hérouxtyville," an intolerant small town). A truck driver (T) from Hérouxtyville suspiciously greets the couple as they exit their car to fill up on gas at the town's only station.[10]

T: Tu parles d'un heure pour conduire en pydjama.
Talk about a time to be driving around in your pajamas.
M: C'est un costume traditionnel.
This is traditional clothing.
T: Parce que l'Halloween c'était y a deux mois.
Because Halloween was two months ago.
(M and W look at each other and laugh)
T: C'est quoi votre char?
What kind of car do you have?
M: Une Hyundai.
A Hyundai.
T: Un char étranger. Bougez pas. (On intercom in truck): Hé le gros. Une famille de tamouls dans un char de chop suey. J'é ramasse-tu?
A foreign car. Don't move. (On intercom in truck). Hey, big guy. A Tamil family in a chop suey car. Do I pick them up?

There it is, the punch line. Yet nothing about this couple remotely suggests a connection with Tamil culture (Indian or Sri Lankan). Having failed to convince the truck driver they are fellow citizens, this couple is labeled as the most enigmatic of ethnic categories in Québec: *les tamouls.*

Analyzing the entire exchange afterward, I notice the poetic juxtaposition between the rough-sounding voice of the nonstandard Québécois French–speaking truck driver—this register is easily identifiable by the hard-sounding [t͡s] in "tu," [dʒ] in "pydjama" (also an anglicism) and [tʃ] in "chop suey," as well as his use of the archaic French word "char," his nonstandard syntax, "j'ai ramasse-tu," "c'est quoi," "un heure," and "ya," and his idiomatic expression, "hé le gros"—and the polite-sounding voice of a well-groomed man speaking a foreign-sounding French with none of these hard sounds. These caricatured voices index an underlying social critique: the truck driver must be culturally ignorant or racist for mistaking the couple's ethnicity as Tamil, which is clearly inaccurate. The narrator affirms this interpretation of the truck driver's xenophobia by proclaiming in a slightly ambiguous register, "À Hérouxtyville, tout c'qui est pas d'icitte on n'en veut pas!" (In Hérouxtyville, whatever is not from here, we don't want it). Except for the one deictic marker "d'icitte" spoken in nonstandard Québécois French to emphasize the inverse, what is actually "not from here" in the (not-so) fictional town of Hérouxtyville (modeled on the real town of Hérouxville), the narrator utters the rest of his line in standard Québécois French. These double-voiced utterances betray the narrator's sarcastic tone and affirm the socially distant relationship that urban folk from Montréal seek to emphasize with the non-cosmopolitan folk of rural Québec.

Although I did not discuss this comedy sketch with my Indian and Sri Lankan Tamil informants in Montréal, I have encountered similar themes and strategies of racism- and xenophobia-motivated social distancing in their own migration narratives. Aditya, a graduate student in his early twenties who experienced caste and class discrimination in his hometown of Pondicherry, makes a candid observation when asked how he discerns Indians from Sri Lankans:

> First their looks even. I can't pinpoint their appearance. But I can find a Sri Lankan person. If I see a person I can tell. The worst one is that I am mistaken as Sri Lankan in and around Montréal. By French people and by English people. They first ask me, "Oh you're from Sri Lanka?" "No I am from India." (*laughter*)

Aditya deduces that his dark complexion predisposes some people to assume that he is Sri Lankan. Although his laughter suggests a possible lack of concern with this, other Indian Tamils react to this misnomer more seriously and attempt to emphasize the vast social distance between themselves and Sri Lankan Tamils to protect their elite mobility. One way this distance manifests itself publicly is by displaying a preference for speaking English instead of French in daily life.

The Elite Mobility of Learning English

Although census information about caste groups in India ceased to be recorded after 1931, social anthropologists Christopher Fuller and Haripriya Narasimhan (2014) argue that the transformation of Tamil Brahmins from a "traditional, mainly rural, caste elite into a modern, urban, middle-class community" was completed by the mid-twentieth century. Writing about "anglophile" Tamil Brahmins living in New Delhi, sociologist Anand Inbanathan (1997) explains how their children commonly attend private English schools or public schools run by the Delhi Tamil Educational Association and study in Tamil for elementary school and English for secondary school. Although this practice is changing, older generations of Tamil Brahmins rarely learned Hindi and relied instead on the *lingua franca*, English, a language they believed allows for greater social mobility. A similar decision-making rationale characterizes first-generation, middle- to high-caste Indian Tamils living in Montréal who choose English as their *lingua franca* and develop only rudimentary knowledge of the civic language, Québécois French. After all, outside of the school system one can easily survive in Montréal without knowing French.

The Sundarans and Viswanathans, both Iyengar Tamil Brahmin families,[11] exemplify this preference by studying and working almost exclusively in English over several generations. Mr. Sundaran, who is from Delhi, and Mrs. Sundaran, who is from Bangalore, first met while completing their doctoral studies at the University of Waterloo in Ontario in the late 1960s. He received a Ph.D. in computer engineering and she in chemistry before they both moved to Montréal, where Mr. Sundaran worked at a pharmaceutical company until his retirement. He now volunteers part-time as a professional hospital interpreter and translator for Sri Lankan Tamil patients, and Mrs. Sundaran teaches chemistry at an English-medium CEGEP (the equivalent of community college).[12] The Viswanathans, both from Bangalore, completed their doctorate and postdoctoral studies at the University of California at Berkeley in the early 1970s before moving to Montréal. These couples' children, Lalitha Sundaran and Mohan Viswanathan, are childhood friends-turned-college sweethearts who recently got married and now work primarily in English as family practice physicians. Mohan's childhood as an English-dominant speaker is relatively straightforward. Growing up in the primarily English-speaking town of Dollard-des-Ormeaux in the West Island, he attended English-medium public schools before enrolling at McGill University, a prestigious English-medium university, to pursue his medical studies. Raised in the mostly French-speaking South Shore town of St-Bruno-de-Montarville, Lalitha developed a different communicative repertoire by attending a French immersion program in English-medium elementary and secondary schools, where, she recalls, "francophone and anglophone students wouldn't sit together in the cafeteria; there were a lot of fights between the two groups."[13] Lalitha works at Jewish General Hospital in Côte-des-Neiges, the English-medium hospital where her father also volunteers part-time as an interpreter and translator of Tamil.[14]

As the only Tamil interpreter among mostly Gujarati and Punjabi coworkers, Mr. Sundaran speaks of a pressing need for Tamil language workers in hospitals due to the growing Sri Lankan patient population. Growing up speaking primarily in Tamil with her family, Lalitha feels at ease conversing in Tamil with her Sri Lankan patients and aspires to establish a family practice clinic serving low-income immigrants and refugees living in the neighborhood where she works. Mohan is much less comfortable speaking in French since he attended English-medium schools all his life, and also struggles to speak Tamil, which he learned to speak later in his life, believing that "Sri Lankan Tamil . . . is a completely different language." Mohan insists that most Indians in Montréal, his wife excluded, would have to study Sri Lankan Tamil as a foreign language, much like English speakers study French. He manages to converse with his Indian in-laws in Tamil yet always uses an interpreter to speak in Tamil with his Sri Lankan patients. Mr. Sundaran tells me that Mohan, who is faced with being assigned to work for several years in an underserved rural community in Québec, wants Lalitha to move with him to the United States, where they can earn more money and raise their future children in English.

Upwardly mobile Indian Tamils frequently emigrate for reasons of education and employment. Aditya arrived in Montréal on September 2, 2001, just a few days before the terrorist attacks in the United States, to pursue a master's degree in building engineering at Concordia University. A Vaishnava Hindu by origin from Pondicherry, Aditya hails from an unconventional family. Raised by a single mother, a homeopathic doctor who used to work for the government, Aditya considers Telugu to be his "mother tongue," since his mother was born in a border town now part of Andhra Pradesh where residents speak both Tamil and Telugu. Aditya generally speaks Telugu with his mother's family and Tamil with his father's family, who is from the Manali district of Chennai, yet confesses to feel less loyalty toward his family in Chennai because "nobody stays there now . . . all of our roots have moved everywhere." Leaving Pondicherry himself at a young age, Aditya first studied architecture at the University of Madras and then worked as an assistant editor for the *Construction Journal of India* in New Delhi before moving to Montréal. He applied to nine master's degree programs in the United States and Canada before eventually deciding on Concordia University, known for its reputable programs in engineering and bioinformatics and providing what he considers to be "the best education for a cheap price." Recalling the few Indian Tamil graduate students at Concordia when he first arrived, Aditya explains:

> Canada was not a hot spot at that time. For Indians, it was still a new place to explore. When I came, I was the only Tamil guy. There were two Tamil guys before, but the year I came, I was the only guy. They came in ones and twos. The next year after my batch, we had at least six, seven people. No more than that, ten people. Ten Tamil people. I am not saying Indian. From Tamilnad. So that was a large increase and that was the time that the U.S. has this problem of restricting the visas. I came on 2nd September. Then people started focusing on Canada. A lot of people started to come to Canada after that.[15]

Aditya created a Yahoo listserv to assist international students in finding apartments near downtown metro stations, obtaining student visas, and locating grocery stores carrying Tamil food products. It is noteworthy that in his social circle, there are no second-generation Indian Tamils. He does not relate easily to Canadian-born Tamils who are, in his opinion, more oriented to classical traditions than he and his friends, who boast of a more modern, Westernized outlook:

> It took me a long time to meet the second-generation Indians that are born here. Not many people I have met so far even. Culturally we are different, though we both are Indians, origins-wise. Their Indian is not synchronized with our Indian. They are more classical. I mean like, if they are Indian, if they take only the Indian part, their only Indian part is very classical. And our only Indian part is more everything. May not be classical even [laughter]. Theirs is more refined.
>
> Not language. Language wise, they only get what their parents speak so, uh, that you cannot really get the pure part of it. But the other part, like the classical music or classical dance, they go for the real pure stuff. I have a couple of friends who go for Bharat Natyam. They are good in it, they do good stuff. I know a person who went back to India to learn *veena*. That is a big surprise for us. That surprises because we don't know that. Maybe 10 or 20% do this, even that 20% who do classical stuff, they don't spend 100% on classical stuff. They have other stuff going on, right? That's not really the common stuff in India, right? There are people who are completely Westernized, in India even.

Aditya's classmate at Concordia University, Arjuna, explains that learning classical Indian arts is "a traditional Tamil Brahmin family thing. So it is compulsory to study." He himself a Brahmin like many of the first-wave Indian Tamil immigrants settling in Montréal in the 1960s and 1970s, Arjuna studied *veena* (a stringed instrument) and learned Carnatic music as a child and is now an active member of the arts association, *Bharatiyar Sangeet Sangam*, in Montréal.

Tamil Brahmins, first and second generation, are less concerned with linguistic purity. Aditya, who studied Tamil literature in India, considers himself the exception for remembering how to write in Tamil. Hemanth also used to write poetry in Tamil in India yet admits to now forgetting some Tamil characters and even how to write basic sentences. Ironically, Hemanth's father was a teacher of Tamil in Chennai, where his modest earnings prevented him from sending his first son to English-medium school. Only Hemanth, the second son, could study in English after his father had saved enough money to pay for private school tuition. Hemanth sheepishly explains this rationale:

> South Indian Tamils are crazy for English. English represents power and superiority. They know Tamil but they speak in English because they see it as a modern thing. People believe that if you don't know English, you can't survive in this world. And knowing English gives you more opportunity to travel.[16]

Choosing to speak in English also creates a bond among non-Hindi-speaking South Indians in Montréal, such as between Aditya and his mostly Telugu-speaking friends. Arjuna, who learned Hindi while residing with his mother's family in Bombay and regularly socializes with Hindi-speaking North Indians in Montréal, is perhaps the sole exception. In 2002, Aditya, Arjuna, and several other graduate students founded the Indian Students Association (ISA) at Concordia University to host cultural shows and social activities emphasizing pan-Indian commonalities.

By invitation I attend a cultural show organized by Indian leaders of the organization, Tamilagam, in celebration of the Hindu holiday, Deepavali, on October 8, 2005. A first-generation female college student from India and a second-generation male teenager born in Montréal perform a series of skits as the show's masters of ceremony. During one of these skits, the woman pretends to be an immigrant mother (*ammā*) teasing her Canadian-born son (*makan*) about his cultural and linguistic ignorance. In a particularly humorous exchange, ammā speaks to makan in Tamil and makan responds to her in a Tamil–English drawl. When makan "fails" to perceive an important phonemic distinction between the long and short "a" in Tamil and mistakes the word "debate" (*paṭṭi manṛam*) for "grandmother" (*pāṭṭi*), parents in the audience are reminded of their own English-dominant children's difficulties in distinguishing Tamil vowel lengths. Even when ammā corrects his mistake, makan continues to "incorrectly" superimpose English stress patterns and intonation contours onto Tamil words, as well as Tamil stress patterns and intonation contours onto English words. The following excerpt showcases makan's ability to seamlessly alternate prosodic laminations while simultaneously switching between codes. Here, I underline the use of English intonation contours (rise–fall–rise) when makan is speaking in Tamil, highlight in bold Tamil intonation contours (fall–rise–fall) when he is speaking in English, and use italics to mark when his Tamil speech is overlaid with English lexical stress.[17] Also, English lexical stress is indicated with accent marks and Tamil vowel length in over score.

(1) *ā'mā* you said something about "*pa'ṭṭi man'ṛam*"
mom you said something about "paṭṭi manṛam"
(2) **what is that**
(3) **is pāṭṭi coming over, I don't know**
is grandmother coming over, I don't know
(4) **oh it's a debate is it**
(5) **oh actually speaking**
(6) *nā kū'ṭa rōm'ba* school debate *pa'ṇṇi tēr'pen*
I love it when we have school debates
(7) ya ya, our favorite, all the time, debate *pa'ṇṇi tēr'pen*
(8) so what's the topic

Skillfully alternating between Tamil-accented English and English-accented Tamil in lines 1–2 and 5–6, the teenager playing makan briefly steps outside of his caricatured role as an ignorant buffoon to expose his true mastery of both languages. Audience members who laugh perhaps detect his challenge of the popular stereotype that second-generation boys are too lazy to speak Tamil properly. Rather, his effortless prosodic alternations imply that a more youthful, laid-back style might be necessary to master multiple languages. No doubt leaders of Tamilagam chose this teenager as the master of ceremonies because of his knowledge of both Tamil and English. However, through the teenager's pretense of linguistic ineptitude, they can also issue a gentle reminder to parents who do not speak with their children enough in Tamil of the consequences that may await them. From a linguist's perspective, the teenager's skillful lamination of Tamil intonation onto English sentences and English lexical stress and vowel length onto Tamil syllable structure demonstrates a heightened level of metalinguistic awareness of the hierarchical organization yet simultaneous presence of segmental phonological forms (that is, vowels and consonants) and suprasegmental features (that is, tone, stress, pitch, rhythm, and intonation) and, moreover, how to manipulate their combination to create a speech register that sounds both Tamil and English, but not exactly like the "Tanglish" popular among the older generation of migrants from India. Rather, this Tamil-English drawl is uniquely the product of Montréal's newest generation of Tamil anglophone elites, who, while facetiously pretending to keep these languages separate, are building multilingual repertoires with greater flexibility for social and geographic mobility.

The Circumscribed Mobility of Learning French

After spending four months living in an English-dominant neighborhood in Côte-des-Neiges, I searched for a different rental in the French-speaking quartier, Villeray, to be closer to the many Sri Lankan Tamil men and women who work in factories there and the Catholic church that offers mass and other ecclesiastical services in Tamil. My new roommates, Mario and Joseph, are twenty-five-year-old childhood friends from Saguenay-Lac-St-Jean, a rural region of Québec that often features as the butt of jokes in urban circles for its reputed preponderance of cousin marriages. The two friends migrated to Montréal in the early 2000s to study computer programming together at the Université de Montréal, yet after trying without success to break into Montréal's thriving video game industry, they now work long hours as electronics repair technicians. A friend of mine who designs at Ubisoft, the largest video game company in Montréal, confirmed that his company prefers to hire English speakers or bilinguals who can communicate with an international clientele. Mario and Joseph, even though they studied English since grade school, cannot hold a simple conversation in this language. Moreover, they speak a variety of nonstandard Québécois French that is unique to the Saguenay-Lac-St-Jean region. I assume that I alone, as an American, have difficulty understanding Mario and Joseph's speech, until one day Joseph's girlfriend tells me that people from the Lac-St-Jean often use archaic idiomatic expressions that Montréal natives, she herself included, cannot readily comprehend.

Since learning more prestigious varieties of French facilitates greater mobility within the circumscribed francophone world, people who command standard Québécois French or International French enjoy better career and life opportunities not available to Mario and Joseph or other native speakers of nonstandard French. Correspondingly, Indian and Sri Lankan Tamils who choose French as their dominant language are also likely to choose a life and career path in Québec or another French-speaking country. Tamils originally from Pondicherry, India, had made a similar decision in 1962 after the French colony joined the Indian union, and elite residents with French citizenship were given the choice to keep their French citizenship and gain privileged access to French health care, education, and retirement pensions, or else become Indian citizens.[18] Although born in Pondicherry, Aditya and his family were never French citizens. Only through my friendship with Marianne, a graduate student of religion at the Université du Québec à Montréal (UQAM), did I learn of an older diaspora of francophone Tamils whose ancestors (maternal in Marianne's case) have roots throughout *la francophonie*.

A mutual friend, David, a student of religion and researcher of Tamil Saivism, introduces me to Marianne when I visit his office at UQAM one day. Learning of our similar mixed-race ancestry—her father is Québécois, my mother is Québécoise; her mother is Indian, my father is Indian—we hit it off and arrange to meet for lunch at a North Indian restaurant on campus on *rue St-Denis*. When I arrive seeing Marianne dressed in a salwar kameez (tunic and trousers) rather than nondescript Western clothes like mine, I realize how proud she is to self-identify as Indian. Through the course of our meal, Marianne shares with me the remarkable history of her maternal extended family, who are all French citizens originally from Pondicherry and currently living in France. Marianne's mother's family comes from an elite lineage of wealthy merchants who resided for five generations in Saigon, Vietnam, during and after French colonial rule in Asia. The children of this family all attended French-medium Catholic schools in either Pondicherry or Saigon, moving back and forth between the cities as the circumstances demanded. Marianne's mother herself returned to Pondicherry with her own mother and siblings after completing her schooling in Saigon and before finding a job in Cambodia; yet when her beloved father passed away, she left Cambodia to join a religious convent in Laos to grieve privately. There, she met Marianne's father, a young missionary from Trois-Rivières, Québec, studying to become a priest. Fascinated with Indian culture, he fell in love with Marianne's mother at first glance through the convent window and gave up the priesthood to work in a commercial role for the Church instead.

The newly married couple traveled extensively throughout the francophone world building a home for their young family. Marianne and her older sister were born in Switzerland and lived there for a few years until the family moved to Vancouver to accommodate his father's itinerant job with the Church. In Vancouver, the girls attended a French-medium public school for French Canadian and French-speaking immigrant children, where the teachers strictly enforced a policy obliging students to speak in French for half the school day (including recess) and the other half in English. Marianne recollects students code-switching and code-mixing and thus infuriating their teachers, who told them, "pick one language and speak it well." Despite their teachers' admonishments, the children did not feel deficient in either language. Marianne nostalgically recalls speaking both English and French with ease in Vancouver. Yet at age fifteen, when Marianne's father was relocated to a suburb of Versailles in France and her mother took her to register for school, she was informed by the teachers there that Marianne's education in Vancouver had insufficiently prepared her for full-time study in French. Her mother disagreed with this assessment and chose to enroll Marianne in a class with her same age cohort rather than hold her back a year. Marianne surprised her teachers with how quickly she picked up Parisian French, yet over the years, lost her conversational ability in English due to a lack of practice. Even at home, her parents speak only in French with one another, and Marianne, in addition to French, only occasionally speaks in Tamil with her mother and her other relatives.

After completing her university studies in France, Marianne moved with her parents back to Canada—yet, this time to her father's home province of Québec—and started her master's degree at UQAM. Now, instead of struggling with French, Marianne struggles with English. She confides in me that that she would not mind living in an English-speaking country, such as the United States or in Asia, where, ironically, she believes she would feel more comfortable than in a French-speaking society like Québec. She makes friends easily with Indians and non-Indians, Catholics and non-Catholics alike. This comes naturally to her since her mother has always had close non-Indian friends. In Vancouver her best friend was a Canadian woman married to a Corsican man, and in Saigon, her closest friends were Vietnamese women. Marianne refers to her North Indian and Indo-Mauritian friends as Hindi people (whether they speak Hindi or not), yet her closest and truest friends are other Catholic francophones. After our lunch together, Marianne brings me to visit the *Centre liturgique de l'ordre des Sœurs Disciples du Divin Maitre* on *rue Sherbrooke* to meet some of the nuns whom she has known since she was a girl in France.

Marianne also invites me to meet her parents, devout Catholics as well, at her home in Saint-Michel, where I spend many evenings enjoying Marianne's mother's delicious coconut chicken curry. Occasionally, I accompany the family to their church, such as on the Day of the Assumption of the Virgin Mary, when we participate in a neighborhood procession touring the streets of Rosemont. Marianne's father also puts me in contact with Father Joseph, the chaplain of the Sri Lankan Tamil Catholic mission and officiator of mass in Tamil at *Église Ste-Cécile* every Sunday, who agrees to let me observe heritage language classes at his church. When I update the family on the progress of my research, they sometimes share their own views.

One day, I tell Marianne and her mother that some people regard Indian Tamil and Sri Lankan Tamil as two distinct languages. This statement provokes different responses from mother and daughter. Marianne concurs and states that Indians speak "Spoken Tamil" and Sri Lankans speak "Written Tamil," which she cannot fully understand because she is illiterate in Tamil. Marianne's mother, upon hearing her daughter's response, clarifies that Sri Lankans speak a more classical style of Tamil than Indians do. Having often socialized with Sri Lankan women at her Catholic church while living in Paris, Marianne's mother is more familiar with Sri Lankan Tamil varieties than her daughter is. Comparing Sri Lankan Tamil to Parisian French on the one hand, and Indian Tamil to Québécois French on the other, she states that the former two languages are purer and more literary-like than the latter two. Both Marianne and her mother speak the prestigious International French, compared to Marianne's father who, as a native of Trois-Rivières, still retains traces of a French Canadian accent, despite many years living abroad.

Marianne, after finishing her master's degree, is looking for a job in education, while her older sister, having always excelled at learning languages, works as an interpreter and translator for the federal government in Ottawa. In demand throughout Canada, trilingual interpreters and translators are especially plentiful in Montréal where, especially if they work for the government, they can make a decent living. Nila, a recent college graduate, is contemplating becoming a translator and interpreter herself. She temporarily works as a waitress and office manager at her sister and brother-in-law's restaurant, Spicy Land, on *rue Jean Talon* in Parc Extension, the neighborhood with the second-largest Tamil-speaking population in Montréal after Côte-des-Neiges. One day in March 2005, I agree to meet David at this restaurant to discuss our plans to tour the Tamil Saivite temples of Montréal where he conducts his research. We are the only other people in the restaurant except for two young boys quietly completing their homework at a nearby table. Nila gives us her undivided attention and, after learning of my research, explains that, like she herself, her nephews, ages nine and ten, speak Tamil, French, and English fluently. To prove this, she calls them over to our table in English and introduces them to us in French. When we ask them about their schoolwork in French, they respond likewise; when their parents call from the kitchen in Tamil to chide them for not working, the boys respond in Tamil and head reluctantly back to their table. As Nila also walks away, David sadly comments that trilingual children are often obligated to translate for their monolingual parents and relatives at doctors' visits, parent-teacher conferences, and other meetings, where they are exposed to adult-sensitive information. He insists that this exposure makes them disrespectful and unruly toward parents.[19]

Later during the meal, Nila informs us that her father works at the *Palais de Justice* as an interpreter and translator of French, English, and Tamil on asylum cases involving Sri Lankan refugees. Born and educated in Sri Lanka and literate in both Tamil and English, upon arriving in Montréal Nila's father took advantage of intensive full-time and part-time courses funded by the provincial government to learn French. Later, after buying a house in a mainly French-speaking suburb in Laval, he became, by necessity, conversationally fluent in French. Nila, sharing the same language competences, says that her father has been pressuring her to join his profession since she graduated from the University of Toronto with a degree in psychology. Yet to secure steady employment, Nila returned to Montréal to decide whether she wants to remain in this city with her family or find work elsewhere in Canada. For now, as the restaurant's office manager, she keeps busy by bringing the establishment into compliance with Québec's language legislations by writing advertisements, translating menus, and conversing with clients in French.

The next evening, David and I visit Montréal's three Sri Lankan Tamil Saivite temples, devoted separately to the worship of Murukan, Durkai, and Ganesha, important gods in the Tamil Hindu pantheon, as well as the pan-Indian temple, Hindu Mandir, where Vaishnavite and Saivite Indian Tamils worship alongside Indians of other ethnolinguistic backgrounds. Under renovation to build a *pūjā* room in the adjoining building that also features a genuine *kōpuram*, which is an ornate monumental tower situated at the entrance of the temple, the *Thiru Murugan Temple* appears particularly bustling that night. David takes me to meet the priests and board members. The youngest soon-to-be board member, Pavalan, a man in his mid-twenties who emigrated from a town near Kopai in Jaffna when he was eleven, agrees to meet with me the following week to discuss his work for the temple. A part-time security guard at Pierre Elliot Trudeau airport finishing his college studies in business marketing, Pavalan still finds time to volunteer as the temple's government liaison. His responsibilities there involve researching government funds, consulting with lawyers about land zoning issues, and collaborating with elected officials and media personnel to educate the wider public about Sri Lankan Tamil culture and religion. Pavalan praises Mayor Gérald Tremblay, a personal friend of his, for expressing genuine interest in Hinduism and attending a temple event three years ago, during which they ceremonially planted three trees together, symbolizing unity between Sri Lanka, Canada, and Québec, at the entrance of the temple. Favorably comparing Montréal to both Toronto and Paris, where many of his relatives reside and he has often visited, Pavalan characterizes Montréal's lifestyle as being "easier, more open, and going with the flow" compared to the "busy" scene of Toronto and the less tolerant milieu of Paris, where he says the dominant French culture is "too strong" to permit religious and cultural diversity to flourish.

Although the first of Pavalan's relatives to immigrate to Canada was a maternal uncle who works as a truck driver in Toronto, his other maternal relatives settled in Montréal after moving to Dubai and Singapore and then sponsored his entire family to migrate directly there. Together, the family has prospered by helping finance each other's homes and businesses. His uncles co-own two Sri Lankan grocery stores, one on *Autoroute Décarie* and another, Jaffna Foods, in the West Island. Pavalan's maternal family's social and geographic mobility deviates from the more precarious fortunes and circumscribed mobility of his paternal relatives living in the United Kingdom, the Netherlands, Norway, and France, where many are forced to remain. One cousin in particular, who emigrated from Jaffna to Colombo and then to Paris, eagerly awaits the Canadian government's final approval of Pavalan's father's request to sponsor him in Québec.

Such restrictions on geographic mobility are common among Sri Lankan Tamil refugees of lower class and caste status, who often do not have the financial resources and social networks to seek asylum in their first country of choice, or even live in their preferred city or neighborhood. Upon arriving in Montréal, Pavalan's parents followed the established pattern of first renting a small apartment in Côte-des-Neiges and then moving to a bigger one in the Sauvé quartier closer to their place of employment. Although Pavalan's father once made a decent salary working as a naval engineer for a Greek-owned cargo ship in Sri Lanka, because his engineering degree is not accredited in Canada, he now works as a low-paid machinist at a textile factory where his wife also packages socks. Saving money fastidiously over the years, the family purchased a semidetached home in the suburb of Dollard-des-Ormeaux not far from the Thiru Murugan Temple. Not satisfied with the size and design of this starter home, they are currently building a larger house that is architecturally designed according to Hindu ritual standards. While waiting for the construction, which has stalled due to a shortage of funds, to finish, the family is living temporarily in a rental apartment, having sold their first home to finance the second.

Pavalan speaks with disgust of English-educated Sri Lankan and Indian Tamil engineers, doctors, and professionals who "show off" their English competence in front of less privileged, monolingual folk like his parents who, having had a harder time joining the middle class, work in factories, restaurants, and other service industries or manage convenience stores, automotive repair garages, grocery shops, video rental shops, clothing and textile stores, and restaurants. His parents vicariously attach their family's aspirations of social mobility to their children's success, which, in Québec, depends largely on them learning both English and French well. Pavalan considers learning French especially important to his future since he hopes to establish a sports apparel business in Montréal. Although he considers himself equally fluent in English and French, Pavalan did not have an easy time acquiring French when he first arrived in the city at age eleven. Since he is now most comfortable in English, this is our language of conversation.

Pavalan explains how in primary school he was automatically placed in a *classe d'accueil* (welcome class) for immigrant children of different ages and ethnic backgrounds and often spent the entire day learning the same elementary lessons in French. This experience lasted for years.

> French is most difficult to learn. When I came to Canada in 1990, I was put into a welcome class. Everyone was put there, grades one, three, five, six, all together in one group, everyday. For one or two years we stay there, then they see how well we pass the tests. It was very difficult. At the same time, my parents were moving around too fast, and I kept going from school to school, so I had to redo several class grades. A lot of kids are repeating because French grammar is difficult.[20]

After graduating secondary school and enrolling in an English-medium college, Pavalan found English much easier to learn than French because, in his opinion, English grammar "has less rules." He gradually switched to speaking in English with most of his friends, including with Sri Lankan Tamils. Although chagrined that he did not learn to read and write Tamil properly, Pavalan admits to the fatigue of being multilingual and wishes for the simplicity of a life totally immersed in Sri Lankan culture and speaking only in Tamil, without fear of the consequences.

Curious to learn how he uses French, English, and Tamil specifically on a daily basis, I inquire and Pavalan explains that when he works at the airport or hangs out in downtown, he does not think twice about ordering food or initiating conversations with strangers in English. Yet if asked a question in French, he will always respond in French. Only with his younger sister and one close friend does Pavalan code-switch and code-mix in English, French, and Tamil:

P: We mix three languages. We mix words. Sometimes we use two languages, sometimes three. And you know what? Me, I use Tamil when I get mad. When I ask questions, I use French. When I answer, I answer in English.
S: That's amazing. Why?
P: I have no clue why. It's a human thing. Just got created.

Pavalan's sister, who is five years younger than he and started school in Montréal in the first grade, never had to attend welcome classes and learned French quickly and easily. However, since she now studies at Concordia University, where she socializes entirely in English, Pavalan's sister is slowly forgetting how to speak French due to her current lack of practice. I share my own difficulties speaking French after leaving home for college, and Pavalan concurs that his French got rusty once when he started working for an English company in Montréal. Since then, by speaking in French regularly with government officials and his business partners, he has re-established his fluency.

Conveying his support for Québec's language laws, Pavalan criticizes immigrants who take advantage of the province's welfare system without doing their part to learn French and, instead, devote all of their time to working and paying off debts. Pavalan came to appreciate Québec's immigration policies last summer when visiting his relatives in England, Scotland, Norway, the Netherlands, and five other European countries, where he witnessed the hardships experienced by Sri Lankan Tamil refugees and immigrants excluded from basic welfare services. Some Sri Lankan Tamils in Montréal, even if they do not speak French, sympathize with the goals of Québécois nationalism and commiserate with the perceived lack of federal recognition for language rights. Pavalan tells me of a special *puja* (prayer ritual of devotional worship) that he is organizing in celebration of the Québécois national holiday, *St-Jean-Baptiste*, to be held in front of the *Sri Durkai Amman Temple* in late June 2005. I am reminded of Kalamathi, a middle-aged Sri Lankan Tamil woman working at a travel agency in Côte-des-Neiges, who admits that she once attended a PQ meeting and wishes she could learn French to better monitor her teenage son's conversations. Yet, at the same time, she asserts without hesitation, her family would move to Toronto if Québec ever became independent. When I ask Pavalan what he thinks of Québec's nationalist politics, he rejects the likelihood of independence and dismisses such terms as "francophone" and "anglophone" as "political talk" that does not capture the true diversity of Montréal.

Calling himself a "Canadian on the outside and Tamil inside at home," Pavalan nonetheless remains vigilant about preserving his religious and cultural identity in a multiethnic society. Though he makes friends with people of different ethnicities and prefers to socialize with Italian-Canadians and Québécois de souche friends rather than Sri Lankan Tamils, he draws the line at marrying a non-Tamil woman since he wants to avoid the inevitable hardships experienced by mixed-race children. At that point, he asks me if being mixed-race is tough. I muster a noncommittal reply, "yes and no," feeling uncomfortable under Pavalan's ethnographic gaze, and abruptly change topics to ask him how he would advise Sri Lankan Tamil youth growing up in Montréal to best learn their language and maintain their culture. In addition to going to temple, watching Tamil movies and shows, and attending cultural events, he urges them to hang out with "Tamil friends, but good friends" who do "not carry guns and knives." I let his statement slide without comment, aware that by saying so, Pavalan is inadvertently perpetuating racist stereotypes depicting Sri Lankans as "thugs" and "terrorists." In this moment, I recognize the incredible impact that racism has in paving divergent pathways of social and geographic mobility among Tamil speakers, circumscribed as these may be in francophone Québec.

The Subversive Mobility of Learning Nonstandard French

Public disbelief that South Asian immigrants and their children would choose to speak French in their everyday lives fuels stereotypes depicting South Asian immigrants and minorities as monolinguals or, at best, bilinguals, who prefer speaking their heritage language and perhaps English over French. This stereotype especially irritates Arun, the fifteen-year-old altar boy at Our Lady of Deliverance Mission, with whom I introduce this book through his clever farewell, "Viens pō, thanks!" Arun also challenges interlocutors who assume that he cannot speak French or English by sarcastically retorting, "*Je ne* speak *pas* English" or "I don't *parle français*," demonstrating his mastery of both grammars. Along with his close friends, Mani and Ram, Arun belongs to a church youth group that participates in community service and intramural sports, among other activities. Arriving from Jaffna two years earlier and quickly becoming fluent in French after being immersed in a French-medium public school, Ram feels slightly ostracized by the English-dominant youth in his church and hangs out mostly with Mani, another teenager educated exclusively in the French-medium public school system. One Sunday afternoon before mass, I sit down with Mani and Ram to discuss the youth group's activities. Speaking in French and occasionally code-switching into Tamil, Ram and Mani explain that they speak in Tamil with adults and English with other boys in the youth group, but never in French with anyone at the church other than each other. When I ask them how adults react to hearing them code-switch between Tamil and French, Mani and Ram grin and say, "They don't like it at all." They realize that Sri Lankans immigrating here as adults may feel threatened by youth who acquire French relatively easily. Little do these adults know that Mani and Ram are not only fluent in Québécois French, but also command a nonstandard variety of Québécois French, which, often depicted as an "authentic" non-elite register, embodies subversive capital if employed in the right contexts.

Due to the less-than-straightforward hierarchy of French varieties spoken in Québec, many immigrant adults readily acknowledge the value of speaking standard Québécois French or International French yet remain confused or ignorant of the popular culture cachet of nonstandard Québécois French. I was living in an apartment in Côte-des-Neiges with Sylvia, a Montréal-born university student of Chinese descent, and Julie, a French exchange student, at the beginning of my research, when all I could speak was nonstandard Québécois French. Sylvia often expressed how bizarre it was to hear an Indian woman from the States speak nonstandard Québécois French with an American accent. Born in Montréal, Sylvia herself alternates between speaking standard and nonstandard Québécois French and English, depending on who her interlocutors are, and code-mixes in all three with close friends. Although familiar with the colloquial language popularized in Québécois films shown in France, Julie was not prepared for the vast differences between Québec's French and France's French and is always shocked to hear students and even professors at the Université de Montréal speak in nonstandard Québécois French. In her opinion, only newscasters on television and radio speak good French in Québec.

In April, when Julie's boyfriend, Marc, arrives from France, keen to see Montréal's tourist attractions, we visit a *cabane à sucre* (maple sugar shack) to share a meal of maple syrup-flavored ham, potatoes, beans, soup, tea, and pie. Afterward, we venture to the barn outside into the still-frigid weather to listen to the farmer explain how he makes *tire*, a type of maple syrup candy that gels after being poured onto snow. Marc and Julie ask me to translate for them from nonstandard to standard Québécois French; they cannot understand a single word the farmer is saying. A few days later, Marc asks Sylvia and me why the Québécois insert "tu" everywhere into their speech. We laugh and explain, more or less, the use of "tu" as an interrogatory marker, similar to the inverted "-t-il," with origins perhaps in the northwestern regional dialects of old French (Vecchiato 2000). Yet when Julie and Marc point out the mispronunciation of *aéroport* as "aréoport," Sylvia and I, both of us guilty of this phonetic inversion, share a moment of defiant solidarity as we defend the phonological and grammatical systematicity of our colloquial language. Historically, the Québécois have enjoyed a complicated relationship with the French and even now are easily rankled by such comments perceived as uppity. Rarely does a Parisian, for whom nonstandard Québécois French is almost beyond comprehension, fail to be startled by the unique traits of Québécois French. And although the Québécois are intimately familiar with Parisian French, rarely do they speak like Parisians, unless they actively cultivate this accent.

I once responded to a graduate school friend of mine, who asked me how a foreigner could learn to speak nonstandard Québécois French, that only by growing up in Québec does a person acquire it. This answer betrays my own childhood language ideology in which I assumed that joual is the only authentic language of Québec and its speakers are the only authentic Québécois. My husband, who speaks standard Québécois French as his mother tongue, takes pleasure in shattering this illusion. Speaking nonstandard Québécois French nevertheless opens many doors for me during my research; it always puts a smile on my interlocutors' face when they realize that I come from an ordinary background like them, despite my elite educational background and career path. Also, when Indian and Sri Lankan Tamil youth hear me speak nonstandard Québécois French, they assume that I share with them similar experiences as ethnic minorities growing up in Québec and informally learning to speak this "language of the people." In fact, I developed friendships with my most self-revealing informants, including Selvamani, who introduces this chapter, by conversing with them in nonstandard Québécois French.

After visiting the Thiru Murugan Temple in Dollard-des-Ormeaux, a Montréal suburb, David and I return to the city to visit another Saivite temple, Sri Durkai Amman, in the urban quartier of Parc-Extension, when after the pūjā David introduces me to a family and explains that the eldest son assists him with his research. David recommends that I exchange contact information with Selvamani, the eldest daughter, only three years younger than me, who helps to organize the Sri Durkai Amman Temple's summer festival every year. Selvamani agrees to meet with me a few weeks later at the temple steps, where her younger sister, Mala, and another friend (who declined to be interviewed) also join us. Through our conversation that day, I learn that Hinduism, both in its ritualistic and in its philosophical aspects, helped Selvamani overcome a difficult childhood of illness and conflict with neighbors and classmates. Although I try to steer the conversation toward language issues and do not dwell on topics pertaining to religion, racism, or war, the latter preoccupy Selvamani and form the most compelling segments of her narrative.

Born in Jaffna, Selvamani and her family first moved to Chennai, Tamil Nadu, in 1985 at the beginning of the civil war in Sri Lanka and, three years later, to Montréal, where her younger sister, Mala, and her two younger brothers, Raja and Sathya, were born. Selvamani self-identifies as Québécoise due to her habitual use of French, and Indian due to her childhood years living in Tamil Nadu. When asked by strangers if she is Sri Lankan, she denies it to avoid recollecting the painful memories of war and having to experience the racism commonly directed at Sri Lankans. In the following segment of our interview, Selvamani animates distinct voices to discuss these issues.

The first excerpt describes Selvamani's daily encounters with racism growing up in Côte-des-Neiges where, I learn, there is a deep-seated animosity between Filipinos and Sri Lankans.[21]

(1) Parce que n'importe quand
Because whenever

(2) quand j'enregistre ma voix, ça l'air d'un garçon.
I record my voice I sound like a guy.

(3) Alors, <u>tsé, je me ferai pas poigné</u>
So, you know, I'm not going to be had.

(4) **ennatā, ennatā, enna rompa cirītā?** (laughter)
What, what, what's so funny?
(5) Alors, qu'est-ce que je disais? Bon, lorsque
So, what was I saying? Okay, when
(6) j'étais adolescente, comme depuis secondaire trois
I was a teenager, like since the 9th grade
(7) j'avais pas de contact avec des gens de
I didn't interact with the people of
(8) mon pays mais, disons que j'en avais mais
my country, let's say I did but
(9) c'était pas des meilleurs, alors, qu'est-ce qu'on
it wasn't the best, so, what we
(10) faisait′, comme, je trouvais ça honteux de mettre
would do, like, I thought it was embarrassing to wear
(11) le *bindi* ou bien de parler dans ma langue ou
a *bindi* (decorative dot on forehead) or to speak in my language or
(12) quoi que ce soit, je trouvais ça comme insultant
whatever, I found it like insulting
(13) pour moi, okay, parce que, tsé, ils nous traitaient
personally, okay, because, you know, they would call us
(14) comme paki, en gé′néral′ dès que t'étais brun
pakis, normally, as long as you were brown
(15) avant c'était le terme paki qui était connu.
before paki was the term that was known.

She explains to me how nowadays, Québécois are more discerning of differences between South Asians like Bengalis, Punjabis, Tamils, and Pakistanis, when Mala interjects in a Parisian accent.

(16) *Ç'a diminué maintenant.*
It's not as bad now.

Repeating what Mala says but in a Québécois French accent, Selvamani then continues her story.

(17) Oui, ç'a diminué maintenant
Yes, it's not as bad now
(18) oui, comparé avant, oui, alors
yes, compared to before, yes, so

(19) tsé, ils nous traitaient, ils disaient des mauvais
you know, they would call us, they would say really bad
(20) mots, carrément, mais des mauvais mots,
words, I mean really, bad words.
(21) Je m'excuse′ mais là′, ils sont des retardés.
I beg your pardon but, you know, they are retarded.
(22) Tsé, ils utilisaient des noms des noms de parties de génitaux
You know, they would use the names of sexual organs
(23) puis ils criaient sur les rues. Pour moi ça . . .
and cry these out in the streets. For me this . . .

Interrupting to ask who are the culprits of this malfeasance, I am surprised by her answer.

(24) C'est toutes les . . . mais beaucoup c'était les filipinos.
It's all the . . . but a lot of them were Filipinos.

"Dans ce quartier ici?" (In this very neighborhood?), I ask knowing that Côte-des-Neiges has a sizeable immigrant population from the Philippines.

(25) Ah ben ici et partout là, ouais, ouais, ouais . . .
Oh well here and everywhere, in fact, yeah, yeah, yeah . . .
(26) dans Montréal c'était en grande partie.
In Montréal it was the majority doing this.
(27) Alors qu'est-ce qui se passe, moi je me suis dit, okay, genre,
So, what happens, I tell myself, okay, like,
(28) Je je révelais pas à eux mon identité.
I I did not reveal to them my identity.
(29) Puis, une autre raison pourquoi j'ai . . . ça c'est plus personnel je m'excuse
And another reason why I . . . this is more personal I apologize
(30) Je. . . .J'ai jamais dit que j'étais sri lankaise. J'ai jamais dit. Non.
I . . . I never said that I was Sri Lankan. Never said. No.

After a short pause following her emphatic "non," I tentatively ask, "Tu disais quoi?" (You said what?).

(30) Soit que je . . . si il me disait. okay, "T'es-tu sud-indienne?"
Either I . . . if they told me, okay, "Are you South Indian?"
(31) j'ai dit, parce que avec mon accent de tamoul ils me reconnaissent pas.
I said, because with my Tamil accent they couldn't place me

(32) La plus grande partie ils vont me dire, "Est-ce que tu viens du sud-Inde?"
Most people will say, "Are you from South India?"

(34) Je dis parce que . . . Lorsque j'étais arrivée ici
I say because . . . when I arrived here

(35) on était deux ou trois familles dans notre coin de Sri Lankais
We were two or three families in our neighborhood of Sri Lankans

(36) puis il y avait deux magasins indiens.
And there were two Indian stores.

(37) C'était le temps qui ont tué Rajiv Gandhi.
This was the time when they killed Rajiv Gandhi.

(38) <u>Y ont</u> carrément commencé (incomprehensible)
They really started to . . .

(39) <u>là</u> j'ai commencé avoir une haine <u>là,</u> inexplicable
since then I started to feel an unexplainable hatred

(40) envers cette gang de sais pas quoi, alors . . .
toward this gang of I don't know what to call them, so . . .

Pressing further for clarification, I ask, "C'était qui?" (Who was it?).

(40) Voilà dire, les terroristes et les gens de ce pays là.
One way to say this is the terrorists and the people of that country there.

(41) Alors, puis, moi aussi j'ai quitté parce que dû à. . . .
So, then, I also left because due to

(42) <u>la</u> problème de guerre tout ça j'avais des problémes de santé.
The problem of war and all that I had health problems.

(43) Alors mes parents ils <u>ont démenagé</u> en Inde.
So my parents they moved to India.

(44) C'est là <u>que</u> j'étais guerie. On a vécu là-bas en Inde. Alors,
That where I was healed. We lived there in India. So,

(45) depuis ce temps-là même comme j'ai été un peu detachée de mon pays natal.
since then and there, even, like, I felt a bit detached from my native country.

(46) Alors, je sais pas
So, I don't know

(47) moi j'ai trouvé plus d'attachement vers . . . avec l'Inde que mon pays . . .
me, I found that I was more attached toward . . . with India than my country

(48) Je respectais mon pays en tant que pays historiquement et pour sa valeur
I respected my country for its history and its value

(49) mais, okay, si ils me considéraient comme une sinhalaise, là, je m'en foutais.
But, okay, if they considered me a Sinhalese, that, I didn't care about.
(50) Mais pour être considérée comme un tamoul et puis me faire insulter,
Yet to be considered as a Tamil and to be insulted by this label
(51) j'étais pas prête. Je me suis dit, non.
I wasn't ready. I said to myself, no.
(52) Okay, puis j'étais pas d'accord avec quoi s'est passé là.
Okay, and I didn't agree with what had happened there.
(53) C'est trop politique, alors, je le laisse.
It was too political, so I leave it alone.
(54) Alors je me suis dit, oui, je suis sud-indienne, okay.
So, I tell myself, yes, I am South Indian, okay.
(55) Ou bien si il me dit je suis nord indienne, je dis oui.
Or otherwise if someone tells me that I am North Indian, I say yes.
(56) N'importe quoi mais pas sri lankaise, je le dis pas.
Anything other than Sri Lankan, I do not say that.[22]

For most of this segment, which lasts approximately three minutes, Selvamani speaks to me in standard Québécois French, our customary language of communication. Only once after making a droll observation about the pitch of her voice does she switch into Tamil in line 4 to pointedly ask Mala why she is laughing at her. This aside, the most linguistically notable features of Selvamani's narrative are her occasional use of nonstandard Québécois French lexicon, phonology, and grammar. With regard to phonology, words like *faisait'* (line 10), *en gé'néral* (line 14), and *Je m'excuse' mais là'* (line 21) have the stress patterns and prosodic accuracy of a native speaker. She also inserts popular idiomatic expressions such as *tsé* throughout the text and *je m'excuse mais là* (line 21), *je me ferai pas poigné* (line 3), and *genre* (line 27) at the beginning or end of clauses or before delivering a subversive comment, such as *ils sont des retardés* in line 21. Only in a few places does Selvamani employ nonstandard Québécois French morphosyntactic constructions, for example replacing "il" with "y" in line 38, conjugating *démenager* with *avoir* instead of *être* in line 43, using *que* instead of *où* as a conjunction introducing a subordinate clause in line 44, and preponderantly using the emphatic particle *là* throughout the text. Overall, with the sole exception of quoting the voice of the Québécois public in line 30, Selvamani carefully avoids using any grammatical constructions, such as the interrogative "tu," that point to the more socially stigmatized features of nonstandard Québécois French, popularly regarded as uneducated speech. As Julie and her boyfriend Marc reveal, the use of "*t'es-tu*" in the phrase "t'es-tu sud-indienne?" would elicit the greatest scorn for its "ungrammatical" construction.

Selvamani's sporadic use of nonstandard French popularly associated with working-class and rural Québec is most striking in juxtaposition with Mala's conspicuous use of a Parisian French accent in line 16. When Selvamani repeats Mala's phrase, she effectively creates an adjacency pair commonly used in Québec discourse for correcting mispronunciations. Yet in this case, Selvamani authoritatively reclaims the narrative floor and later teasingly insinuates that Mala is only posturing to be a speaker of Parisian French since she has only visited France two or three times. Mala is embarrassed and remains quiet, yet in this sisterly squabble, Selvamani and Mala reveal their combined range of stylistic variation and competence in French. In fact, Selvamani displays exceptional skill in incorporating just enough expressions and sounds from nonstandard Québécois French to authenticate her mockery of those whom she deems to be less capable of integrating into francophone society, namely, "Sri Lankan terrorists" and "Filipino racists." In this comment Selvamani makes clear that she does not include herself among *them*.

Forty minutes into our conversation, we are discussing Selvamani's awakened interest in Hinduism after the age of eighteen when she began worshipping regularly at the temple, reading Hindu mythologies and texts, and eating vegetarian food to heal her body from a mysterious illness afflicting her since childhood, when abruptly I ask her if she wants to visit Sri Lanka.[23]

(1) **I want** . . . je veux aller . . . aux trois temples.
I want . . . I want to go . . . to three temples.
(2) <u>Y</u> a trois temples que je veux aller
There are three temples that I want to visit
(3) et malheureusement c'est à . . . au Sri Lanka
and unfortunately they are . . . in Sri Lanka
(4) et je suis pas capable d'y aller.
and I am not able to go there.
(5) J'ai une phobie. J'ai une phobie.
I have a phobia. I have a phobia.
(6) Parce que, lorsque j'étais petite, vois-tu,
Because, when I was a young girl, do you see,
(7) c'est là qu'ils ont commencé la guerre
that is when they started the war
(8) et <u>j'ai tombé</u> malade avec la guerre, puis . . .
and I became ill with the war, and then . . .

(9) et depuis ce temps-là . . . oui, c'était comme une peur.
and since then. . . .yes, it was like a fear.
(10) Lorsque j'étais petite dès qu'il y avait quelques chose qui me plaisait pas
When I was a young girl whenever there was something that displeased me
(11) je tombais malade. J'étais comme ça.
I became ill. I was like that.
(12) <u>T'es comme</u> j'avais . . . <u>t'es comme</u> une fièvre . . .
It was like, I had . . . it was like, a fever . . .
(13) <u>t'es comme</u> qui me tuait là, tout le temps.
it was like, that was killing me, all of the time.
(14) C'était une fièvre qui commençait puis à la fin j'étais à terre
It was a fever that started and then at the end I was on the floor
(15) alors, ils pouvaient pas continuer à me voir comme ça.
so, they could not continue to see me like this.
(16) C'est là qu'ils <u>ont démenagé</u> en Inde.
That is when they moved to India.
(17) Alors, depuis ce temps-là j'ai eu une phobie qui m'a . . . je peux pas.
So, since that time I have had a phobia that makes me . . . I cannot.
(18) <u>Tsé</u> <u>y a</u> deux fois que je suis allée en Inde.
<u>You know</u> two times I went to India
(19) les deux fois . . . les deux dernières fois j'avais **Sri Lanka transit**.
the two times . . . the last two times I had a transit in Sri Lanka.
(20) <u>Tsé</u> je prenais ma..**my [ceinture?]** I was going "beep."
You know I was holding onto to my . . . my seatbelt. I was going "beep."
(21) Juste à savoir **I am landing on Sri Lanka**
Just knowing I am landing on Sri Lanka
(22) j'avais une peur que je pouvais pas décrire même maintenant.
I felt a fear that I could not describe even now.
(23) Même maintenant <u>té comme</u> ma mere, <u>a</u> disait,
Even now it was like my mother she said,
(24) cet été là on va aller en Inde et comme Sri Lanka pour . . .
this summer we are going to India and like Sri Lanka to . . .
(25) elle voulait faire un . . . je sais pas
she wanted to do a . . . I don't know
(26) **she took a [wall?] for me and she wanted to do something.**
(27) **I was like, "no!"**
(28) <u>Je suis je suis je te dis</u> . . . je peux pas. Je peux pas.
I was I was I am telling you . . . I cannot. I cannot.
(29) C'est pas que j'aime . . . maintenant c'est pas que j'aime pas le pays.
It is not that I like . . . now it is not I don't like the country.

(30) Si si j'avais une haine, oui. Mais là je respecte le pays.
If I felt hatred, yes. But now I respect the country.

(31) Mais je sais pas, j'ai une peur en dedans moi que je peux pas l'expliquer.
But I don't know, I felt fear inside of me that I cannot explain.

Similar to the previous excerpt, Selvamani uses nonstandard Québécois French at key junctures in this narrative. For example, when her speech falters due to the emotional toll of recollecting her past sickness or the dread of returning to Sri Lanka, Selvamani speaks almost entirely in nonstandard Québécois French (lines 12–13), except when she switches into English (lines 18–21 and lines 23–28) to bare her deepest feelings. This pattern of code-switching cannot be explained by presuming Selvamani's identification with English, which is not true. In fact, she barely spoke in English until college and still prefers speaking in French, even if this irritates elder patrons at the temple. Proving this point, our conversation is interrupted when an older Sri Lankan Tamil man exiting the temple elicits a contemptuous reaction from Selvamani. Once again switching into English, she expresses disdain for this man, who often chastises her and her sister for switching into French on sanctified temple grounds, even though he does the same with his daughter in English. Ironically, only code-switching between Tamil and French, not Tamil and English, annoys him. Selvamani surmises that he esteems English above French and is reminded of his exclusion from Québécois society for not speaking French.

Yet even Selvamani and her sister do not agree on what constitutes the right way to code-switch and code-mix in French, Tamil, and English. Although both sisters complied with Bill 101 in attending French-medium primary and secondary schools, afterward they embarked on different life trajectories. Selvamani studied in English at McGill University and now considers herself literate in English and French and conversationally fluent in nonstandard Québécois French, standard Québécois French, English, and Jaffna Tamil. She regularly code-switches and code-mixes in French and English or Tamil and English with her friends depending on their ethnicity, French and Tamil with Mala, and French, English, and Tamil with her younger brothers, Raja and Sathya. Born in Montréal seven years after Selvamani, Mala instead self-identifies as francophone and Hindu. Eschewing English entirely and socializing with friends who are either French- or Tamil-dominant speakers, she prefers to mix neither these two social groups nor their languages.[24] In September Mala plans to become the first Sri Lankan to voluntarily attend a French-medium college in the quartier of Ahuntsic, she informs me with pride, joining her close friends who are mainly francophones of Arab descent. With sisterly affection, Selvamani chides Mala for making a major life mistake and implies that she will not be as competitive for jobs in science, her chosen career path, without expertise in English.

After we finish our hour-and-a-half-long conversation, Selvamani invites me to visit her home the following weekend to observe her and her sister's efforts to tutor their younger brothers and neighbors in French. Similar in layout to my own apartment in Côte-des-Neiges that I share with two college students, their three-bedroom apartment is cramped for a family of seven. In the tiny extra room opening out to the balcony overlooking the playground of a primary school, Selvamani works with her younger neighbors on grammar lessons while Mala coaxes her brothers to complete their homework in the living room. I go to the living room first to chat with Raja and Sathya in English, their language of preference. Raja tells me that after attending primary school in French and secondary school in English, he feels that he is equally proficient in both languages. Most of his friends of South Asian and Caribbean descent in the neighborhood code-switch and code-mix between nonstandard Québécois French and a Canadian variety of African American English. Yet the youngest brother, Sathya, who had attended a primary school in English in Western Canada where he lived with relatives before moving to Montréal and beginning anew at a French-medium public school, is still struggling to adjust to the new curriculum. Eager to discuss with me his love of hockey, Sathya confides that he self-identifies as Canadian and speaks in English whenever possible, much to Mala's apparent dismay.

I leave the living room to next observe Selvamani's lesson in the balcony room. The three tutees, two sisters and one cousin, attend the English-medium public school located right across the street from Selvamani's apartment, which features a French immersion program and heritage language classes popular among Tamil-speaking students. Compared to schools that offer ninety minutes of French instruction per day, immersion programs instead provide 100-percent instruction in French during the first two years and increasing periods of English instruction thereafter. Despite their initial "immersion" in French, however, the girls continue to make basic grammatical mistakes that Selvamani attributes to a lack of conversational practice. The oldest girl in the fourth grade shows me her score of 80 percent on a quiz requiring that she differentiate between the pronoun *on* and the verb auxiliary *ont*. Upon finishing the tutoring session, Selvamani declares to me that students attending this English-medium school have no chance of learning French well, unlike she herself, who began the first grade in mainstream classes in a French-medium public school where she does not recall having any difficulty learning the language. Although she studied cellular biology and religion in English at McGill University, she feels comfortable working in French in a toxicology lab at a biotechnology company in a small town in Québec close to Ottawa. Both sisters credit their parents' good judgment for insisting that their children attend primary or secondary schools in French, even if they transition into English in later grades, as three of them have done without noted difficulty.[25]

A year later, when returning to visit Montréal during the summer, I telephone Selvamani and learn of her impending marriage to a man residing in the Indian city of Trichy in Tamil Nadu. I congratulate her heartily on the happy news, even though she qualifies this by saying that she cannot visit him in India because of her refugee status and he cannot visit her in Montréal until he has a visa. All of her life Selvamani has sought to differentiate herself from Sri Lankans, not only by embracing the use of standard Québécois French but by subversively using nonstandard Québécois French to narrate her dream of living a fulfilled life, from beginning to end, in India. I recall a segment of her narrative from one year ago in which she expresses this desire:

(1) Seulement si j'avais une autre vie là
Only if I have another life
(2) je souhaite de pas en avoir,
I don't wish to have another one,
(3) je veux naître en Inde.
I want to be born in India.
(4) Même comme une pauvre paysanne je m'en fous,
Even as a poor villager I don't care,
(5) mais pour naître en Inde **you should be gifted and it is not an easy thing.**
but to be born in India you should be gifted and it is not an easy thing.
(6) Pour moi je suis pas née en Inde, je veux mourir en Inde.
As for me I was not born in India, I want to die in India.
(7) C'est c'est le plus plus le plus gros cadeau que je peux avoir.
It's it's the biggest biggest biggest gift that I could have.

Again, by incorporating nonstandard Québécois French idiomatic expressions into her overall speech yet avoiding some of its more stigmatized features, Selvamani gives poetic form to her self-conscious transformation from a young girl paralyzed by war and racism to a young woman empowered to be multilingual on her own terms. Of all the interviewees featured here, Selvamani most vividly testifies to the power of narrative to realize one's own vision of mobility.

Becoming Multilingual

Asking the question of how pathways of social and geographic mobility overlap with strategies of multilingual language acquisition, this chapter has focused on Indian and Sri Lankan children and youth between the ages of ten and thirty and analyzed interviews and conversations featuring their migration narratives to highlight the unpredictable trajectories of mobility, language learning, and ethnonational identification characterizing Montréal's Tamil diaspora. Tamil youth who figure out how to navigate Montréal's Anglo-Franco rivalries and "get a leg up" on their less perceptive or verbally skilled friends and family members often feel more empowered to narrate highly personalized life histories and future trajectories, even if their expressed lack of preference for or fluency in English or French challenges social expectations. Simultaneously, the underlying disputes about the prestige, authenticity, and "street cred" of International French, Canadian English, nonstandard Québécois French, and African American English that lurk as "shadow conversations" (Irvine 1996) give rise to double-voiced utterances indexing the intertwined experiences of mobility and immobility of this diaspora.

This chapter has also established that racist stereotypes about LTTE sympathizers, gangsters, and undocumented immigrants indiscriminately target both Indians and Sri Lankans and irrevocably drive the ethnolinguistic and ethnonational differentiation of this diaspora. Becoming multilingual is dangerous since, if executed improperly, a person can step outside the bounds of Tamil and Québécois normativity and challenge prescribed ideals of nationhood and modernity. The enigmatic use of "tamoul" as a racial epithet, implying both visual and aural foreignness in Québec, suggests that unknown Tamil migrants, regardless of which languages they speak, are always suspected of being disloyal to Québec's nationalist regime. The next chapter further explores the visual and aural dimensions of linguistic integration and belonging by tracing the different manifestations of a language ideology through which Sri Lankans self-identify with "Written Tamil" and Indians with "Spoken Tamil" as their heritage languages.

4 A HERITAGE LANGUAGE INDUSTRY

In May 2005, Father Joseph, the chaplain of the Sri Lankan Tamil Catholic mission, agrees to Marianne's father's request to assist me with my research investigating Tamil heritage language schools in Montréal. This is a major turning point for me; earlier I had faced a disappointing setback when two francophone principals denied me permission to observe their schools' heritage classes in Tamil. One fine spring afternoon, Father Joseph meets with me at his office on the first floor of *Église St-Vincent-Ferrier* on *rue Jarry* to discuss the history of Our Lady of Deliverance. His private quarters are on the second floor of the mission house, located three blocks from my apartment in Villeray and four blocks from Église Ste-Cécile on *avenue Henri-Julien*, where Father Joseph officiates over mass in Tamil every Sunday afternoon. After listening intently to me explain why I want to observe educational programs for Tamil children, Father Joseph invites me to attend language and catechism classes when they resume in September and, at the end of summer, witness the Marian peace procession to take place in Rigaud, Québec. Since during the week Father Joseph also works as a chaplain for Indian and Filipino Catholic seamen at the Port of Montreal, I volunteer to be his assistant and drive the seamen to and from their ships and the designated recreational and shopping areas near the port.

As the summer progresses, Father Joseph occasionally calls on me to assist him with paperwork dealing with the attempted purchase of an old church for the Sri Lankan Tamil Catholic mission. One afternoon I stop by the mission house to help him translate the church's building inspection report from French into English. Offhandedly, I ask Father Joseph if he ever tried to learn French in the last four years that he has been in Montréal. He replies that he was keen to learn French at first and had once asked Father André, the Québécois de souche priest in charge of St-Vincent-Ferrier's mission house, to tutor him, but Father André insisted that he is not qualified. How could a native speaker not be qualified, Father Joseph wondered, thinking of the volunteer language teachers at his church who do not have any special training in Tamil. Puzzled by Father André's response, Father Joseph reassured him that he must know his mother tongue well enough to teach him, yet Father André countered that what he lacks is academic, not vernacular expertise. Father Joseph let the matter drop and did not bother to try learning French again.

Fathers Joseph and André's contrasting views on linguistic expertise stem from their different conceptions of the relationship between spoken and written languages. Father Joseph and most of the language teachers at the Our Lady of Deliverance mission primarily grew up in the Jaffna province of Sri Lanka and are not only literate in Tamil, but also conversant in a supposedly literary style of Jaffna Tamil. Their didactic authority comes from believing that their speech reinforces several millennia of written tradition. Only in the upper grades when children are expected to write essays and read literature does Father Joseph use teachers with academic credentials in Tamil. As a foreigner, Father Joseph would be equivalent in rank to a novice and require only a native speaker to teach him the rudiments of spoken and written French, or so he believes. I instead gather that Father André, though trained by the Catholic Church and undoubtedly literate in French and Latin, speaks a nonstandard variety of Québécois French and worries that he may unwittingly teach Father Joseph the "incorrect" grammar of his vernacular.

This misunderstanding reminds me of a similar discrepancy between the "mother tongue" teachers of Asian languages and the certified teachers of European languages who are hired to teach in Montréal's publicly funded heritage language education program. The PELO (*Programme d'enseignement des langues d'origine*) director of the English Montreal School Board (EMSB) explained to me that, although they strive to find teachers with academic credentials, when they cannot find any—which is often the case with Tamil, given the few certified teachers available—they will hire "mother tongue" speakers instead. Due to pressure from community leaders, however, Italian, Greek, and Portuguese teachers are almost always certified. This double standard underscores salient differences in conceptions of expertise that inform discourses about linguistic heritage locally and globally.

The most international of these discourses derives from UNESCO's notion of "intangible heritage," which argues that oral folkloric traditions require urgent "preservation" and "revitalization" to ensure their future survival (Schmitt 2008; UNESCO n.d.a).[1] Whether wittingly or not, such humanitarian efforts often deny coeval status to the verbal repertoires of so-called "timeless" peoples (usually indigenous and rural communities) by contrasting them with "literate" societies in possession of written traditions (Bauman and Briggs 2003). As a classical language, Tamil does not qualify as "intangible heritage." Yet another discourse prevalent in diasporic communities characterizes future generations of immigrants and ethnic minorities as progressively incompetent, first in the written and then in the spoken "heritage language" of their ancestors. National policies promoting the documentation and education of endangered heritage languages, therefore in one way or another, reproduce temporally dichotomous views of speaking and writing. By mapping the use and knowledge of spoken and written languages onto different timescales, global discourses and national policies suggest that speaking one's mother tongue might be beneficial for the present, yet in order to truly memorialize the past and command the future, expertise in writing and knowledge of literary languages are needed (Das 2011).

These insights speak to recent linguistic anthropological writings on temporality, which articulate how language ideologies mediate people's perceptions of the past, present, and future, as well as the presumed linear relationship between these temporal dimensions (see Inoue 2004a). Ideologies depicting heritage languages as purified "written" artifacts or degenerate "spoken" vernaculars posit the greatest temporal divergence between "text" and "talk" and ossify these as different codes rather than as mere communicative modalities. Moreover, institutional practices associated with heritage language education, including the auxiliary printing of dictionaries and pedagogical materials, the distribution of these multimedia goods to merchants and vendors, and their consumption by teachers and students, altogether bespeak an organized and profitable industry that creates state-sponsored or community-supported programs to preserve or revitalize heritage languages in ways that are compatible with the circulation of global capital.

Such is a time-sensitive business, though. For example, Canada's Tamil heritage language industry has grown slowly, though steadily, through public and private investments by government officials and Indian and Sri Lankan community leaders over the past fifteen years, yet investors must accomplish two things to ensure the industry's longevity. First, books and schools seeking to preserve Tamil must convince students that their spoken language resembles an ancient and reputable literary tradition; in contrast, books and schools seeking to revitalize Tamil must prove that the colloquial language can have a vibrant oral tradition of its own. Moreover, each codified and standardized variety of the heritage language must elicit strong affiliative sentiments, or what Ramaswamy (1997) calls "language devotion," to ensure that the next generation of Canadian-born children will maintain the use of Tamil into the future. In other words, children must self-identify as speakers of pure Tamil or cosmopolitan Tamil and be devoted to studying these as heritage languages. This is no easy task in Québec, where neoliberal policies challenging the value of heritage language education for global trade cast the future relevance of Tamil in doubt and pose significant obstacles to the industry's longevity (Das 2015).

Another dimension of the temporality of heritage language education consists of discourses depicting it as a recent phenomenon arising out of the post–World War II world order. This view is supported by the history of minority language education in twentieth-century North America, where immigrant leaders initially established privately funded community schools taught by native speakers to compensate for the relative lack of federal recognition and financial support for instruction. Yet there is also plausible evidence of heritage language educational initiatives during the colonial period. For example, a school for the children of Indian Tamil indentured laborers working in the spice plantations of mid-nineteenth-century French Guiana was possibly gifted bilingual dictionaries, grammar books, and other texts, translated from French and Latin into Tamil and authored by Catholic missionaries in Pondicherry, India, to teach Tamil. Yet only in the context of present-day Montréal, Québec do public and private schools teach two distinctly codified and standardized varieties of Tamil, known as Written Tamil and Spoken Tamil, to two ethnonational populations of Tamil-speaking migrants, Sri Lankans and Indians, respectively.

This chapter explores the book-printing and educational practices of the Tamil heritage language industry, drawing on archival and ethnographic evidence from over one and a half centuries and across South Asia and the Americas, to highlight the variable social and political contexts in which empires, nations, and diasporas make decisions about how to codify and standardize colloquial or literary registers of Tamil. I argue that Anglo-Franco imperial conflicts in colonial South India, which perpetuated old and instigated new linguistic rivalries over what counts as the best Tamil typography and orthography, entailed four enduring outcomes. First, the colonial categories of High and Low, Classical and Modern, and Written and Spoken Tamil merged with the precolonial categories of literary, oratorical, and colloquial Tamil on the one hand, and notions of pure and corrupted Tamil on the other. Second, the colonial description of Tamil as a diglossic language with a classical tradition established the narrative foundation for twentieth-century Indian and Sri Lankan Tamil nationalist leaders to argue for the antiquity and indigeneity of Dravidian peoples and languages. Third, by basing their scholarship on high-caste pandits' analyses of classical Tamil texts, European scholars valorized expert knowledge of written languages, whereas Tamil nationalists adopted a stance valuing the everyday knowledge of spoken vernaculars by non-Brahmin leaders. Finally, in quibbling over how to represent graphically what sounds like minor degrees of lexical, phonological, and grammatical contrast to nonnative speakers, European scholars demonstrated to future language activists in South Asia and the diaspora how to blur or exaggerate formal differences between colloquial and literary Tamil to promote their own political and ideological agendas. Consequently, a spirit of rivalry now characterizes the efforts of Indian and Sri Lankan Tamil teachers and authors who, in response to Anglo-Franco nationalist conflicts in Québec, work to standardize and codify two heritage languages by differentiating between the colloquial and literary-like forms of Tamil.

One could similarly argue that the Tamil heritage language industry in contemporary Canada owes its rise and (possible demise) to a language ideology of temporality emerging from the contentious language politics of the mid-nineteenth century, which established that written languages embody ancient expertise and spoken languages embody contemporary knowledge. Preserving written Tamil and revitalizing spoken Tamil as differentiated heritage languages emblematic of two distinct ethnonational groups, Sri Lankans and Indians, thus offers alternative yet complementary pathways to achieving global modernity, albeit one that shares the same vision of a diasporic future requiring the past to be preserved. Furthermore, Canada's Tamil heritage language industry adopts the unconventional view that any mother tongue speaker, who commands sufficient knowledge of literary Tamil or speaks multiple colloquial Tamil varieties, as do most adult immigrants living in Montréal, can teach basic literacy and conversational skills to children. Therefore, rather than simply imitating the scholarly practices of colonial-era pandits, the teachers of Tamil schools and authors of Tamil textbooks in the Canadian diaspora are increasingly emulating the populist style of the charismatic South Indian "movie star-politicians" of the twentieth century (Dickey 1993:341) to reinvent an industry facing incessant challenges.

Printing Tamil Books in Colonial French India

By all accounts, French India was a failed colonial project that enjoyed a brief heyday from the mid-seventeenth to the late eighteenth century when the French East India Company, after receiving a royal charter from King Louis XIV in 1664, founded five commercial outposts in British-controlled Bengal (that is, Chandernagore) and the Madras Presidency (that is, Yanan, Pondicherry, and Karikal), as well as the Kingdom of Mysore (that is, Mahé). After a series of wars between France and England occupying most of the eighteenth century resulted in smaller skirmishes in India and intermittent periods of British rule over French Indian territories, the Treaty of Paris in 1763 unequivocally restored all Indian territories to France on the condition that the country relinquish any future imperial ambitions in the subcontinent. Agreeing to these terms, the king liquidated the French East India Company in 1769 and unified the five *comptoirs* (branches) of French India into a single administrative unit headquartered in Pondicherry.

Despite vanquishing the French in India, the British Raj rightly suspected them of committing ongoing seditious activities by secretly forging alliances with princely states, converting Hindus to Catholicism, and propagating republican critiques of colonialism, especially in the period after the French Revolution. Indeed, a strong sense of French religious, linguistic, and national identity prevailed, especially among elites in the Tamil-speaking cities of Pondicherry and Karaikal, which belatedly joined the independent state of India in 1962. There, the early work of Catholic missionaries in vernacular printing and education had accentuated the positive reputation of French officials among Indians, at least regarding their patronage of the Tamil language. British officials, in comparison, lacked any notable Tamil scholarly expertise until the early to mid-nineteenth century, when the Madras School of Orientalism sponsored a "revival of letters" to translate and print books in Tamil and English (Trautmann 2006:197).

During the mid-nineteenth century, when the demise of colonial French India was all but certain, Catholic missionaries and French government officials pursued modest experiments in bilingual education and printing in French and Tamil, primarily to deter the further encroachment of British Protestant missionary activity in the French Indian cities of Pondicherry and Karikal. Taking stock of the problems facing the Catholic Church in French India, the First Synod of the Apostolic Vicariate of the Coromandel Coast, which convened in Pondicherry in 1844 "to decide what would be best for the good of the Missions" (Archdiocese of Pondicherry and Cuddalore n.d.), prioritized educating boys and girls, opening minor and major seminaries, training catechists, caring for Christians and missionaries, and printing books in Tamil and French. Consequently in 1840, Abbot Louis-Savinien Dupuis of the Catholic Mission of India received permission to operate a small press in Pondicherry and printed several hundred copies of books written in French, Latin, and Tamil "for the good of the colonies," as he specified in a letter written to the Governor of French India in 1863. Enclosing a catalog of recent works published by the press in this letter, Dupuis suggested that these books would be equally useful for European officers living in India and France as they are for immigrants and indentured laborers living in overseas French plantations and colonies, where the promotion of the knowledge of Catholicism is an undeniable "good."

> . . . in order to let the metropolitan government decide if the products of our printing press, of which I am enclosing a catalog, could be of use in learning Tamil in the various colonies where many populations that speak this language could render it useful to government officials; whether these could be useful also for Tamil classes offered in Paris and paid for by the government, and, most of all, whether these could be greatly useful in

> teaching and inculcating morals to the large number of immigrants who work in the colonies, nevertheless if his Excellency the Minister judged that the "good" this printing press produces deserves some encouragement, it would be welcome with gratitude and could contribute even more to the general good. (Inde 1863)

By emphasizing the press's mission to deter the spread of Protestant propaganda throughout Christendom, Dupuis sought to create new reading publics among Tamil-speaking diasporas in Sri Lanka, Mauritius, Burma, Malaysia, Hong Kong, and Aden, where many Catholics lived.

Close examination of this catalog reveals a comprehensive list with titles, authors, prices, and brief descriptions of the books' target audiences (see Figure 4.1) (Inde n.d.). Dupuis even indicates which alphabets, proverbs and fables, and simple lessons in French and Tamil are intended for children. Topping the list are two Tamil-French and French-Tamil dictionaries that Abbot Dupuis co-authored with Abbot Louis-Marie Mousset. Linguistic anthropologist Joseph Errington explains that dictionaries, grammars, and other descriptive linguistic projects first became resources for "figuring and naturalizing inequality in the colonial milieu" in the sixteenth century (2001:20). In the context of eighteenth- and nineteenth-century South India, Catholic and Anglican/Lutheran presses competed to standardize Tamil in the image of rival European print techniques and classificatory schemas and claim that their own texts were the most accurate, aesthetically modern, and, hence, authoritative. This rivalry also led to authorial disagreements over Tamil typography, orthography, metalinguistic labels, and alphabetic ordering. More than just copyediting matters, at stake in these debates were conflicting French and British stances on whether to preserve tradition or facilitate modernization in South India, and how to best do so.

Up until 1800, Jesuit missionaries had written most grammars and dictionaries in Tamil. A Lutheran press in Tranquebar printed without permission the most celebrated of these texts, a Tamil-Latin dictionary written in 1738 by their Jesuit rival, the Italian priest Father Beschi. To write this dictionary, Beschi closely studied the *Tolkappiyam*, the oldest known Tamil grammar book, which is divided into expository sections on alphabet, lexicon, phonology, morphology, and poetics. The *Tolkappiyam* is especially strong in its attention to phonetic detail and orders the Tamil alphabet, starting with the letter "k," according to a markedness hierarchy of "distinctive features" based on place of articulation in the vocal cavity (from back to front), voicing, and aspiration.[2] Beschi's first innovation reinterpreted the *Tolkapppiyam*'s label koṭun tamiḻ (which means crooked Tamil) as Low Tamil, and ceṉtamiḻ (which means pure Tamil) as High Tamil. Secondly, he adopted the Latin alphabet order, overturning centuries of Indian

FIGURE 4.1 Book catalog printed by the Catholic Mission of India.

phonological and textual analysis to open the way for Europeans to introduce other orthographic and typographic innovations.[3]

For example, whereas Jesuit missionaries had transliterated Indian vowels using the Italian alphabet and Indian consonants with the English alphabet, British printers changed this system by transliterating vernacular Tamil entirely into English and classical Tamil into Italian. French Catholic missionaries like Dupuis and Mousset, emphasizing their use of new and old transliteration standards, adopted Beschi's Latin alphabetic order yet, with regard to vowels, rejected the Indian conventions practiced by scribes and the Latin conventions preferred by Beschi in favor of new French ones. Thus, they wrote /u/ as <ou> rather than <u> or <oo>. Although British transliteration conventions globally prevailed over the French, in a dictionary reprinted in 1895 after Dupuis's death, Mousset continued to experiment with different transliteration practices by embracing the use of "High Tamil orthography," depicted as more representative of classical Tamil words than "Low Tamil" (1895:xxii).[4] Also, by differentiating between entries of "tamoul vulgaire" and "tamoul poétique" in the dictionary, despite making the disclaimer that these represent a linguistic continuum, the authors helped to conflate "spoken" and "corrupt" qualities with Low Tamil, and "written" and "poetic" with High Tamil.

> In order to make it more beneficial for everyone, we have gathered in alphabetical order the greatest number of *tamoul vulgaire* and *tamoul poétique* words that we could find. These two idioms of the same language, we could say almost two distinct languages, even though they come across as fairly distinct from one another, are not distinguished by absolute markers that are stark enough for us to separate them in a dictionary, without causing frequent difficulties for those who study one or the other. (Mousset and Dupuy 1895:v)

Such metalinguistic labels affirmed the existence of "two distinct languages" that, even if they differed phonologically and grammatically only in degrees, still "come across as fairly distinct."

In a colonial newsletter published in 1855 featuring Dupuis' catalog, a column contrasts the aesthetic features of older, classical typesetting characters in Tamil with newer, more modern ones invented by the Catholic Mission (see Figure 4.2). In a letter sent to Paris, Dupuis proudly asserts that both Frenchmen and Englishmen applauded his typography as the new standard:

> English experts who saw such a clear and easy victory instead of the confusion that existed previously, have been amazed, no doubt that this reform will introduce among their ranks, and I reckon that France will have to take the same path of making major improvements and reforms of typography, which originate with one of its subjects and colonies. (Inde 1855)

Also, in the preface to the Tamil-French dictionary that Dupuis co-published with Mousset in 1850, the authors describe their text as the most thorough and systematic dictionary to date, surpassing earlier versions by Indian scholars and

CARACTÈRES TAMOULS.

CONFECTIONNÉS PAR LES FONDEURS INDIGÈNES DE LA MISSION,

SOUS LA DIRECTION

DU PROVICAIRE APOSTOLIQUE CHARGÉ DE L'IMPRIMERIE.

NOUVEAUX CARACTÈRES	ANCIENS CARACTÈRES
SELON LE TYPE DONNÉ PAR LE PROVICAIRE.	SELON LE TYPE ORDINAIRE DU PAYS.
CORPS 11.	CORPS 12.
ORAISON DOMINICALE.	ORAISON DOMINICALE.

பரமண்டலங்களிலேயிருக்கிற எங்கள் பி
தாவே உம்முடைய நாமம் அர்ச்சிக்கப்படுவ
தாக, உம்முடைய ராச்சியம்வருக, உம்மு
டையசித்தம் பரமண்டலத்திலே செய்யப்ப
டுமோப்போல் பூமியிலேயும் செய்யப்படுவே
தாக, அன்றன்றுள்ள எங்கள்அப்பம் எங்க
ளுக்கு இன்றுதாரும்...

SALUTATION ANGÉLIQUE (interlignée).

பிறியதத்தத்திறுலே பூரண மரியாயேவா
ழ்க, கர்த்தர் உம்முடனே, பெண்சாதிகளு
க்குள்ளே யாசிர்வதிக்கப்பட்டவளுநீரே, உ
ம்முடைய திருவயிற்றின் கனியாஜெயேசு
ஆசிர்வதிக்கப்பட்டவருமாமே, அர்ச்சியசி
ஷ்டமரியாயே சர்வேசுவரனுடையமாதா
வே பாவிகளாயிருக்கிற எங்களுக்காக...

பரமண்டலங்களிலேயிருக்கிற எங்கள் பி
தாவே உம்முடையநாமம் அர்ச்சிக்கப்படுவ
தராக, உம்முடைய ராச்சியம்வருக, உம்மு
டையசித்தம் பரமண்டலத்திலே செய்யப்
படுமோப்போலப் பூமியிலேயும் செய்யப்ப
டேதராக, அன்றன் முள்ள எங்கள்அப்பம்...

SALUTATION ANGÉLIQUE (interlignée).

பிறியதத்தத்திறுலே பூரணமரியாபேவா
ழ்க, கர்த்தர் உம்முடனே, பெண்சாதிகளுக்
குன்னே யாசிர்வதிக்கப் பட்டவளுநீரே, உ
ம்முடைய திருவயிற்றின் கனியபேசேசு
ஆசிர்வதிக்கப் பட்டவருமாமே, அர்ச்சியசி
ஷ்டமரியாயே சர்வேசுவரனுடைய மாதா
வேபாவிகளாயிருக்கிறஎங்களுக்காக...

CORPS 9.
SALVE REGINA.

இருபதயாபத்துக்கு மாதாவாயிருக்கிற வெங்
களிராக்கினியேவாழ்க, எங்கள் திவேமெ பெங்கள்
தஞ்சமே பெங்கள் மதுரமெவாழ்க, பரதேசிகளா
யிருக்கிற நாங்களேவைபின் மக்கள் உம்மைமப்பா
ர்த்தன் கூப்பிடுகிறேம், இந்தக்கண்ணீனிர்க் க
ணவாயிலேநின்று பிரலாபித்தமூது, உம்மையே
நோக்கிப்பெருமூச்சுவிடுகிறேம், ஆதலால்எங்கள்
க்காக வேண்டிமன்ருடுகிறதாயே, உம்முடைய த
யாபமூன்ள திருக்கண்களே எங்கள்பேர்லே....

ORAISON (interlignée).

சர்வசத்தியுடையவருமாய் நித்தியருமாயிருக்கி
ற சர்வேசுவரா, முத்திபேறுபெற்ற கன்னிந்தாயா
ன மரியாயியுடைய ஆத்துமமூஞ்சர்ரமு மிலிமிர்
த்துசாந்துவினை நுக்கிரகத்திறுலேதேவரீருடையதி
ருக்குமாரனுக் இயொக்கியமான பிடமாவிறந்த
ஏந்கனவேநியமித்தருளினீரே, அந்தந்திவ்வியதா
யை நிணைத்துமகிழ்கின்றநாங்கள்அவளுடைய...

CORPS 9.
SALVE REGINA.

ஈருபதயபாபத்துக்கு மத்ராவாயிருக்கிற பெங்கள்ரா
க்கினியேவாழ்க, எங்கள்திவேமெபெம்தஞ்சமேபெங்க
ள்மதுரமெவாழ்க, பரதேசிகளாயிருக்கிறநாங்களேவை
பின்மந்தன் உமமைமப்பார்த்தக் உப்பிடுகிறேம், இந்த
க்கன்னினிர்க் கணவாயிலேநின்று பிரலாபித்தமூது, உ
ம்மையேநோக்கிப் பெருமூச்சுவிடுகிறேம், ஆதலால்எங்க
ளுக்காகவேண்டிமன்ருடுகிறதாயே, உம்முடைய தயா
பமூள்ளஎடிருக்கன்னை பெங்கள்பேர்லே இருப்பி....

ORAISON (interlignée.)

சர்வசத்தி புடையவருமாய் நித்திய ருமாயிருக்கிற சர்
வேசுவரா முத்திபேறுபெற்ற கன்னிந்தாயான மரியாயி
புடைய ஆத்தமமூஞ்சர்ரமு மிலிபிர்த்துசாந்துவினைந்தக்
கிரகத்திறுலேதேவரீருடைய திருக்குமாரனுக் இயொக்கிய
மான பிடமாயிருக்க எந்கனவே நியமித்தருளினீரே, அ
ந்தத்திவ்வியதாயை நிணைத்துமகிழ்கின்றநாங்க எவளு
டைய விசக்குமூன்ன மன்ருடுகிறுலே...

ÉCHANTILLON
DE CHAQUE CARACTÈRE TAMOUL
ENVOYÉ A L'EXPOSITION.
CORPS 11 (interligné)

அ ஆ இ ஈ உ ஊ எ ஏ ஜ ஐ ஒ ஓ கி
கி கூ க் ங்ஙி யி ஈ ஙூ ஞ் சி சே சு ச் ஞ் ஞி ஞீ
ஜீ து தூ ண் டி டீ டெ ண் ண ணி ணீ
ணூ ணூ ண் ண்த தி தீ து தூ த் ந் நி நீ நு
நூ ந்ப பி பீ புபூ ம் ம மி மீ மூ ய் ய யி
யுபூ ர் ரி ருருூ ல் லி லீ லு லூ ல்ல வ்
வி விவு வுூ ழ் ழி ழீ ழு ழூ ள் ள ளி ளீ ளு
ளூ ள் ற ற்றி றீ று றூ ன் ன்னி னூ
ண் ஃ க்ஷ கி க்ஷீ ஷ் ஷி ஷீ ஜை ஜ் ஸ்ஸ்ரீ க
உ ச ஷ ஹ எ அ கூ ஜா ணே.

ÉCHANTILLON
DES CARACTÈRES TAMOULS
DU SIÈCLE DERNIER.

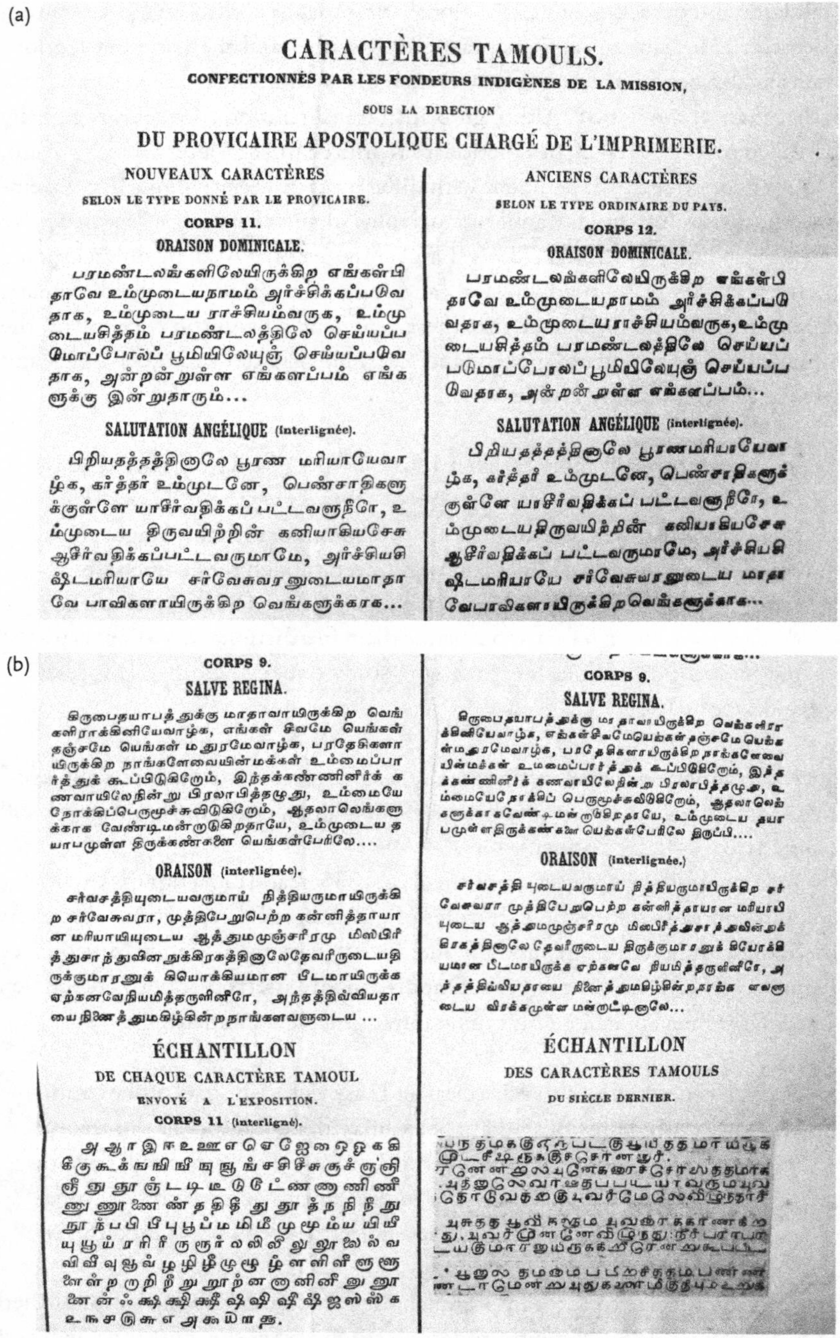

FIGURE 4.2 Typographical standards in writing Tamil ca. 1855.

British writers plagued by copyist errors. This boasting of typographic and orthographic innovations underscores the rival efforts taken to produce distinctly French and British brands of Tamil scholarship in the mid-nineteenth century, which collectively reinforced diglossic views of a language yet enabled deviations from the literary language to be evaluated according to different scalar metrics and social hierarchies. Hence, today, Arjuna, a speaker of Chennai Tamil, can argue that Sri Lankans' habitual use of [l] rather than [ɻ] proves the greater phonological purity of Indian Tamil, and Sri Lankans can retort that morphological reduction in Indian vernaculars instead demonstrates their lesser antiquity.

Such contestations did not become commonplace until new nationalist publics emerged in South Asia and the diaspora in the late nineteenth and twentieth centuries to accommodate the growing domestic and transnational demand for Tamil texts previously limited to British, French, and high-caste elite readers. From 1835 through the 1880s, Indian-operated or -controlled presses printed many new books and periodicals exclusively in Tamil, causing the premature demise of French- and British-controlled presses and forcing them to publish mostly in European languages. Afterward, French-Tamil dictionaries became mere curiosities, perused only by the odd customer years later, such as Selvamani, who bought one of Dupuis' dictionaries while living in Chennai in anticipation of immigrating to Montréal. Yet the social life of these books also has a hidden chapter. In 1865, a single shipment reached French Guiana to become among the first collections of bilingual books to be traded across the far-flung peripheries of an empire. Heeding Dupuis's request that the book catalog be forwarded to the governors of Réunion, Martinique, Guadeloupe, and Cayenne overseeing Tamil indentured laborers, the Governor of French India wrote to the Minister of the Navy and Colonies in Paris about the press on Dupuis's behalf:

> My attention focused especially on the Tamil-French dictionary and grammar that was just published, important works long in the making that are due to the science and the irrepressible zeal of two members of the Mission. After examining these works, I ask the Head Father if the colonies with Tamil-speaking immigrants have been informed of the resources that are being offered by such an institution, as much as for easing relations between owners and workers as much as to guarantee the functioning of courts and tribunals. Since no positive response was given to me concerning this request, I ask to be given an update about this situation and the works of the printing press, as well as the book catalog that could be given either to other colonies: Reunion, Martinique, Guadeloupe, Cayenne, or to scientific institutions of the Metropole. (Inde 1863)

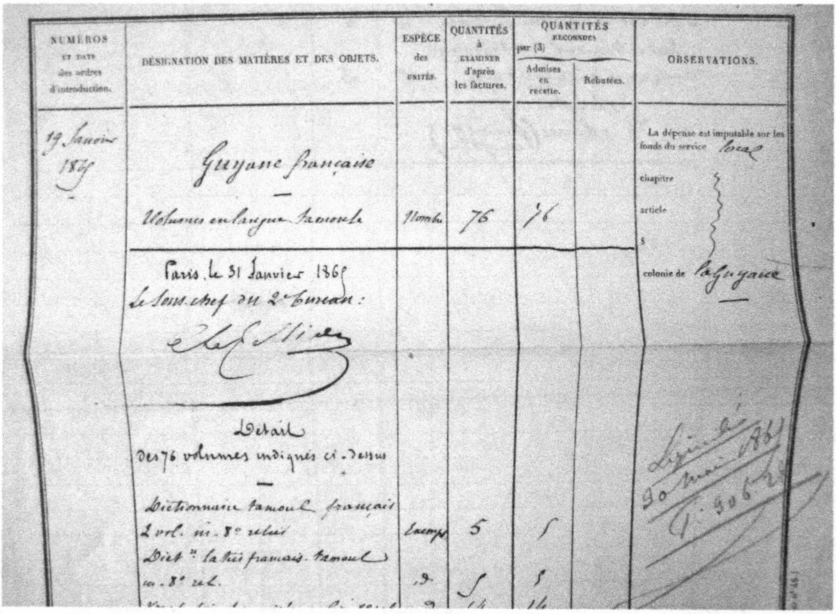

NUMÉROS ET DATE des ordres d'introduction.	DÉSIGNATION DES MATIÈRES ET DES OBJETS.	ESPÈCE des UNITÉS.	QUANTITÉS à EXAMINER d'après les factures.	QUANTITÉS RECONNUES par (3) Admises en recette.	Rebutées.	OBSERVATIONS.
19 Janvier 1863	Guyane française — Volumes en langue tamoule	Nombre	76	76		La dépense est imputable sur les fonds du service local chapitre article § colonie de la Guyane
	Paris, le 31 Janvier 1863 Le Sous-chef du 2e Bureau:					
	Détail des 76 volumes indiqués ci-dessus — Dictionnaire tamoul français 2 vol. in-8° relié	Exempl.	5	5		
	Dict. latin français-tamoul in-8° rel.	d°	5	5		

FIGURE 4.3 Purchase order of Tamil-language books for French Guiana, 1863.

Of all the Governors contacted, only French Guiana's governor responded affirmatively and ordered seventy six volumes of books, including dictionaries, grammars, workbooks, catechisms, Biblical stories, and copies of *Arabian Nights*, written or translated into Tamil from French or Latin (see Figure 4.3). What their purpose was for the colony, one could only venture a guess.

In French Guiana, even before the abolition of African slavery in 1848, Father Louis Sénégal had inquired into acquiring Indian laborers of a spice cultivator caste from the Malabar Coast, where spices grow aplenty, to cultivate cinnamon and pepper in their forested hinterlands.

> We should bring to French Guiana approximately 1,100 Indian farmers along with their wives, some Cholas from Ceylon who are of the caste specially trained in cultivating cinnamon and preparing its precious bark, farmers from the Malabar coast and Sumatra who are used to cultivating pepper, to introduce into Cayenne these two crops and judge which one among them we should prefer. (Guyane 1819)

Because "Tamoul" and "Malabar" were used interchangeably by European bureaucrats and scholars up until the mid-1800s to characterize, one, the Tamil language, two, the coastal peoples of Sri Lanka, and three, the western coast of

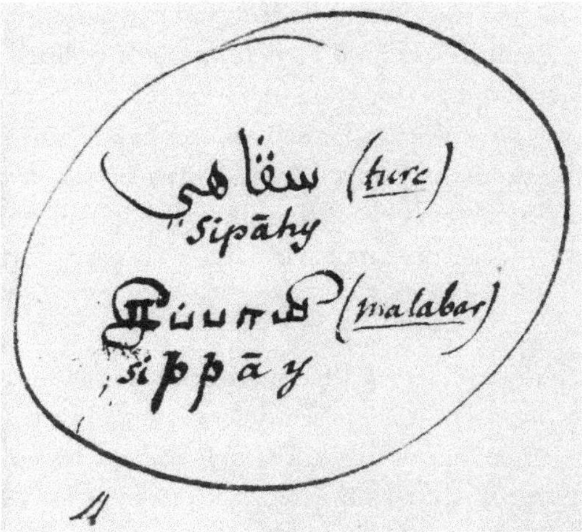

FIGURE 4.4 "Sippay" in Tamil and Arabic script labeled as *malabar* and *turc.*

India (Inde 1831) (see Figure 4.4), the Governor made the costly mistake of conflating the Malayalam-speaking inhabitants of the Malabar Coast and the Tamil-speaking inhabitants of Sri Lanka, both of whom are spice cultivators, with the Tamil-speaking inhabitants of the Coromandel Coast. Ultimately, to circumvent their British rivals stationed in Colombo and Madras ports, the French selected laborers from among the east coast residents of French India, who had no prior experience working with spices, to migrate to French Guiana.

> The Tamil language is better known under the name *malabare* among the French, and it is the Tamil lineage that Balby calls by the family name *Malabare* in his geography dictionary. (Mousset and Dupuy 1895)

Between 1856 and 1877, a recorded 6551 Tamil-speaking rice cultivators, masons, shepherds, weavers, and servants from villages and towns near Pondicherry and Karikal, mostly men and women between the ages of fourteen and thirty, were cajoled with false promises of lucrative and hospitable work conditions or simply kidnapped onto French-owned ships en route for Cayenne. In 1857, Tamils comprised a quarter of French Guiana's total population (Singaravélou 1991).

Children who accompanied their mothers to this colony or were born in French Guiana may have attended schools founded by the sisters of St. Joseph de Cluny at Sinnamary and Mana plantations for the children of freed slaves. These schools taught reading, writing, arithmetic, and Christian morality in

French and Creole and, in 1858, awarded grammars, dictionaries, and other books printed in Latin, Greek, and French, specially ordered from France, to students as end-of-year prizes for good performance. When the school became secular in 1863, it is possible that Tamil books replaced Latin and Greek books as prizes. The testimony of Lotus Vingadassamy-Engels, a third-generation Guadeloupean of Tamil ancestry writing about the Indian Antillean diaspora, confirms that knowledge of Tamil had largely disappeared within a single generation.

> We lost a lot, but we preserved what was essential. We lost our languages. Coming from all over India as we did, we spoke different languages and communication was not easy. For practical reason we adopted the common language of the island, Creole. It served as a common vehicle between all races there—whites, blacks and mixed blood. For some time we kept using our own languages, but the new generations born on the island lost touch with them very soon. Our priests and the more educated among us did try in the beginning to teach children their original mother tongue, but several factors contributed to condemn these attempts to failure. (Assisi n.d.)

If priests and parents sought to teach children of Tamil descent their "original mother tongue," books would have been instrumental to this endeavor. The lack of records in French Guianese archives of the Mission of India's shipment leaves one to conclude that these books were not intended for colonial libraries or given to plantation owners and had a more singular function.

The archives also do not mention anything about the linguistic repertoires of indentured laborers other than to presume that villagers recruited from Pondicherry and Karikal spoke Creole and understood French, even if this was not always true. In fact in 1877, the British Raj outlawed Indian Tamil migration to French Guiana when it became obvious that countless men, women, and children (around 50 percent) had unnecessarily died of diseases aboard ships and in plantations because the French had ignored the overseeing British government's requirement to hire Tamil-speaking interpreters to assist medical doctors (Guyane 1862). After most Tamil laborers were repatriated to India and only a few remained in French Guiana, French plantation owners welcomed the change in policy as an opportunity to recruit "hardier" Asian laborers, having decided that Tamils were a weak race unsuitable for hard labor. Ironically, though numerically eclipsed and outlasted by Tamil indentured laborers in Guadeloupe (population 42,326) and Martinique (population 25,509) from 1854 to 1889, only French Guiana, despite its horrid reputation for mistreating Tamil laborers, saw value in Tamil books. Not until the early twenty-first century would the transnational trade of Tamil books be revived for the purpose of educating migrant children, but this time it would take place between the Canadian cities of Montréal and Toronto, where Tamil speakers have inherited a different colonial history yet one also shaped by an enduring Anglo-Franco rivalry.

Funding Heritage Language Education in Québec

In 1977, the Canadian federal government lent modest financial support to community heritage language programs following the dissemination of the *Non-Official Languages Study* (O'Bryan et al. 1976) indicating strong interest among ethnic minority communities.[5] However, because education falls under provincial jurisdiction, the federal government could not implement these programs in public schools. Ontario was the first province to offer fully funded heritage language instruction in public schools in Toronto starting in 1977 (Cummins 1992).[6] Not to be outdone by its anglophone rival and hoping to mitigate ethnic minority leaders' outrage over the recent passage of Bill 101 (*Loi 101*), Québec's Ministry of Education, Leisure, and Sports implemented its own heritage language program, known as the PELO, in 1978 (CECM 1998; McAndrew 1991). In 1979, a few children of European ancestry began taking classes in Greek, Italian, Portuguese, and Spanish at select public schools, first French-medium and then English-medium, in Montréal. Parents needed at least twenty-five signatures to petition their principals to offer additional classes and, upon receiving approval, collaborated with local school board officials to hire teachers from their own communities. Courses in Algonquin, Vietnamese, Laotian, Hebrew, Arabic, Tagalog, Hindi, Urdu, Bengali, Sinhala, and Tamil joined the roster over the years (see Table 4.1) (Commission scolaire de Montréal n.d.). "Les enfants de la loi 101" refers to an entire generation of bilingual or trilingual children born after 1977 who learned French as their civic language in public schools, English through informal means, and their heritage language in PELO or community schools.

Since 1998, Sri Lankan children have had the choice of taking Tamil PELO classes offered at five French-medium and three English-medium public schools in Montréal. Indians, seeking to avoid contact with Sri Lankans, have opted out of PELO classes entirely. Despite the effects of this rivalry between Indians and Sri Lankans, Tamil ranks as the fifth most popular heritage language in Montréal, with 221 total students and the largest incoming class of preschool students enrolled in 2007–2008 (Ministère 2008).[7] When I contacted the PELO directors of the Commission Scolaire de Montréal (CSDM) in June

Table 4.1 PELO classes offered at the CSDM in 2007–2008

Heritage Language (Year First Offered)	Percentage of Students	Number of Students
Italian (1978)	47%	3215
Greek (1979)	2.2%	160
Portuguese (1979)	2.1%	143
Spanish (1979)	12%	816
Arabic (1985)	20%	1373
Hebrew (1985)	4%	267
Vietnamese (1983)	3.2%	221
Tamil (1998)	3.3%	225
Others (2001)	2.3%	160
Total		6832

2002 and the EMSB in June 2005 to broach the possibility of conducting research at one of their schools, both directors, who are well versed on research about heritage language education in Canada, sent me articles discussing the PELO's merits for integrating minority children into the majority francophone or anglophone society.[8]

PELO classes are offered two or four times a week (before school, during lunch, or after school) for two and a half hours total and come in a variety of curricula. Since third-generation minorities of European ancestry mostly speak in English or French at home, their curriculum focuses on teaching basic speaking skills and listening comprehension. PELO classes for recent immigrant children who already speak the heritage language at home instead work on improving their reading, writing, and oratorical speaking skills in the literary standard. The Tamil PELO, in addition to teaching literacy in Tamil, also promote Sri Lankan students' self-identification as speakers of literary Tamil. In 1998, a CSDM official, Françoise Binamé, collaborated with a senior Sri Lankan Tamil teacher, Nesananthar Sundararajah, to write the Tamil PELO curriculum for both elementary and intermediate levels. The EMSB adopted the same curriculum and translated it from French into English, restating the global objectives and aims as follows:

> Global Objectives (ORAL and WRITTEN)
> The main objectives of this program are: to preserve the heritage language and culture, to enable students to communicate in a standard language in situations related to their environment, and to learn the written language.

> Aims (ORAL and WRITTEN)
> The role of this program is to: maintain and improve the student's basic knowledge of the language and his or her specific language abilities, and to help the student develop the attitudes required to cultivate an interest in the heritage language and to appreciate and identify with the culture. (CECM 1998:12)

By asserting in the same sentence that students should learn to "communicate in the standard language" and "learn the written language," the Global Objectives imply a close relationship between colloquial Sri Lankan Tamil and the written standard. Furthermore, by stating that the "role of the program" is to "help the student develop the attitudes required to cultivate an interest in the heritage language and to appreciate and identify with the culture," the Aims explicitly conflate students' ethnic identities with their heritage languages. Elsewhere, the curriculum specifies that "the student should be able to communicate orally (in standard language) to persons familiar to him or her, on the following topics": me, you, and our families; my school; seasons; time; health and hygiene; recreational activities; food and drink; animals; clothing; my home; and special celebrations. Lessons falling under "Me, You and Our Families" require the student to "be able to talk about basic personal identification and family (using standard language) with persons who are familiar to him or her" by asking information such as name, family relationships, age, address, telephone number, and place of birth (CECM 1998:13). With respect to literacy skills, the elementary curriculum further specifies that "the student should be able to understand texts that relate to the themes presented in this program" and "write texts relating to his or her needs and interests, and to the themes presented in the oral modules" (CECM 1998:14). Overall, the Tamil PELO curriculum emphasizes speaking skills and basic literacy skills, yet its main objective is to encourage students to self-identify with a standardized variety of literary Tamil to "preserve the heritage language and culture" (CECM 1998:12).

In July 2002, I telephone a high-ranking official at the *Commission scolaire Marguerite Bourgeoys* in the West Island to ask about the future of heritage language education in Québec. Speaking of the PELO as a relic of the past, she informs me of new programs on the horizon to teach "international languages," though she does not explicitly define what these would be. The Ministry of Education, Leisure and Sports offers the following rationale for their shift in priorities:

> In the present context of globalized trade and communication, knowledge of many languages represents a major asset since it allows a person to communicate with interlocutors of various cultural communities and develop

> an attitude of openness, respect and tolerance toward these communities. (Belzil 2006:69)

Arguing that children who are fluent in multiple languages would better compete in the global market and enable Québec's economy to prosper, the Ministry proposes that all Québécois children, and not just ethnic minorities, should learn a third language. Urban elites had made a similar argument in 1988 in petitioning the Ministry to allow children of all ethnic backgrounds to attend PELO classes, yet relatively few parents have taken advantage of these opportunities (and none at all in Tamil classes) after the Ministry approved the request. In 2007, the Ministry funded a new initiative called "Spanish as a Third Language Program" (*Programme d'espagnol, langue tierce*) to teach Spanish to public school children of explicitly non-Hispanic descent.

> Intended for students with minimal to no competence in the assigned language, courses that teach a third language introduce students to a new language and associated culture. The Spanish program therefore seeks to help non-Hispanic Québécois students to communicate in this language, familiarize themselves with its related cultures, and develop an interest in the language that will endure beyond high school. (Belzil 2006:69)

This policy, however, unfairly segregates Hispanic children, who can only study Spanish in PELO classes, from other non-Hispanic children, who can study Spanish in both programs. Considering the steady attrition of government funds for the PELO since 1994, the future of provincially funded heritage language education in Québec does not appear especially bright.

The CSDM denied my request to conduct research on PELO classes in French-medium schools after one principal in Côte-des-Neiges expressed concern that my project had "*trop un contenu politique*" (too much political content), and the other principal simply refused to return my phone calls. Despite my initial discouragement, I decided to later apply with the EMSB, whose PELO director, after hearing of my earlier difficulties, hinted that the CSDM might be suspicious of my political allegiances. To be fair, my proposal did exhibit an implicit bias against Bill 101's policies toward immigrants. I had been unaware of this "problem of tone" until several Québec studies scholars reviewing my work brought it to my attention. After modifying my proposal to focus squarely on questions of pedagogy and language acquisition, I received permission from the EMSB's PELO director and principal to observe Tamil classes at Parker Elementary School.

Teaching Tamil at Parker Elementary School

In January 2006, in anticipation of my impending fieldwork at Parker Elementary School, I move into an apartment in Parc-Extension that I share with a Moroccan-French nurse and an international student from Mexico, located only ten minutes' walking distance from Parker. Three blocks south of Parker is *École de la Montagne*, a French-medium public elementary school attended by many of the Sri Lankan children living in the neighborhood (see Figure 4.5). Every Tuesday and Thursday afternoon from January to March, I carefully walk along the icy sidewalk, past de la Montagne's imposing three-story building to reach Parker's more modest two-story building, arriving before the 2:05 pm bell rings to avoid the mad rush of schoolchildren in snowsuits bursting through the front doors to board their school buses or walk home (see Figure 4.6). Heading straight for the teacher's lounge, I wait there until Vasanthi and Nilima, the two Tamil PELO teachers, arrive. Usually, the other Bengali, Hindi, Urdu, and Greek PELO teachers are already there, casually chatting with one another in English while preparing their class materials. Yet Vasanthi and Nilima, who speak little English, seldom join in this camaraderie.

Nilima is an accredited teacher from Jaffna, where she previously taught home science and geography at a high school. Currently, she teaches Tamil at Parker and a French-medium public school in Côte-des-Neiges where, she assures me, the curricula are the same. Although Vasanthi's bachelor's degree in commerce from Sri Lanka is not accredited in Canada, she was hired to teach Tamil at Parker Elementary despite not having any prior teaching experience or credentials. On

FIGURE 4.5 École de la Montagne in Parc-Extension.

FIGURE 4.6 Parker Elementary School in Parc-Extension.

Tuesdays I accompany Vasanthi to her elementary classroom, where she teaches first- through third-grade students, and on Thursdays I visit Nilima's intermediate class of fourth- through sixth-grade students. To avoid distracting the students, I sit as unobtrusively as possible in the back of the classroom, where I set up my microphones and minidisc recorder. Sometimes, after class ends at 3:30 pm, Nilima and I walk part of the way back home together to wait for her two sons, Selvan and Kaushik, who speak with one another in French as they exit de la Montagne, before greeting me in English and their mother in Tamil. Although more Sri Lankan Tamil students attend de la Montagne than Parker, this French-medium school does not offer Tamil instruction. Nilima was eligible to send her sons to Parker yet chose La Montagne for its superior French instruction. When she and the other Sri Lankan parents petitioned La Montagne's principal to offer Tamil PELO classes, they were dismayed to learn that he had allocated all of the PELO funds for teaching Arabic, the majority heritage language of students at this school.

According to Vasanthi, out of the forty or so Sri Lankan children attending Parker Elementary, less than half participate in the Tamil PELO. She attributes this low enrollment to the parents' preference to send children to after-school tutoring sessions in French rather than Tamil. I once overheard a fifth-grade student inform her teacher, Nilima, that she would have to miss Thursday's class to go to French tutoring. I also heard from Selvamani that two of her young tutees quit the Tamil PELO after the third and fourth grades because their mothers had asked them to work on improving their French skills instead. When I inquired with Selvamani's cousins if this was indeed true, they added that they could not keep up with the literacy lessons, although one girl insisted that her mother still tutors her in Tamil at home. The transition between the third and fourth grades is a particularly critical time when many students stop attending PELO classes, especially those struggling with reading and writing. At Parker, Karthik is the only fourth-grade student in the elementary class to have failed the matriculation exam to pass onto the intermediate class. Vasanthi often gives him special lessons to keep him motivated.

Hoping to speak candidly with some of the elementary students, ages 6 through 9, about their desires to learn Tamil, I arrange to lead a group question-and-answer session at the end of class on January 26.[9] I begin by asking the students how they feel about learning Tamil, and several of the girls and boys respond in chorus, literally jumping out of their seats in eagerness, "I like it, I like it, I like it!" One boy further specifies, "I really like it. Because I never heard of these new words" and another girl says, "I like Tamil class. I like to read and write. I like to say hard words." Most students find speaking in Tamil relatively easy but reading and writing more difficult. When I ask, "Who do you speak to in Tamil?" almost everyone chimes in to say, "*Ammā appā*!" (Mom and dad!) Vasanthi confirms that mothers and fathers often help out with Tamil homework and speak to their children about Sri Lankan culture. I count five students (in a class of nine) who claim to have previously visited Sri Lanka. One says, "I love Sri Lanka. The culture, it's good." When pressed further to explain why, he responds, "I don't know. I like it."

English is another favorite language of theirs. When I ask them why they converse with their friends and brothers and sisters in English, one girl replies, "They said to me in the Tamil language, I don't want to say it in Tamil, I want to say in it English." In this English-medium school where French instruction begins in the second grade, many students find French more difficult to learn, especially those who did not attend French-medium preschool or do not speak in French with their friends. The level of excitement in the classroom rises once again when I ask about code-switching and code-mixing. "Do you mix sometimes Tamil?" "Yes." "Sometimes English?" "Yes!" "Sometimes French?" "YES!" the children shout with increasing pitch and intensity. Building on this excitement, I ask them about their favorite Tamil film and movie stars and witness all orderliness vanish as the children gleefully shout out the names of famous actors ("Rajinikanth!") and the latest Tamil movies they watched on satellite television at home.

One mother who often helps out Vasanthi in the classroom agrees to let me interview her son, Preetam, and daughter, Anita, together. Anita (A) is a precocious soon-to-be eight year old in the first grade who speaks Tamil and English, but not French, yet. Her older brother, Preetam (P), an articulate nine year old in the second grade, informs me that, after attending French-medium preschool and kindergarten, he now speaks all three languages, yet with different abilities. Without any prompting, Anita and Preetam begin the interview by referring to Tamil as their mother tongue, which to them literally means the language spoken by their mother.

(1) S: If someone asked you, "Why are you learning Tamil? What do you like about the language?" How would you describe the language?
(2) A: Cause it's my mother's language. Because it's our language!
(3) S: Good, good.
(4) P: It's my mother's language. It's my language. And I need to study it. Also also my father's father's language. So we had to study it. But we don't know lots... much. That's why we had to go to Tamil PELO.
(5) S: Okay. Did you want to go or did your parents tell you to go?
(6) A: Where?
(7) P: No, we want to go and they let us go.
(8) A: We were babies. How could we decide? We weren't even born!
(9) S: Okay, good answer. (*laughter*)

Tickled by Anita's precociousness, I ask about their difficulties in learning Tamil.

(10) S: Okay. Um. Do you think the Tamil language is difficult, easy?
(11) A: Easy easy easy.
(12) S: Easy for you. How about you?
(13) P: It's easy for me to speak but writing is kinda hard. And like reading . . .
(14) A: Reading. I know to read.
(15) P: Yeah, she knows more than me.

Later, I prompt Anita and Preetam with a leading question about their feelings toward Tamil.

(16) S: Do you think it's a pretty language, beautiful language?
(17) A: Old language.
(18) P: Yeah it's nice. It sounds like. Sounds familiar. Like we are in Sri Lanka.
But my mother says it's always hot in Sri Lanka. She said she said she said it's so hot. It's always like you never see any birds soaring around in the sky because like it burns and dies it's so hot.
(19) S: When you speak it how do you feel?

(20) A: Nothing because I always speak.
(21) P: I feel like I'm a guy in Sri Lanka.
(22) A: But I don't feel hot.

Once again, Anita's answer demonstrates beyond-her-years intelligence and confirms her status as the star pupil of Vasanthi's class, surpassing even her older brother in reading and writing.

Note that Anita describes Tamil as "old" even though I prompt her with adjectives such as "pretty" and "beautiful." Perhaps the PELO class has reinforced her belief that Sri Lankans speak an old or classical style of Tamil, or perhaps she learned this from her family. Heart-warmed by Anita and Preetam's obvious affection for one another, I ask them to describe how they communicate as siblings. Anita says, "When we talk together our dad says, 'Don't talk in English at home, talk in Tamil.'" I assume this means that their father wants Preetam and Anita to speak only in Tamil at home, but Anita clarifies, "Not only Tamil, little bit." As monolingual Tamil speakers, their parents cannot understand when Preetam and Anita converse in English (and apparently the two are always talking with each other) and prefer that they speak at least some of the time in Tamil. Yet for the most part, Preetam explains, his parents do not bother them with their private conversations. "They do their stuff and we do ours." Preetam is quite serious about learning Tamil, even though his family does not plan to return to Sri Lanka, and states decisively, "I like Tamil because it is my mother's language and we are Tamil people. We will stay here or we'll go to Toronto or something. Yes, we will use Tamil in the future."

Vasanthi, their teacher, only speaks in Tamil during class, and insists that her students do the same, assuming that all can speak and understand Tamil equally. Her primary objective is to teach them basic literacy skills in Tamil, starting with reading and writing the alphabet. Despite her attempts to conduct the class solely in Tamil, I estimate that only 70 percent of student responses to Vasanthi's questions are in Tamil. Usually, the students speak with one another in English, excluding some brief interruptions in Tamil. One girl, Sarmini, and one boy, Tharshan, do not speak in Tamil at all. Sarmini remains silent during the entire period and Tharshan frequently asks his friend seated next to him to translate Vasanthi's instructions into English. When Vasanthi returns a graded quiz on the alphabet, Prakash, one of the more conversationally fluent students in the class, notices that Sarmini received a score of 2 out of 20 and embarrasses her by asking loudly, in English, why her score is so low. Overhearing this exchange, Vasanthi instructs Sarmini and Tharshan, who also received a low score, to practice writing the alphabet while she teaches the rest of the class how to write words and construct simple sentences in literary Tamil. After class when I ask Vasanthi about Sarmini's and Tharshan's poor performances, she attributes their inferior writing skills to a lack of encouragement from their parents. Never once does Vasanthi acknowledge that they might have trouble comprehending or speaking in Tamil.

The following week, Vasanthi works on identifying consonants that many elementary and intermediate students cannot regularly distinguish because they do not exist in French or English. These sounds include (1) [ʈ] (written here in Tamil notation as "ṭ") and [ð] (written as "t"); (2) [ɳ] (written as "ṇ"), [n̪] (written as "ṉ"), and [n] (written as "n"); (3) [ɻ] (written as "ḻ"), [ɭ] (written as "ḷ"), and [l] (written as "l"); and (4) [r] (written as "ṛ") and [ɾ] (written as "r")—as well as long and short vowels. For "ṭ" Vasanthi clearly enunciates [ʈ] and writes <ட> on the board; for "t" she enunciates [t] and writes <த>. She then asks the students to come up with as many words as possible ending with the syllable "ṭai" <டை>. After each student example, Vasanthi demonstrates how to correctly pronounce the word using the [ʈ] sound and writes it on the board. Here is the final list produced by the class, along with my translations:

கடை	*kaṭai*	store
குடை	*kuṭa*	umbrella
கூடை	*kūṭai*	basket
நடை	*ṉaṭai*	gait
வடை	*vaṭai*	cutlet snack
படை	*paṭai*	force
உடை	*uṭai*	breach
சடை	*caṭai*	plaited hair
இடை	*iṭai*	between

For the second and third examples, she dramatically exaggerates the difference between the short and long *u* or [ʊ] so that students can better discern the phonemic contrast between *kuṭai* (umbrella) and *kūṭai* (basket). Vasanthi then repeats the entire exercise by asking for new words ending in "tai" <தை>. The students catch on quickly and, I estimate, confuse <த> with <ட> only about 10 percent of the time. Yet this knowledge must be reinforced every year, even among intermediate students who continue to make the same mistakes. On January 24, the intermediate teacher, Nilima, distributes a worksheet asking her students to write words ending with the syllable *āy* <ஆய்> in order to solve a riddle. The first riddle asks, வாலை ஆட்டி நன்றி செலுத்தும் (that which wags its tail in gratitude.) The correct answer is *ṉāy* (dog), pronounced as *ṉāyi* in colloquial Jaffna Tamil. On their worksheets, some of the students incorrectly write *ṉai*, a nonexistent word that mimics the short vowel sound of a colloquial-like pronunciation, rather than the long vowel sound of the literary word, *ṉāy*. Seeing this mistake appear several times on her students' worksheets, Nilima collectively addresses the issue:

(1) N: *n̲ai illɛ n̲āy*
not n̲ai n̲āy
(2) *el̲utu pāppōm n̲āy*
let's try writing dog

To illustrate the mistake graphically, Nilima writes the word in Tamil script on the board and enunciates the phonemic contrast between the long vowel *ā* <ஆ> and short vowel *ai* <ஐ>. Only then do students understand how to pronounce the literary word and the colloquial word differently.

Vasanthi, who is more of a purist than Nilima, also makes an effort to expose students to less commonly spoken words in Tamil. During the second half of class on January 19, Vasanthi distributes a worksheet with pictures of a radio, television, telephone, newspaper, fax machine, and other household objects commonly referred to by their English names (see Figure 4.7). She asks for more examples of English loanwords and aids them to identify the Tamil equivalents.

stamp	முத்திரை	*muttirai*
letter	தபால்	*tapāl*
post office	தபாலகம்	*tapālakam*
bank	வங்கி	*vaṅki*

The students do poorly on this exercise. After class, when Nilima walks over to Vasanthi's classroom to chat, I suggest to both of them that Vasanthi's students may have never heard these words before because they and their families are accustomed to using only the English names. Nilima and Vasanthi agree, yet when I ask them to compare how Sri Lankans and Indians incorporate English into their everyday speech, they express contradictory observations. Vasanthi believes that Indians use "pure" Tamil words for technological or modern objects, whereas Nilima insists that Indians use English words more often. Vasanthi humbly defers to Nilima, who is more familiar with Indian varieties of Tamil since she listens to radio programs, television shows, and films produced in Chennai, and has first-hand experience interacting with Indians in Montréal. Due to the ethnonational segregation of Indians and Sri Lankans, teachers with little contact with Indians may mistake their pedagogical styles and standardization practices in competitive terms.

When directing her students to stop speaking in English, Vasanthi uses the Sri Lankan expression, *kataikku kuṭātu*, by employing the classical Tamil word, *kataikka*, "to speak," whereas Indians would say *pēcā kuṭātu*. However, this single word choice does not prove that Jaffna Tamil is a classical language. When Vasanthi teaches her students how to write sentences in subject-object-verb order

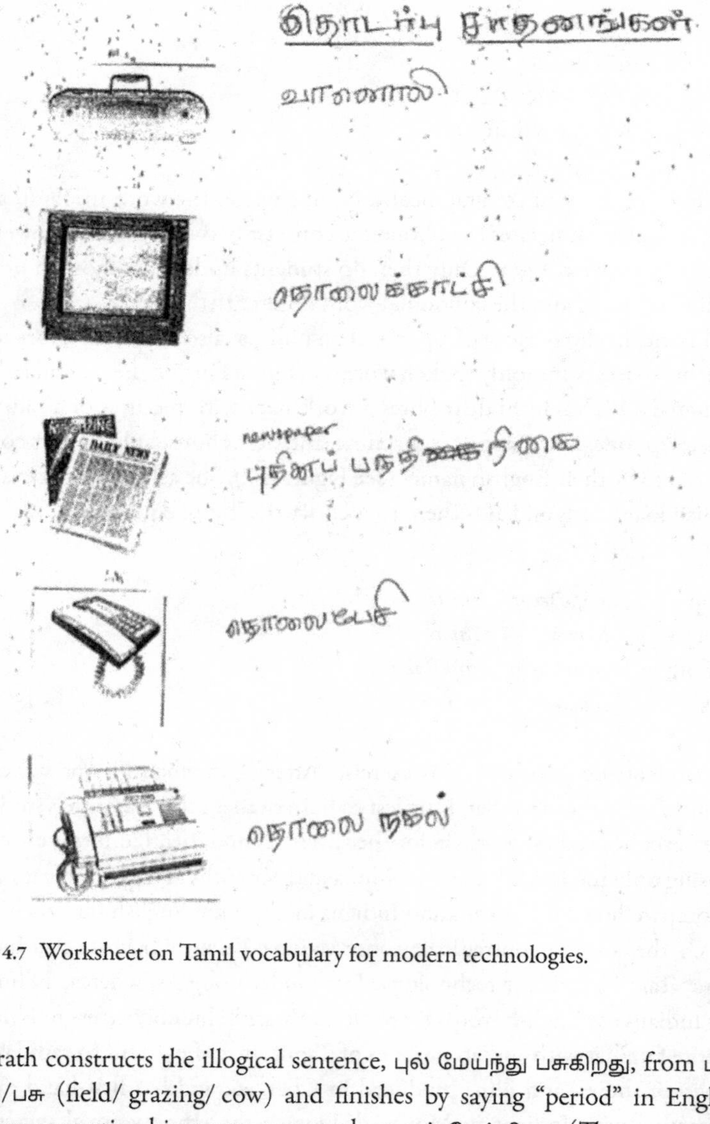

FIGURE 4.7 Worksheet on Tamil vocabulary for modern technologies.

and Sharath constructs the illogical sentence, புல் மேய்ந்து பசுகிறது, from புல்/ மேய்ந்து/பசு (field/ grazing/ cow) and finishes by saying "period" in English, rather than correcting his sentence to read பசு புல் மேய்கிறது (The cow grazing on the field), Vasanthi insists that Sharath say "muṭṭu pulli" instead of period, even though punctuation is a European neologism introduced into Tamil literature only in the late nineteenth century (Kandiah 1978). Therefore, although curricular discourses adopted by teachers like Vasanthi (and perhaps internalized by students like Anita) imply that Sri Lankans speak an older style of literary Tamil than Indians, who are depicted by some teachers as speaking the more modern language, the Sri Lankan Tamil vernacular spoken in Montréal is better described, in linguistic terms, as a Jaffna style of colloquial Tamil that has retained more classical lexicon and literary morphosyntactic features than regional Indian styles.

Reading storybooks written in literary Tamil bought from *Nickes Fantaisies*, a store owned by Nilima's brother on rue Jean-Talon in Parc-Extension, Vasanthi always paraphrases and translates these stories into colloquial Jaffna Tamil for her students. One day, Jeevitha and her older brother Prakash summarize the tale of a monkey and a bee from a book that Vasanthi read in the last class. Prakash also writes all of the nouns that he recollects on the board in Tamil:

பெயர்ச்சொல்	*peyarccol*	noun
குரங்கு	*kuraṅkɨ*	monkey
தேனீ	*tēnī*	honeybee
தேன்	*tēn*	honey
மரம்	*maram*	tree

Vasanthi then asks Prakash to convert the nouns from their singular to plural forms. For the first three nouns, this involves simply adding the morpheme *-kaḷ* to the end of the word, a task that Prakash easily accomplishes. Yet when faced with the last two nouns, Prakash cannot proceed because he does not know the literary *sandhi* rules for converting [m] and [n] to [ŋ] before [g].[10] When Prakash expresses his chagrin, Vasanthi reassures him that he will learn these rules soon.

Yet intermediate students who know the *sandhi* rules still struggle to recognize them in writing. When reading texts out loud, students often sound out each word, syllable-by-syllable, in a colloquial Jaffna pronunciation. Often they do not fully understand the text until Nilima translates it for them into colloquial Jaffna Tamil. On January 24, Nilima announces to her students' (S) vast displeasure that they will take turns reading from the story assigned for homework.

(1)	N:	*ippo niṅka vāciccu*
		now that you have read (the story)
(2)		*ruci vāciruṅka*
		prove it by reading (out loud)
(3)	S:	no teacher, no teacher, please

As further incentive, Nilima promises to award points to students based on their individual performances. Nitya (S), enticed by the prospect of winning the competition, volunteers first.

(1) S: *mayil paṛavaikaluḷ mikavum*
The peacock is the most beautiful bird.
(2) *alakanatu mayil*
beautiful peacock
(3) *itu iḷaṅkai intiyā mianmār malēsiya pōnṛa nāṭuviḷē vāḻkiṛatu*
It lives in the countries of Sri Lanka, India, Myanmar, and Malaysia.

Nitya stumbles over unfamiliar loanwords, such as *intiyā, mianmār*, and *malēsiya*, as well as sounds specific to literary Tamil, such as the "ṛ" or [r] in *pōnṛa* and "ḻ" or [ɻ] in *vāḻkiṛatu*. Yet since she completes her recitation in 31 seconds, the fastest speed so far, she receives the highest possible score of four points. Following Nitya is Naveen, the most fluent student in the intermediate class, who completes the same recitation in 45 seconds to receive only three points. In addition to stumbling over the same words as Nitya, Naveen has a hard time saying *mikavum* (*rompa* is used in colloquial Jaffna Tamil), *nāṭuviḷē*, (*naṭulɛ* is used in colloquial Jaffna Tamil), and *alakanatu*. This competition exemplifies how PELO teachers evaluate success according to how quickly students bridge their competence gap between colloquial Jaffna and literary Tamil.

To facilitate students' comprehension of literary Tamil, a language more-or-less unfamiliar to them, PELO teachers will draw on students' existing knowledge of colloquial Jaffna Tamil and then demonstrate how to convert colloquial words into literary Tamil. At the same time, to promote students' ethnolinguistic identification with literary Tamil as their heritage language, teachers may sometimes blur grammatical differences between literary Tamil and Jaffna Tamil. These conflicting goals result in colloquial and literary forms of Tamil being mixed in ambiguous ways. I hesitate to label these practices as "code-mixing" or "code-switching" because students do not always perceive, nor are they taught to perceive, colloquial and literary Tamil as different codes. I also avoid labeling many of these utterances as "bivalent" since teachers may want to emphasize their morphological hybridity. Rather than explaining these practices by inferring the teachers' intentions, I instead explore the alternative possible meanings of the sequential ordering of colloquial and literary forms. In some cases, a lesson may appear to naturalize the developmental trajectory of acquiring first oral and then literary competency by emphasizing the knowledge gap between novice children and expert teachers; for example, a student volunteers an answer in colloquial Jaffna Tamil and the teacher transliterates it (that is, converts the word from Roman into Tamil script) and translates it into literary Tamil. In other cases, the lesson may appear to diagram in historical time the grammatical degeneration of colloquial Tamil from its (imagined) pure, literary source; thus, the teacher first introduces a word in literary Tamil and then dissects it into the colloquial Jaffna Tamil parts.

Nilima (N) illustrates both of these strategies in a series of lessons on January 24. She begins class by writing "24 தை 2006 செவ்வாய்" on the board and stating in literary Tamil:

(1) N: *okay n̲ān dēṭu el̲utukir̲atu*
okay I am writing the date

Here, Nilima employs the phonologically assimilated English word for date, *dēṭu*, instead of the Tamil word, *tēti*, giving the phrase a slightly colloquial flavor. Naveen (S) then eagerly calls out:

(2) S: *tīcher iruvatinālu tai cappay kilamɛ*
teacher, Tuesday the 24th of Tai month

In this sentence, Naveen speaks entirely in colloquial Jaffna Tamil, using sounds such as "p" rather than the literary "v," "ɛ" rather than the literary "ai," and "l" rather than the literary "l̲," and also epenthesizing (that is, adding) "ɨ" after *-nal* (Schiffman 1999). When Nilima repeats Naveen's response, she translates only select words of his into literary Tamil (in bold):

(3) N: *iruvatinālu tai* ***cevvay kilamai***
Tuesday the 24th of Tai month

Thus, *iruvatinālɨ* retains its colloquial form, while *sevvay* assumes a new literary form and *tai* functions as a bivalent form bridging both words on either side. Functionally, this sequence diagrams how to convert from colloquial Jaffna Tamil into literary Tamil. Positioned at the end of this sentence is *kilamai*, a word that combines the distinctly colloquial Jaffna Tamil sound of "l" (rather than literary "l̲") with the literary Tamil sound of "ai" (rather than colloquial "ɛ"). Most probably, Nilima and her students would hear this word as exclusively literary Tamil because Sri Lankans generally perceive "l" and "l̲" ([l] and [ɻ]) as allophones. Coincidently, by hybridizing the sounds of colloquial Jaffna and literary Tamil to create the word *kilamai*, all prior phonological variations become even less perceptible to students, who are left with the impression that colloquial Jaffna Tamil is not very different grammatically from literary Tamil.

Later in the lesson, when teaching students how to construct compound words, Nilima writes "கத்திரிக்காய் = கத்திரி + காய்" and explains the meaning of this phrase in literary Tamil:

(1) N: ***kattirikkāy enr̲āl*** *eggplant*
kattirikkay means eggplant

Sonali (S) then answers the second question on the worksheet asking for the compound word for "banana" in colloquial Jaffna Tamil, and Nilima transliterates this by writing "வாழைப்பழம் = வாழை + பழம்" and twice repeating Sonali's response in literary Tamil:

(2) S: *vālēppalam*
banana

(3) N: ***vāḻaippaḻam vāḻai paḻam***
banana banana

In this didactic exchange, Nilima emphasizes the distinction between "l" and "ḻ" ([l] and [ɻ]) to train Sonali's ear to distinguish between colloquial Jaffna and literary Tamil pronunciations. For the remainder of the lesson, whenever Nilima reiterates and corrects her students' pronunciation, this turn-taking highlights an intergenerational gap in their linguistic competences and promotes the view that, without Nilima's assistance, students cannot convert their everyday knowledge of colloquial Jaffna Tamil into the more specialized and valued knowledge of literary Tamil. A few students do not submit willingly to this lower status. For example, when Nilima explains the conditions under which bananas and plantains in Sri Lanka become sweet, Sonali audaciously interrupts her to say, "Teacher, I have never went to Sri Lanka," forcing Nilima to change the topic by surrendering, "Okay, another example *collu*" (Okay, tell me another example).

Nilima sometimes enunciates a word first in colloquial Jaffna Tamil if her students cannot readily decipher the literary Tamil example, such as in the case of "மணியோசை = மணி + ஓசை."

(1) S: *appaṭinnu enna tīcher*
what is the meaning teacher

(2) N: *maniyōcɛ ding ding*
bell sound ding ding

(3) S: bell bell sound
bell bell sound

(4) N: *ippo n̲ān colradɛ ellām collu*
now all of you say it like I say it

(5) N: ***maniyōcai*** *mani ōcɛ*
bell sound bell sound

(6) N: ***n̲āṅkal*** *appatinnu* ***colluvōm***
we will say it in this manner

(7) N: ***maniyōcai***

Although Nilima utters *maniyōcɛ* in line 2 in colloquial Jaffna Tamil, she does so to establish a familiar footing for students who cannot recall this word from their everyday vocabulary. After they correctly guess the meaning in line 3, though, Nilima repeats the entire word in literary Tamil in line 5 (*maniyōcai*) before breaking it down into its lexical components in colloquial Jaffna Tamil (*mani ōcɛ*). This sequence suggests two possible interpretations. The pairing of *maniyōcai* and *mani ōcɛ* could imply the grammatical simplification from literary Tamil to colloquial Tamil, or, rather, the phonological similarity of colloquial Jaffna Tamil and literary Tamil. It is this very ambiguity that helps to promote the PELO ideology that Sri Lankans speak a literary language.

Analyzing these lessons thus reveals unresolved ideological tensions not made explicit in the PELO curriculum. First, we learn that teachers do not always agree with one another about how to represent the relative purity of Indian and Sri Lankan Tamil varieties. Second, individual teachers inconsistently blur or exaggerate the boundary between colloquial Jaffna Tamil and literary Tamil, whether in speech or writing, in their lessons. Third, teachers create lessons that highlight how certain sounds, grammatical forms, and words are emblematic of a pure, literary style of Sri Lankan Tamil yet ignore many other non-purist forms or neologisms in colloquial Jaffna speech. Overall, interactions in the PELO classroom exemplify how teachers maintain their didactic authority by exploiting the underlying tension between principles of simultaneity and hierarchy in two codes, whether seen as bivalent or diglossic, and either highlighting or minimizing the phonological and grammatical differences between literary Tamil and colloquial Jaffna Tamil. Though not exactly what we would call charismatic teachers, Vasanthi and Nilima nonetheless embody a type of "populist" expertise that is derived from their first-hand experiences growing up in Sri Lanka.

At the end of my research, I ask the students to complete a survey evaluating their reading, writing, and speaking skills in Tamil, using a scale from 0 to 5 to indicate minimal to highest-level expertise. Four respondents are in the first grade (six year olds), two in the second grade (seven year olds), two in the third grade (eight year olds), three in the fourth grade (nine year olds), and two in the fifth grade (of the two ten year olds, one had just started taking Tamil PELO classes). Table 4.2 itemizes the results of this survey according to grade level, and Table 4.3 ranks the overall ease and frequency of each activity (1 indicates the easiest or most common activity). Entries in italics refer to activities requiring specialized knowledge of literary Tamil. Although these results are not statistically significant due to the small sample size (and possibly due to the young age of the respondents, who may not fully understand the questions), they do highlight two interesting patterns. First, the higher grade levels do not

Table 4.2 Self-evaluation survey of Tamil PELO students' language skills and activities

	1st grade	2nd grade	3rd grade	4th grade	5th grade
Read Tamil comics or fiction	3.75	1.5	2.5	2.33	2
Read Tamil newspapers	0	2.5	2.5	1	4
Read Tamil store signs	4.25	2.5	5	4	3
Read personal letters in Tamil	1.5	1.5	2.5	4.67	3.5
Read poetry, literature, or religious books	3.5	1.5	2.5	3	1.5
Understand lyrics to Tamil songs	5	4	4.5	5	4.5
Understand dialogue in Tamil movies	3.75	5	5	5	4.5
Understand Tamil news on TV	5	2.5	4	2.67	2.5
Understand a priest's speech	0	0.5	2.5	3	3
Understand relatives speaking in Tamil	4	2.5	5	5	4.5
Speak to parents or grandparents in Tamil	4.5	5	5	4	5
Speak to priest or elders in Tamil	3.75	1.5	5	3	5
Speak with friends or siblings in Tamil	4.5	4	4.5	1.67	5
Write name in Tamil	3.5	5	4	4.67	3
Write Tamil alphabet	4.25	5	5	5	3
Write short stories or poems in Tamil	2.74	1.5	1	4	1

Table 4.3 Tamil PELO students rank the ease of language activities (those in italics require knowledge of literary Tamil)

	Average	Rank
Speak to parents or grandparents in Tamil	4.7	1
Understand dialogue in Tamil movies	4.65	2
Understand lyrics to Tamil songs	4.6	3
Write Tamil alphabet	4.45	4
Understand relatives speaking in Tamil	4.2	5
Write name in Tamil	4.034	6
Speak with friends or siblings in Tamil	3.934	7
Read Tamil store signs	3.75	8
Speak to priest or elders in Tamil	3.65	9
Understand Tamil news on TV	3.34	10
	2.734	11
Read Tamil comics or fiction books	2.416	12
	2.4	13
	2.048	14
Read Tamil newspapers	2	15
Understand a priest's speech	1.8	16

display greater confidence in their language skills than do the lower grade levels. In fact, some of the highest scores belong to six and seven year olds, who were by far the most enthusiastic students. Second, activities scoring lowest among students tend to require greater knowledge of literary Tamil, whether for reading, writing, or speaking. In addition to suggesting that the PELO has only made modest gains in teaching literacy and oratorical skills in literary Tamil, this survey reinforces the importance of examining attitudinal factors to understand how children reflexively acquire a heritage language. Sri Lankan children attending the PELO may be learning to self-identify with literary Tamil, yet they are still far from being considered proficient in speaking, reading, and writing in this purist register.

Teaching the WTM Curriculum

At most Sri Lankan Tamil political functions in Montréal, a representative of the World Tamil Movement (WTM) exhorts parents in the audience to speak to their children in Tamil at home and send them to schools to learn to read and write Tamil. Although I do not know the official statistics, I would estimate that less than a quarter of Sri Lankan children in Montréal learn Tamil in schools and most attend for three years or less. Children who do not attend Tamil schools can still learn to speak colloquial Jaffna Tamil by conversing with their relatives, yet they do not usually become literate. Generally, children literate in Tamil attend schools run and funded by the WTM, which also receive 10 percent of their financing from Québec's Ministry of Cultural Communities (Canadian Education Association 1991).[11] In 2003, WTM leaders from around the world convened to draft a standardized curriculum for teaching literary Tamil to Sri Lankan children growing up in Western countries. Recognizing that the children of refugees residing in countries such as Canada, France, Denmark, Norway, and Australia have different educational objectives and linguistic skills to master than children growing up in India or Sri Lanka, the WTM developed unique pedagogical materials, including a syllabus, student workbook, teacher's manual, and home instruction CD-ROM, adapted to diverse diasporic contexts. The Academy of Tamil Arts and Technology and the Ontario Academy of Fine Arts in Mississauga manufacture and distribute most pedagogical materials required for use in WTM schools around the world (see Figure 4.8).

WTM schools, taught by former schoolteachers and parent volunteers and overseen by nationalist leaders from Jaffna, explicitly link the reproduction of Sri Lankan Tamil heritage with the elevated status of literary Tamil as a classical language. Offering instruction from the first through tenth grades, these more time-intensive schools make fewer allowances for mistakes in the oral use of literary Tamil and impose greater expectations for reading and writing in literary and classical Tamil with each grade level than do PELO classes. Also, advanced students learn to read classical Tamil literature from teachers with education in this subject. In Montréal, there are two Hindu temples, one Catholic mission, and one Protestant church, as well as the WTM headquarters in Côte-de-Neiges,

FIGURE 4.8 Educational CD-ROMs produced near Toronto, Canada.

which offer classes in Tamil following this curriculum. Although the WTM is a secular organization and many of its leaders are atheists, priests and ministers collaborate with WTM leaders to adapt the curriculum to meet religious education goals.

With approximately 125 students, the Thiru Murugan Temple's School of Heritage Studies in Dollard-des-Ormeaux is one of the largest WTM-run heritage language programs in Montréal (Saiva Mission of Quebec, Canada n.d.). In the spring and early summer months of 2005, I was invited to observe and audio-record classes held from 4:00 to 5:30 pm in the basement hall of the temple (Thiru Murugan Temple n.d.). Mrs. Ramanathan, the director of the Sunday language school and Saturday religion school and once an esteemed school principal in Jaffna, exemplifies the linguistic expertise of a Hindu scholar.[12] Every week at the onset of class, Mrs. Ramanathan leads the children in offering a prayer to the goddess of Tamil, *Tamiḻttāy*, after which children place *kunkumam* (vermillion powder) on their foreheads, signifying their sixth *chakra*, or third eye, opening up to the divine in the spiritual pursuit of knowledge, before joining their teachers at tables situated around the hall. Exclusively Sri Lankan in its assembly, the Thiru Murugan Temple strictly follows the philosophical tenets of Shaiva Siddhanta, a religious philosophy valorizing the ritual worship of Tamiḻttāy, Siva, and Murukan as the original deities of Hinduism, and these basic tenets permeate every class.

On March 27 I begin my observations at the temple school by visiting each class for fifteen to twenty minutes and jotting down notes on their main lessons and general student characteristics. I am particularly keen to note students' gender distribution, use of textbooks, and code-switching practices, and whenever possible, to talk to them informally about their lessons (see Table 4.4). I immediately notice a few trends. First, whereas teachers permit kindergarten and first-grade students to speak in colloquial Jaffna Tamil for conversational practice, they increasingly obligate older students to read out loud and write in the literary standard. Similar to a new curriculum adopted in Sri Lanka for teaching Tamil as a Second Language to Sinhalese students, instruction in Spoken Tamil is emphasized in the early years and Written Tamil is reserved for the intermediate and advanced levels (Davis 2014). As a rule, WTM teachers do not translate texts written in literary Tamil into colloquial Tamil. In contrast to Vasanthi's practice of paraphrasing storybooks into colloquial Tamil to assist in her students' comprehension, the first-grade teacher at the School of Heritage Studies reads a story to her young students entirely in literary Tamil and requires them to repeat each phrase, verse by verse. The PELO and WTM's curricula diverge the most after the third grade, when WTM students begin

Table 4.4 Notes of lessons by grade level at the Murugan Temple School

Kindergarten (1 girl, 2 boys)
Female teacher leads the children in a nursery rhyme song. She asks them to repeat each verse several times. Then she asks her students the meaning of basic vocabulary words, such as city, country, and world. A girl around age three or four is the most enthusiastic participant. A boy has difficulty understanding the teacher.

1st grade (5 girls, 5 boys)
Female teacher narrates a story written in literary Tamil from the textbook verse by verse, and asks her children to repeat each word or phrase.

2nd grade (5 girls, 5 boys)
Students write the letters of the Tamil alphabet in their workbooks. Some children speak to their classmates in French and to the female teacher in Tamil.

3rd grade (7 girls, 2 boys)
Male teacher dictates short phrases and sentences in literary Tamil and students write these down in their notebooks.

4th grade (3 girls, 2 boys)
Female teacher asks children to read a short story and answer comprehension questions in their workbook. Two girls take turns reading a short story from their workbooks. The girls claim that they are better than the boys in Tamil and are proud to speak Tamil. The boys in the class appear to have difficulty reading and speaking Tamil. One boy cannot understand English and prefers to speak in French. Another boy says he is proud to be fluent in French, even if he is not in Tamil.

6th grade (2 girls)
I interrupt their lesson to speak to two female students, who converse with one another in French, to me in English, and to the female teacher in Tamil.

8th grade (4 girls)
Female teacher reviews a quiz in which students have to write a short essay in literary Tamil. Today they will learn how to compose letters to parents discussing the difference between Tamil and Canadian holidays. One girl says that she is proud to speak Tamil because it makes her feel special. She thinks that learning Tamil makes it easier for her to learn French, and vice versa. Three of the girls attend French-medium schools and one girl attends an English-medium school.

9th and 10th grades (1 girl, 2 boys)
Male teacher reads several pages from a Tamil literature book to students and asks them to write a several paragraph summary in literary Tamil for homework. This advanced class meets only once a month. The teacher is studying for his MA in engineering at Concordia University. While living in Jaffna, he used to write literary articles in Tamil and dabble in composing classical Tamil poetry.

reading in literary Tamil with greater fluency and phonological accuracy than students in the intermediate PELO class at Parker Elementary School. By the fourth grade, children can read short stories and respond to oral comprehension questions entirely in literary Tamil and, by the ninth grade (which is not offered by the PELO) children can compose and recite original essays in literary Tamil.

In May 2005, I learn that two tenth-grade students have passed the standardized matriculation exam, taken each year on the same date by Sri Lankan children around the world, to receive a certificate signed by WTM leaders recognizing their mastery of literary Tamil. After the exams are finished, attendance at the School of Heritage Studies drops precipitously as many families leave town for summer vacation, some visiting their relatives in Jaffna, newly opened to travelers during the ceasefire. One Sunday afternoon I count only seventy students in attendance. During the pre-class assembly, Mrs. Ramanathan stresses the importance of devoting oneself to language study through group prayer, song, and moral exegesis. I audio-record this event and later, with the assistance of K. Karunakaran and S. V. Mahadevan, who helped me to translate and interpret the meaning of the specific prayers and stories, I analyze the assembly's temporal structure to argue that Mrs. Ramanathan enacts a primordialist narrative of modernity celebrating the purity of Sri Lankan Tamil through the worship of Siva, Murukan, and Tamiḻttāy. Through voicing and register contrasts that serve to differentiate between, on the one hand, classical and literary Tamil, values of religious morality, and elders' expertise, and on the other hand, modern and colloquial Jaffna Tamil, values of secular morality, and novices' knowledge, the vernacular appears as if it has been spiritually elevated and purified as it emerges from and succeeds the classical Tamil (see Table 4.5).

Table 4.5 Pre-class assembly at the Murugan Temple School

	Language	Genre	Theme
Part One	Classical Tamil	Written prayer	Religious devotion
Part Two	Literary Tamil	Written song	Preserving Sri Lankan Tamil language and culture
Part Three	1) Literary Tamil 2) Colloquial Jaffna Tamil	Oral folktale	1) Medieval and colonial secular fable 2) Contemporary moral lesson

Rather than beginning class with a recitation from the secular book of poetry considered to be a masterpiece of Sangam literature, *Tirukkural*, as is traditionally done in Tamil schools in South Asia, Mrs. Ramanathan instead begins the assembly by leading her students in reciting religious scripture from the ninth-century bhakti hymnbook, *Tiruvacakam*, written in Classical Tamil.[13] Teachers and students then sing the school song in literary Tamil and, afterward, Mrs. Ramanathan narrates two well-known fables. The first fable takes place in a generic medieval Tamil kingdom and the second in a colonial Sri Lankan town visited by Gandhi. After reciting each story, the principal code-switches into colloquial Jaffna Tamil to comment on the moral lesson. In sum, the assembly starts off in a classical register, transitions into a literary register, and finishes off in a colloquial register that emerges seamlessly from the prior literary one. From pure to impure, classical to modern, and literary to colloquial, earlier linguistic forms are temporally depicted as being primordial to, and higher in status, than contemporary linguistic forms.

Specific turn sequences and footing shifts establish this metapragmatic framework for interpreting temporal change (both historical and intergenerational) as degenerating linguistic form or decreasing knowledge. When Mrs. Ramanathan utters a line from the *Tiruvacakam* prayer and waits for her students to repeat it, this exchange entails an intergenerational footing authorizing the elderly principal's greater expertise. Students standing in stationary rows of increasing height and age facing the principal are also positioned such that taller and older students flank shorter, younger, and less advanced students. Moreover, when Mrs. Ramanathan walks slowly around the assembly to monitor individual student performances, the circular movement diagrams her all-encompassing knowledge of classical, literary, and colloquial Tamil varieties, compared to the students' more limited knowledge of the vernacular. Finally, Mrs. Ramanathan speaks in literary Tamil when she narrates each fable to embody the voice of the "primary source," and code-switches into colloquial Jaffna Tamil when commenting on the moral message to exemplify its oral exegesis. This shift in footing anchoring the language of prayer and morality in the classical period and the language of secular commentary in the modern period diagrams how to maintain a link between the past and present as a pathway to religious truth.

For example, after describing in literary Tamil (bold) a medieval kingdom where Tamil language, culture, and arts once flourished, Mrs. Ramanathan shifts mid-word into Jaffna Tamil (italics), inserting colloquial morphemes and words (italics) to emphasize proper moral behavior.

(1) **pellārum nallavarkalāyitaṉum naṉmaiyē***ceyyōnum*
we must act in a way that benefits everyone

Using the Jaffna Tamil morpheme *-ōṉum* (meaning "we must") rather than the literary *-āṉum* or Indian *-āṉū* entails a shift in region and period from the generic past to the Sri Lankan present. Similarly, after narrating the fable of Gandhi's visit to colonial Sri Lanka in literary Tamil, Mrs. Ramanathan punctuates the end of each phrase with a colloquial suffix to emphasize its moral.

(1) **adāvadu tīya ceyalkalɛ pārkkātɛ**
therefore you should try not to do bad things

(2) **keṭṭadɛ pēcādɛ—pēca**paṭādu
or speak badly—don't speak badly

Through the inclusion of literary sounding "r" or [ɾ̥] and colloquial sounding [ɛ] in *pārkkātɛ* (instead of saying the colloquial word *pākkātɛ*), and the combined use of the generic *pēca* and the Jaffna-specific *paṭādu* in *pēcapaṭādu* (rather than saying *kūṭādu* as do Indians), these hybrid constructions, beginning in literary Tamil yet ending in colloquial Jaffna Tamil, hint at the close phonological and morphosyntactic affinity of literary Tamil with its Sri Lankan descendant.

The school song, through the use of deictic pronouns, further outlines the boundaries of a Sri Lankan Tamil Saivite identity and differentiates it from other rival Hindu and non-Hindu Tamil communities. In classical and literary Tamil, one distinguishes between exclusive "we" and "our" (*nāṅkaḷ* and *eṅkaḷ*) and inclusive "we" and "our" (*nām* and *nama*); colloquial Tamil employs only exclusive first-person plural pronouns. Although the school song is sung entirely in literary Tamil and inclusive *nām* (capitalized) is used initially to refer to the collective, when singing of the association's excellent qualities, the exclusive pronoun *eṅkaḷ* is instead employed.

(1) **paṉbāri kalaikal tamiḻ pēṉal**
by nurturing Tamil culture, arts, language

(2) **pāṅkuraṉ māṉam NĀM uḻaippōm**
with honor we will toil

(3) **cērṉdiram ellām tamiḻ vaḷarkkum**
everyone, joining together, Tamil will grow

(4) *eṅkaḷ* **cīriya paṉpinai kāttiruvōm**
we will safeguard our excellent qualities

(5) **vāḻiya vāḻiya vāḻiyavē**
prosper, prosper, prosper long!

(6) *eṅkaḷ* **kalaikaliṉ kalvi kaḻakamadu**
our arts education association

This shift to the exclusive "we" may accentuate pride in specifically belonging to the Murugan Temple community, rather than other Hindu, Catholic, Protestant, and Muslim communities in Montréal, among which language purism may be less emphasized. Thus, for Tamil Eelam to prosper, one needs the Murugan Temple to "safeguard our excellent qualities" by preserving the classical and literary languages, requiring both an expert principal and "mother tongue" teachers to do so.

My observations of WTM classes held at the Our Lady of Deliverance Mission reveal an identical curriculum, minus the overt focus on Hinduism. Every Sunday afternoon from 2:30 to 5:00 pm, 156 Catholic children participate in Tamil-language class, followed by catechism class, in the basement hall of Église Ste-Cécile in Villeray. Similar to the Murugan Temple school, first- through tenth-grade classes are comprised of groups of six to twelve students occupying nine workstations (the ninth and tenth grades are taught together), each with their own tables and whiteboards. As is the custom, women teachers of younger grades wear long skirts and modest blouses or salwar kameezes, and men who teach the older students are casually adorned in polo shirts and pants. (At the Murugan Temple, women wear saris and girls wear salwar kameezes.)

On September 4, teachers instruct the kindergarten and first-grade students to describe their summer vacations in colloquial Jaffna Tamil and the older students to work on lessons in their workbooks. The third-grade teacher also uses the workbook to review vocabulary words beginning with the letter "k." Pointing to objects around the room, she asks students to write their names in literary Tamil on the whiteboard. She then stresses the correct pronunciation of each word by emphasizing phonemic distinctions between the sounds "ṇ," "ṉ," and "n" ([ɳ], [n̺], and [n]); "ḻ," "ḷ," and "l" ([ɻ], [ɭ], and [l]); and "ṛ" and "r" ([r] and [ɾ̺]). Students in the intermediate grades practice constructing simple sentences and paragraphs, whereas ninth- and tenth-grade students individually read short stories and answer reading comprehension questions in their workbooks. One of the boys informs me that every December, the advanced classes compose original poetry and dramas in literary Tamil to recite at the *oḷiviḻā* (Festival of Lights) celebration.

After class finishes, the children reassemble into two rooms, with the older children staying in the basement and the younger children going upstairs, to be instructed in the catechism by Father Joseph and another senior church member. I observe Father Joseph's jovial yet futile attempts to instruct the older students, gossiping among themselves, about the lives of saints in English. After class, I ask Father Joseph about his laid-back teaching style with adolescents. He confesses that he prefers working with the older children because the younger ones often do not speak much English. Once, due to popular demand, Father Joseph brought in a French-speaking nun to teach the catechism in French and offer French classes to the parents. To transform this into a more permanent arrangement, however, he insists that he would have to find someone with advanced knowledge of French, Catholicism, and Tamil—not an easy feat in Montréal.

At both the Catholic mission and Saivite temple schools, teachers emphasize the connection between speaking and writing in literary Tamil and practicing one's religion. At the Murugan Temple this was achieved through morning prayers to the goddess *Tamiḷttāy*. At Our Lady of Deliverance, oratory performances in literary Tamil at religious festivals such as oḷivilā and peace processions in Rigaud (to be discussed in chapter 6) underline one's devotion to the Virgin Mary. Although the WTM is not a religious organization, since many Sri Lankans consider religion just as important as language in defining who they are, the organization provides enough flexibility in its curriculum to permit both aspects of self-identification. Learning Tamil is thus a way to become properly Catholic or Hindu in a specifically Sri Lankan sense. Where parents choose to send their children to learn Tamil is also a sign of their commitment to a larger collective, whether religious in the case of attending the Murugan Temple or Our Lady of Deliverance mission schools, or political in the case of attending the WTM headquarters' school in Côte-des-Neiges. Moreover, acquiring knowledge of literary and classical Tamil is a means of suggesting that the contemporary life of diasporic Sri Lankans emanates from a deeper historicity. Protecting the boundary between colloquial and literary Tamil is thus paramount for WTM leaders, unlike for the Sri Lankan and Québécois coauthors of the Tamil PELO curriculum, who permit the blurring of these linguistic boundaries to assist and encourage children to learn and self-identify with literary Tamil as their heritage language.

Tutoring in Tamil by Tamilagam Elders

As a rule, Indian Tamils never send their children to WTM schools, viewed as Sri Lankan spaces of religious and political indoctrination, or Tamil PELO classes, offered in lower-income neighborhoods where mostly Sri Lankans, and not Indians, reside. However, by distancing themselves socially and linguistically from Sri Lankans and positioning themselves as rivals, Indians relinquish access to government funding for Tamil heritage language education in Montréal. Lalitha and Mohan, happy that the Québec government pays for Tamil instruction, do not anticipate needing this public assistance. Instead, Lalitha plans to follow her parents' model by speaking only in Tamil to her future children. Mohan concurs that speaking to young children in Tamil comes naturally to him, even if with adults it does not. Lalitha's father harbors greater concern for Indian parents who speak to their children in English and others who, despite their best intentions, cannot oblige their children to speak in Tamil at home. To render Tamil literature more accessible among the diaspora, Dr. Sundaran is participating in a transnational effort, involving more than two hundred expatriates with professional degrees in computer science, to transliterate classical literature from Tamil into Roman script and post these onto the web.

Dr. Sundaran also cofounded, along with several other elders, the Québec Tamil Association (also known as Tamilagam) to promote "awareness of the culture of Tamil Nadu (India) in [the] Montréal area" through the "celebration of traditional festivals in [the] Montréal area, promoting cultural awareness among youth, Tamil-language education, supporting Tamil cultural activities, helping newcomers to [the] Montréal area, and cooperating with other cultural organizations" (Tamilagam n.d.).[14] Under the category of Tamil-language education on the Tamilagam website, Dr. Sundaran has posted links to Internet resources such as "making children speak Tamil," "Ram S. Ravindran's Web Based Spoken Tamil," "U of Penn-Web assisted Tamil Course," "South Asian Vowels and Consonants," and "Sound like a native with these simple rules." There is also an advertisement for private tutoring classes offered by R. A. Krishnan, another founding member of Tamilagam. In 2004, Krishnan published a textbook series, *Spoken Tamil Grammar Book*, written in Roman script to teach Tamil to second-generation children (see Figure 4.9). These learning resources collectively stress the mastery of colloquial speech and downplay the importance of learning literary Tamil in the diaspora.

Replete with grammatical lessons on nouns, verbs, prepositions, adjectives and adverbs, and sentence construction, as well as a glossary of commonly used nouns, sample dialogues and conversations, and annexes on verb conjugations and conventions for transliterating Tamil into Roman, Krishnan's book is quite the accomplishment for a former engineer with no prior knowledge of Tamil linguistics. *Spoken Tamil Grammar Book* is entirely the product of "mother tongue" expertise, albeit one cultivated over the years through Krishnan's autodidactic study of Tamil sociolinguistic variation. The book's pedagogy exemplifies a language ideology that, since the seventeenth and eighteenth centuries, has equated "precise, plain and unadorned, rational ways of speaking" with progressive and modern minds (Bauman and Briggs 2003:7). The work of purification, Krishnan explains in his introductory preface, involves rectifying

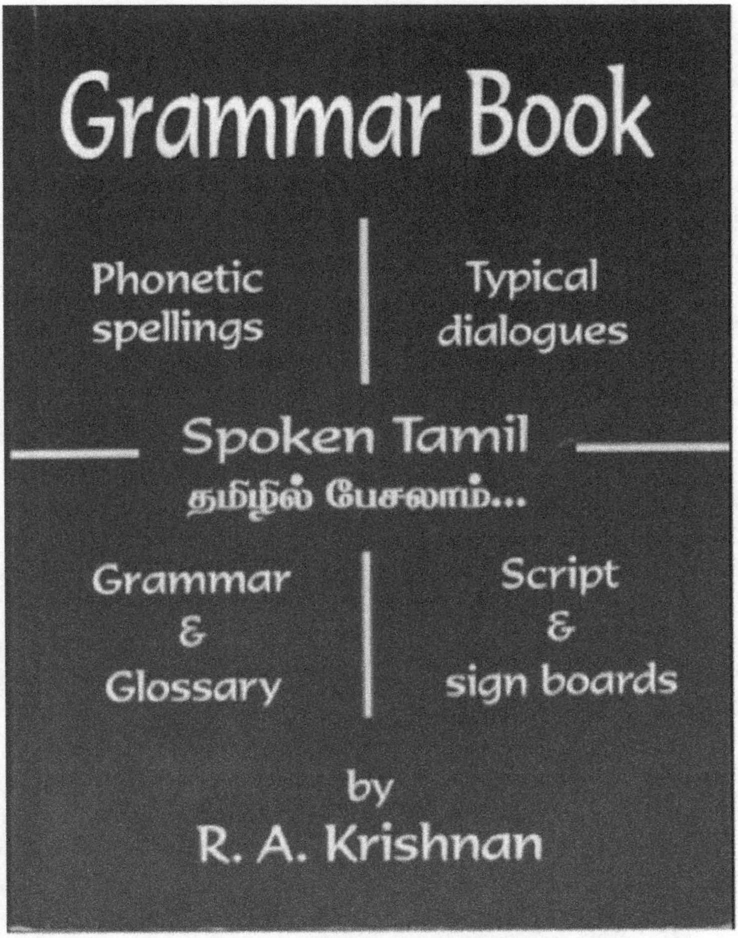

FIGURE 4.9 Front cover of *Spoken Tamil Grammar Book*.

"problems" of diglossia by writing the book in the more efficient style of colloquial or "Spoken Tamil":

> Another distinct special feature of Tamil is that the spoken language is quite different from the written one. This has come up because the written part, particularly the verb forms and case endings, is very complicated to use practically, especially when spoken in the rapid rate that day-to-day life requires. To solve this problem, different communities in various Tamil speaking regions have shortened it in their own way for ease of

> expression. As a result of this, the spoken language widely differs by both region and community. (Krishnan 2004:5)

By stating that literary Tamil is "very complicated to use practically," Krishnan implies that morphological reduction enhances the communicative function and accessibility of the colloquial language. The difference between regional registers, he states, is due to the idiosyncratic choices made by communities to elide sounds or clusters of sounds in the rapid pace of everyday speech.

> While speaking many words are joined with or without linking alphabets suiting the accent of communication. Similarly some alphabets are ignored or left out depending on the accent. These needs (*sic*) to be observed and learnt from the community with whom one has dealings. Though the above feature is common in all languages this is very much prevalent in [the] Tamil language. (Krishnan 2004:75)

As textbook standard he adopts "the spoken language used by street shopkeepers in Chennai, the capital and the largest city of Tamil Nadu, India" (2004:5). Even though most people in South Asia would attest to the impurity of Chennai Tamil, Krishnan instead embraces it as a mixed code, popularly called Tanglish, and explains the rules for mixing English with Tamil:

> There is a way to talk in Tamil using the equivalent verb in English. This method can be used very effectively till you learn all the verbs in Tamil. This is adopted by the educated persons even if they know the words in Tamil well and is quite popular. The equivalent English verb followed by the verb "seyya" or "paNNa" (to do) in the proper verb form is adopted. Example 1. Naan angE swim paNNeREN / wash seyyaREn (I am swimming / washing there) . . . *Exception* It is not a practice to use this method for the verbs "go" and "come." Example one does not say. 1. "naanga angE go seyyaROm." (we are going there). (Krishnan 2004:76)

Therefore, rather than exhibiting a purist attitude and admonishing students who code-switch or code-mix in Tamil and English, he instead encourages them to code-switch for greater ease of communication. As a Brahmin Indian Tamil, Krishnan has inherited a legacy of code-mixing with Sanskrit and English and, though he might appreciate the idea of preserving the purity of Tamil, also recognizes the ability to alternate between Tamil and English as its own kind of expertise. The textbook even acknowledges specific word classes, such as "Fruits and Vegetables of European origin like Cauliflower, Carrot, Beans, Apple, etc."

and travel-related ones, like "engine, train, guard, ticket checker, compartment," better stated in English (2004:22–24).

Among his compatriots, Krishnan is also unusual in valuing knowledge of French and using it to draw comparisons with grammatical categories of Tamil unfamiliar to his French-dominant students. Along with Nila's father, Krishnan works as a certified interpreter and translator in French, Tamil, and English for the *Palais de Justice* and is comfortable in all three languages. Krishnan also tailors his lessons to suit his students' regional dialects. Most familiar with varieties specific to Kerala, Chennai, Coimbatore, Delhi, Kuala Lumpur, and Jaffna, places where he has either personally lived or visited, Krishnan includes notes on their peculiarities:

> The tamil (*sic*) months start from the middle of the equivalent English months indicated above. In Srilanka (*sic*) the tamil equivalent of the english (*sic*) month is straightaway adopted even if the date falls on first half of English month. Example for jan 6th, thai 6th is adopted though it actually falls in the month of "margazhi." In India and Malysia (*sic*) the exact tamil months and corresponding tamil dates are only adopted. (Krishnan 2004:16)

At times he develops textbook supplements for students interested in studying a specific regional variety. For example, one student wanted to study the colloquial variety of Tamil spoken near the border between Tamil Nadu and Kerala; since his own family is originally from this region and his mother speaks this variety natively, writing this supplement came easily to Krishnan.

In the summer of 2005, I sit in on several of Krishnan's tutoring sessions and work with him individually to improve my own conversational use of Indian Tamil. Over conversations at the Food Court in the *Complexe Desjardins*, I learn that Krishnan does not singularly reject the importance of writing in Tamil; he simply believes that children should become literate after they have mastered the spoken language. Because many Indian children in Montréal cannot speak Tamil well, learning to write in Tamil would hinder their progress, Krishnan believes. He uses an orthographic system of "phonetic spelling" different from the conventions standardized by the University of Madras Tamil Lexicon established in 1936.[15] The prerogative to innovate partially stems from his caste background as a Brahmin, who is historically less concerned with issues of linguistic purity. Also, perhaps his boldness comes from him being a charismatic teacher and activist, for which he has received public acclaim by being featured on television documentaries about South Asians in Canada and recruited by a local university to teach college-level Hindi. Several North American school districts are also considering using his textbooks, which are currently being distributed in major Indian cities. Krishnan informs me that his books sell the most among urban elites attending English-medium schools because they highly value acquiring knowledge of colloquial Indian languages for the purposes of business and travel. As author, teacher, translator, and interpreter, Krishnan can be considered an exemplary figure of the Tamil heritage language industry, epitomizing the type of charismatic South Indian activist whose "personality politics" (Dickey 1993:349) also involves expertise and involvement in language modernization.

A Division of Language Labor

This chapter's comparison of printers, teachers, schools, and books in Tamil in contemporary Canada and colonial India has revealed how Anglo-Franco conflicts fostered the formation of local and transnational publics that played critical roles in standardizing and codifying Tamil as a diglossic language. In the case of colonial India, a linguistic rivalry between imperial powers boasting of their minor contributions to an ancient Tamil scholarship had given rise to the transnational distribution of bilingual dictionaries and grammar books reinforcing European views of Spoken Tamil and Written Tamil as distinct codes. In contemporary Canada, a linguistic rivalry between neighboring cities championing the cause of minority language education has instigated the formation of an ethnonationally divided Tamil heritage language industry in which Indians and Sri Lankans competitively invest in different schools and publish their own pedagogical materials to preserve the purity of literary Tamil, revitalize colloquial Tamil, or promote self-identification with one or the other heritage language. Ultimately, this industry naturalizes a division of language labor in which Indians work toward revitalizing Spoken Tamil by teaching from pedagogical materials written in Roman script, and Sri Lankans preserve Written Tamil through lessons emphasizing oratory and literacy using Tamil script.

Through historical and ethnographic analysis, I have also explored how debates about typography, orthography, and script accentuate the diaspora's unresolved questions about the social construction of linguistic expertise and the ideological nature of linguistic boundaries. Contrary to folk beliefs and some scholarly views, there is no categorical distinction between Sri Lankan and Indian regional varieties, or even colloquial and literary registers of Tamil. Beyond lexical contrasts, most linguistic differences are based on slight morphosyntactic and phonetic distinctions that some users, expert or not, interpret as discrete, and others as continuous. Though Indians in Montréal generally respect Sri Lankan values of purity and Sri Lankans applaud Indian innovation, a spirit of rivalry has developed from these comparisons. The following chapter examines the amplifying effect of linguistic rivalries by analyzing how neighborhoods compete for fame and fortune by inscribing urban spaces with signs written in literary or colloquial Tamil.

5 INSCRIBING THE ŪR

The Sri Lankan Tamil restaurant Spicy Land opened and closed its doors for business within the span of only a few months. Despite being ideally situated across the street from a busy Tamil-owned grocery store, *Marché Thurga*, and located on a major commercial thoroughfare in Montréal, *rue Jean-Talon*, Spicy Land did not survive long in this city's politicized business climate. Rumor has it that the restaurant's demise was due to its inability to attract a regular neighborhood crowd or citywide clientele. However, the owners had also mishandled Québec's language policies. One day when I visited the restaurant a few months before it shut down, I offhandedly commented to Nila how hard it was for me to find the restaurant at first since the building does not have a storefront sign. She explained that her brother-in-law was still waiting for her to translate the sign that he wrote in Tamil into French and English before he could affix it outdoors. As a recent refugee from Jaffna and monolingual speaker of Tamil who knows little English and no French at all, her brother-in-law did not feel confident enough to write the sign on his own without making grammatical mistakes and typographical errors. Bill 101 explicitly mandates that business owners post outdoor signs written in French that are accurate and display bigger, bolder, and more front-and-center French characters than text written in any other language. Unfortunately, Spicy Land shut down before the owner could demonstrate his legal compliance.

Other nearby grocery stores, jewelry shops, and restaurants owned by Sri Lankans have fared better with the fickleness of customers and the scrutiny of politicians, partly by visually inscribing them with multilingual signs written in French, Tamil, and English, to become more-or-less permanent fixtures in the neighborhood. These outdoor signs attest to the growing visibility and tangibility of the Sri Lankan Tamil character of Parc-Extension, one of several *quartiers* or neighborhoods in Montréal arguably undergoing transformation into a Tamil *ūr* (hometown). Graffiti on the nearby metro station map in Villeray that reads "Little India" over the *Boulevard Acadie* stop at Parc-Ex is misleading since more Sri Lankans, Bangladeshis, and Pakistanis actually reside there than Indians (Cauchy 2003). Bounded by rue Jean-Talon on the south, Boulevard Acadie on the west, *Autoroute Métropolitaine* on the north, and *Parc Jarry* on the east, Parc-Ex is also famous for being the most densely populated neighborhood in Canada.

In 1994, when the municipal government adjoined Parc-Ex with its neighboring quartiers, Villeray and St-Michel, to create a single *arrondissement* (borough) out of three ethnically and socioeconomically dissimilar ones (see Figure 5.1), the middle-class residents of Villeray, mostly of European or Québécois de souche descent, vociferously bemoaned this decision:

> Don't go telling a resident of Villeray that his neighborhood bears the new name of Villeray/Parc-Extension. He will give you a look before retorting a bit disdainfully, "Don't associate us especially with Parc-Extension . . ." And if you make the same statement to a resident of Parc-Extension, he will certainly laugh. It is not because the citizens of these two neighborhoods adjoined by the Bourque administration in 1994 are totally against the idea, but they think that they are so different from one other that they cannot speak of one single neighborhood. (Trottier 1998)

For the Sri Lankan residents of Parc-Ex, however, this rezoning allowed them to extend the boundaries of their neighborhood beyond the confines of their residential quartier. *Parc Jarry*, a large municipal park dividing Parc-Extension and Villeray, has now become one of the centers of neighborhood life, especially on weekends and summer evenings when families stroll along its trails and youth play cricket tournaments on its fields (see Figure 5.2). Few Sri Lankan Tamil families reside in Villeray, yet many adults do work in the jewelry and furniture factories located on *Boulevard St-Laurent* on the Villeray side of the park, right next to *École Lucien-Page*, the French-medium high school attended by Ram and other Sri Lankan Tamil youth of his age.

Parc-Ex, like many immigrant neighborhoods around the world, densely populated with affordable housing located close to residents' workplaces, is home to ethnonational groups who predominantly speak in languages other than English. The immigrant neighborhood where I first grew up in South Jersey was similar to Parc-Ex, until our apartment complex was transformed into higher-priced condominiums and everyone left to purchase single-family homes in town or rent apartments elsewhere where prices were cheaper. Today, this neighborhood is but a shadow of its former conviviality in the 1980s. Yet in Montréal, new waves of immigration and the steady assurance of depressed rental prices (Montréal's housing and rental prices are far below the national average) ensure that the

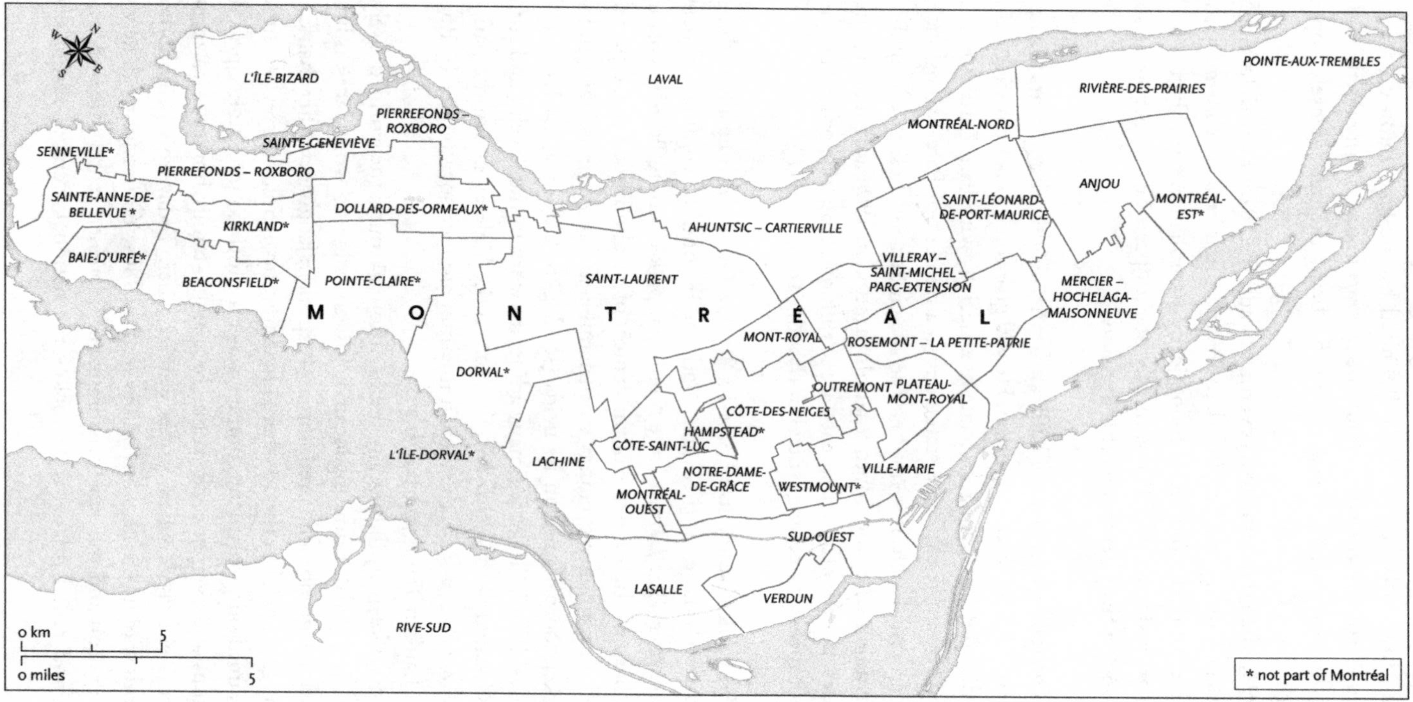

FIGURE 5.1 Map of Montréal's boroughs and neighborhoods.

FIGURE 5.2 View of the south side of Parc Jarry.

diverse linguistic, ethnic, and racial character of this lower-income neighborhood remains intact even if its specific composition is in flux. Parc-Ex, once a quintessentially Greek neighborhood, is now typecast as exclusively South Asian, despite the increasing number of African and Maghrebian residents living there since the last decade. Storefront signs written prominently in Tamil, Hindi, Urdu, Arabic, Bengali, and, to a lesser extent, Greek, English, and French, signal some of these demographic transitions, whereas other languages written in Roman script, lacking the same visible alterity, fly under the radar.

I am compelled by Parc-Ex's motley and transitory social history to inquire into the semiotic mechanisms influencing how outsiders and insiders could possibly interpret this neighborhood's urban character. In addition to the competition over city services and housing prices, I ask, what other local or transnational rivalries impinge on the changing façades of diasporic neighborhoods where Tamil speakers in Montréal reside? Is there something *linguistically* unique about the everyday sociality of Sri Lankans living in Parc-Ex and other urban neighborhoods that differs from the experiences of more affluent Indians living in visually nondescript, suburban neighborhoods? Can certain quartiers in Montréal truly aspire to be Tamil *ūrs* in the idyllic South Asian sense? And do diasporic neighborhoods in Montréal differ substantively from other North American ones because of the province's language laws? In short, the answer to all of these questions is yes.

The rest of Québec views Montréal at best as an anomaly and at worst as a thorn in its side. Certainly, the argument goes, if Montréal were as ethnically, linguistically, and racially homogenous as most of the province, Québec would be a sovereign nation by now. Also, if one adopts this viewpoint, immigration is at odds with nationalism and immigrant neighborhoods are veritable bastions of federalist activity. Yet from a diasporic perspective—one not necessarily rooted in the here-and-now—multiple allegiances can coexist in neighborhoods where residents of different ethnic and racial backgrounds learn to cohabitate as well as comply with provincial and federal laws. Migrants to Montréal quickly learn the political salience of visual linguistic cues through their daily encounters with signage legislated by Bill 101, which promotes and protects the status of French above that of English in Québec. Among South Asians, Sri Lankans have in particular capitalized on the visuality of their written language (that is, "Written Tamil") through signage to display their competing political allegiances in both clever and partially concealed ways. Indians, who instead identify with a colloquial language (that is, "Spoken Tamil") and rely primarily on aural cues to assert their ethnonational identity, do not similarly aspire for their neighborhoods to be visually identifiable.

Writing legally compliant signs in Montréal is also fueled by a spirit of rivalry between Sri Lankan Tamil neighborhoods seeking recognition as "Little Jaffnas" around the world. This chapter investigates the confluence of nationalist language legislation and transnational language activism to illuminate how (and to what extent) immigrant neighborhoods can be and are being transformed into Tamil hometowns. Referred to by Eisenlohr (2006) as "diasporization," such a process, within the context of Montréal, relies on two "semiotic ideologies" pertaining to beliefs about the materiality of writing (Keane 2003).[1] One belief asserts that tangible and visible objects such as writing are more durable compared to the more intangible, aural phenomena of speech. Another related idea presumes that diasporic communities that visibly mark their neighborhoods by inscribing them with writing in a heritage language insinuate their presence there in the past and seek to guarantee it well into the future. Embodying qualities of both visibility and tangibility, therefore, writing is believed to confer durability and longevity to an immigrant neighborhood. Furthermore, since Sri Lankans claim to be custodians of a Jaffna style of literary Tamil with a celebrated classical legacy, inscribing this legacy onto their streets and buildings not only makes Sri Lankan neighborhoods appear more visually palpable as diasporic spaces, but the inscriptions also highlight the antiquity, fame, and respectability of their profitable and up-and-coming establishments. Diasporas hence partially emerge through the material sedimentation of literacy practices.

Linguistic anthropologists and sociolinguists conducting research on literacy in urban, multilingual contexts have often remarked how textual facades act as potent signifiers directed at differently scaled addressees (Blommaert et al. 2005; Daveluy and Ferguson 2009; Frekko 2009; Gade 2003; LaDousa 2002; Romaine 2001). Likewise, I argue that not everyone who walks through the streets of Parc-Ex and other Sri Lankan Tamil neighborhoods in Montréal has the requisite multilingual competence to appreciate subtle nuances in their inscriptions. Tourists may simply remark the exotic character of the multilingual signage, whereas state officials and neighborhood watch groups that scrutinize signs for mistakes in French may seek evidence of residents' political disloyalty. Local residents instead search for information about merchandise or clientele. For example, Sri Lankans observing building signs in Parc-Ex may infer clues about their intended addressees—are they Hindu or Catholic, high or low caste, World Tamil Movement (WTM)–affiliated or unaffiliated? Only community leaders who carefully choose, position, and write signs in the right codes, scripts, and orthographies, placating both provincial politicians and transnational activists, may then dare to pursue more ambitious goals. Whereas elite Indians invest in acquiring symbolic capital by personally pursuing high-prestige careers, less elite Sri Lankan Tamils instead collectively seek respectability, profit, and fame as the prizes for transforming their diaspora neighborhoods into legally compliant quartiers as well as morally authentic Tamil ūrs.

Rival Tamil Ūrs

Exploring the multivalent concept of the *ūr* to articulate non-Western theories of space, time, agency, and personhood, anthropologist E. Valentine Daniel, in his ethnographic study of the Kalappūr village in Tamil Nadu, India, writes, "One of the most important relationships to a Tamil is that which exists between a person and the soil of his ūr" (1995:63). Acknowledging difficulties in translating ūr, usually glossed in English as "place of residence" or "native village," he instead defines it as "a named territory that is (1) inhabited by human beings who are believed to share in the substance of the soil of that territory, and (2) a territory to which a Tamil cognitively orients himself at any given time" (1995:63).[2] Daniel concludes that the ūr is not just a spatio-territorial concept but also represents a "person-centric view of reality" mediated by the material properties of both human and nonhuman inhabitants (1984:70). Among these properties are *kuṇam* (intrinsic qualities) and *putti* (surface-level consciousness), which refer to how the soil makes the ūr more or less compatible with certain jāti groups.[3] Diane Mines (2005), who conducted ethnographic research in the village of Yanaimangalam in Tamil Nadu, India, confirms that villagers there referred only to the dominant jātis as *ūrmakkal* (people of the ūr). The implications of this research are the following: if indeed the ūr's character is based on the soil's composition and reinforced by local caste hierarchies, changing its character would require nothing less than a total environmental or sociological overhaul.

The typical layout of a village ūr includes a well-demarcated center, with alternating streets lined with family homes and shops marking where the dominant (higher) jātis (caste subgroups) live, eat, and work. Village caste hierarchies also determine where subordinate (lower) jātis can build their homes, usually in smaller segregated neighborhoods nearer to the forest. Named after a patron goddess, the ūr is protected by her temple, which is positioned at the forest periphery to defend villagers from ghosts, spirits, and uncivilized beings lurking therein, and other temples and shrines devoted to the fierce gods, which dot the village landscape and extend outward into the agricultural fields where the lower-ranking jātis cultivate. Increasingly, this village layout represents only an idealized type in urbanizing South India and war-torn Sri Lanka, where in the latter case the widespread scarring of land has even challenged the traditional conceptualization of "landscape" (*thinai*) as one of the defining tropes of Tamil identity (along with language and ancestry) (Cheran et al. 2007).[4] Thiranagama, who interviewed internally displaced Muslims expelled from Jaffna in the 1990s, cautions against relying on too-abstract notions of the ūr and instead recommends paying attention to ideas of "hometown" in the context of practical life as an "everyday language of love, affection, sentiment, and memory" (2011:19) generative of new forms of historicity and personhood. For example, Muslims are now renegotiating dowry practices of property transmission from mother to daughter in light of their loss of land during the war. With land no longer as central to the reproduction of identity as it was before, Vellālar cultivators, who were once considered to be the exemplary figures of Sri Lankan Tamil ūrs (Pandian 2007), are now more easily surpassed by rival caste and social groups.

Recent historiographies of South Indian villages and towns also attest to the fluidity in caste hierarchies shaped by colonial and postcolonial rivalries (Dirks 2001). For example, although five hundred years ago Yanaimangalam, a *brahmadeya*, was a village granted by the king to his Brahmin supporters, over the centuries subordinate jātis supplanted the power of local Brahmins by participating in nationalist and labor reform movements that reshaped the "social and spatial contours of their local lives and their village" and extended their clout and ritual privileges (Mines 2005:22). Reflecting how "social relations of dominance are embedded in the spatial rendering of the ūr," the current layout of Yanaimangalam has shifted to accommodate rising jātis and exclude newly shunned ones (2005:49). Mines thus concludes that the ūr is to be understood as a living sign with multiple meanings "refracted through the lens of different social, political-economic, and even existential orientations" (2005:4). Daniel concurs with this analysis and further suggests that, as a living sign, the ūr's "institutions can generate an agentive moment as long as they contain within them the signs of a human being" (1984:190). Through written signage, for example, the ūr can "speak" in a distinctly colloquial or literary voice to proclaim its greater compatibility with a social group.

Social relations in the ūr, although primarily instantiated under the local gaze of fierce gods and mother goddesses, have also always drawn on national and transnational migrant networks of patrilineal kin and jāti members who, though leaving their *conta ūr* (ancestral village), are not doomed to a lifetime of feeling out of place as the diaspora literature often implies. Historically, even though late eighteenth-century colonial conditions had ill afforded Tamil-speaking indentured laborers much choice concerning their final destination or overseas compatriots, by the early nineteenth century the implementation of the *kangani* (overseer) system permitted higher-caste middlemen to consider issues of ūr compatibility when recruiting laborers from villages in India and Sri Lanka. Even today, many Sri Lankan Tamil refugees pay middlemen to facilitate their voyages overseas, while others rely on familial, caste, and broader social networks to research the compatibility between caste and final destination. It is widely believed that if one's kinsmen or jāti members encountered success in a place, so too will the new migrants.

> This attempt to locate one's own people in a new ūr is not motivated by any desire to establish ties of friendship or even acquaintance with the people. Rather, it is based on the assumption that if the new ūr is compatible with one of one's own, there is a good chance that it will also be compatible with oneself. (Daniel 1984:82)

Although Daniel suggests that new migrants who belong to subordinate jātis might be inclined to enhance their ūr compatibility by changing their own *putti* or altering the town's *kuṇam*, since dominant jātis generally resist such efforts, instead more commonly subordinate jātis will temporarily adopt a subservient role until they can locate a new ūr and establish themselves there as its dominant caste.

Certainly this dynamic of fission is evident in Montréal, where new waves of immigration fuel the emergence of more affluent Sri Lankan Tamil neighborhoods in the West Island suburbs (where older migrant cohorts purchase single-family homes) and somewhat less affluent neighborhoods in central and east Montréal (where newer cohorts rent apartments or purchase multi-family homes). Overall, Montréal has become a desirable destination for Sri Lankan Tamil refugees arriving in transit from European and Australian cities, such as Paris, Marseille, London, Hamm, Bern, Zurich, Brussels, Bergen, Skanderborg,

Sydney, and Canberra, in eager anticipation of higher-paying jobs, government welfare, and an overall better life.[5] Although some refugees bypass Montréal en route straight to Toronto, others express particularly favorable attitudes toward the malleability of its urban character, such as Pavalan, who as a child riding his bike past the Murugan Temple's construction site in Dollard-des-Ormeaux in the 1990s, proudly witnessed this impressive religious structure transform his suburb into one that now rivals many of Toronto's more affluent Tamil neighborhoods. Visible edifices inscribed with Tamil script further highlight this neighborhood's rising prominence among the diaspora.

Nationalist discourses in Sri Lanka linking the rise or fall of a neighborhood with its dominant jāti community suggest that the moral conduct of girls and women also plays a role in this process. In the words of a prominent female Tiger soldier interviewed by social anthropologist Øivind Fuglerud in Jaffna, the ideal feminine persona (*karpu*) embodies qualities of chastity and conjugal fidelity such as "shyness, timidity, ignorance, passiveness, and obedience" (1999:109). Unmarried Tamil men, seen as threatening the integrity of the domestic sphere, are relegated to work and other outdoor spaces. Yet gender segregation is not automatic in the diaspora, where women often labor alongside men in restaurants, factories, and shops. Christopher McDowell (1996) explains how upper-caste Sri Lankan Tamil families in Switzerland avoid temples where unmarried Tamil men worship. Similarly in Montréal, some high-caste Catholic Tamil families choose to attend mass in English at the multiethnic St. Kevin's Church in Côte-des-Neiges instead of in Tamil at Église Ste-Cécile to prevent their daughters from mingling with lower-caste boys. Second-generation Sri Lankan Tamil children are generally not encouraged to marry one another. Young women, tainted by presumptions of their improper sexual contact, instead wed men from abroad, and men seek women from upwardly mobile castes in Jaffna, where there is still a "strong preference for marrying children out of the country, particularly daughters" (McDowell 1996:102).

One Sunday afternoon during catechism class at Église Ste-Cécile, I witness these gender dynamics at play. Father Joseph is discussing Biblical history and Christian morality with five girls and six boys, ages fourteen through sixteen. The boys, seated together on one side of the table, enthusiastically respond to Father Joseph's questions, whereas the girls, seated on the other side, gossip and make snide comments. When Father Joseph asks a young girl what new or unusual thing she discovered during her recent trip to Sri Lanka, I am astonished to hear her curt reply, "Nothing is different. Everything is good" and go back to gossiping unabashedly with her friends. Two weeks later, Father Michael replaces Father Joseph, who has to return to Sri Lanka to renew his visa, in teaching the catechism. Having just completed his seminary studies in Rome, Father Michael exhibits a no-nonsense approach in dealing with the adolescents. At the beginning of class, he asks two of the girls to recite the opening prayer. They deflect responsibility onto a third girl, who finally whispers the prayer in a soft voice. Next, Father Michael asks the students to summarize the story of the "calming of the seas" from the Gospel of Mark. Though they were instructed to review this story at home, it is obvious that none of the students have done so. At least most of the boys have brought their textbooks with them to class; not a single girl has her book. Father Michael, exasperated by the side conversations that he overhears, finally reprimands the girls, who sit in stony silence for the remainder of class. Venting in fury afterward, Father Michael tells me, never in his career has he encountered such disrespect, especially from girls! Unable to understand how young Christian Tamil women did not learn to speak to adults with proper etiquette, he blames their moral laxness on the spiritual decrepitude of Québécois society, a sinful place where profit trumps virtue and Catholic cathedrals are being sacrilegiously converted into shopping centers.

Indian Tamils exhibit less alarm about changing gender dynamics in the diaspora. I met two single female graduate students attending Concordia University and Université de Montréal who live alone in Montréal. According to Hemanth, they speak "good Tamil" and enjoy a positive reputation in the community. Hemanth reserves his criticism for women in Chennai who exhibit notoriously sexually forward behavior and mix Tamil and English to sound "modern."

> I asked girls, why? Everyone does it. The underlying reason is that they want to show their modernity. Just modern. Even guys do, but it is mostly seen in girls. But guys don't, they can't do it very well. Guys make fun of this. If a guy meets a girl in the city, he will want to speak to her in English. And the same person when he goes home he will speak proper Tamil.

Although first-generation Indian Tamil immigrants still seek out marriage partners in India, it is more common for second-generation Indians growing up in Canada, such as Lalitha and Mohan, to marry other Canadians. In contrast with Sri Lankans, Indians are under fewer obligations to sponsor overseas kin through marriage and share money, travel documents, and information about job prospects with them. Generally more relaxed about reproducing the moral virtue of their communities than Sri Lankans, Indians also do not seek to visibly replicate the attributes of their conta ūr in Montréal, but instead prefer to live dispersed in downtown quartiers and suburbs and rely on aural cues, by identifying with a colloquial heritage language, to assert their ethnic identity. Indians may visit and shop in Sri Lankan neighborhoods, but they do not belong there.

Traditional Québécois Villages

Compared to the ideal Tamil ūr, the layout of the traditional Québécois village is practically the inverse: the village center is the parish church, regarded by villagers as their moral compass for maintaining kin relations and social order, flanked by a business district and then encircled by residential homes extending outward to the forest, river, or sea. My mother's childhood home in *Île Bizard* is an illustrative example. Now a suburban island community incorporated into the greater region of Montréal, originally when my mother's family moved there in the 1950s, Île Bizard was a picturesque countryside refuge for Québécois de souche fleeing the congestion, noise, and pollution of the big city. After crossing a bridge from the West Island, a small dirt path and bridge connect Île Bizard with the tiny island community of *Île Mercier*, where my grandfather built one of the first houses with his own labor. Twenty or so houses now dot the inner and outer perimeter of this island, along with many one-bedroom summer cottages used by vacationers camping on the *Rivières-des-Prairies*.

Until the age of eleven, I spent most of my summers in Île Mercier playing with the children of summer vacationers or accompanying my grandmother on her daily walks around the island (*faire le tour de l'île*). We often had tea with neighbors relaxing on their balconies before making our way to my eldest aunt's house, located on the riverfront a hundred yards or so behind my grandmother's house. I adored the greenery, quietude, and intimacy of village life, where everyone knows everyone else, so different from the concrete jungle of my own immigrant neighborhood in South Jersey. Although I am not Catholic—the only child in my mother's family not to be baptized in this faith—I gladly followed my grandmother to Sunday mass at the village church, content with the promise of her buying me a Caramilk chocolate at the *dépanneur* (convenience store) afterward. Everyone else in the family had given up on the Church. Illiterate in French and unfamiliar with Catholic liturgy, I passed as a Catholic by repeating "prends pitié de nous" (take pity on us) and following everyone else's lead in standing, kneeling, and sitting at the right times. Except for brief moments of self-consciousness when I had to remain in my pew as everyone else, my grandmother included, got up to receive communion from the priest, mass was an enjoyable experience. Next to the church on the main road is the hair salon where the stylist set my grandmother's hair every week and gave me my first perm, a popular hairstyle in the eighties. Down the road to the only grocery store in town, I often rode my bike and fetched items for my grandmother, who liked to pick her own vegetables from the community garden in Île Mercier and have milk delivered in plastic bags to her front door. My cousins and I swam in the river at a private beach on Île Mercier until the homeowners fenced off the beach, and afterward, we skipped rocks, caught frogs, and fed the ducks on my aunt's dock to pass the time.

At first it did not matter to me that my family members were the only Americans not of *pure laine* (white race) on the island, since I made friends easily with the other little girls who also spoke in nonstandard Québécois French. Yet my attitude slowly changed as I got older and overheard my aunt, who worked for the municipal government of Ste-Geneviève across the river, complaining that the area was becoming more anglophone and immigrant in character. Accustomed to seeing Île Mercier as a linguistically, ethnically, and racially homogenous community, especially compared to my hometown in South Jersey, I was confused by this remark. One summer day, my grandmother noticed the dark pigmentation around my fingernails and forced me to scrub my hands with soap in the bathroom until "j'ai enlevé toute la saleté" (I got rid of all the dirt). Knowing that I was one of her favorite grandchildren, whom she lavished with gifts and affection that I cherish still today, made it easier for me to deal with this painful experience. I find it ironic, though, that she would focus her attention on my coloration when her own pigmentation, a product of Native descent, was also dark. This incident abruptly opened my eyes to the broader context of race and ethnic relations in Québec.

When I visited my grandmother's natal village of Petite-Rivière-Saint-François, ninety kilometers east of Québec City, for the first time in June 2005 with my mother and her younger sister, we asked the first person exiting the parish church to escort us to the Lavoie family home (see Figure 5.3). In this small hamlet of about 700 residents of all French Canadian descent, the Church continues to exert tremendous influence over village life and parishioners know everyone else's family genealogies. Through my grandmother's kin, the townsfolk of Petite-Rivière-Saint-François knew of me long before I had ever visited or learned of them. Curious to discover new family members and see my grandmother's natal home, planted fifty yards from the Saint Lawrence River, this picturesque village felt far removed from our way of life in Montréal. Today, no one in my family remains in Petite-Rivière, having moved to Montréal or passed away. The depopulation of Québec's countryside, in conjunction with current immigration trends, ensures Montréal's expansion while contributing to the isolation of the rural population.

Respectable Montréal Neighborhoods

Despite Montréal's designation as *une ville aux cent clochers* (a city with a hundred church towers), contemporary life there no longer pivots around church activities. Historically, Montréal grew through the amalgamation of small villages such as Île Bizard that were gradually transformed into urban or suburban quartiers

FIGURE 5.3 Church in Petite-Rivière-St-François near the St. Lawrence River.

while retaining their traditional village layout. Deirdre Meintel et al. (1997), Cécile Poirier (2006), and colleagues at the Université de Montréal describe Côte-des-Neiges and Parc-Extension as Montréal's quintessential immigrant neighborhoods. Since the early-twentieth-century annexation and post–World War urbanization of these farming villages into the expanding Montréal metropolis, different waves of immigrants have claimed separate residential pockets in Côte-des-Neiges and Parc-Extension as their own. In the 1980s and 1990s, Sri Lankan Tamils established a residential neighborhood in the northwestern corner of Côte-des-Neiges, bounded by *chemin Côte-des-Neiges* on the east, *rue Victoria* on the west, *rue Jean-Talon* on the north, and *chemin Côte-Ste-Catherine* on the south. Occupying a central position is the *Eelam Tamil Association de Québec* (Quebec WTM) building headquarters on *rue Van Horne*, a residential street bisecting this neighborhood. Compared to the dimensions of Côte-des-Neiges, Parc-Ex features a smaller, poorer, and more recently established diasporic neighborhood first settled by Sri Lankan Tamils in the 1990s. By the 2000s, even though Greek-Canadians owned most of the real estate in Parc-Ex, the real estate agents and shop owners were chiefly of South Asian descent.

Sri Lankan Tamils, especially those residing in the urban quartiers of Côte-des-Neiges and Parc-Extension, have taken advantage of their neighborhoods'

FIGURE 5.4 View of Église Ste-Cécile in Villeray from Parc Jarry.

downtrodden and liminal status as transitory immigrant spaces to transform them into contending Tamil ūrs. These efforts are, however, constrained by the fact that Sri Lankans live in a multiethnic and multilingual milieu where social relations with other racial and ethnic minorities must be carefully tended, especially with neighbors who share the same schools, churches, residential streets, and shops. Notwithstanding, community leaders face mounting pressure to found organizations and erect buildings that will attract more immigrants from Jaffna and elsewhere in the diaspora, knowing that growth in population, territory, and wealth builds the ūr's reputation of "bigness" (*perumai*) and "honor" (*mā<u>n</u>am*) and, by attracting newcomers, promises greater prosperity for all residents (Mines 2005). Such desires, though, also incite competition between rival Sri Lankan neighborhoods in Montréal.

As the physical layout of the ūr expands, so does the oratorical use of literary Tamil. A couple blocks east of Parc Jarry, Father Joseph delivers mass in literary Tamil at Église Ste-Cécile (see Figure 5.4); a couple blocks south of this park, Hindu priests recite mantras in literary Tamil at the Sri Durkai Amman Temple. As more Sri Lankan children grow up in these neighborhoods, classes offering instruction in a literary style of Jaffna Tamil also expand in size, number, and type. In Côte-des-Neiges, where most Sri Lankan Tamils reside in Montréal, the Tamil PELO is now offered at three schools—*École-des-Nations, École Simonne-Monet*, and Coronation Elementary School[6]—in addition to Tamil classes offered at the WTM headquarters on rue Van Horne. Currently, Parker Elementary is the only school to teach Tamil in Parc-Ex. The most recently added Tamil PELO class is offered at *École Nesbitt* in the predominantly French-speaking neighborhood of *Rosemont* in east-central Montréal. This quartier, where Sri Lankans are now purchasing houses, working in factories, and attending schools, is an up-and-coming one in the diaspora.

Many first-time Sri Lankan homeowners are attracted to Rosemont, despite its peripheral location, because of its more affordable houses and less crime-ridden streets, in comparison to those in Parc-Ex or Côte-des-Neiges. Located three blocks away from École Nesbitt is the office of Kanthan Vilvaratnam, a real estate agent with *Groupe Sutton-Acces Inc.*, whose advertisement I found tucked under my car windshield wiper at the peace procession organized by Father Joseph at Rigaud in July 2005. Written in French on one side and English on the other, the advertisement concludes with the signature, "your friend Kanthan," written in Tamil (see Figure 5.5). This minimal use of Tamil script, along with Kanthan's self-portrait, guarantees him the patronage of Sri Lankan Tamil clients. Cheran (2007) writes that Sri Lankan real estate agents are ubiquitous in Toronto and publicize their services aggressively through online business directories and widely distributed flyers. In Montréal, where housing prices are depressed and post-secondary education is affordable, agents have profited greatly from the wartime increase in Sri Lankan Tamil migration to Canada. Private investments in real estate, however, have public costs. Agents and buyers must be literate, to a certain extent, in three languages—Tamil, English, and French—and have extensive knowledge of Québec's language policies. In this case, Kanthan Vilvaratnam is savvy enough to write a sign in French and Tamil on one side, and English and Tamil on the other, without mixing French and English together or otherwise

FIGURE 5.5 Advertisement for a real estate agent in east Montréal.

sacrificing the advertisement's clarity and aesthetic appeal. His business also contributes to the respectability of the middle-class Sri Lankan Tamil community in Rosemont, where potential homeowners are attracted to buy even though the neighborhood is far from being recognized as a "Little Jaffna."

Profitable Business Districts

Despite the few shops and businesses scattered throughout Rosemont and the West Island suburbs, only Parc-Ex and Côte-des-Neiges have discernible Sri Lankan business districts. Much like the petty shops in South Asia located on main roads or boulevards bordering residential neighborhoods, men, women, and children in Montréal can easily walk to buy daily incidentals and share news and gossip in shops not far from their homes.[7] Parc-Ex's business district, located between rue Jean-Talon on the south, *rue Jarry* on the east, *rue Saint-Roch* on the west, and *rue Liège* on the north, is about two-thirds the size of Cte-des-Neiges' three business districts combined, one of each centered on *rue Victoria* (see Figure 5.6), *Chemin de la Côte-des-Neiges*, and *Plaza Côte-des-Neiges*.[8] Table 5.1 lists all of the Sri Lankan-owned venues on rue Victoria, where Tamil store names are written in Roman and Tamil scripts and translated into French.

Studies of Sri Lankan Tamil-owned shops in Toronto have exposed how owners rely heavily on kinship ties to amass the credit, workforce, and clientele needed to run their businesses (Cheran 2007). This observation is confirmed by most of my informants in Montréal, who know of at least one or two relatives who own or work at such shops. For example, Nilima, the Tamil PELO teacher at Parker Elementary, helps to staff her brother's clothing and variety store, *Fantaisies Nickes*, on evenings and weekends (see Figure 5.7). The parents of one of Nilima's students own the popular grocery store *Marché Jeevini* in Parc-Ex. *Marché Jeevini*'s main competitor is *Marché Thurga*, a medium-sized grocery store owned by the older brother of Muthu, president of Concordia University Tamil Mantram (CUTAM). Arun, the altar boy at Église Ste-Cécile, has two uncles who manage an auto repair shop in Parc-Ex, and Pavalan's uncles share ownership of *Jaffna Fruits & Légumes*, a grocery store located next to the Murugan Temple in Dollard-des-Ormeaux.

Cheran attributes the relative success of Tamil grocery stores to nostalgia for homeland goods.

> Cultural alienation and nostalgia . . . has economic advantages for diasporas . . . It is no wonder then, the price of vallarai, murungai, and ponnankaani—leafy vegetables that grow in abundance in Sri Lanka and India which consumers generally pick themselves at will, are among the most expensive produce at Tamil grocery stores! (2007:162)

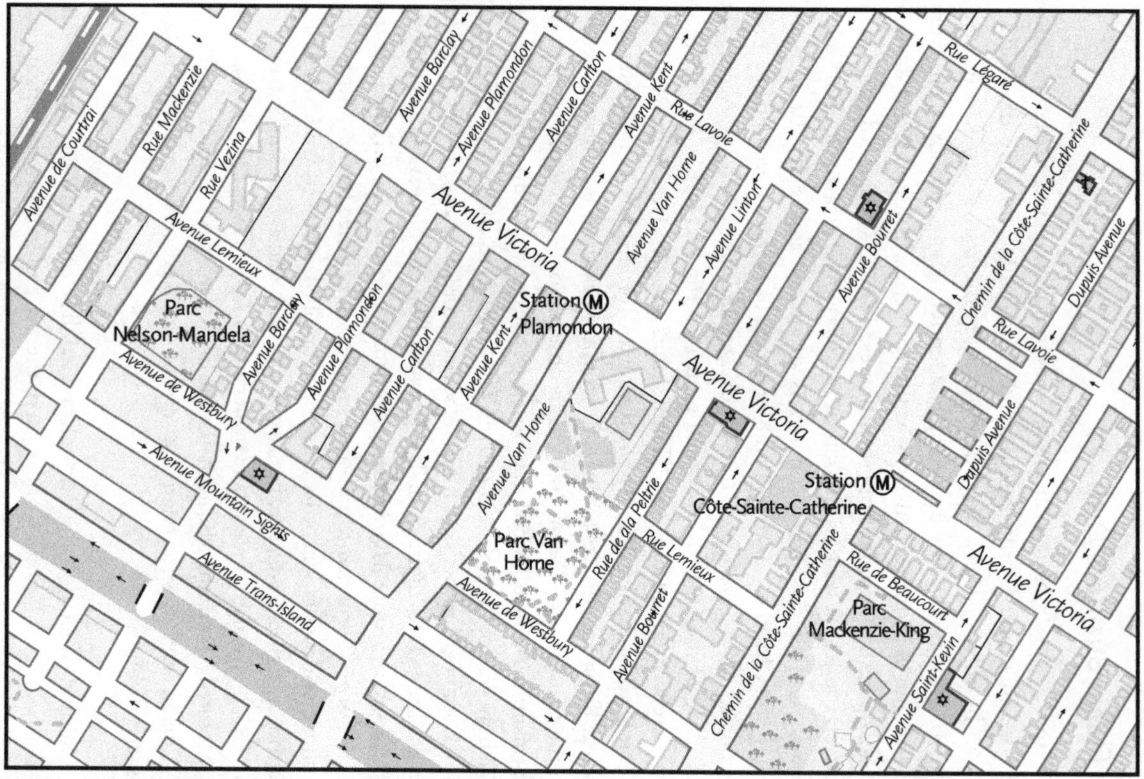

FIGURE 5.6 Map of avenue Victoria in Côte-des-Neiges.

Table 5.1 **Tamil shops along avenue Victoria in Côte-des-Neiges**

Street Intersection	Name of Establishment	Type of Shop
Bouchette & Barclay	Aliment Exotiques	Grocery store
Plamondon & Carlton	A.S. Poissons	Fish market
	Marché Emmy	Grocery store
	Resto-Bar	Restaurant
	Voyage Ceican	Travel agency
Carlton & Kent	Marché Victoria	Grocery store
	Oriental ENG	Grocery store
Linton & de la Peltrie	Boutique Pirapa	Clothing store
	Restaurant Ruby	Restaurant
	Bijouterie KPS	Jewelry store
de la Peltrie & Bourret	Lucky Telecom	Convenience store
Côte-Ste-Catherine & Dupuis	Marché Rebecca	Grocery store
Dupuis & St-Kevin	Marché Jolée	Grocery store

FIGURE 5.7 Fantaisies Nickes store in Parc-Extension.

Savvy marketing strategies also generate demand. *Vanikam* (2008) is an online directory that publishes a list of Sri Lankan– and Indian Tamil–owned businesses in Montréal, Ottawa, Toronto, Vancouver, and New York City. Even though the authors claim to have updated this directory twelve times since 1997 for accuracy, the 2008 edition lists all grocery stores in Côte-des-Neiges but only mentions the one grocery store, Marché Jeevini, in Parc-Ex. Marché Thurga and *Marché Abinaya*, bereft of *Vanikam*'s publicity, instead compensate by diversifying their merchandise and selling Indian, African, Chinese, and Caribbean, in addition to Sri Lankan, goods (see Figures 5.8a and 5.8b).

Usually, the presence of Tamil script on storefront signs sufficiently indicates Tamil business ownership. When seeking to attract a more diverse clientele, however, shop owners may also display additional scripts and languages. Regardless of their make-up, all store signs must comply with Bill 101's typographical criteria. The first criterion mandates that the store's name be written in French at the very top of the sign. Second, the font size of words written in French script must be significantly larger than any other language's script. Most signs adopt a conventional bilingual format, where the smaller Tamil script is positioned underneath the larger French script (see Figure 5.9a). Less common are signs that adopt a

FIGURE 5.8a Marché Abinaya in Parc-Extension.

FIGURE 5.8b Marché Thurga in Parc-Extension.

FIGURE 5.9a Model bilingual sign in Parc-Extension.

FIGURE 5.9b Model trilingual sign in Côte-des-Neiges.

trilingual format, with English words typically written in an even smaller-sized font and situated near the bottom of the sign (see Figure 5.9b).

Already suspected, as South Asians, of preferring English over French in their everyday lives, Sri Lankan Tamil shopkeepers are under pressure not to write signs that could be publicly interpretable as disloyal to linguistic nationalist policies. From a political standpoint, it makes sense to include the least amount of English possible on storefront signs, yet from a commercial standpoint, the inclusion of English words assists shopkeepers in marketing their merchandise to anglophone clients of diverse South Asian, African, Caribbean, and Middle Eastern descent. Because it can be safely assumed that government officials in Montréal cannot read Tamil, shopkeepers do not feel pressured to faithfully translate or transliterate French words into Tamil or Tamil words into French. For example, when reading the Tamil name, *ēñcal dekkayar* for *Angel La Garderie du Bon Berger* out loud, I notice that it is phonetically transliterated directly from the English name, "angel daycare," rather than *Angel La Garderie*. So, even though this sign appears to follow the conventional bilingual format of writing the establishment's name in French on the top and Tamil on the bottom, closer inspection reveals it to be a trilingual sign addressed in French to government officials, yet also in English to customers who are perhaps literate in Tamil and accustomed to code-mixing with English. Whether by signaling that this venue is an English-friendly store or by attracting upwardly mobile shoppers who speak predominantly in English, this choice of orthography demonstrates one of the strategies by which Sri Lankan business owners seek greater margins of profitability while also complying with provincial legislations.

Comparisons of temple and commercial signs with the same name "Durga" (see Figures 5.10 and 5.8b) further reveal how business owners and religious leaders employ contrasting approaches to handle conflicts between nationalist prescriptions and professional or organizational aspirations. On the sign posted on the exterior wall of the Sri Durkai Amman Temple, the choice of script and orthography signals the temple's greater devotion to Tamil nationalist ideals of linguistic purism, reinforced by its strict adherence to the Shaiva Siddhanta philosophy. In contrast, the commercial sign written for the grocery store Marché Thurga (named after the goddess), uses non-purist characters and orthographies more recognizable to a broad public, especially when transliterated into French or English. For example, though both temple and commercial signs adhere to literary Tamil sandhi conventions by writing the goddess's name with two "k's" (<க்க>),

FIGURE 5.10 Sri Durkai Amman Temple in Parc-Extension.

only the temple sign faithfully transliterates this voiceless velar stop as "k" into French, whereas the commercial sign uses "g," a voiced velar stop, to write "Thurga" in an orthography familiar to mostly South Asians. The temple sign also employs the literary character <ஐ> transliterated as "ai" in Roman script, in contrast with the commercial sign that uses the colloquial character <அ> transliterated as "a" to produce a colloquial-sounding name, "Thurga."

Differences in participation frameworks partly explain these choices. In addressing an ethnonationally homogenous audience of Saivite devotees, temple managers would be expected to display their primary commitment to safeguarding the antiquity of their religious heritage by writing the temple's name strictly in literary Tamil. Also, though community organizations are exempt from Bill 101, the temple nonetheless adheres to this law by writing its French name in a larger-font-size Roman script. Not exempt is Marché Thurga, which has produced a sign with the requisite French transliteration written front and center and the Tamil name written at the bottom. For the purpose of soliciting customers who are relatively less concerned with religious causes and Tamil nationalist politics and more interested in buying consumable goods, store owners can get away with writing a colloquial-sounding name masked in Tamil script. Temple priests may discern and disapprove of this subtle distinction revealing that "Written Tamil" is not synonymous with "literary Tamil," but the average customer probably does not.

Recall that Marché Thurga, a medium-sized grocery owned by Muthu's older brother, is not advertised in *Vanikam* and caters to a more diverse clientele than Marché Jeevini, the grocery store featured in *Vanikam* that enjoys a primarily Sri Lankan Tamil clientele. Marché Thurga's storefront sign also features the foreign Grantha character <ஷ>, used to transliterate the non-Dravidian phoneme [ʃ], as "ch" in "marché" (see Figure 5.8b). Only customers literate in Tamil could read this character as indicating a potential lack of loyalty to the purist ideology of the nationalist regime of Tamil Eelam, sponsored by the WTM in Montréal. Given Muthu's devotion to humanitarian relief yet preference to run CUTAM as an apolitical organization, plausibly his older brother is also less interested in catering to nationalist politics than in running a profitable business in Montréal. This reasoning would explain the store sign's non-purist style of writing.

Sometimes, orthographic mistakes arise when transliterating between French and Tamil due to the lack of a transliteration standard, despite Abbots Dupuis and Mousset's best efforts to create one in the mid-nineteenth century.[9] One common type of error is caused by the phonetic transliteration of Tamil into nonstandard Québécois French. Comparing signs for Marché Jeevini in Figures 5.11a and 5.11b, for example, one notices that the store's name is alternatively spelled with an "i" ("Jeevini") in the *Vanikam* advertisement (Vanikam 2008) and

FIGURE 5.11a Advertisement in *Vanikam* for Marché Jeevini.

"e" ("Jeeveni") on the storefront sign. This choice to transliterate <இ> (short [ɪ·]) as "i" in written French is more phonetically accurate if spoken in nonstandard Québécois French, which sounds like [ʏ·], rather than in standard French, which sounds like [iː]. Also, by transliterating short [ɪ·] as "e," which sounds like [ə] in nonstandard Québécois French and standard French, both pronunciations sound wrong compared to the standard Tamil pronunciation. Given these equally problematic options, I would conclude that "Jeeveni" instead follows an English orthographic standard for representing <ஈ> (long [iː]) as "ee" and <இ> (short [ɪ·]) as "e." Shopkeepers thus bridge the unfamiliar relationship between French and Tamil by veiling English words in Tamil script.

FIGURE 5.11b Marché Jeeveni in Parc-Extension.

A different conclusion to be drawn from this comparison is that Sri Lankan Tamils, although often illiterate in French, are nonetheless demonstrating their familiarity with a variety of nonstandard Québécois French commonly spoken in Montréal. Looking closely at the storefront sign for Marché Jeeveni in Figure 5.11b, one notices that the voiced uvular fricative [ʁ] has been omitted from the Tamil transliteration of "marché" when writing "mācē" as <மாசே>. The *Vanikam* ad in Figure 5.11a instead substitutes uvular [ʁ] with the alveolar flap [ɾ̥] and writes "mārcē" in Tamil script using the character <ர்>. No government official would notice that the word "macé," written in an inscrutable Tamil script, reflects a highly stigmatized pronunciation associated with the Québécois de souche underclass. Even nonstandard Québécois French speakers who say "maché" would write "marché." Ironically, comparing the above-mentioned examples, there is one sign (see Figure 5.8b) in which standard French is transliterated into a nonpurist Tamil script using the Grantha character (<மார்ஷே>), and another sign (see Figure 5.11b) that transliterates nonstandard French into a purist Tamil script by using only Dravidian characters (<மாசே>).[10] The resulting combinations are two hybrid signs that either look like or sound colloquial-like when read or spoken out loud. Choices of code, script, and orthography thus demonstrate how multiple participant frameworks, which can be laminated onto competing writing conventions, enable community and business leaders to send overt and covert messages to different government officials, nationalist leaders, and clients about how their business legitimately makes a profit.

Famed Religious Peripheries

As the prior analysis of the Sri Durkai Amman Temple's sign illustrates, language ideologies about the antiquity of written language are closely intertwined with communal efforts to globally showcase the fame of a neighborhood's church or temple through publicity written in literary Tamil (in Tamil script) and English (in Roman script). In contrast to how business owners in Parc-Ex/Villeray, Côte-des-Neiges, and Dollard-des-Ormeaux strive for legitimacy under the vigilant gaze of the Québec state, religious leaders instead seek recognition of their establishment's fame and glory through the eyes of devotees living transnationally. Due to Sri Lanka's protracted civil war, recent efforts to rebuild churches and temples destroyed or demolished in Jaffna have been sluggish and precarious, and many religious leaders have focused instead on erecting new edifices in the diaspora. Even though several aspiring "Little Jaffna" neighborhoods in Montréal can claim respectability for their middle-class residential quartiers and profitability for their thriving business districts, none can allege to be a proper Tamil ūr without a patron mother goddess, fierce god, or saint (like Durkai, Murukan, or the Virgin Mary) watching over them.

Montréal's Sri Lankan Tamil population is religiously diverse with 66 percent Saivite Hindus, 27 percent Roman Catholics, and the remainder Protestants and Muslims (Statistics Canada 1991a).[11] In Sri Lanka the leadership of the Liberation Tigers of Tamil Eelam (LTTE) is reputedly predisposed toward Karaiyar Catholics and Vellālar Hindus; the same can be presumed of Montréal's WTM leadership. Hindu and Catholic leaders, despite participating in different religious networks, often collaborate to augment the fame of their jointly inhabited neighborhoods. Concurrently, competition between co-residing members of dominant and subordinate jātis within a single neighborhood threatens to cause fissures in religious communities. Examining the social history of Tamil Saivite temples and Catholic churches in Montréal elucidates this dialectic of collaboration and competition.

At our initial meeting, Father Joseph shared with me the origin story of the Our Lady of Deliverance mission. The first Tamil Catholic priests to settle in Montréal, he explains, were Fathers Arulmoli and Selvan, who emigrated from India in the late 1990s to study at a seminary in this city. Offering private masses in literary Tamil to Sri Lankan families on the side, they eventually registered the fledgling mission with the archdiocese of Montréal. Before Father Selvan moved to the United States, he issued a request with the Jaffna diocese to send a replacement priest as soon as possible. Months passed before this request was filled. First, the Jaffna diocese required Sri Lankan Tamil Catholic families in Montréal to register their query directly with the Holy See in Rome. After the Jaffna diocese appointed Father Joseph, then parish priest of Mullaitivu, as the mission's new chaplain, he needed to procure a visa to live in Canada. In 2001, Tamil Catholics in Montréal welcomed their new priest to a mission in utter disarray. Armed with an incomplete list of the addresses of former parishioners, Father Joseph traveled door-to-door canvassing families to rejoin the revitalized mission of Our Lady of Deliverance. By 2005, he registered 258 families, 80 percent of whom began to attend mass regularly in Tamil on Sunday afternoons at Église Ste-Cécile. Believing Sri Lankan children and youth to be easily tempted by "Western culture and values," Father Joseph also wasted little time in organizing educational programs and recreational activities to foster their moral, spiritual, and social development. In addition to Tamil-language and catechism classes held on Sundays, the church offers Carnatic signing and bharatanatyam dance classes every Saturday and sponsors field trips and cricket tournaments once a month.

Father Joseph deplores how his parishioners still heed caste distinctions, even though the mission and Catholicism in general reject these social hierarchies before the eyes of God. Yet according to Father Joseph, the first question Catholics will ask of other Catholics is the name of their ūr and church in Sri Lanka to infer their interlocutors' caste status. He also laments how caste politics have divided his congregation between St. Kevin's Church in Côte-des-Neiges and Église Ste-Cécile in Villeray.[12] St. Kevin's Church, frequented mostly by Filipino and Caribbean immigrants, is presided over by Anglo-Canadian priests and an Indian Tamil deacon who ministers to the Sri Lankan parishioners. Indian Catholics usually attend Sunday mass in their own neighborhood churches yet enlist Father Joseph's and Deacon Adolfo's services to officiate in Tamil over the major sacraments of baptism, marriage, communion, confirmation, and funeral. Occasionally, Father Joseph receives special permission from the Port of Montreal to bring Indian seafarers of Catholic faith to attend mass in Tamil at Église Ste-Cécile.

Father Joseph's hard work in revitalizing the mission and expanding its membership has been so successful that the space rented at Église Ste-Cécile is no longer adequate. Father Joseph tells me that his goal is to raise $400,000 to purchase *Église Ste-Thérèse-de-l'Enfant-Jésus*, an empty church located on *rue Mistral* in northeast Villeray, and establish an autonomous Sri Lankan Tamil parish there. By the summer of 2005, much to the consternation of Father Joseph, the mission has only amassed $150,000 in donations from local families (who each gave $1000) and small businesses in Montréal and Toronto (who each gave $5000 or $10,000). In 2009, I learn that the mission has instead purchased *Église Christ-Roi* on *rue de Louvain est* in Ahunstic. This mixed residential and industrial neighborhood is close to where many Sri Lankan Tamils work in the textile factories, due north of Parc-Ex/Villeray and across from the *Autoroute Metropolitaine*. Less than a year after purchasing the church, volunteers finished constructing the water tank, parking lot, and Stations of the Cross and began working on the interior renovations to fully transform the building into a Sri Lankan Tamil church. Each stage of the transformation was visually documented with pictures and captions written in Tamil that are posted on the mission's website (see Figure 5.12a–5.12c) (Our Lady of Deliverance n.d). Inviting the world to see what priests traveling from Toronto and Jaffna, Trincomalee, and Batticaloa in Sri Lanka personally witnessed at the church's consecration,

FIGURE 5.12a Our Lady of Deliverance Mission at Église Christ-Roi in Ahuntsic.

FIGURE 5.12b Photos of important Catholic ceremonies with Tamil captions.

this digital publicity heralds the fame of a rising ūr connecting the quarters of Parc-Ex, Villeray, and Ahunstic, where Sri Lankan Tamils respectively live, work, and worship.

Bordering this ūr on its southeast side in Parc-Ex is the Sri Durkai Amman Temple, one of the earliest Sri Lankan Tamil Hindu Saivite temples built in Montréal. When Sri Lankans first arrived in Montréal in the 1980s, they worshipped alongside other Hindus at the Hare Krishna Temple and the Hindu Mandir. Sri Lankan Hindu Saivites soon began holding separate Friday services, and by 1985, different factions had developed among these devotees. One group formed the Saiva Mission of Québec and purchased several acres of land to build the Thiru Murugan Temple in Dollard-des-Ormeaux (see Figure 5.13a). Another group purchased a smaller plot of land in Parc-Ex to build the Sri Durkai Amman Temple (see Figure 5.13b). A few years later, a priest relocating to Montréal after living in Toronto for several years founded the Sri Maha Ganapathi Temple Society and built a small Ganesha Temple near his home in Ahunstic.

FIGURE 5.12c Photos of important Catholic ceremonies with English captions.

Selvamani, who worships regularly at the Sri Durkai Amman Temple, cites tensions due to caste relations between its devotees and those of the Murugan Temple, where she occasionally worships for special pūjās. Caste distinctions in diasporic contexts are often exacerbated by the absence of cultural and institutional sanctions ensuring the de facto segregation of jāti groups, Daniel (1995) and McDowell (1996) argue. Without such sanctions, different jātis compete to elevate their ritual status through a process that anthropologist M. N. Srinivas first identified as "Sanskritization." Sanskritization occurs when "low Hindu caste, or tribal or other group, change[s] its customs, ritual, ideology, and way of life in the direction of a high, and frequently, 'twice-born' caste" (Srinivas 1952:6). To achieve the contrary effect, Vellālar elites in Switzerland actively shun temples built by lower-caste Hindus to deter the latter's aspirations for ascendancy.

> In 1993 there was a campaign to halt the building of temples in every Swiss town because, campaigners believed, it was an initiative by a group of "untrained and unworthy priests to suck money from the community." However, more importantly, it represented a development in which Hindu

FIGURE 5.13a Thiru Murugan Temple in Dollard-des-Ormeaux.

FIGURE 5.13b Sri Durkai Amman Temple in Parc-Extension.

priests were seen to be actively engaged in assisting lower-class Tamils to improve their caste status, to adopt a new class identity through the employment of low-rank priests and the use of usurped caste symbols, thus breaking the bond between the Vellala and their Brahmins, which for so long underpinned the Vellala dominance in Tamil society. (McDowell 1996:229–230)

Whereas in Switzerland higher-caste elites maintain their caste dominance by limiting the building of new temples, in Montréal elites instead self-segregate and avoid non-elites, who create their own or join other caste-specific temples and churches.[13] This difference in strategy can be attributed to Tamil Brahmins (who are all Indians in Montréal) and Vellālar and Karaiyar Tamils (who are all Sri Lankans) not sharing the same reciprocal relationship of ritual service as they do in Sri Lanka or Switzerland. Building ethnonationally segregated Indian and Sri Lankan Tamil temples in Montréal is thus an effective strategy to ensure the caste segregation of Brahmins and non-Brahmins.

Each temple exalts the unique qualities of its devotees and, by extension, enhances the glory of the neighborhood or quartier. For example, the architectural grandeur of the Thiru Murugan Temple reflects and adds to the wealth and respectability of its patrons, who mostly live in or near the suburb of Dollard-des-Ormeaux. Built in two phases, the temple's latest feature includes an addendum built according to *ākama cattiram* (ritual prescriptions for building South Indian temples followed by Vaishnavites and Saivites). Importing the right stones, statues of gods, and caste laborers from India, the board finished the construction in 2006 and celebrated what they hailed to be the largest Saivite temple in North America and the only South Indian temple in Montréal to have an authentic kōpuram. The official consecration ceremony attracted priests and devotees from all over Canada, India, Sri Lanka, Denmark, and the United Kingdom (Thiru Murugan Temple n.d.). Prices listed in Canadian dollars, US dollars, euros, and pounds encouraged international visitors to purchase a Canadian stamp to commemorate this exceptional event. The board made no secret that building the temple cost a fortune; since 1985, the Saiva Mission of Québec has spent over four million dollars on the complex. Yet Pavalan assures me that the board members anticipate recuperating the entire sum, mostly donated to the temple by wealthy businessmen from Jaffna.

Similar to the Our Lady of Deliverance's website, the Murugan Temple's website visually chronicles the building's history through pictures and short narratives written in both English and Tamil. By highlighting the authenticity and grandeur of ritual practices and architectural features, this digital publicity elevates the temple's fame and celebrates the renaissance of a second Tamil ūr among the diaspora. During the two-week annual summer festivals held sequentially, first at the Sri Durkai Amman Temple in June, then at the Ganapathi Temple in July, and finally

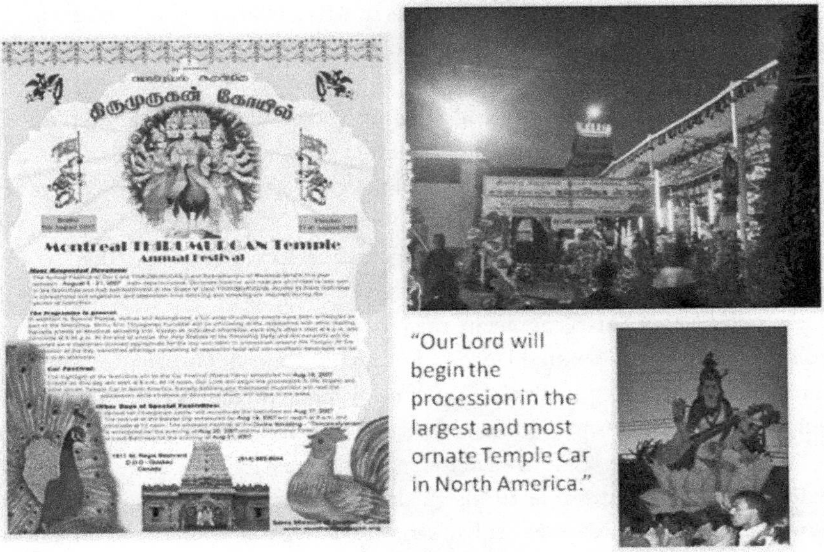
"Our Lord will begin the procession in the largest and most ornate Temple Car in North America."

FIGURE 5.14 Annual festival at the Murugan Temple, 2005–2007.

at the Thiru Murugan Temple in August, devotees from all three temples visit, witness, and evaluate for themselves the blessings bestowed by the gods and goddesses onto their devotees. Government officials also make brief appearances at these festivals to convey their support for the Sri Lankan Tamil Hindu community. Outdoor events, including music performances and food fairs, attract Catholic Tamils, including Father Joseph, and Indian Tamils as well. Rumors circulate widely about which temple has the largest, richest, and most elaborate festival of that year.

At the Murugan Temple festival that I attended in August 2005, tens of thousands of people from all over the tri-city region of Montréal, Ottawa, and Toronto mingled inside and outside the temple building and wandered through a crowded football-sized field to watch *kāvaṭi (kavady)* devotees purging themselves with spears, musicians playing on a makeshift stage, and vendors selling sweets and snacks at kiosks.[14] Two years later in 2007, an online poster promises to reveal the "largest and most ornate Temple Car in North America" at the opening procession of the summer festival (see Figure 5.14):

> The highlight of the festivities will be the Car Festival (Ratha Yatra) scheduled for Aug 18, 2007. Events on this day will begin at 9 a.m. At 12 noon, Our Lord will begin the procession in the largest and most ornate Temple Car in North America. Kavady dancers and ceremonial musicians

will lead the procession while chanters of devotional music will follow in the wake. (Thiru Murugan Temple n.d.)

This image of vibrant sociality and religious fervor alleges to rival even scenes from Jaffna, which was then a homeland under siege, with superlatives highlighting features of the temple contributing to the glory of the Tamil Saivite heritage preserved in Montréal. Embellishments on the puja sanctum and temple façade further testify to the global scale of its grandeur. On March 28, 2008, Shaiva Siddhanta devotees and priests from South Asia and around the world once again convened in Montréal to consecrate the Murugan Temple's newest acquisition, a golden *vel*, the sharp-pointed lance of Lord Murukan symbolizing "penetrating spiritual knowledge," specially imported from India, to add "significant value in our spiritual consciousness" (Thiru Murugan Temple n.d.).

Appropriately, the last festival of the summer is held in Dollard-des-Ormeaux, which enjoys the status of featuring the largest Saivite Hindu temple in North America. Compared to other Sri Lankan Tamil neighborhoods in Montréal, although Dollard-des-Ormeaux lacks a well-defined business district or residential core, as *the* preferred destination for upwardly mobile Sri Lankans, this suburb rivals all others. David, the graduate student who studies Tamil Saivism, believes that a spirit of rivalry between Sri Lankan Tamil communities in Montréal and Toronto will galvanize the construction of a larger Saivite temple in Toronto, back and forth, so on and so forth. Overall, competitive temple festivals showcase the spiritual ascendancy of the city of Montréal as a preferred destination for refugees, and its specific neighborhoods or quartiers as leading contenders for being recognized transnationally as Tamil ūrs, where famed churches and temples offer the promise of future blessings from saints, gods, and goddesses to their devotees.

From Quartier to Ūr

I began this chapter by asking how linguistic rivalries drive transformations in an urban neighborhood's character or, in this case, reconstruct Montréal's quartiers into potential Tamil ūrs. Because previous scholars have argued for viewing the ūr as a dynamic living sign that endures despite changes in the overall social, economic, and political conditions, it is important to consider how Sri Lankan Tamil homeowners, business owners, and religious leaders visibly attest to the durability and longevity of their up-and-coming neighborhoods by inscribing cues of their respectability, profitability, and fame. In the act of choosing between foreign or native, impure or pure, and standard or nonstandard characters, scripts, orthographies, and codes to write the storefront signs, advertisements, and websites featured and analyzed in this chapter, Sri Lankan community leaders exhibit varied stances with respect to nationalist policies and transnational prescriptions yet all reinforce the same semiotic ideology asserting that literacy practices promote the material sedimentation and thus enhance the transnational reputation of a diasporic community.

Sri Lankans, compared to Indians, invest more heavily in replicating their homeland in Montréal precisely because their conta ūrs (ancestral towns) have been under siege by the Sri Lankan army for decades, and their churches, temples, shrines, and memorials are still being razed to the ground. Also, compared to the experiences of urban diasporic communities elsewhere in North America, Sri Lankans living in Montréal face greater public scrutiny for their compliance with language laws. No business, temple, church, or school in Québec survives for long unless its leaders pay tribute to the province's nationalist movement and, more importantly, do so in writing. Many Sri Lankans also partake in profitable transnational alliances that require additional displays of loyalty. Though Montréal's Tamil-speaking diaspora is not alone in how it negotiates these conflicting nationalist and transnational politics, the manner in which Anglo-Franco rivalries have engendered new linguistic rivalries between businesses, temples and churches, and residential neighborhoods is indeed unique. In the next chapter, I compare Indians' and Sri Lankans' performative enactments of globalist imaginaries to explore how this diaspora conceptualizes the relationship between homeland and host society through narratives about a primordialist territory, "Tamil Eelam," and a cosmopolitan realm, "Tamilagam." My point is that although Indians and Sri Lankans may publicly appear as "rivals" in Montréal, their pursuit of prosperity collectively boasts of a global modernity that rivals all other "civilizations'" in both primordiality *and* cosmopolitanism.

6 NAVIGATING THE COSMOPOLIS

South Asian geographies have always exhibited tendencies toward the fabulous. Over the last century and a half, Indian and Sri Lankan Tamil nationalists have proudly embraced their millennia-long histories of migration as evidence of an unparalleled cosmopolitanism, expressed by famed Sangam poet, Kaniyan Poonkundran, when he writes, "Every country is my country; every one is my kinsman" (*Yātum ūre; yāvarum keḷir*) (quoted in Cheran 2007:150). Ignoring the periods of forced immobility and encounters of racism, incarceration, sickness, death, torture, dispersal, and loss of language that expose more sordid travails, nationalists instead praise the vast empires of fabled Tamil kings of long ago and leaders still-to-come. Earlier in this history, Sri Lankan migrants fared better than Indians in navigating the globe;[1] later, Indians did. Documenting these changing tides reveals the spatial contours of a Tamil-speaking world that has, since ancient times, imagined itself in expansive and even globalist terms. This chapter explores the discursive construction of the "fabulous" global imaginaries of Tamil speakers living in Montréal by analyzing their recollections and re-enactments of travel and pilgrimage. Featuring roving priests, devotees, and statues sanctifying the sites of temples, festivals, and processions from around the world, these narratives and rituals entail a unique vision of an unfettered cosmopolis, connecting new and old homelands and host societies.

Accompanying and often supplanting the routes of globetrotting priests, devotees, and statues are circulating discourses—oral stories and written records—that not only transcend the boundaries of time and space but also actively reshape them. Capturing this creative capacity of language through the concept of chronotope, Mikhail Bakhtin (1981) describes how narrative devices of character voicing and emplotment entail envelopes of space and time that transform perceptions of the very nature of reality. Linguistic anthropologists have demonstrated that chronotopes of modernist narratives often posit an irreducible break between the past and present to occlude other coexistent temporalities and geographies in the ethnographic and archival record (Agha 2005a; Basso 1996; Eisenlohr 2006; Inoue 2004b; Irvine 2004; Lempert and Perrino 2007; Silverstein 2005; Woolard 2004). Included among these discounted temporalities and geographies are diasporic narratives, such as those in Mauritius that emphasize the cyclical nature of "messianic" time (rather than linear "historical time") and depict the host society as imbued with the "ever-present quality of heroic and virtuous ancestors" (Eisenlohr 2006:242). When embedded in historical tales, such as among the Western Apache, sacred geographies can also act as roadmaps guiding listeners toward moral, spiritual, and social improvement and "work in important ways to shape the images" that listeners "have—or should have—of themselves" (Basso 1996:62). Chronotopes further invite the suspension of belief about the causality of events and the proximity of things through narrative devices (see Irvine 2004:103). In doing so, they create the impression of "virtual space-time 'movement' and 'travel'" by implying the existence of similitudes and simultaneities between people, places, and things that would be otherwise understood as more spatially distant or not coeval to one another (Lempert and Perrino 2007:207).

With regard to Montréal's Indian and Sri Lankan Tamil diasporas, despite possessing different views of a cosmopolitan future, the two share similar views of a primordial past due to their common literary heritage. Historian Sheldon Pollock (2006) describes this mutual literary legacy as dating to at least the beginning of the Common Era, when Sanskrit was both the liturgical language of priestly Hindu castes and the literary language of kings and emperors. He writes, "For the next thousand years, it is the voice of Sanskrit poetry that would be heard in politics from the mountains of Peshawar to Prambanam on the plains of central Java" (1998:10). These vastly different empires required a language of cosmopolitan character, with power derived from its "aesthetic capacities, its ability to make reality more real—more complex and more beautiful" (1998:13), in order to function as a "code for the expression of key symbolic goods—the most important among these being fame" (1998:14). Across the Indian Ocean to Burma, Thailand, Cambodia, Laos, Vietnam, Malaysia, and Indonesia, Sanskrit also bestowed fame upon rulers who emulated the glorious temples, city planning designs, and epic literatures of Indian imperial aesthetics, proving that the reign of Sanskrit differed substantially from that of other cosmopolitan ancient languages, such as Greek and Latin, which had gained influence through conversion, conquest, and colonization instead.

Most notable among the "cosmopolitan vernaculars" emerging in the wake of Sanskrit's retreat from the disintegrating South Asian empires of the ninth and tenth centuries was Tamil, patronized by local Chola rulers who "appropriated a Sanskrit aesthetic and a range of its literary models . . . for both political and imaginative expression" (Pollock 1998:28). These models included prescriptions for how to standardize Tamil grammar, rhetoric, and metrics and infuse Tamil poetry with the authority of textuality and modes of writing, rather than that of oral speech. Contact between Sanskrit and Tamil literatures, therefore, generated precursor ideas to modern-day concepts of diglossia. Pollock explains these and other consequences of language contact "as part of the repertory of a global Sanskrit, the sign precisely of Sanskrit's transregionality: They were local colorings that were produced translocally, and thus were an index of Sanskrit's pervasion of all local space" (1998:18). Such a "supralocal space of political-cultural reference" was based on the landscapes of the *Mahabharata*, a narrative chronicling the Iron Age war between the Kaurava and Pandava princes of India, which utilized an epic-like chronotope to situate the field of character development and political activity within a cosmos of hazy temporal and spatial boundaries.

Tamil intellectuals borrowed liberally from these cosmopolitan idioms in Sanskrit literature to construct their own chronotopes of homelands. Among these, the most "fantastic and fabulous spatial imaginary" (Ramaswamy 2000:578) is the antediluvian landmass of Lemuria (also known as *Kumari Nadu* [virgin country] or *Kumari Kandam* [virgin territory]), regarded as the birthplace of all human civilization and the progenitor of Dravidian languages. Variable narrative accounts of the size of Lemuria's landmass in twelfth-century and late-nineteenth-century texts permitted readers to imagine for themselves that Kumari Nadu extended far beyond the present-day borders of Tamil Nadu, even reaching across the Indian and Pacific Oceans to join together the Asian, Australian, African, and Antarctic continents. Such an account of Lemuria is taken from the children's book *Our Nation*, written by Kandiah Pillai (1945:2–3):

> Where the Indian Ocean exists today, once there was a vast land expanse. This was called Navalan Teevu. Europeans called it Lemuria . . . At its center stood Mount Meru. One of its peaks was (Sri) Lanka. Just as the continent of Asia lies in the north today, Navalan Teevu or Lemuria lay in the south . . . There was intense volcanic activity on Navalan Teevu. Several of its regions disappeared into the ocean. (Quoted in Ramaswamy 2000:586–587)

According to this text, before the mythical flood had entirely wiped out the first and second Sangam civilizations between 30,000 and 16,000 B.C.E., small communities of Dravidian-speaking peoples lived across the different continents. Over time these language families naturally diverged, yet only in Kumari Nadu, where the Pandyan kings ruled, did the inhabitants preserve the grammatical features of the original Lemurian language, later renamed as Tamil (Arudpragasam 1996; Ramaswamy 1998).

Almost as grandiose are tales of a post-diluvian *Tamilagam* (land of Tamils), a territory inherited by the Pandyan, Chola, and Chera empires ruling South India and Sri Lanka, ranging from the Tirupati Hills in the north to the coastal tip of Kanyakumari in the south and from the west to east coasts, and dating from the third Tamil Sangam (ca. 100 B.C.E.—C.E. 300) to the fifteenth century. In the late nineteenth and early twentieth centuries, Indian Tamil nationalists circulated cartographic images of Tamilagam to legitimate the idea of a sovereign nation, *Dravida Nadu* (Dravidian country). Although Kanyakumari is currently located at the southernmost tip of Tamil Nadu, nationalists also suggested that prehistoric Tamilagam extended much further south to "land's end," called the "southern Kumari." Ramaswamy explains, "For Tamil fabulists, the very ambiguity of this latter phrase has offered a strategic opportunity to insist that 'Kumari' here refers not to the 'Cape'—the land's end of today—but to the antediluvian river that ran through Kumari Nadu and that served as *its* southern boundary" (1998:586). Like Lemuria before it, Tamilagam's hazy boundaries allowed for this homeland to grow or shrink in scale, unconstrained by actual geological factors and geopolitical limits, to suit the imagination.

Cultural anthropologist Dennis McGilvray, a scholar of eastern Sri Lanka, describes Sri Lankan Tamils' view of history as "not so much a record of personalities and events as a collective sense of a timeless and eternally valid Dravidian heritage" (2008:55). Historically, Sri Lankans have referred to the Jaffna province as *Ceyagam* (land of the child) to emphasize its privileged position within the realm of Tamilagam (Sivathamby 1995). Yet in the twentieth century, nationalists rejected this association to instead affirm the existence of an autonomous Tamil civilization in ancient Sri Lanka (Pfaffenberger 1994). Searching for a homeland with realistic, rather than fantastic, geopolitical and geological boundaries, nationalists identified the medieval Hindu kingdom of Jaffna, which was ruled by the native Aryachakravarti dynasty from the thirteenth to seventeenth centuries and survived military assaults by both Vijayanagara kings from South India and Kandyan Sinhalese kings from Sri Lanka, as their ideal candidate (Rajanayagam 1994). They also proclaimed medieval Jaffna to be the reincarnation of Eelam, a prehistoric Dravidian homeland, which, based on vague textual references and controversial archeological evidence, is thought to date to the sixth century B.C.E. prior to Sinhalese-Buddhist migration from North India (Arudpragasam 1996). Arguing that the remnants of Eelam's ancient glory lies in the purity of the Tamil language preserved in Jaffna from ancient times through the present, Sri Lankan Tamil nationalist narratives construct a chronotope that challenges statist as well as scientific conceptions of time and space, by linking the people and languages of prehistoric Eelam with medieval Jaffna, contemporary Jaffna, and the future sovereign territory of Eelam.

Yet the mental act of traveling from the supra-continental landmass of Lemuria to the trans-continental realm of Tamilagam and the subcontinental territories of Eelam and Tamil Nadu also instantiates a profound loss in scale and glory. Ramaswamy (1998) writes of twentieth-century Indian intellectuals sorrowfully standing on the edge of land in Kanyakumari and looking outward to the sea, letting their minds wander to far-away places as they contemplate the splendor of past Tamil civilizations. Despite their different recollections of the past and dreams for the future, Indians and Sri Lankans have never truly defined their homelands separately from one another. In fact, their narratives and rituals of pilgrimage and travel often feature both Sri Lankan and Indian characters, who voyage across each other's homelands to explore the meaning of belonging, especially during unpredictable times. Ho explains, "Like genealogy, pilgrimage is movement given moral meaning: the former gains meaning through time; the latter, across space" (2006:xxv). He further suggests that narratives that objectify mobility are subject to biases that create "the conditions of possibility for movements to be channeled, controlled, diverted, and argued over" (2006:23). The following vignettes describe how narratives and rituals of travel and pilgrimage in Montréal are written and orchestrated to challenge hegemonic notions of the "global" and memorialize the excursions of both hypermobile Indians and immobile Sri Lankans in search of knowledge and peace in a turbulent world. Hence, rival groups of Tamil speakers coresiding in Montréal can collectively proclaim a global modernity rivaling all other civilizations, by showcasing Sri Lankans' preservation of a literary language with a primordialist birthright, and Indians' revitalization of colloquial languages with more cosmopolitan ambitions.

Ram and Sita Journey through Tamilagam

Tamilagam, the nickname given to the Québec Tamil Association, best exemplifies the entrepreneurial spirit revered by globetrotting Indian Tamils who travel far and wide to realize their personal aspirations of social mobility. Krishnan, one of the founding members of this organization, is its archetypal character. His paternal great-great-grandfather, who was originally from a Brahmin community in a village in the Coimbatore district of northwestern Tamil Nadu, moved to Burma in the early nineteenth century in search of work. He and his family remained there until the economic downturn of World War II, after which Krishnan's father married his mother and resettled in her hometown in Kerala, India. Born a few years later, Krishnan attended a Malayalam-medium school and grew up speaking a Kerala variety of colloquial Tamil with his mother, while to his father Krishnan was instructed to speak in the Brahmin caste dialect. Moving to New Delhi during his teenage years after his father obtained a government job, Krishnan attended a Tamil-medium school there and learned to speak in Hindi with his friends; yet his father, ever the Tamil loyalist, forbade him to speak Hindi at home and hit him once for disobeying this rule. Also, although most of Krishnan's friends married local Hindi- or Punjabi-speaking women, his father arranged for him to marry a Brahmin woman from the city of Trichy in Tamil Nadu. Krishnan's wife, who grew up speaking a Tanjavore variety of Tamil, could not understand her mother-in-law's dialect at first.

Throughout his career as a civil engineer, Krishnan has traveled the world in search of lucrative job opportunities. Gainfully employed by Exxon-Mobil Corporation for most of his professional life, he has lived abroad for different periods of time in Africa, Europe, Asia, the Middle East, and North America, making between $100,000 to $150,000 a year in non-taxable income. Krishnan enjoys learning languages and recounts to me with pride how in the Congo he learned a bit of Lingala, and while working with Bengali colleagues in Delhi he learned to converse in Bengali. Now, retired from engineering and permanently settled in Montréal where he works part-time as a court-certified translator and interpreter of French, English, and Tamil, Krishnan has familiarized himself with Colombo and Jaffna colloquial varieties of Tamil (adding to his expertise in the Malaysian, Tanjavore, Delhi, and Kerala varieties that he already knows well).

Of his three children, one daughter works as a teacher and is married to a neurologist in Mississippi, another daughter is a housewife and lives in Montréal, and one son lives in Bangalore where he is a senior manager at Intel Corporation. Krishnan is proud that his family, although geographically scattered and pursuing their own ambitions, remains true to its Tamil heritage. Himself trained as a Carnatic music singer, Krishnan informs me that his daughter and grandchildren living in Montréal are world-traveling bharatanatyam dancers. When his children were young, Krishnan (like his father before him) insisted that they speak to him in Tamil at home. Now, his children apply the same method of Tamil immersion in raising his grandchildren, who, Krishnan asserts with satisfaction, all "speak Tamil beautifully," especially compared to the descendants of Indian immigrants who arrived in Montréal in the 1960s and 1970s and are now "literally crying in regret because they have lost their culture." One day in October 2005, after our evening tutoring session is finished, Krishnan invites me to attend the upcoming Deepavali celebration at Concordia University to observe how the organization Tamilagam celebrates the richness of Indian Tamil Hindu heritage. He will play the role of a *sannyasi* (Hindu ascetic) in a drama, coauthored by himself and several university students, exploring the evolving practice of Hinduism in a globalizing world.

I meet another one of the drama's writers at a social event held for graduate students at India Beau Village Restaurant a few weeks before the Deepavali celebration. Siva, a Ph.D. student at the *Université de Montréal*'s bioinformatics department who invited me to attend, leads me to the women's table, where I introduce myself to Aditi, one of Siva's bioinformatics colleagues. Originally from Hyderabad, Aditi speaks Telugu as her mother tongue and learned Tamil while studying at Kamaraj University in Madurai. Although Aditi always wanted to study abroad, inspired by her family's frequent travels throughout India as UNICEF volunteers, she initially had a hard time adjusting to life in Montréal. During the first few months when she lived at her advisor's house, Aditi shared the space with a man from Cameroon who, she confesses, scared her. The two eventually became friends and played Scrabble together in French, yet when Aditi saw an advertisement written by a Tamil girl, Usha, looking for a roommate, she responded immediately. Usha is seated next to Aditi and speaking with a woman named Vanathi in Tamil, when another woman joins their conversation and responds in Malayalam. I realize that the South Indian women are all seated together on one side of the table and the Hindi- and Urdu-speaking North Indian women on the other. Despite their different mother tongues (Telugu, Tamil, and Malayalam), all of the South Indian women know Tamil to some extent and, therefore, could claim to belong to Tamilagam (the cultural realm and not the organization), even if they are not ethnically Tamil.

Hearing the men at the table behind us speaking animatedly in Tamil, English, and Hindi about language politics, the women's table tentatively broaches a similar conversation in English. Usha begins by conjecturing that French is close to Hindi because they share similar gender systems, yet Roshni, a North Indian girl who grew up in Canada, disagrees and explains that French and Hindi are completely different grammatically. The Malayalam-speaking woman interjects to say that South Indian languages sound uncouth compared to North Indian languages. Roshni agrees, yet Usha, after sharing a meaningful look with Aditi, retorts that never before has she heard a South Indian describe her language in such derogatory terms. "Usually people say how sweet our languages sound," Usha insists and Vanathi vehemently agrees. An awkward pause follows and the conversation stalls, until the North Indian women return to speaking with one another exclusively in Hindi and Urdu, and the South Indian women (and me) in English and Tamil.

To change the subject, Usha mentions the upcoming Deepavali celebration hosted by Tamilagam at Concordia University, which all of the South Indian women at the table plan to attend. Dressed in a royal blue salwar kameez with the *dupatta* (shawl) modestly covering her chest, Usha explains that, although her father will not allow her to wear a sari until she gets married, this Saturday in honor of Deepavali he has given her special permission to wear one for her role as Sita in a modern-day adaptation of the *Ramayana*. When Siva asks Usha what the play is about, she hints of references to the Ayodhya temple controversy. He teases her, "I hope it won't be anything against Hinduism, or else we will have to come in brandishing our Shiv Sena flags."[2] Earlier, Krishnan had explained to me that the drama uses Ayodhya as a dramatic foil to condense two thousand years of history into a single narrative depicting the mythical god-heroes, Rama and Sita, touring modern-day Tamilagam in search of Deepavali's true spiritual meaning. The heroes leave heaven by *pushpaka vimana*, a mythical flying palace, to stop at the cities of Colombo in Sri Lanka, Rameswaram and Chennai in Tamil Nadu, and finally Ayodhya in Uttar Pradesh in North India. Following the advice of the god-sage, Narada, returning from the International Jazz Festival in Montréal, Rama and Sita gather information about a temple built on the site of Rama's birthplace on top of the now demolished Babri Mosque in Ayodhya. Although tainted by the recent exchange of gunfire between terrorists and Indian police at the temple-mosque complex in July 2005, this year's celebration of Deepavali nonetheless commemorates the triumph of good over evil by the lord Rama and other Hindu gods.[3]

On the day of the performance, the MC introduces the thirty-minute drama, entitled *rat yāttirai,* in the following words translated from colloquial (Indian) Tamil: "We have compiled imaginary experiences of the God in case He comes to the Earth, in the form of a drama. Sri Rama and his wife are about to land on earth to see the temple being built for them. The events on the tour they take to travel to earth are called *rat yāttirai.*" Below, select scenes are translated into English, followed by brief descriptions of the omitted scenes. Although the play is written and performed entirely in colloquial (Indian) Tamil, there is one character, a Sri Lankan cricket fan played by a Sri Lankan youth from Montréal, who speaks in a stereotypically Jaffna voice.[4] Krishnan explained to me that the Sri Lankan accent is the only one that Indians like himself cannot mimic. In addition to poking fun at the incomprehensibility of Sri Lankan Tamil, the drama uses language issues as humorous asides to accentuate the corruptibility of Indian Tamil, the demise of Tamil scholarship, and the ungodliness of Hindi. Although Rama laments the current age's lack of religiosity, overall he personifies a cosmopolitan voice through his comments, travels, and lifestyle choices.

In the first scene, Sita and Rama, who are enjoying the tranquility of domestic bliss following hundreds of thousands of years of marriage, engage in a bit of lighthearted bickering.

SITA: Hello! What are you doing in these early hours of the day?
RAMA: I am doing what everyone else does in the morning.
SITA: Meaning?

RAMA: Checking my email on the Internet.

SITA: Who are they from? Are they from Lava and Kusa?[5] What does my daughter-in law say?

RAMA: Oh, slow down. Everyone is okay. As the Tamil poet, Kannadasan, said, "Everyone will be happy if they remain in their designated place."[6]

SITA: Hello? You appear to be making a sarcastic remark at me.

RAMA: So what? You left for the forest immediately after getting married. You have three mothers-in-law, but haven't experienced any mother-in-law bickering yet.

SITA: Did I volunteer to go? It was your dad who ordered you to live in the forest for fourteen years. I was worried that you would be lonely. I thought that you would have nothing to eat except for leaves and other forest stuff and suffer from hunger.

RAMA: Fourteen years. I was thrilled that I was going to be free and joyful. Then you followed and came along. Okay, but did you keep quiet? You were adamant in asking for that damn deer, and I only went after it to get some relief. That Mareekshan tricked us, and you yelled at Lakshmana and he went away. He couldn't take it. Yet you didn't keep quiet. You left like a fool, and Ravana took you away to his place. I had the best of intentions to prevent Ravana from suffering the way I had and told him to release you. But that idiot misunderstood me and fought and waged a war with me. He got his entire race killed. Poor guy.

SITA: Why pity him? Why should you pity him? You started by saying that to be happy forever, everyone should remain in their designated place, and you went on to narrate the entire episode of the *Ramayana*. It is your birthday today. I was going to cook some special food for you.

RAMA: Wow. What's the menu?

SITA: Chicken drumstick *sambar* (lentil soup made with tamarind).

RAMA: Aha.

SITA: Eggplant fry.

RAMA: Super.

SITA: *Rāsam* (pepper soup).

RAMA: *Balē balē balē* (yay yay yay).

SITA: *Vaṭai* (lentil fritter).

RAMA: Wow, wow.

SITA: *Pāyasam* (vermicelli milk pudding).

RAMA: Aha.

SITA: All of these I was about to cook. Now I have changed my mind. Nothing.

RAMA: So I won't get *vaṭai*, *pāyasam*, and all? I made a mistake. I should have kept quiet.

After establishing their playful dynamic, the drama introduces the main storyline. Rama and Sita, while perusing the Internet, are upset to learn that there are no temples dedicated in their honor.

SITA: Okay, what other things were you looking at on the Internet?

RAMA: Nothing. There's a website called "hindutemples.com." I cannot find any temples in my name. Krish, Venkat, and everyone else have many temples built for them. Why not for me?[7]

SITA: Why grumble? Do we lady gods have temples built for us? In Tamil Nadu there is someone called Kushboo.[8] I learned that people have even built a temple in her name. Later on it was demolished, for some reason.

RAMA: Did you notice something? Temples are built for all of the deities. Nobody is left out. Someone by the name of Vairamuthu mentioned in a song lyric in the movie *Kadhalan* that goes like this: "There is no vegetarian among cats and no Rama among men."[9] There is even a temple for Kannaki. But no temple for Sita.

SITA: How dare this Vairamuthu say something like this? Today's songs have become intolerable. So Vairamuthu knows better? Anyhow, based on what you've said, I've started thinking, why don't we have a temple in our names?

RAMA: We'd better contact Narada to find out the reason. Let me call him using your cellphone.

SITA: Why? What happened to your phone?

RAMA: It's an outdated model. Yours is the latest. Also, you pay for it.

SITA: Finish the conversation fast. You do not know where and on what planet this gentleman is now. Roaming charges are terribly high.

RAMA: Hello, is it Narada? Can you drop by our place?

NARADA: *nārayāṇā nārayāṇā.*

RAMA: What man, what happened to your *kuṭumi* (lock of hair) and *tambura* (musical instrument)? I can't see them.

NARADA: I was passing over the skies of Montréal. The jazz festival is going on there. Someone was selling a guitar for very cheap. I thought, why carry this heavy tambura around all these years? So I threw it away and purchased this guitar. And, it was too hot on Earth because of the greenhouse effect and global warming. I thought it fit to remove my long hair also. Then I got this cap also. These days people need to be up-to-date. I purchased these Levi jeans and Reebok shoes also. What do you think?

RAMA: Wow. Looks good.

Affirming popular gender stereotypes, this scene establishes Rama as the forward-thinking and technologically modern one in contrast with the more conservative

Sita, aptly portrayed by Usha. Also by depicting Narada, a preeminently world-traveled sage who is considered to be the source of all knowledge among Hindu gods, as willing to give up several millennia of tradition for the novelties of Montréal, the play establishes its favorable stance toward a modernizing lifestyle.

NARADA: Okay, why did you make me hurry here? By the way, many happy returns of the day.

RAMA: Thank you so much. The reason why you came here is, Sita and I have a serious concern. Why don't we have temples in our names on earth? The other guys, Krish and Venkat, have a lot. Why?

NARADA: That's a good question. Let me find out. (*internal monologue*) "Come on Narada. Let's have fun now. Let me find a solution to the problem in Ayodhya through him." Are you aware of a temple being built in your name in India?

SITA: Go on. I too am anxious to see this temple being built in our names.

NARADA: Okay, do you remember your birthplace?

RAMA: It's been too many years. I completely forgot.

SITA: If this is the case, I believe you may start to wonder who I am. It is Ayodhya, don't you remember?

RAMA: No, no. I do remember. I just checked to see if you remember, that's all.

NARADA: My job is over. All that remains is to watch and enjoy.

RAMA: Narada, it seems like you intend to start a problem.

NARADA: No, no. Nothing like that. How can I start a problem with you? Even so, a problem created by Narada always ends well. You are aware of that.

In the next omitted scene, Rama and Sita agree to travel to the temple in Ayodhya without Lakshmana, Rama's younger brother, and hope to avoid running into the demon brothers, Ravana and Kumbhakarna. Narada believes that once Rama witnesses the current religious strife in Ayodhya, a kingdom that was once the exemplar of just rule under Rama, he will find a solution to the conflict.

Packing their bags and some "modern clothes" to fit in with the current times, Rama and Sita set off on their *pushpaka* plane, but not before planning their itinerary on "Northwest.com." Sita is alarmed to learn she is traveling to Sri Lanka, where the demon Ravana had once kidnapped her.

SITA: Hey man, what's this place? Where have we landed?

RAMA: It is better not to land directly in Ayodhya. I have plans to visit a few more places.

SITA: Can you tell me what they are?

RAMA: First Sri Lanka, then Tamil Nadu, and lastly Ayodhya.

SITA: Sri Lanka? Why did you bring me here? I am very much afraid of this place. I have wild memories.

RAMA: That was when you were alone. Now I am here with you. Don't panic.

SITA: I see Ravana's face in everyone here.

RAMA: Don't worry. He made a mistake once. He wouldn't dare do it again. I am told that he feels bad even now for having kidnapped you. I sent Hanuman as my envoy to bring you back. That man lit fire to his tail and spread it all over. He still has to file his report as to why he did that.

SITA: Stop joking. Someone is over there. Ask him how to reach Asoka Vanam. That is where I was kept under house arrest. I wish to have a look at it.

SITA: Gosh, there comes Ravana!

RAMA: Keep cool, he had ten heads. But this person only has five.

CRICKET FAN: Hello, may I help you?

RAMA: Can you guide us to Asoka Vanam?

CRICKET FAN: What are you saying? I can't understand.

RAMA: It's Asoka Vanam, Ravana's Garden. Don't you know?

CRICKET FAN: Who's Ravana? What's your problem? I know no Ravana. All I know is Atapattu, Muralitharan, Jayasuriya.[10]

SITA: Darling, who are they?

RAMA: They seem to be cricketers. Hold on a second.

CRICKET FAN: Okay, where do you come from?

RAMA: We are from heaven.

CRICKET FAN: Where is that? Near Colombo or Jaffna?

RAMA: How can I make him understand?

CRICKET FAN: Okay, okay. What does Asoka Vanam look like?

SITA: Full of trees, lots of people.

CRICKET FAN: Now I get it. It must be Premadasa Stadium. I am going there. Come with me. There are players from India who have come. Let us go see.

RAMA: Let us also come with you. This is not the place that we told you about. Look Sita, it's called Asoka Vanam. You wanted to see it. It's been converted into a stadium.

CRICKET FAN: Oh, this is not the place that you were looking for? Sorry, I want to see the match. I can't come along with you anymore.

RAMA: It's okay. Can you tell me the score? Also, tell me who is going to win the World Cup this year.

CRICKET FAN: It is Sri Lanka, for sure.

RAMA: No, I hope England wins.

SITA: Hey man, do you know this game?

RAMA: Simple. There is a website called "Cricketboard.com." I learned about it from there. In our era it was all about wrestling, catapult, and more.

CRICKET FAN: Catapult, we play that still today. Can we play now?
RAMA: No, we are busy with other things. We must leave you.

Upon meeting a Sri Lankan man, Rama asks him for directions to Asoka Vanam, speaking in colloquial Indian Tamil. "Ingē acōka vanattukku eppaṭi pōkaṇumnu teriyumā?" (Can you guide us to Asoka Vanam?) The man does not understand at first and responds in colloquial Sri Lankan Tamil, "Enna kataikkiṟīr? Viḷangavē illē." (What are you saying? I can't understand.) In this sentence, not only is the man's choice of *kataikka* (to say) exclusive to colloquial Sri Lankan Tamil (literary Tamil and colloquial Indian Tamil instead use *pēca*), but also *kataikkiṟīr* (he is saying) is closer to the literary Tamil construction, *kataikkiṟīrkaḷ*, than the colloquial Indian one, *kataikkiṟinga*. This initial turn sequence thus establishes the uniqueness of Sri Lankan Tamil as a literary-sounding language compared to all other regional varieties spoken within Tamilagam.

Rama and Sita then land in Rameswaram, across the Gulf of Mannar and at the closest point in India to Sri Lanka. Legend has it that Rama rested there while preparing to rescue Sita from Ravana. They meet a drunken man on the beach who mistakes them for South Indian film stars.

RAMA: We were staying here before we saved you. We had a lot of things to plan. This is Rameswaram.
SITA: Oh, what did you do here?
RAMA: Nothing. We built a temple here for Siva. I'm looking for the route there.
LOCAL: What's this? Not getting enough booze. They told me it is a sachet of arrack. Not much of interest here. Hey look! Who is that with the long *pañca* (men's garment) and *madicār māmi*.[11] She looks like the heroine in the film *Anniyan*. Come on, let's have some fun.
LOCAL: It's just for fun. Don't get angry. You are . . . you look like the Telugu film, *MGR*, hero N.T. Rama Rao. But it's been a long time since he breathed his last breath.
SITA: I thought he would recognize us. But he is confused.
RAMA: No man, I am the real God Rama. She is Sita, Lady God.
LOCAL: All I know is *parāṭṭā* (fried bread) and gravy. What is this, Sita and Gita?
SITA: Why the hell did you tell him everything?
LOCAL: Okay, you say you are Rama. Is he the one who cheated everyone, who said that he had discovered something called Herbal petrol?[12] Are you a cheat? Hey cheat!
RAMA: Stop talking to him. Here's where we built the *cēttu* (bridge). It's not here now. I can't even find it.
LOCAL: Hello, what are you looking at in the sea? Expecting a tsunami?

RAMA: What's a tsunami?

LOCAL: A turbulence in the ocean. It brought in a hell of a lot of floodwaters onto the land and destroyed everything.

RAMA: No, no. I built a cēttu from here to Sri Lanka. I am searching for it.

LOCAL: What is a cēttu? Is it the name of a movie with our actor Vikram?[13] How can this man build it? Maybe he is the director of the movie. Sir, please give me a chance to act.

RAMA: He doesn't understand what cēttu is. It means "bridge" in your language.

LOCAL: Now it is clear. Long ago that bridge was built by a Mr. Rama with the help of monkeys. My grandfather used to tell me stories about that.

RAMA: It's me, the same Rama.

LOCAL: Do I look stupid? He is a god, you look like a human.

RAMA: No man, it's me.

LOCAL: This god confuses me very much. He may have a multiple personality disorder like the hero in the movie *Anniyan*. Let me leave before he does something bad to me.

Through the actions of a drunken man, the authors of the drama establish exactly what is wrong with the current epoch: the lack of respect for the gods and knowledge of Hindu tradition, the obsession with popular culture and modern vices, and the decreasing use of the Tamil language.

Afterward, Rama and Sita travel northward to Chennai, a city known for its unbearably hot weather and water shortages, where they meet a man, singing beautifully in Tamil, who explains to them that he makes more money selling tea than he did as a former Tamil teacher.

SITA: Garbage everywhere. What an ugly city! Where are we now? Rama Rajyam was said to be the benchmark for rulers.[14] People ruling here need to learn from you.

RAMA: That's it. You have finally accepted my glory at last.

SITA: Do you know who is king here?

RAMA: No king. Only a queen. Everyone utters the word "mom" twice and goes away. Looks like mom is not taking care of her children.[15]

SITA: It is very hot indeed. Can you get some water from somewhere?

RAMA: Wait. Let me go see.

TEA VENDOR: Tea, tea, tea. Did you call me?

RAMA: Yes. Can you give me some water?

TEA VENDOR: Where are you coming from?

RAMA: Meaning?

TEA VENDOR: I am asking you if you were in jail for some time.

RAMA: No. Why?

TEA VENDOR: How dare you ask for water at the Central Railway Station? It has been a long time since we've seen a glimpse of water. But I can give you some hot water.

RAMA: You say there is no water at all. How can you make it hot?

TEA VENDOR: It is called tea. There is not much difference between hot water and tea. Anyhow, it is good for your health. I have even written a poem about it. Listen. (*He sings.*)

RAMA: So much boasting for this damn tea? Sita, your tea is far better.

SITA: At least we are agreed now.

RAMA: Gentleman, your song seems better than your tea. You sing very well. How did you learn to sing?

TEA VENDOR: I am a retired Tamil scholar. Compared to teaching Tamil, I earn more by selling tea. So I am now a tea vendor and do not waste my time. Okay, why do you wear such a long *pañca* and *sari* in this scorching Madras sun?

RAMA: We are coming from heaven.

TEA-MAN: The place where Rambha and Urvashi dance?[16] Are you from there?

RAMA: There's a whole reception committee in heaven. There are more divisions. Kailayam, Indrapuri, Thirupparkadal, etc., etc.[17]

SITA: What does that mean, "etc. etc."?

RAMA: I have no idea of the rest. I know only this much.

TEA VENDOR: This means that you are a god?

RAMA: Yes, I am Rama, this is Sita.

TEA VENDOR: *Cittarkaḷ* (saints) say that insane people usually get relief from drinking tea. Maybe it works in the reverse as well. Hello, are you crazy?

RAMA: What do you mean?

TEA VENDOR: (*Internal monologue*) "That crazy man must have added a drink to his tea."

RAMA: What a pity. Come on Sita. Let's move on to Ayodhya, my birthplace. Let's see if someone there recognizes us.

TEA VENDOR: Go to Ayodhya, or Ayodhyakuppam.[18] Pay me for my tea before leaving.

Declaring Tamil scholarship to be waste of time and failing to recognize Rama's and Sita's true identities, the tea vendor betrays his cultural and religious ignorance as the gods take their leave for Ayodhya.

SITA: Ouch. Damn that travel. It was so difficult.

RAMA: Why do you say that?

SITA: We did not travel by Ayodhya Express. We were robbed by the worst people. All of your weapons and my adornments are gone. All of my best dresses are gone. Thank god I hid the money in my hip. At least that is safe.

RAMA: Anyhow, people here are not so patient. Reserved people can travel only for a short while. Most of the time unreserved passengers take over the train.

SITA: Come on, man, let's see where the temple is.

SITA: Okay, okay, come on. Let's find the temple and leave here fast.

RAMA: I cannot find where the temple was built.

PUBLIC: *rām rām satya hē rām rām satya hē*. Let's do it or die. We will build a temple for Rama. Let's do it or die.

RAMA: What's this? Everyone is shouting, "Rama, Rama." Nobody bothers to notice us. I can't understand what they are proclaiming.

SITA: You made Sanskrit the governing language. What these people are speaking is neither Sanskrit nor Tamil. What language are they speaking?
We are safe in that at least we know Tamil.

Sita's not-so-subtle rejection of Hindi as a language incomprehensible to the gods locates Ayodhya on the fringes of Tamilagam, the Tamil-speaking realm. Fortunately, a *sannyasi* there speaks Tamil and explains to Rama and Sita why devotees are rallying near Rama's temple.

In his explanation, the *sannyasi* emphasizes the role played by South Indian devotees in rediscovering the Hindu temple in Ayodhya one hundred and fifty years prior. Like Rama and Sita's current pilgrimage to discover the truth about Ayodhya, South Indian devotees had undertaken a similar pilgrimage to find knowledge about Rama and share it with the world. The drama ends abruptly with the *sannyasi* fathoming Rama and Sita's divine identities with Narada's aid and experiencing nirvana, after which Rama resolves to end the conflict in Ayodhya once and for all.

SANNYASI: Are you new to this place? What do you want?

RAMA: Oh good, we can at least understand what you are saying. We came here in search of the Ram Temple. But is there some kind of rally going on here? What is it for?

SANNYASI: These are Rama's devotees. They are saying that they will not rest until a temple is built for Rama. This is why they are shouting.

RAMA: That means there is no temple here.

SANNYASI: Yes, yes, there is. Come on. I will take you there. Come on. Look at it. This is the temple. Everyone calls it Ammaji temple.

SITA: Why is Rama's temple named after a woman, Ammaji?

RAMA: What? This is quite puzzling.

SANNYASI: The story goes like this. There was once a lady by the name of Singaramma. It was possible to complete this temple only because of her help. Earlier it was called Singaramma temple. Now it is called Ammaji temple.

SANNYASI: Yes, it is a long story. I will tell you. Listen.

SITA: Look man. Without the help of a woman even a temple can't be built. Don't you realize this?

RAMA: Yes, yes. This is only a half-hour drama. Make it fast. We have to end it.

SANNYASI: Okay, let me try. Long ago the *āḻvārkaḷ* (devotional poets) visited the temple and wrote sonnets describing its beauty. You must have known the great man, Mr. Sri Ramanujar.[19] He also visited the temple. For reasons unknown, people did not visit the temple for many centuries. However it is said, some one hundred fifty years ago, pilgrims from South India came here to visit the temple.

RAMA: Like us?

SANNYASI: Don't be hasty. Allow me to complete the story in full. You may ask these questions when I finish. Okay, when people from South India visited the temple, the old temple described by the *āḻvārkaḷ* was not there.

RAMA: So they started rallying?

SANNYASI: No, no, but they were smart. There was a great man, Parthasarathy Iyengar. He asked for help from the British Indian government and King Sethupathi. He dreamt of an incident where the idols of Rama were kept buried under the sand in a place called Thiruppullaani near Rameswaram. That was the place where Lord Rama stayed and rested when the cēttu was built. Are you aware of it?

RAMA: You are telling me my own history?

SANNYASI: Look. We have reached the place. This is where the idols were brought to the banks of River Sarayu and where the rituals were performed and where the temple was built. It is a hundred and one years old now.

RAMA: This means there is no temple at all. Then why all this bullying?

SANNYASI: Their intention is to build a temple at the birthplace of Ram. This temple rests on the place where Sri Ram was praying. No, no, where he did godly things. Tell me. Which is more important? The birthplace or the place where good deeds were done? Isn't it where good things happened?

RAMA: Yes.

SANNYASI: Even for human beings it's the deeds that they do that is most important.

NARADA: *nārayāṇā nārayāṇā.*

SANNYASI: Oh, you too are a devotee of Rama, like me? I am happy to meet you.

NARADA: You've gotten the entire benefit out of your devotion to Lord Sri Ram.

SANNYASI: What are you saying?

NARADA: Who do you think stands before you? It is the real God Sri Ram and his wife, Sita.

SANNYASI: Oh, what a surprise! I can't believe my eyes. This is the first time that I have ever felt nirvana. It is a hundred and one years since this temple was built. It gives me pride that you, the Lord, have descended and are presiding before me. I am in ecstasy.

SITA: At least this person can realize who we are.

RAMA: It takes maturity to realize us. He has it. So happy to meet you, gentleman. Okay, bye. Mr. Narada, we came here on your suggestion to see the temple being built for us. We are very happy.

NARADA: But the main reason for suggesting that you come here is only for you to understand the actual situation. You came here to see the temple built for you. You have seen all the bullying done in the name of building a temple for you.

RAMA: I have seen the temple already built, and I have also seen the bullying. Anyhow, I need to take on another incarnation. For this purpose I have called for a GBM.

NARADA: What is a GBM?

RAMA: General Body Meeting.

NARADA: Very happy to hear it. I sent you here only to take this decision. Can I attend the General Body Meeting?

RAMA: No rains, no grains. Sure you are invited. Okay. My long weekend is coming to an end. I want to travel back in my *pushpaka* plane. Come on, let's go.

Returning to heaven on their magical plane, Rama and Sita promise to assume new avatars to deal with the turmoil in Ayodhya. It is implied that only through travel could they have acquired the knowledge required to appease this religious conflict. On this day of Deepavali, Indian Tamils in Montréal are instructed to look toward Rama and Sita, who speak Tamil, the only living language of the gods, and who epitomize spiritual truth and material wealth in addition to adopting a cosmopolitan lifestyle, as the ideal man and woman. Also, by bestowing virtue along the way, Rama and Sita's pilgrimage sanctifies the boundaries of the continuously changing and ever-expanding realm of Tamilagam.

Our Lady of Madhu Finds Eelam

On April 3, 2008, an article on Tamilnet captures my attention with the headline, "Our Lady of Madu [*sic*] has become a refugee in her own land" (Tamilnet 2008a). It explains how the statue of the Virgin Mary was safely removed from the shrine of Madhu after being targeted by hostile fire from the Sri Lankan army.

Leaders of the Liberation Tigers of Tamil Eelam (LTTE) call on the international community, singling out allies in Tamil Nadu and Norway in particular, to condemn this latest act of violence against the "holy land" of Madhu (Tamilnet 2008b, 2008c). In particular, the LTTE criticizes the government's strategy of targeting religious sites as a form of "ethnic cleansing" intent on achieving nothing less than the "temporal and spiritual conquest of Tamils" (Tamilnet 2008d). *Lankaweb.com*, the diasporic voice of Sinhalese-Buddhist nationalists, counters that the Madhu shrine is not a holy land since it was built less than two hundred years ago on top of a temple, *Pattini Devale*, frequented by both Buddhists and Hindus (Gamage 2008). The LTTE retaliates by accusing Sinhalese-Buddhist nationalists of portraying Catholicism as a non-indigenous religion to "Sinhalicize" the region and downscale the shrine's history as a haven for Catholic Tamils that have fled religious persecution since the seventeenth century. Reminding the public of how the Sri Lankan army has previously targeted Catholic churches and Hindu temples used as sanctuaries during the war, the LTTE denounces the government's response as polemical rhetoric.

During intermittent periods of peace, including the ceasefire between 2002 and 2006, Sri Lankans of different faiths undertook peace pilgrimages to Madhu to pray for healing and an end to war. Legend has it that the shrine's soil, where devotees first planted the statue of the Virgin Mary in 1670, possesses miraculous properties that can cure even poisonous snakebites. The power of performing miracles is intrinsic to the wooden statue of Our Lady of Madhu itself, venerated by pilgrims from all over the country. In 1870, the Bishop of Mannar established June 2nd as the annual feast day for Marian devotees to visit this shrine. When he later moved the feast to the Day of the Assumption on August 15th, massive crowds convened in Madhu to attend what has become one of most important pilgrimage events in the Sri Lankan Catholic calendar.

Father Joseph, a former parish priest of the Mullaitivu diocese in northeastern Sri Lanka, sought to recreate the sacred geography of the Madhu pilgrimage by continuing the practice, first established by his Indian predecessors in the late 1990s, of organizing an annual peace pilgrimage to the Marian shrine in Rigaud, Québec. Rigaud is a small agricultural town located seventy kilometers west of Montréal that was named after the last governor of New France, Pierre François de Rigaud, the Marquis of Vaudreuil-Cavagnal. Even though Marquis Rigaud surrendered Montréal to the British after the end of the Seven Years' War in 1760, this part of rural Québec remained devoutly Catholic. Legend asserts that God transformed a field of potatoes in Rigaud into stones to punish farmers who did not observe the Sabbath under British rule. Also in 1874, Brother Ludger Pauzé, inspired by the story of Bernadette at Lourdes in France, planted a statue of Our Lady of Lourdes on the hillside of *Mont-Rigaud* (Sanctuaire

Notre-Dame-de-Lourdes de Rigaud n.d.). Since then, Marian devotees have prayed on this soil. It is said to possess miraculous properties like many of the other pilgrimage sites visited by devout Catholics throughout Québec, including the churches of *Sainte-Anne-de-Beaupré* near Québec City, *Cap-de-la-Madeleine* in Trois-Rivières, and *Oratoire St-Joseph* in Montréal, which all began as small shrines in the early years of French colonization (Dickinson and Young 2000). My own French Huguenot maternal ancestor converted from Protestantism to Catholicism after she experienced a miracle at Sainte-Anne-de-Beaupré in the late 1600s.

On July 30, 2005, between two and three thousand Catholic and Hindu devotees arrived from Montréal, Ottawa, and Toronto to participate in the second Marian peace procession organized by Father Joseph at the *Sanctuaire Notre-Dame-de-Lourdes* at Rigaud (see Figure 6.1). This penultimate pilgrimage transpired one week before the final pilgrimage was to take place at Madhu in Sri Lanka. Invited by Father Joseph to attend, I ask Marianne to accompany me to Rigaud since she has visited the sanctuary before and attended many Marian processions in France, and could shed a comparative perspective. This, however, is her first procession organized by a Sri Lankan priest and conducted entirely in literary Tamil. In France, she tells me, Indian priests from Pondicherry organize

PETITE HISTOIRE DU SANCTUAIRE

Le sanctuaire Notre-Dame-de-Lourdes est un lieu de pèlerinage situé au flanc de la colline de Rigaud, dans un paysage d'une rare beauté.

Dédié à la Vierge de l'Immaculée Conception, il rappelle les apparitions de Marie à Lourdes en France en 1858 et le message qu'elle confia à la jeune Bernadette Soubirous.

En 1874, seize ans plus tard, l'appel de la Vierge à Bernadette trouve un écho dans le cœur d'un religieux du Collège Bourget, le frère Ludger Pauzé, Clerc de Saint-Viateur. Il choisit un coin discret dans la colline de Rigaud pour y loger une statuette de Notre-Dame-de-Lourdes.

Son supérieur, le père François-Xavier Chouinard, des professeurs et des élèves fervents reçoivent la confidence et viennent avec lui prier la Vierge. Les jeunes sont les premiers pèlerins. Un véritable culte marial prend ainsi naissance et n'a cessé de se développer depuis.

A BRIEF HISTORY OF THE SHRINE

Our Lady of Lourdes Shrine is a pilgrimage centre in Rigaud. Its hillside location is renowned for its natural beauty.

Dedicated to the Immaculate Conception of the Virgin, the Shrine stands as a reminder of the apparitions and message of Mary to Bernadette Soubirous in Lourdes, France, in 1858.

Sixteen years later, in 1874, Mary's call to Bernadette echoed in the heart of brother Ludger Pauze, Cleric of Saint Viator, a member of the staff of College Bourget. He found a discreet location on the hill to place a small statue of Our Lady of Lourdes.

His Superior, Father François-Xavier Chouinard, other teachers and fervent pupils shared in the secret and were led to pray the Virgin. Youth were the first pilgrims. A true Marian devotion was born and has continued to flourish since then.

Sanctuaire Notre-Dame-de-Lourdes
C.P. 158 Rigaud (Québec)
J0P 1P0 CANADA

Tél. : 450-451-4631
Fax : 450-451-0655

www.csviateur.qc.ca
lourdesrigaud@videotron.ca

SANCTUAIRE
Notre-Dame-de-Lourdes
Our Lady of Lourdes
SHRINE
Rigaud (Québec)
2005

Un Sanctuaire sous les arbres
animé par
les Clercs de Saint-Viateur

A Haven Under the Trees
in the Pastoral Care of
the Clerics of Saint Viator

FIGURE 6.1 Pamphlet of the Sanctuaire Notre-Dame-de-Lourdes in Rigaud.

the Marian processions (attended by both Indians and Sri Lankans) and the homily is translated into French for the benefit of young children. We arrive at the sanctuary at 8:34 am to find only three other cars parked in the upper lot. I watch as a few families wander down to the lower parking lot where men are busy setting up a food tent. Marianne and I decide to explore the sanctuary and head to a cave lined with prayer candles and featuring a carved rock basin holding holy spring water. We each light a fifty-cent candle and say a prayer. Four women kneel outside the cave in front of a stone relief of the Virgin Mary to recite the rosary in Tamil, and the outdoor altar, where six seats await the priests, remains empty.

Marianne comments how South Asian masses always have more priests than in Western masses. She also notifies me that whenever you visit a new church, you should say the prayers, "Notre père," "Je vous salue Marie," and "Gloire au père," each three times. Seating ourselves in the first pew, we silently recite the prayers. A few adolescent boys walking noisily past the altar irritate Marianne, who wonders aloud why no one respects the signs posted everywhere exhorting visitors to maintain the silence. At 9:00 am I estimate there are between sixty to one hundred people milling on the sanctuary grounds. Marianne and I climb Mont-Rigaud to inspect the original chapel that was built above the outdoor altar and admire the view of the entire valley from this elevation. After this mini excursion, we return to the lower arena, where at least three hundred people are seated on the benches and waiting, now 9:30 am. I notice that Father Joseph has arrived and point him out to Marianne, who has never met him before and only heard of him through her father's work with the Church. At 10:00 am, with four hundred people waiting in the pews, a young boy brings the priests' garbs carefully hung on a rack to the altar and they don their robes.

Father Joseph begins speaking in colloquial Jaffna Tamil using a microphone to project his voice throughout the outdoor arena with the assistance of stereo speakers. Unable to fully understand what he says, I ask Marianne to repeat as best she can (she herself has difficulty understanding the speech of Sri Lankan Tamils). She tells me that Father Joseph informed everyone who wants to join the procession to walk down the hill or take the bus to *Église Madeleine*. He personally is going there to meet everyone and join the procession transporting the statue of Our Lady of Madhu back to the main altar. I look around but no one moves. He repeats the same message five minutes later informing devotees that it is not too late to join the procession. We leave our bench and head downhill to find the procession and realize that hundreds of people have gathered in the lower parking lot and more are standing along the main road. A van transporting the priests slowly passes us on the road followed by a crowd of devotees. I watch as a French-speaking security guard unsuccessfully attempts to coax the crowd to not block traffic, until a young Sri Lankan man, who briefly speaks with the security guard in French, informs everyone in Tamil to move over to the side of the road. I glance at my watch. It is 10:30 am. I estimate that at least one thousand people have now joined the procession. Marianne and I wait at this junction until the church bells rings at 11:00 am, signaling the start of mass.

Originally, we plan to join the procession halfway as it makes its way up the road to the altar, yet by 11:30 am we grow anxious that we will not find good seats and decide to return to the outdoor arena. While walking we pass in front of a LTTE stall, easily recognized by its small red flags, where men are selling CDs. I point out the stall to Marianne, who is surprised to see the LTTE at a religious event. When we sit down I check my phone messages and realize that Father Joseph has called me to see if I have arrived. Marianne is dismayed that the event is running late. In France, she states, mass would have started at 11:00 am sharp, though she concedes that the priests would have advertised the beginning of mass for 10:30 am since Indians are notoriously late. Four other clergymen have since joined Father Joseph near the altar, including Deacon Adolfo of Saint Kevin's Church in Côte-des-Neiges, two visiting Sri Lankan priests from Jaffna and Australia, and Father André, the Québécois de souche priest who runs the mission house at Église St-Vincent-Ferrier. Marianne points out the contrast between the plain-clothed Québécois de souche priest and the Tamil priests, who, she says with slight disapproval, are wearing extravagant robes with golden shawls and borders of different shades that do not correspond with the colors of the calendar of saints as they should.

The crowd at this point has surpassed three thousand. Almost all of the men are dressed in pants and dress shirts or cotton polo shirts. Women of marriageable age are wearing saris or long skirts, and unmarried women, teenage girls, and children are in long skirts, salwar kameezes, *pāvāṭai* (embroidered skirts), or party dresses. As the day progresses, more adolescents and teenagers arrive, with girls attired in tight shirts with short sleeves and skirts and boys in sports gear. Young girls and women are decked in gold jewelry, a display of finery that Marianne finds offensive. The previous night she had called to instruct me to wear a long skirt and simple shirt with sleeves. She herself made a special point to dress in blue and white, the colors of the Virgin Mary. I notice that a middle-aged woman in the bench next to us is dressed in a sari of the same colors.

By 12:00 pm the procession makes its way up the hill to the main shrine (see Figure 6.2). Arriving first is the statue of the Virgin Mary, dressed in a blue and gold embroidered robe and a pointy golden crown, carried in a golden makeshift altar featuring a series of pillars ending in an upward peak and a pink and white garland draped over it. Young boys and men wearing blue and white robes and holding blue-trimmed white flags are walking behind the altar, followed by women singing hymns in Tamil. We move up to the third pew to witness the mass

FIGURE 6.2 Procession of the Virgin Mary at the Sanctuaire Notre-Dame-de-Lourdes, Rigaud.

up close and I turn on my audio recorder. Five priests are carrying the statue to the main altar as Father Joseph begins to recite the mass in literary Tamil. Three young girls dressed in red and yellow half-saris cast a circle with candles and incense and throw flowers onto the floor. Marianne whispers to me in reproach that they have incorrectly tied their saris with the tail end of the cloth conspicuously showing in the back. When one woman puts kunkumam on Father Joseph's forehead, Marianne is aghast that a woman dare touch a priest so brazenly. She attributes this permissiveness to the "over-Hinduization" of the Catholic liturgy, something that would never happen in France or India, and blames the incident on the event's organizers, and not the priests.

As Father Joseph finishes reciting the mass in literary Tamil, many of the women sitting near us in the front pews sing along with the hymns, kneeling and sitting in proper synchrony. I notice that the pious woman clothed in a blue and white sari remains on her knees throughout the mass, praying with her head bowed and eyes closed. After mass, Father Joseph introduces Father André in English and thanks him for attending the function, even though he was hospitalized two weeks earlier. Father André speaks of the message of peace and brotherhood that the Virgin Mary, as everyone's mother, brings to all people, Christian and non-Christian alike. Deacon Adolfo from St. Kevin's Church blesses the crowd with incense, and the two visiting Sri Lankan priests deliver homilies in literary Tamil,

FIGURE 6.3 Priests genuflecting before the statue of the Virgin Mary in Rigaud.

exhorting devotees to pray for an end to the war in Sri Lanka. Father Joseph encourages everyone to donate at least ten dollars toward purchasing a new church for Montréal's Catholic Tamil mission, and then the priests lift the statue of Our Lady of Madhu from the makeshift altar and gingerly place her on the main altar, where they genuflect in front of her (see Figure 6.3). A few moments later she is returned to the makeshift altar and carefully carried down the steps to the middle of the front pew, where crowds of people surround her to touch the holy statue believed to manifest miraculous powers. Finally, Father Joseph performs the Eucharist and the devotees walk up to the altar to receive communion.

As the crowds thin out, we leave to pay our respects to Father Joseph and touch the statue of Our Lady of Madhu before heading to the tents and vans, where volunteers are distributing bananas and sweet buns. Hearing a person on the loudspeaker directing people to the parking lot to donate money to the church, we slowly walk there to find people lining up in front of the Tamil Rehabilitation Organization table, where cotton candy and snacks are being sold. Next to this table volunteers are distributing plates of rice, pickle, chutney, *paruppu* (lentil soup), and a bun filled with chickpeas. By 2:30 pm, visitors speaking French, English, and other languages start to arrive. A few Sri Lankan families continue to mingle in the parking lot, where Tamil music emanates from vehicles with license plates from Québec and Ontario, featuring crosses hung from rearview mirrors and the flyers of Sri Lankan businesses tucked under windshield wipers.

The following week, Our Lady of Madhu returns to Madhu, Sri Lanka for the Day of the Assumption feast attended by two to three hundred thousand devotees, Christians, Hindus, and Buddhists, praying for peace in the midst of rumors of impending war. Father Joseph, who has to return to Jaffna in the fall of 2005 to renew his visa, finds himself unexpectedly detained there for more than half a year and cannot organize the follow-up Marian procession in Rigaud in 2006.

Also that year, an increasingly aggressive Sri Lankan army erects a military checkpoint in Madhu, deterring pilgrims from reaching the shrine and blockading tens of thousands of people for several days after the festival's end (Tamilnet 2006). In 2007, few pilgrims dare return to the shrine of Madhu, which is caught in the crossfire between LTTE and Sri Lankan forces and, by spring 2008, the Sri Lankan army has invaded Madhu and forced the Mannar bishop to flee with the statue, first to Jaffna and then to Goa. In 2007 and 2008, Father Joseph reinstates the peace procession and annual pilgrimage to Rigaud, even though the Our Lady of Madhu statue cannot return to her spiritual homeland in Madhu, under siege.[20]

The timing of the Marian processions held in Madhu and Rigaud during these few years reflects the impact that civil war has on the volatile relationship between homeland and host society. Initially, Rigaud's pilgrimage was modest in size compared to Madhu's pilgrimage, occurring first and preparing the way for the triumphant return of the statue of the Virgin Mary to her Sri Lankan homeland, where her miraculous powers were originally transubstantiated to the soil. During the resurgence of war, Rigaud became one of several alternative homelands for the itinerant statue. Sacred geographies enacted through resemblances, including the likeness of the soil of the Marian shrine in Rigaud to the one in Madhu, the similar origin stories of the foundation of the shrines, and the shared peace missions of pilgrims visiting both shrines at around the same time, allowed for the statue to temporarily sojourn in Rigaud and sanctify the growing material and spiritual presence of Eelam, the ancient Sri Lankan Tamil homeland, on Canadian soil.

After Prime Minister Stephen Harper banned the LTTE and World Tamil Movement (WTM) in Canada, Sri Lankan Tamil memorials had to be less explicit in promoting their agenda for a sovereign Eelam. On July 25, 2006 at a public square in Parc-Ex, several hundred Sri Lankans commemorated the victims of the anti-Tamil pogrom in Colombo on July 23, 1983, known as "Black July," and simultaneously protested the prime minister's policy. Similar protests had been planned in Europe and Australia (Tamilnet 2007; Whiteman n.d.). Using visuals and allegory to dramatically re-enact the pogrom experience, showcase gruesome pictures of mutilated bodies, and criticize Canada's foreign policy, this memorial presented a causal chain of acts of violence and discrimination, starting with Colombo's pogrom in the 1980s, followed by Jaffna's civil war in the 1990s, Batticaloa's military assault in the 2000s, and Canada's censorship of the LTTE in 2006 (see Figures 6.4a–6.4c). No mere coincidences, these events constituted a unitary narrative of many acts of injustice against the Tamil people.

Father Joseph also does not believe in coincidences. A few months after the Marian procession, he invites me, along with his altar boy, Arun, on a "faith-sharing" mission to Ottawa to assist at a mass with another Sri Lankan Tamil priest soliciting money for tsunami victims. We plan to drive onward to

FIGURE 6.4a Drama reenacting the Colombo pogrom on Black July 2006.

FIGURE 6.4b Images of massacred women and children on Black July 2006.

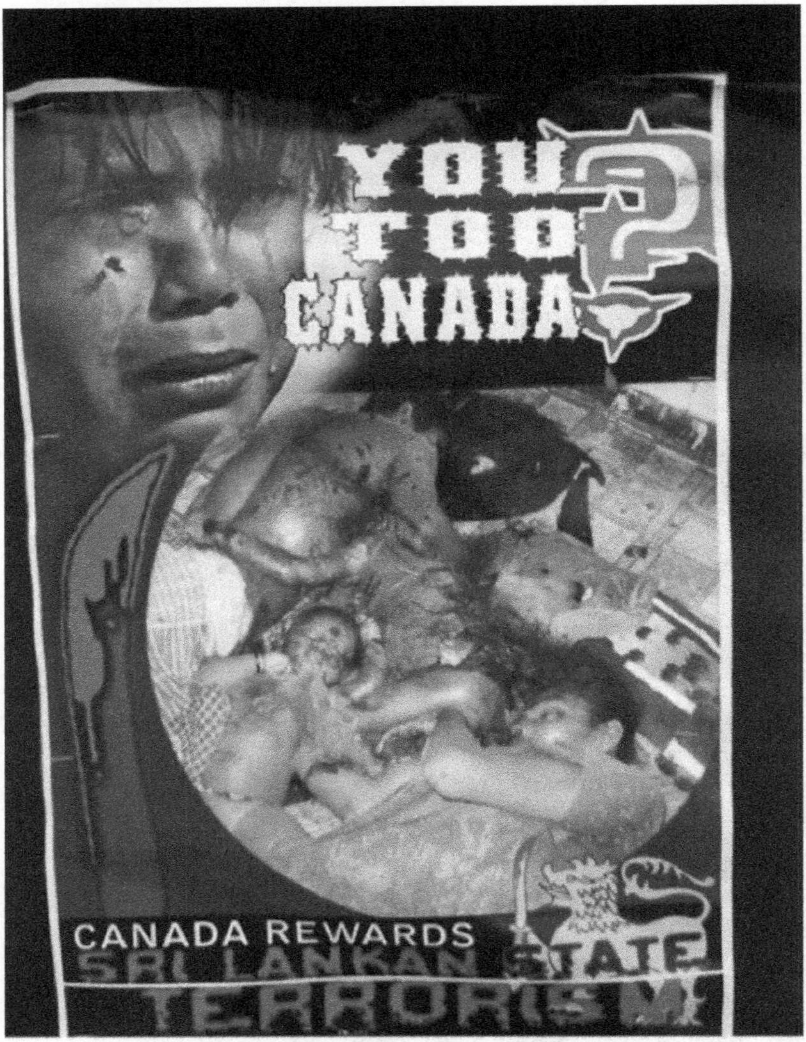

FIGURE 6.4c Poster critiquing Canadian foreign policy on Black July 2006.

Toronto to preside at a baptism and visit Father Joseph's older sister who lives there. During the car ride to Toronto, Father Joseph asks me to share my "faith story." Not knowing the genre, I explain that I was born in Montréal in 1977 to a French Canadian mother, who is Catholic, and an Indian father, who is Hindu, although I was raised agnostic. When my mother became ill with leukemia when I was twelve years old, she asked me to embrace God. To fulfill her wish now that I am back in her homeland, I decided to learn the catechism from Father Joseph.

Sensing my nervousness, Father Joseph assures me that this is a good story and falls silent. After a few minutes, he shares with me his own account of joining the priesthood. Although I did not record what he said, I jotted down the story in my notebook later that night and paraphrase it here below.

> When I was six years old, my mother was pregnant with child. I very much wanted to have a little sister and I wagered with all of my relatives that the child would be a girl. On the day of her birth, all of my relatives assembled at the hospital to wait. I was overjoyed to hear that I had a little sister. Her name was Ananthi. I collected money from the wager and bought a gold chain for her with it. I didn't know it at the time, but my father was sick with blood cancer. Three years later when I was nine years old and my sister was three, my father died of cancer. My four brothers and sisters and I were gathered around his deathbed when my father requested that one of his sons become a priest.
>
> The parish priest of my village, which is near the town of Palali in northern Jaffna, was an old French missionary. He often asked the local boys to help him with mass. One day when the priest did not arrive to the church in time for mass, everyone sent me to go out and look for him. I found the priest fallen off his bicycle. I helped him get up and brought him back to our church. As we were walking the priest said to me, "I am looking for a young boy to become a priest and follow in my footsteps. We need native priests to serve the people here." Most priests in Jaffna at the time were European missionaries.
>
> Both the priest and my father's requests stayed with me until, when I was twelve, I joined the seminary. Though the seminary was within walking distance of my home, I lived at the seminary hostel. I missed my little sister very much. I didn't realize that she had become sick until one day, in 1977 when I was fifteen years old, they came to my hostel to tell me that Ananthi had also died of blood cancer. She was only nine years old.

It is a somber and chilling story, and I cannot help but notice similarities in our experiences. Both of us have close relatives afflicted with leukemia; both of us had formative childhood encounters with French Catholics. After the baptism that day, Father Joseph takes Arun and me to visit his sister's home in Mississauga where we spend the night and I am asked to share my faith story once again. I think nothing more of it until we return to Montréal the next day and drop off Arun with his parents. Father Joseph then confesses that he invited me to travel with him to Toronto because he wanted his eldest sister to see my face. Apparently, I bear a striking resemblance to their little sister, Ananthi, who passed away the same year that I was born. I learn that the events of my life mysteriously fill in the missing pieces of his biographical timeline, and Father Joseph is more convinced than ever of his destiny to migrate from Sri Lanka to Québec.

I am stunned by this admission and do not respond. As a Catholic, certainly Father Joseph does not believe that I am the reincarnation of his little sister? I recall how Father Joseph once told me that when he became the parish priest of Mullaitivu in the late 1990s, he toured the town church to exorcise the ghosts of soldiers whose corpses once littered the grounds. Perhaps he believes that the ghost of his sister lives on through me? This transcendental possibility reminds me of Ho's assertion that pilgrimage gives moral meaning to movement, and Bakhtin's argument that narrative devices can reconfigure time and space to construct new realities. For Father Joseph, Tamils and the French have always been spiritually and politically connected. Perhaps our meeting is just another reminder of how Tamil global imaginaries can and are being nourished on Québec soil.

Global Modernities

The ethnographic and archival study of Tamil mobility and immobility aims to expose the dialectic relationship of elite and non-elite global modernities, defined here as language ideological projects in which speakers and writers objectify dimensions of time and space through the use of scalar metaphors. What this chapter has specifically demonstrated by way of ethnographic vignettes and narrative analyses is how, based on the chronotopic depiction of Tamilagam and Tamil Eelam as two different (though sometimes overlapping) homelands with dimensions that are not easily plotted onto Cartesian space and linear time, pilgrimage and travel conjuring up images of ancient landmasses and global terrains are accounts of linguistic rivalries writ large. Indian and Sri Lankan nationalists share pride in demonstrating that Tamil-speaking civilizations not only preceded most other ancient civilizations, like the Greeks and Romans—hence their primordialism—but also surpassed them in geographic scale—hence their cosmopolitanism. Narratives of the self-proclaimed hypermobile and upwardly mobile Indian elites celebrating their regional linguistic diversity, and rituals venerating the religious icons and priests of Sri Lankans who value linguistic purity, therefore attest to a collective vision of "primordial cosmopolitanism" informed by a language ideology of Tamil diglossia. In Montréal, where the politics of Anglo-Franco conflicts and Tamil migration have given rise to the belief that Indians speak a colloquial variety of Tamil and Sri Lankans speak a literary variety of Tamil as their respective heritage languages, stories and dramas about linguistic rivalries can also grow to assume the scale of civilizations.

7 CONCLUSION

Inviting readers to contemplate the politicization of ethnic, racial, linguistic, and national identifications from a comparative and historical perspective, this book has demonstrated that imperial and national rivalries only make sense in the *longue durée* and within a transnational context. A common thread running through the analysis of ethnographic and archival evidence presented in this book is that anglophone and francophone conflicts in South Asia and North America have motivated other linguistic rivalries, in this case, between and among Indian and Sri Lankan Tamil migrants residing in Montréal and elsewhere in the diaspora. What makes the city of Montréal such a compelling place to study these social and political processes is that its inhabitants do not take for granted the ontological reality of French, English, and Tamil as standard languages, and, therefore, are more attuned to their aesthetic dimensions, pragmatic functions, and creative capacities for social reproduction and transformation. For example, Tamil speakers in Montréal, who quibble over the significance of minor degrees of phonological and grammatical difference between "colloquial" and "literary" Tamil, are also making ideological claims about these languages' durability and the directionality of their own ethnolinguistic identification practices in ways that reflect upon or change social and geographic mobilities.

The unexpected and little-noticed effects of Anglo-Franco conflicts on Tamil migrants and the spoken and written languages with which they identify can be bifocally examined by looking at activities at the peripheries of empires. In early nineteenth-century colonial South India, despite the British having reduced the French to tiny pockets near the posts of Pondicherry and Karikal, French sponsorship of Tamil scholarship still surpassed that of the British. French Catholic missionaries, much like their Portuguese and Italian Jesuit predecessors, worked closely with high-caste Tamil pandits studying classical texts, writing poems, and analyzing the language's grammar. To catch up, British officials in Madras raided Pondicherry for the best

Tamil teachers, types, and printing presses. Much like elsewhere in the colonial world in the early- to mid-nineteenth century, French and British officials then continued to compete with one another in printing new dictionaries, grammars, and Bibles that promised them greater facility in learning native languages, authority in governance, and clout in evangelization.

What specifically resulted from this nineteenth-century feud between British and French printers of Tamil books was the merger of precolonial Indian language ideologies about the beauty, purity, and antiquity of different Tamil varieties, and colonial European language ideologies about the functional and grammatical differences between High and Low, and Classical and Modern Tamil. When nationalist leaders finally exercised their license to publish Tamil books and periodicals condemning the missionary and colonial administrative practices of Europeans in the mid-nineteenth century, they nonetheless endorsed these language ideologies, reworked as the concept of linguistic diglossia, by positing that Spoken Tamil and Written Tamil are grammatically distinct registers of a single language that also has a proud classical tradition. Even at the turn of the century, Tamil nationalist leaders from India and Sri Lanka agreed that colloquial or Spoken Tamil was the more modern and impure register, and literary or Written Tamil was the older and purer one, even if they disagreed on exactly which standardization strategies were needed to render both of these languages worthy of soon-to-be sovereign nations.

Different political climates lessening linguistic rivalries in one country yet exacerbating them in another eventually led elite Tamil Brahmin emigrants from India and non-elite Jaffna Tamil emigrants from Sri Lanka, hitherto little known to one another, to meet in the diaspora. There they came to regard Indian Tamils as embodying the modernizing virtues of a hybridizing colloquial language, which itself is emblematic of the globalist vision of Tamilagam as a cosmopolitan cultural realm. The purist virtues and classical provenance of literary Tamil, reinforcing the primordialist vision of Tamil Eelam, instead personified Sri Lankan Tamils searching for a safe and secure homeland.

Yet in Montréal something unusual happened. Rather than focusing on obvious differences in national, religious, caste, and class status to justify their self-segregation and alternative prospects for social mobility, Indian and Sri Lankan Tamil leaders have instead developed (or at least appear to have developed) a new type of rivalry. Since Anglo-Franco conflicts in Canada have naturalized the idea that all people belong to distinct ethnolinguistic communities, Indian and Sri Lankan Tamil leaders have invested in one of two grammatically distinct codes, Spoken Tamil and Written Tamil, and claimed these as their respective heritage languages to differentiate themselves ethnonationally. This linguistic rivalry encompasses all of the schools, businesses, and religious institutions that use either colloquial or literary varieties of Tamil, each with their own orthographies and scripts, to convey both overt and covert messages about political allegiances and gain respectability, profit, and fame for neighborhoods seen as up-and-coming ūrs. A shared belief in the unparalleled glory of primordial Tamil homelands nonetheless transcends these modern-day quarrels to highlight an older rivalry among cosmopolitan civilizations.

Speakers who are compelled to visually and aurally discern phonological and grammatical markers of linguistic variation in discrete or not-so-discrete terms, therefore, participate in the discursive and ideological reproduction of different global modernities. First-generation Indians and Sri Lankans, who display lesser competence in French and English than in Tamil, adopt narratives of global modernity that address the uncertainties of war and displacement and enable them to contemplate how to achieve material prosperity and spiritual enlightenment for themselves and their kin. More English- and French-savvy Canadian-raised or born second-generation Tamil Canadians, who have variable expertise in speaking and writing in Tamil, draw on their multilingual repertoires to instead grapple with problems of racism and limited resources for mobility. Despite the prevailing attitudes of language purism adopted by nationalist leaders in Québécois and Tamil societies, a lot of code-switching and code-mixing occurs in Montréal, though circumscribed in style and form. Tamil and French may be mixed with English to increase the former languages' prestige, but rarely are the former languages mixed together (except by Sri Lankan children attending schools in French), because to do so invites the contempt of community leaders and government officials invested in maintaining the idea of separate Indian and Sri Lankan Tamil, and anglophone and francophone worlds.

To live in Montréal is thus to be confronted with the obligation to profess one's language loyalties in mutually exclusive terms, even though more and more residents of different age cohorts, ethnicities, and political leanings are opting not to align themselves with rigid identity categories altogether. I began and ended this book with vignettes of my road trip from Montréal to Ottawa and Toronto with Arun and Father Joseph to highlight the creative and unexpected ways of reconciling these sociolinguistic and metaphysical discontinuities by constructing unusual bridges between worlds. Through the writing process, I was often reminded of how ethnographers require more than just an attentive eye and empathetic ear; they must be willing to experience the discomfort of being included or Othered by other people's narratives. Arun told me during the trip to Ontario that the church elders, his parents included, were puzzled by my presence and referred to me as the "Filipina woman" to make sense of my complexion and interest in the church. Though I am not Tamil, as a multilingual person of South Asian and Québécois ancestry born in Montréal yet raised as an American, I have been open about the personal nature of this project to my informants and my readers, hoping that the stories featured in this book will resonate widely among different minority communities in Montréal and across other urban, multilingual contexts. Perhaps I, like Father Joseph, chose to fill in the gaps of this ethnographic account primarily about Tamil migrants with personal recollections of my life in Québec to rethink the scales of our global belonging.

Finally, I wrote this book to model a comparative methodology in linguistic anthropology useful for understanding complex sociohistorical phenomena. Based on semiotic perspectives about the processual nature of language and communication, this methodology approaches the archival and ethnographic analyses of linguistic evidence as indispensable and complementary counterpoints to one another. By acknowledging that diasporas, nations, and empires are interdiscursively constituted and, therefore, cannot be studied as autonomous or noncontemporaneous polities, exploring their converging and diverging histories helps to illuminate the role of language in society and politics. Also, I have shown how the ideological construction and contestation of different hierarchical scales evaluating sociolinguistic phenomena, ranging from measures of the purity and prestige of languages to the fame or respectability of heritage language institutions, depends on how the material relationship between social and linguistic signs is felt, inferred, and rationalized. Although the semiotic mechanisms of ethnolinguistic differentiation analyzed here are specific to the experiences of Tamil migrants navigating the aftermath of colonial and post-colonial Anglo-Franco conflicts, the more global themes of exclusion elucidated by this book also point to investigative problems that could benefit from closer collaboration between policymakers and scholars of language, migration, ethnicity, and globalization. I conclude by mentioning one such possibility.

Since December 6, 2011 in Québec, applicants for permanent resident status in the Regular Skilled Worker category must pass an official language examination of oral and written comprehension and production in French (to receive sixteen maximum points) and English (to receive six maximum points) (Immigration, Diversité et Inclusion Québec n.d.). This policy follows in the wake of a Canadian law that has been in effect since June 26, 2010 and requires proof of language competence in *either* English or French. Although language tests for naturalization are not uncommon throughout the world, this latest derivative is a relative novelty. The first country to require immigrants to pass the TESOL was the United Kingdom in 2007. Not to be outdone, other English-speaking Commonwealth countries, including Canada, Australia, and New Zealand, implemented similar policies in subsequent years. Only a handful of non-English-speaking countries, such as the Czech Republic, Germany, and Thailand, test immigrants in basic conversational proficiency, but never in reading comprehension or writing.

Québec is the first francophone society to implement a language test for immigrants, and, apparently, it is not an easy test. For now, refugees and unskilled workers have been spared these stringent immigration requirements. What will be the consequences of this latest rivalry between anglophone and francophone nations over the language loyalties of migrants? In Montréal, what will happen to the social relations between elite immigrants, such as Indian Tamils, who would be required to master French and English at a higher level than non-elite refugees, such as Sri Lankan Tamils? Will public support for heritage language education programs still ensure the political loyalty of minority leaders? Since each policy change brings along with it multiple and conflicting language ideologies, both policymakers and scholars are needed to explore the ramifications of this linguistic rivalry for the livelihoods of Tamils and other migrants.

APPENDIX

DEEPAVALI DRAMA

PART 1

SITA: ennā, aṅka enna kālaṅkāttāla paṇṇiṭṭirukkēḷ?

RAMA: kālaṅkāttāla ellārum enna paṇṇuvāḷō atattān nānum paṇṇinṭirukkēn.

SITA: appaṭinnā?

RAMA: iṇṭarneṭṭilē imeyil chek paṅṅinṭirukkēmmā

SITA: yārukiṭṭēruṉtu vaṉtirukku. lavakucāttēruṉtā? enna colṛāḷām en māṭṭup poṇṇū?

RAMA: metuvātān kuṭukkaṛatu. ellārum caukkiyam. tamiḻkkavi kaṇṇatācan conna mātiri yārum irukkumiṭattil iruṉtu vaṉtāl ellām caukkiyamē.

SITA: enna. ētō kuttikkāṭṭaṛamātiriyirukku

RAMA: unakkennā? kalyāṇam āna uṭanē jāliyā kāṭṭukku vaṉtiṭṭē. oṇṇukku mōṇu māmiyār iruṉtum māmiyār koṭumaiyē illai.

SITA: nānā varēnnu connēn? patinālu varusham uṅkappā kāṭṭukku pōnnuṭṭār. nīṅka taniya kashtappaṭap pōṛēḷē. cāppāṭṭukku veṇum ilaiyum taḻaiyum cāppiṭṭu kashtappaṭap pōṛēḷēnnu kūṭa vaṉtēn.

RAMA: patinālu varusham. haiyā jālinnu kiḷampinen. nā varēn. nā varēnnu nīyē vaṉtuṭṭa. cummā iruṉtiyō. aṅka vaṉtu iṉtakshaṇam aṉta mān vēṇumnu aṭam piṭicca. mānaik koṇṭu vaṉtā-tān ennai nimmatiyā irukka viṭuvēnnu nān aṉta mānukku pinnālēyē pōnēn. appa aṉta mārīkshan paṇṇa koḷaṛupaṭiyilē nī lakshmaṇanai pāttu aṉtat tiṭṭu tiṭṭinē. avanum miraṉtu pōy viḻuṉtaṭicciṭṭu vaṉtuṭṭān. cummā irukka vēṅṭiyatutānē. ippaṭiyē acaṭu mātiri veḷila vaṉtē. tūkkinu pōyiṭṭān rāvaṇan. cari nān paṭaṛa kashtam avan paṭa vēṇṭāmēnnu colli viṭṭuṭaccolla connēn. avan ennamō nān avanōṭa caṇṭaikku varēnnu nenacciṭṭu ennōṭa yuttam pōṭṭu avan kulattukkē camāti kaṭṭiṭṭān. pāvām.

SITA: enna pāvam vēṇṭik kiṭakku? cummātān kēkkaṛēn. enna pāvam vēṇṭi kiṭakku? ellārum irukkum iṭattil iruṉtu vaṉtāl ellōrukkum caukkiyamnu ārampiccu muḻu rāmāyaṇattaiyē colli muṭiccuttēḷ. innikku uṅkaḷukku part dēvā irukku. ēthāvatu speshalā paṇṇalāmnu iruṉtēn.

RAMA: bēsh. enna menu?

SITA: muruṅkaik kāy cāmpār.

RAMA: āhā?

SITA: kattarikkāy poṭitta kaṟi.

RAMA: cūppar.

SITA: miḷaku rācam.

RAMA: balē, balē, balē.

SITA: vaṭai.

RAMA: bēsh, bēsh.

SITA: pāyacam.

RAMA: āhā.

SITA: itellām paṇṇalāmnu iruṉten. Ittanaiyum kēkkaṟappa ellām kaṭṭu.

RAMA: vaṭai pōccu, pāyācam poccu. ethaiyō collappōy. en nākkula cani.

PART 2

SITA: cari. iṇṭarnetlē vēṟenna pāttiṭṭiruṉtēḷ?

RAMA: atoṇṇumillēmmā, hiṉtu ṭempiḷs ṭāṭ kāmnu oru vepcaiṭ. atala pōy pāttā. enakkunnu pūlōkattilē taniyā kōyilē illai. krish, venkaṭ ivāḷukkellām ēkappaṭa kōyil. atu ēnnu teriyaliyē.

SITA: ēn kampiḷeyinṭ panṟēḷ? eṅkaḷukku maṭṭum neṟaya kōyil irukkā enna. tamiḻnāṭṭilē kushpōnnu yārōvām! avaḷukkum kūda kōvil kaṭṭināṅkaḷāmē! appaṟam ētō pākkiyam aṉtak kōvilai iṭiccuṭṭāṅkaḷām.

RAMA: oṇṇu kavanicciyō? eṅkē kōvil kaṭṭinālum nāma ellāraiyum vaccitān kaṭṭaṟōm. yāraiyum viṭaṟatillē. yārō vairamuttuvām. avar kātalanṟa paṭattilē. ūrvaci, ūrvaci. ṭēk iṭ īsinnu oru pāṭṭu. atila enna colliyirukkārnā? pūnaiyil caivam kiṭaiyātu, āṅkaḷil rāmar kiṭaiyātu. kaṇṇaki cilaitān iṅkuṇṭu. cītaikku taniyā cilaitān ētu?

SITA: evvaḷavu tairiyam aṉta vairamuttuvukku? iṉtak kālattilē varṟa pāṭṭellām kēkkavē cakikkalē. atukku vairamuttu pāṭṭu evvaḷavō tēvalai. ānā, nīṅka connata yōciccu pāttā namakku ēn avvaḷavā taniya kōyil illē.

RAMA: itukku rīcan kaṇṭupiṭikkaṇumnā. pesṭṭu nāratar tān. iru un cel-fōnla avaraik kūppiṭuṟēn.

SITA: ēn? uṅka cel-fōn ennāccu?

RAMA: atu paḻaiya mādalmā. itānē lēṭṭasṭ mādal. pilla nīyilla kaṭṭaṇum.

SITA: cīkkiṟam pēciṭṭu vaiyuṅkōnnā. enta lōkattilē irukkārō avar? rōmiṅk cārjas-lām payaṅkaramā irukku.

RAMA: halo nāratarā? ippa eṅka āttukku vaṉtuṭṭup pōṟēḷā?

NARADA: nārayāṇā nārayāṇā.

RAMA: enna nāratarē. talailē kuṭumi, kaiyila tampurā etaiyum kāṇōm?

NARADA: reṇṭu mācattukku munnāṭi iṉta māṇṭiril vaḻiyā cañcāricciṭṭiruṉtēn. aṅkē jās festival naṭaṉtuṭṭiruṉtatu. avan frīyā, cīppā giṭṭar vittiṭṭiruntān. ettana nāḷakki tan iṉta tampurāvaiyē māṭṭiṇṭu irukkaṟatunnu colliṭṭu tūra eṟiñciṭṭu kiṭṭār vāṅki māṭṭiṇṭuṭṭēn. appaṟam pūlōkattilē kirīn havus efakt guḷōpal vārmiṅknu colliṭṭu orē cūdā vērttuk koṭṭaṛatā? carinnu hērkaṭṭaiyum paṇṇiṇṭuṭṭēn. atukkappaṛam iṉta toppiya vāṅki māṭṭiṇṭuṭṭēn. ippallām lēṭṭā vaṉtālum lēṭṭasṭṭā varaṇumēnnu colliṭṭu iṉta līvais jīncu, rībōk shūvellām vāṅki māṭṭiṇṭuṭṭēn. eppaṭi?

RAMA: bēsh bēsh rompa nallāṛukku.

PART 3

NARADA: āmā. ennai rombpa avacaramā kūppiṭṭēḷē. colla maṛaṉtuṭṭēn. meni-mōr hāppi riṭarns āf ti ṭē. piṛaṉta nāL vāḻttukkaḷ.

RAMA: rompattāṅks. uṅkaḷa etukku iṅkē varacconnēnnā. enakkum cītaikkum oru payaṅkara davuṭ. ēn eṅkaḷukku pūlōkattilē avvaḷavā taniyā kōyil illē. kirish veṅkaṭṭukkellām ēkappaṭṭa kōyil irukkē atu ēn?

NARADA: itu oru nalla kēḷvi. itukku kāraṇam kaṇṭupidikkaRēn. nāratar kalakattukku, vēlai vaṉtāccu. ayōttiyāla irukkara piraccanaikku oru colyūshan ivar mūlamā vara vaikkiṛēn. uṅkaḷukku iṉtiyāla oru kōyil kaṭṭiṇṭu irukkāḷē. atap patti teriyumō?

SITA: colluṅka. eṅkaḷukku kaṭṭiṭirukkaṛa aṉtak kōvila pōy pākkaṇumnu rompa ācaiyā irukku.

NARADA: appaṭiya? uṅkaḷukku nīṅka poṛanta iṭam ñāpakam irukkō?

RAMA: rompa nāḷ āccā. maṛaṉtu pōccu.

SITA: itē rēṭla pōnāl innum koñca nāḷ ānāl ennaiyē yārunnu kēppēḷ. ayōttiya. nnā. aṛaṉtuṭṭēḷā?

RAMA: illɛ illɛ. enakku ñāpakam irukku. unakku teriyutānnu ṭesṭ paṇṇēn. avvaḷavutān.

NARADA: nān vaṉta vēlai muṭiñcutu

RAMA: nāratarē nīṅka colṛatap pāttā oru kalakatta uṇṭākkinatu pōlat teriyatā?

NARADA: ayyō appaṭiyellām oṇṇumilla. uṅkakiṭṭa nān kalakam paṇṇa muṭiyumā? appaṭiyē nāratar kalakam nanmaiyiltān muṭiyumnu uṅkaḷukkut teriyātā?

PART 4

SITA: ēnnā enna iṭam itu eṅka vaṉtirukkōm nāma?

RAMA: ayōtyava ṭārkeṭṭā vaccukiṭṭu varṛataviṭa nāma nālu iṭam cutti pākkalāmnu piḷān pōṭṭu vaccurukkēn.

SITA: eṅkeṅkē pōlāmnu aidiyā?

RAMA: mutalla ilaṅkai, atukkappaṛam tamiḻnāṭu, atukkappaṛam tāmmā ayōtyā.

SITA: ilaṅkaiyā, ēnnā ennai iṅkē aḻaicciṭṭu vaṉtēḷ? iṉta iṭattaip pāttālē enakku payamā irukkunnā. paḻaiya ṅapakam ellām varutu.

RAMA: appō nī taniyā iruṉtē. ippōtān nān unkūṭa irukkēnla. ēn payappaṭaṛē?

SITA: yāraippāttālum enakku rāvaṇan mātiri teriyaṛannā.

RAMA: oru taṭava paṇṇina tappai innoru muṛai ceyya māṭṭaṅka. appa unna tūkkinu vaṉtuṭṭu, ēṇṭā kaṭattiṭṭu vaṉtōmnu ippakkūṭafil paṉrānnā pāttukkayēn. unna viṭaccolli anumāra tūtanuppiccēn. avar avarōṭa vāllē tīya vaccār. cummā iruṉtārō avar. vīṭu vīṭā pōy aṉtattIya spireṭ paṇṇiṭṭār. ēn tīya spreṭ paṇṇārnu nān vicāraṇai kamishan veccā, atukku innikkukūṭa innum ripōrṭ capmiṭ paṅṅalayām. atukkutān connēn.

SITA: pōtum kēli. aṅke oruttan varān. avaṅkiṭṭa iṉta ashōka vanam eṅka irukkunnu kēḷungō. ennai rompa nāḷ kaitu paṇṇi vacciruṉta iṭamnā. pōy pākkaṅumnu ācaiyā irukku.

SITA: aiyō rāvaṇan.

RAMA: payappaṭātē. avanukku pattu talai ivanukku ivanukku añcu talaitānē irukku. vaṇakkam.

CRICKET FAN: vaṇakkam. uṅkaḷukku enna vēṇum.

RAMA: ingē acōka vanattukku eppaṭi pōkaṇumnu teriyumā?

CRICKET FAN: enna kataikkiṟIr. viḷangavē illē.

RAMA: acōka vanmappā. rāvaṇanōṭa gārṭan. acōka vanam teriyatā?

CRICKET FAN: yār rāvaṇan. umakkenna vicanai? rāvaṇan enakku teriyātu. enakku teriñcatellām aṭṭappaṭṭu, muraḷitaran. jeyacūryā.

SITA: ivāḷllām yāru?

RAMA: kirikkeṭṭars pōla irukku. iru.

CRICKET FAN: cari eṅkēruṉtu vāriṅka.

RAMA: nāngaḷ thēvalōkattilērṉtu varṟōm.

CRICKET FAN: atu eṅke irukku? koḻumpu pakkatlayā. illa jāfnākku pakkatlayā?

RAMA: eppaṭi colli puriya vakkaṟatunnē teriyalai

CRICKET FAN: cari cari acōka vanam eppaṭiyirukkum?

SITA: neṟaya marangaḷ neṟaya manushā.

CRICKET FAN: ā nīṅka kataikkaṟata pāttā atu pirēmatācā sṭēṭiyamāttān irukkum.

CRICKET FAN: nān aṅkatān pōṟan. nīṅkaḷum vāṅkō. iṉtiyālērntu āṭṭakkāraṅka vaṉtirukkāṅka. vāṅka pōy pākkalam.

RAMA: nāṅkaḷum varṟōm.

RAMA: nāṅka conna iṭam itu illēppā. pāru cītā. nī tēṭi vaṉta acōka vanam ētō kirikkeṭ sṭēṭiyamā māriṭuttu.

CRICKET FAN: ō nīṅkaḷ tēṭi vaṉta iṭam itu illaiyā? mannikka vēṇum. enakku uṭanaṭiyā pākkavēṇum. cari inime nān uṅkaḷōṭa vara ēlātu.

RAMA: paravāllai. āmā mēṭclē skōr ennāccunnu teriyumā? appiṭiyē iṉta varusham vōrlṭ kap yār vin paṇṇuvā?

CRICKET FAN: kaṇṭippā ilaṅkai tān jeyikkum.

RAMA: enakkennavō iṅkilāṉtutān jeyikkumnu nenakkiṟen.

SITA: ēnnā. ungaḷukku āṭṭam teriyumā?

RAMA: oṇṇumillēmmā. kirikkeṭ pōrṭ ṭāṭ kām nu oru vep cait. atilē pōy kattuṭṭēn. namma yukattilellām kuttu caṇṭai, killi kōli iṉta viḷaiyāṭṭutānē iruntatu.

RAMA: killi kōli ippavūm viḷaiyāṭuṟam. ātuvamā?

RAMA: illēṅka. eṅkaḷukku neṟaya vēlai irukku. nāṅka keḷampaṟōm.

PART 5

RAMA: cītā unnai mītkarṟatukku munnāṭi iṅkētān taṅkiyiruṉṭōm. unnai mītka neṟayā tiṭṭam pōttōm. itānmā rāmēsvaram.

SITA: ō. ennanā paṅṅiṅṭirukkēḷ?

RAMA: illamā. iṅkē civanukku oru kōvil kaṭṭinōm. atukku rūt pāttiṭṭirukkēn.

LOCAL: innādā carakku itu. aṭiccā kikkē ēṟa māṭṭēṅkutu. pākkeṭ cārāyamnu iṭṭāṉṭāṅga. kikkē ēṟa māttēṅkutu. iṅkē pāṟṟā. pañcakaccamum aṅke oru maṭicār māmiyum cōkkā nikkiṟāṅka. namma anniyan paṭam catā mātiryillē. uṭṭu kalāykkalāmā.

LOCAL: cummatānē pāṭinu pōṟōmpā.nāṅka yār teriyumā. ippa kaṇṭukkabā. nī vaṉtu iṉta rāmar vēshattaik kaṭṭaṟa teluṅku em ji yār en ṭi rāmarāvtānē? ānā avar ṭikkaṭ vāṅki rompa nāḷ āccē?

SITA: cariya kaṇṭupiṭicciṭṭānnu nenaccēn. koḻappaṟāne.

RAMA: illappā. nān tān orijinal rāmar. ivaṅka cītāp pirāṭṭiyār.

LOCAL: enakku teriñcatellām kuttup parāṭṭōvum cālnāvumtān. atēnnatu pirāṭṭiyāru.

SITA: ivanukku. muḻu pēr inṭrōṭakshan vēṇumō.

LOCAL: cari nī rāmarnu colṟa. yāru iṉta mūlikaip peṭrōlunu colli ūra ēmāttinānē rāmar piḷḷai. aṉta ṭubākkūrā. ṭēy ṭubākkūrā. ṭēy.

RAMA: ivan kiṭṭē enna pēccu? iṅkeye iruṉtu iṉta cētu kaṭṭinōmmā. ippa kāṇumē. eṅkētānnu teriyaliyē atu.

LOCAL: innānga kaṭalaiyē pāttuṭṭirukkīṅka. cunāmi varappōkuta?

RAMA: cunāmiyā? appaṭinnā?

LOCAL: kaṭal koṉtaḷippupa. taṇṇi appaṭiyē uḷḷē vaṉtu ellāttaiyum appaṭiyē nācam paṇṇiṭucci.

RAMA: illappā. iṅkēruṉtu ilaṅkaikku oru cettu kaṭṭinēn. ataitān nān tēṭiṅṭirukkēn.

LOCAL: innātu cettuvai nīṅka kaṭnīṅkaḷā? cettu namma cīyan vikram naṭicca paṭamṅka. atu epiṭiṅka ivar kaṭṭa muṭiyum? oru vēḷai aṉtap paṭa ṭairakṭarā iruppārō? Cār enakku naṭikka cāns kuṭuṅkaḷēn.

RAMA: ivanukku cettuvellām puriyātu. uṅka pāshaiyila piriṭjuppā.

LOCAL: appaṭi teḷivā collu. piriṭju vaṉtu rompa kālattukku munnāṭi. rāmarnu oruttaru, vānaraṅkaḷa vacci kaṭnatā eṅka tāttā kata colluvāruppā.

RAMA: aṉta rāmarē nāṉtānpā.

LOCAL: enaiya enna kēṇainnu nenacciyā? avuru cāmi. nī ācāmiya alla irukkē.

RAMA: illappā nāntān atu.

LOCAL: teḷivā koḻapparānē. oru vēḷa anniyan paṭattilē varṟa malṭṭi percanāliṭi dicārṭarā irukkumō. irukkum. apṭinnu colli tiṭṭaṟatukkuḷe nān ōṭiṭaṟēnpā.

PART 6

SITA: eṅkē pāttālum orē kuppaiyum kūḷamumāttān irukku. enna ūrnā itu? Eṅkē vaṉtirukkōm nāmpa? rāma rājyam oru pench mārknu colluvā? iṅkē āṭtci paṇṟavāllām uṅkakiṭṭa ṭireyniṅk eṭuttukkaṇum pōla irukku.

RAMA: appā. nalla vēḷai ippavāvatu ottuṅṭayē.

SITA: uṅkaḷukku teriyumā. iṅka yār rājānnu.

RAMA: rājā illammā. rāṇi. yārek kēṭṭālum ammā ammā nu colli reṅṭu taṭava āṭṭiṭṭu pōṛān. ānā iṅke irukkaṛa nelamayap pāttā ammā tan koḻaṉtaya cariyā kavaniccukkalēnnu nenakkiṛen.

SITA: orē veyyilā irukkunnā. appaṭiyē eṅkayāvatu taṇṇi keṭaikkaṛatānnu pāruṅka.

RAMA: irummā pāttuṭṭu varēn.

TEA VENDOR: cāyā. cāyā. cāyā. kūpṭṭīṅkaḷā.

RAMA: eṅkaḷukku kuṭikka taṇṇi iruṉtā koṭuṅka.

TEA VENDOR: enna uḷḷa iruṉtīṅkaḷā?

RAMA: appaṭinnā?

TEA VENDOR: ille jeyilla iruṉtīṅkaḷānnu kēṭṭēn.

RAMA: illiyē. ēn kēkkaṛē?

TEA VENDOR: pinne cen ṭrallē vaṉtu taṇṇi kēṭṭā enna arttam? iṅke taṇṇiyap pāttu pala varushaṅkaḷāccu. vēṇumnā cuṭu taṇṇi taṛen.

RAMA: taṇṇiyē illēṅkaṛe. ateppaṭi cuṭā taramuṭiyum.

TEA VENDOR: atutān cāyāṅkaṛatu. atukkum cuṭu taṇṇikkum periya vittiyācam oṇṇumillē. tī cuṭu taṇṇi mātiri iruṉtālum mikavum nallatu. atappattiyē kavitaiye eḻutiyirukkiṛēn. atap patti oru kavitayē eḻutiyirukkēn. kēḷuṅka. *(pāṭukiṛar)*

RAMA: iṉte ṭī-kku iṉta pilṭ-ap tēvaiyā? unnōṭa ṭī evvaḷvō tēvalai.

SITA: ippavāvatu ottuṇṭēḷē.

RAMA: aiyā. nāṅka pāṭaṛa pāṭṭu uṅka ṭīya viṭa nāllā iruṉtatu. nallā. cūpparū pādaṛēḷe atu eppaṭi?

TEA VENDOR: nān oru riṭayarṭu tamiḻ paṇṭitar. tamiḻ ṭiyūshan eṭuttu cambātikkaṛataviṭa ṭī vittu cambātikkaṛatu atikam. atanālē. kālattai vīṇākkāma ṭī vikka vaṉturukkēn. āmā iṉta matarās veyyillē pañcakaccamum maṭicārumā nīṅka yāru? veḷiyūrō.

RAMA: ille nāṅka tēvalokattilēṉtu vaṛōm.

TEA VENDOR: enna aṉta rampai ūrvaci ṭaans āṭuvāṅkaḷē aṅkērntā?

RAMA: atellām tēvalōkattile risapshan kamiṭṭī. tēva lōkattilē. pala ṭivishan kaḷ irukku. kailāyam, iṉtirapuri tiruppāṛkaṭal eṭceṭrā eṭceṭrā.

SITA: atennannā eṭceṭrā eṭceṭrā?

RAMA: itukku mēla enakku teriyātummā. ivvaḷavutān enakkut teriyum atukkutān appaṭi connēn.

TEA VENDOR: appa nīṅka kaṭavuḷaa?

RAMA: nān rāmar. ivar cītai.

TEA VENDOR: iṉtat ṭī kuṭiccā paittiyam teḷiyum. cittarkaḷēllām connā. cāri kaviñanarkaḷ. nīṅka pēcaṛatap pāttā paittiyam puṭicca mātiri irukkē.

RAMA: enna colṛēḷ nīṅka?

TEA VENDOR: oru vēḷai paittiyam ṭī kalakkumpōtu viski pirāṉti kalaṉtuṭṭānō?

RAMA: kashtam. vā cītā nāma ayōttikku pōka vēṇṭiyattutān. nān piṛaṉta iṭamāccē. aṅkayāvatu yārukkunnālum aṭaiyāḷam teriyutānnu pāppōm.

TEA VENDOR: ayōttiyākku vēṇālum pōṅka. ayōttiyā kuppattukku vēṇālum pōṅka. pōṛatukku munnāṭi ṭī kuṭicca kācu. paṇam kuṭuṅka.

PART 7

SITA: eppaṭā cennailēṟṉtu ayōtyā varuvōmnu āyiṭuttunnā.

RAMA: ēn appaṭi colṛē.

SITA: ayōtyā ekspirā atu ayōkya ekspirasnu vaccirukkalām. ellāttaiyum tiruṭiṭṭup pōyiṭṭā. uṅka nalla āyutam ellām pōccu en nalla ṭiras ellām pōccu. kācu maṭṭum iṭuppila coruki vaccatunālē tappiccutu. illēnnā atuvum pōyirukkum.

RAMA: iruṉtālum iṅkirukkaṛa manushāḷukku rompa poṛumaimmā. pāti nēṛam ṭireyinla ricarv paṇṇavāḷattvuttu miccavātānē tirāval panṛā.

SITA: vāṅkōnnā kōvil eṅkērukkunnu pāppōm.

PUBLIC: *rām rām catya hē. rām rām catya hē. karēṅkē yā marēṅkē. srī rāmchaṉdarji kē liyē ham mantir panāyēṅkē. karēṅkē yā marēṅkē.*

RAMA: ennatu itu? ellārum rāmā rāmānnu kōsham pōṭṭuṭṭu pōṛā. yārumē nammaḷak kaṇṭukkavē illaiyē. enna colliṅṭupōṛānnu kūṭa puriyalaiyē.

SITA: camskiritamtānē nīṅka iṅkē āṭcī moḻiyā paṇṇinēḷ. evā pēcaṛa pāshai camskiritamum ille. tamiḻum illai. enna pāshaila pēcaṛānnē puriyalaiyē. ētō namakku tamiḻ teriñcatunālē tappiccōmnā.

PART 8

SANYASI: nīṅka ūrukku putisā. enna vēṇum uṅkaḻukku?

RAMA: appā nalla vēḷai nīṅka pēsaṛatāvatu puriyutu. nāṅka iṅkē rāmar kōvilai tēṭiṅṭu vaṉtōm. ānā iṅkē ellārum ārpāṭṭam paṇṇiṇṭirukkāḷē. etukku?

SANYASI: ivāḷellm rāmrōṭa. nāṅkaḷ kōvil kaṭṭiyē tīruvōm. ceyvōm. illainnā maṭivōm. apṭinnu kōsham pōṭṭuṭṭupōrā.

RAMA: appō iṅkē rāmar kōvilē illaiyā?

SANYASI: irukku irukku. nīṅka vāṅkō. nān aḻaicciṭṭu pōṛēn. nīṅka vāṅkō. itō itutān kōvil. pāruṅkō. itukku ippō ammāji mantir appaṭinnu colṛā.

SITA: ēn rāmar kōvilukku ammāji mantirnu pēru.

RAMA: enna itu puriyāta putirā irukku?

SANYASI: atu ennānnā. ciṅkārammānnu oru ammaṇiyām. avarōṭa utaviyālētān iṉtak kōvila kaṭṭi muṭikka muṭiñcutu. motallē itukkum ciṅkārammā kōvil appaṭinnu colliṅṭiruṉtā. ippō ammāji mantir appaṭinnu colṛā.

SITA: pāttēḷānnā. oru peṇmaṇi utavi illāma oru kōvil kūṭa kaṭṭa muṭiyalai.

SANYASI: āmā. atu oru periya kāthai. colṛē. kēḷuṅkō.

RAMA: āmā. cīkkiram colli muṭiyuṅkō. itu arai maṇi nēra ṭirāmātān. ṭirāmāvai muṭikkaṇum.

SANYASI: cari colrēn. pala āyiram varushaṅkaḷukku munnāḷē āḻvārkaḷellām iṅkērukkaṛa rāmar kōvilap pāttu. tamiḻla aḻakā varṇittu pācuraṅkaḷ ellām eḻuti vaccirukkāṅka.

makān srī rāmānujar irukkārē. avar kūṭa. iṅka vaṉtu aṉtak kōvila pāttārām. ānā atukkappaṟam pala varushaṅkaḷā. iṅka yārum vara muṭiyāmal pōccu. camīpat tulē oru nutti ampatu varushattukku munnālē. tenniṉtiayāla iruṉtu cila yāttirikarkaḷ aṉta āḻvārkaḷ colṟa kōvila pākkaṟatukku vaṉtirukkā.

RAMA: eṅkaḷai mātiriyā?

SANYASI: avacarap paṭātīṅkō. avacarap paṭātīṅkō. ennai kataiya muḻukka muṭikka vacciṭtu appaṟam iṉtak kēḷviyellām kēḷuṅka. cariyā? aṉta tenniṉtiyālērṉtu vaṉta yāttirīkarkaḷ vaṉtu pātta pōtu. iṉtak kōvil. atāvatu aṉta āḻvārkaḷ conna kōvil aṅkē illai.

RAMA: enna uṭanē ārpāṭṭam paṇṇa ārampiccuṭṭāḷō?

SANYASI: ille. illē. illlēlla. avāḷēllām rompa smārṭṭu. appō pārttacārati aiyaṅkārnu oru makān iruṉtār. avar enna ceytār. avar biriṭṭish iṉtiya arācāṅkattaiyum rāmānātapuram cēttupati mannar avarkaḷaiyum utavi kēttār. avar tiruppullāṇiyila iṅkē irukkaṟa mūlavaraiyum uṟcavaraiyum maṇalilē kuṟaiṉtu vaikkaṟatā kanavulē kaṇṭārām. tiruppullāṇiyilē tānē rāmar iṉta cēttuvai kattikkoṇṭiruṉta pōtu tūṅkiyiruṉta iṭam. uṅkaḷukku teriyumō illiyō.

RAMA: tiruppatike laṭṭuvā? cari cari colluṅka.

SANYASI: aṉta. itō vaṉtuṭuttē iṉta iṭam. atukkappaṟam iṅkē koṇṭu vaṉtu iṅkē carayu natikkaraiyila kōvillaik kaṭṭi piratishtai ceytu,nūttiyōru varushaṅkaḷ āccu.

RAMA: appa ikē kōvilē illaiyā. iṅkē etukku ārpāṭṭam?

SANNYASI: ivāḷukku srīrāmar piṟaṉta iṭattilē. kōvil kaṭṭaṇumām. iṉtak kōvil srīrāmar viḷaiyāṭuna illē. tiruviḷaiyāṭan. ceykinṟa iṭattil irukku. nīṅkaḷē colluṅkō. piṟappai viṭa tiruviḷaiyāṭaltānē vicēsham?

RAMA: āmām.

SANYASI: manushanukkuk kūṭa avanōṭa piṟappai viṭa avanōṭa ceykaitānē mukkiyam illaiyā?

NARADA: nārayāṇā nārayāṇā.

SANYASI: nīṅkaḷum ennai mātiri rāma paktarā? uṅkaḷai caṉticcatulē rompa caṉtōsham.

NARADA: uṅkaḷōṭa paktikku innikku pripūraṇa palan kiṭaiccuṭiccu.

SANYASI: nīṅka enna colṟēḷ?

NARADA: uṅka munnāṭi yār nikkiṟānnu nīṅka nenakkiṟēḷ? cāṭcāt rāmapirānum cītappirāṭṭiyārumtān.

SANYASI: appaṭiyā? enna āccariyam en kaṇṇē ennālē kūṭa nampa muṭiyalliyē? iṉta oru taṭavaitān manacukku rompa caṉtōshamāyirukku. iṉtak kōvilak kōvilak kaṭṭi nūttiyōru varusham āccu. nīṅka iṅkē vaṉtu munnālē en mūlamā eḻuṉtaruḷēḷnu ne-naccu paramānaṉtamā irukku. paramānaṉtamā irukku.

SITA: appā ippavāvatu avarukkāvatu namma mēla nampikkai vaṉtuthē.

RAMA: nammaḷap puriñcukka oru mutircci vēṇum. atu avarkiṭṭē irukku. uṅkaḷa caṉticcatulē rompa caṉtōsham. pōyiṭṭu vāṅkō. nāratarē nīṅka connattukkāka iṅkē kaṭṭina kōvila vaṉtu pāttōm. rompa caṉtōsham.

NARADA: ānā uṅkaḷai iṅkē anuppiccatu iṅkirukkaṟa nelamayap puriñcikkaṟatukkuttān. ippa vaṉtu ippa uṅkaḷukku kaṭṭina kōyila pāttēḷ. kaṭṟatukku ārppāṭṭam panṟa kōyilap pāttēḷō?

RAMA: kaṭṭina kōyilayum pāttēn. kāṭṭātataiyum pāttēn. ārppāṭṭattaiyum pāttēn. ānā aṅkē piraccanaiyait tīrkka innoru avatāram eṭukkaṇum. atukku. reṇṭu nāḷakku appaṟam nān jī bi em ai kūppiṭṭurukken.

NARADA: atenna jī bi em.

RAMA: jenaral pādi mīṭṭiṅk

NARADA: rompa caṉtōsham. nīṅka iṉta muṭiva eṭukkaṇumkaṟatukkākattān uṅkaḷai iṅkē anuppiccēn. jenaral pāṭi mīṭṭiṅkukku nān varalāmō?

RAMA: paruppillāmak kalyāṇamā? kaṇṭippāvāṅkō. lāng vīk eṅṭ muṭiyappōṟatu. pushpaka vimānattilē riṭarn paṇṇanum. vāṅkō pōlām.

NOTES

CHAPTER 1

1. Among the 17 percent of Canada's population that speaks both French and English, most live in Québec, Ontario, and New Brunswick. According to Marmen and Corbeil (1999), there are nine times more speakers of three or more languages residing in Québec (46.8 percent of all multilinguals) than in any other Canadian province. Only 5.4 percent of Canadians identify themselves as multilingual on the census. Lamarre and Dagenais (2004) have compared trilingual speakers in Vancouver and Montréal and concluded that 44 percent of speakers of heritage languages in Montréal are trilingual in that they speak both French and English, whereas in Vancouver only 4 percent can speak both official languages. See Lamarre et al. (2002) and Sarkar and Winer (2006) for further discussions of the pragmatic factors and social contexts influencing trilingual Montréalers' code-switching practices.
2. Although code-switching and code-mixing are defined in many ways, I define code-switching as the *inter*sentential alternation of more than one language variety, and code-mixing as the *intra*sentential alternation of more than one language variety. I adopt Gumperz's (1982) distinction between metaphorical, that is, unmarked simultaneous code-switching, as being intrasentential, and unmarked, that is, alternating code-switching, as being intersentential (18).
3. Tamil Eelam is a territory in northeast Sri Lanka located on the site of the medieval Hindu kingdom of Jaffna. Twentieth-century Tamil nationalists have proposed this territory as the future site of a sovereign Tamil-speaking nation.
4. Exceptions are Tamil-owned grocery stores, restaurants, and Protestant churches that cater to both Indians and Sri Lankans.
5. Paris's "Little Jaffna" neighborhood in the tenth arrondissement features businesses owned by Pondicherry Indian Tamils and Sri Lankan Tamils.
6. Because Sri Lankan Tamils vastly outnumber Indian Tamils in Montréal, ten to one, the francophone media treats Sri Lankans as the presumptive Tamil-speaking

group and uses *tamoul* and *Sri Lankais* interchangeably (see Blanchette 2005; Chamberland 1998; Régis 1999; Trottier 1998). In Toronto "Sri Lankan" and "Sinhalese" are more commonly used interchangeably.

7. Referred to as "enregisterment," Agha defines these as "processes whereby distinct forms of speech come to be socially recognized (or enregistered) as indexical of speaker attributes by a population of language users" (2005b:38).
8. Charles Sanders Peirce (1955) explains that the principle of iconicity is based on the representation of similar qualities or shared essences between a representamen (the sign) and its object to generate a new interpretant, that is, an icon.
9. The third Sangam literary corpus comprises eight anthologies (*Eṭṭutokai*) and ten poems (*pattuppāṭṭu*). The grammar book (*Tolkāpiyam*) was written during either the second or the third Sangam. All works from the first Sangam are believed to have been lost during a mythical flood (Cheran 2007).
10. The Indian government later recognized Sanskrit, Telugu, Kannada, Malayalam, and Odia as classical languages, based on the criteria that they have an original literature at least 1500 to 2000 years old and that these classical languages and literatures are distinct from modern ones.
11. This translation comes from a CBC video archive of Jacques Parizeau's speech to his supporters immediately after the referendum. CBC provided a simultaneous translation in English through closed captioning during Parizeau's speech in French that is different from other non-simultaneous translations of Parizeau's concession speech.
12. In Montréal, residents living in predominantly wealthy, Jewish, and anglophone ridings, which is the term used to refer to electoral districts in Commonwealth countries, voted overwhelmingly against Québec's secession.
13. The head of the Parti québécois, Pauline Marois, became the first woman premier of Québec in September 2012. She promised to hold a new referendum to decide if Québec should secede from Canada, yet this referendum never took place since, eighteen months later, the Parti libéral, led by Premier Philippe Couillard, succeeded Marois.
14. The concept of a diaspora originally referred to the dispersal of Jews from Israel into Babylon in the sixth century B.C.E. and the forcible expulsion of Africans during the sixteenth- through nineteenth-century Atlantic slave trade.
15. According to the 2006 census, there are 13,895 Tamils who currently live in Montréal, among whom 11,530 speak Tamil as their "mother tongue" (Statistics Canada 2006b). These statistics include first-generation skilled, semiskilled, and unskilled immigrants and refugees from Sri Lanka, India, Malaysia, South Africa, and Europe (in decreasing population size), as well as their descendants. Given that many Tamils from Sri Lanka are undocumented in Canada, these statistics vastly underestimate the actual population size of Sri Lankan Tamils (Rudhramoorthy 2000:189). According to my sources, there are between twenty to thirty thousand Sri Lankan Tamils and two to three thousand Indian Tamils currently living in

Montréal. Tamilnation.org claims that 300,000 Sri Lankan Tamils reside in all of Canada (Tamilnation 2007). The 2001 Census cites fewer Canadian Tamils, using labels such as "Sri Lankan" to perhaps refer to the Sinhalese and "Tamil" to refer to Sri Lankan Tamils. The census counts 91,670 Sri Lanka-born Canadians, 84 percent in the province of Ontario and more than 10 percent in Québec, including 61,315 Sri Lankans and 39,075 Tamils. In Toronto, 72,000 people were born in Sri Lanka, 45,240 self-identifying as ethnically Sri Lankan and 33,145 as Tamil. In Montréal approximately 10,000 people were born in Sri Lanka, 8,465 self-identifying as Sri Lankan and 2,920 Tamil (Statistics Canada 2001). Because the labels "Tamil" and "Sri Lankan" are used interchangeably in some parts of Canada, and "Sinhalese" and "Sri Lankan" in other parts, it is hard to make sense of this data.

16. Canada signed the United Nations "Convention relating to the Status of Refugees" on June 4, 1969. The United States has ratified only the 1967 Protocol that removed time limits and geographic restrictions on refugee claims.
17. There are multiple definitions of linguistic or language ideologies (see Woolard and Schieffelin 1994). I adopt Irvine's definition because it emphasizes the political and moral dimensions of language ideology formation.
18. I would like to acknowledge Judith Irvine for making this point in response to papers presented at the 2013 American Anthropological Association (AAA) panel, "Scaling Linguistic Diversity: Language Standardization as a Scale-Making Project," held in Chicago.
19. Susan Gal (2005) argues that the original concept of "iconization" should be replaced by "rhematization" to describe indexes whose interpretants are instead taken to be icons. Peirce defines a rheme as "a Sign which, for its interpretant, is a Sign of qualitative possibility, that is, is understood as representing such and such a kind of possible Object" (1955:103).
20. When he became president in 2004, Muthu transformed CUTAM from a political organization involved in the civil war to a cultural organization that sponsors movie nights, sports competitions, and talent shows for students and their families.
21. In 2006, Human Rights Watch published an investigative report on the LTTE's fundraising activities in Toronto and the United Kingdom, claiming that extortion and coercion are part of the LTTE's, and quite possibly, the WTM's door-to-door fundraising tactics (Becker 2006).
22. A telephone survey commissioned by the World Tamil Movement found that 74 percent of Tamils living in Toronto support sovereignty for Tamils in Sri Lanka (Smaller World Communications 1996). All Tamil-language newspapers and radio stations use Tamil Eelam as their reference point for home (Cheran 2000:170). Anti-LTTE factions who voice dissent toward the LTTE's ideology do so underground and at great personal cost.
23. The Canadian Tamil Congress (CTC) is a non-profit organization based in Toronto that sponsors mayoral debates in Scarborough, hosts walk-a-thons to

raise money for displaced war victims, and educates the Canadian public about Sri Lankan politics (Canadian Tamil Congress n.d.). In February 2014, a Sri Lankan newspaper quoted security expert Professor Rohan Gunaratna of Nanyang Technological University in Singapore, a man of Sinhalese descent, falsely stating that the Canadian government is investigating the CTC for terrorist activities. Suing him for libel, CTC leaders were vindicated when the Ontario Superior Court ruled in their favor in the sum of $53,000 (Westhead 2014). Yet after the United Nations banned sixteen Sri Lankan Tamil diaspora organizations, including the CTC, for suspected terrorism in April 2014, the CTC's membership plummeted by half.

CHAPTER 2

1. When I was living in Madurai, I heard Chennai residents refer to Madurai residents as speaking "village Tamil."
2. Most sociolinguistic research discusses the differences between Tamil social dialects (Karunakaran 1978; Karunakaran and Sivashanmugan 1981; Sivashanmugan 1981), regional dialects (Kamatchinathan 1969; Zvelebil 1959a, 1959b, 1960a, 1960b, 1961, 1964a), and caste dialects (Bean 1974; Bloch 1910; Bright 1960, 1966, 1968; Bright and Ramanujam 1972; Southworth 1975). Some sociolinguists, such as M. S. Pillai (1965), Kamil Zvelebil (1964a), and Harold Schiffman (1978), have analyzed both dialectal and caste variation in Tamil.
3. Britto's (1986) analysis draws on representative works from ancient, middle, and modern Tamil literary history, including Brahmi and Tamil *vaṭṭeḻuttu* inscriptions; the *Tolkappiyam*; grammars and prose written by Beschi (1822), Caldwell (1856), and Pope (1904); Sethuppillai's (1979) compilation of bardic, epic, and devotional poetry; and various folk literatures.
4. Bhakti poems also criticized the corrupting influence of Sanskrit on the Telugu-speaking Nāyaka court in Madurai, which ruled from the sixteenth through the eighteenth century.
5. Dominant castes, according to Indian anthropologist M. N. Srinivas, are numerically larger than other caste groups and "wield preponderant economic and political power" in their village or region (1952:18). In most of northern Sri Lanka, Vellālas (though technically among the lowest caste, *Sudra*) are the dominant caste (see Sivathamby 2005).
6. See Ishimatsu (1999) for a discussion of the historical origins of Saivism in central and western India.
7. This view represents what historian Thomas Trautmann (2005) refers to as the "immigrant Aryan" position. The alternate view, the "indigenous Aryan" position, argues that Aryans are indigenous to India and were the original inhabitants of the Indus Valley civilization, ca. 2600–1900 B.C.E.. These different reconstructions of

pre-Vedic and Vedic history are based on literary interpretations of the Rig Veda, written ca. 1200 B.C.E., and seals found in the Indus Valley.

8. See Barnett (1976) and Weiner (2001) for a discussion of the linguistic evidence found in Indus Valley excavations.
9. Sixteenth-century bhakti poets described Tamil as a divine and sovereign male persona who performed miraculous acts and earned the homage and adulation of the gods.
10. For example, the Swadeshi movement in the early 1900s and the Non-Cooperation Movement in the 1920s and 1930s delegated to desexualized and morally virtuous yet literate mothers "the task of reproducing the nation not just biologically, but culturally and linguistically as well" (Ramaswamy 1999:2). Mohandas K. Gandhi himself publicly extolled the emotive qualities of learning the mother tongue by equating it with nursing at the mother's breast (Pattanayak 1981).
11. Specifically, this formula proposed teaching in (1) the regional or mother tongue (if the latter was different from the former), (2) Hindi (or another regional language if the school is located in a Hindi-speaking area), and (3) English (or another European language of choice).
12. In 1881, the census defined "mother tongue" as the "language spoken by the individual from the cradle," and in 1961, as the "language spoken in childhood by person's mother." Of the original 849 mother tongues identified in G. A. Grierson's 1928 *Linguistic Survey of India*, only 622 reappeared in the 1961 census, and these answers ranged widely from Sanskrit to the names of castes, villages, and religious sects (Goel and Saini 1972; Pattanayak 1981). The 1981 census recorded 105 mother tongues (much fewer than the 1,652 mother tongues recorded in 1961), of which 19 were Indo-Aryan, 17 Dravidian, 14 Austro-Asiatic, and 53 Tibeto-Burmese languages (Khan 2000). The Central Institute of Indian Languages (CIIL) now emphasizes that "mother tongue" is not the same as "regional language" and advocates increasing government funding for "non-regional mother tongues" (Rao 2000).
13. For example, the 1951 census asked villagers living halfway between West Bengal and Orissa to choose one of three mother tongue affiliations: Bengali, Oriya, and Santali (a tribal language) (Arputhanathan 1955; Mitra 1956). Villages with a majority of Bengali speakers were incorporated into the province of West Bengal and villages with a majority of Oriya speakers into Orissa. The provinces formerly belonging to the Madras Presidency in South India followed a similar protocol.
14. In 1969, the CIIL urged the federal government to officially recognize fifteen regional "mother tongues" and exclude all foreign languages, non-script-based languages, non-spoken languages, and dialects from consideration (Rao 2000). In 1971, mostly heeding this advice, the Indian Constitution ratified eighteen

languages (including Sanskrit, Urdu, and Sindhi) as the official languages of regional business and administration in India (Goel and Saini 1972).

15. The British found it difficult to classify ethnic groups residing along the east and west coasts due to their mixed Tamil and Sinhalese parentage. The east, due to its majority Tamil-speaking Moor or Muslim population, was included as part of the Tamil northeast, and the west coast became designated as Sinhalese and part of the southwestern region (Arudpragasam 1996).
16. The British also favored Burghers, who are Sri Lankans of mixed Sinhalese, Tamil, and European descent.
17. Although most Sri Lankan Tamils are Sudras, the caste system is further stratified by socioeconomic distinctions. The dominant agriculturist Vellāla caste in Jaffna accentuates minor caste differences to highlight their socioeconomic privilege. Therefore, rich Jaffna Tamils perceive poor plantation Indian Tamils as lower in caste, regardless of their actual caste status. Kenneth David (1977) describes the Jaffna caste system as composed of castes that are either bound or unbound in service to Vellālas. Even Brahmins, though few in number in Sri Lanka, are bound to provide the Vellāla caste with temple services. One could discuss strategies of "Vellālarization" and not "Sanskritization" or "Kshatriyaization" as a means of upward mobility in Sri Lankan Tamil society.
18. Ten years later, the government passed the Tamil Language (Special Provisions) Act to amend the Official Language Bill. Bandaranaike, who drafted this amendment, stated that Tamils should have the right to correspond in Tamil without infringing on the official status of Sinhala (Rajan 1995). This amendment did not improve Tamil-language services much and provided few translators, typists, and stenographers for monolingual citizens. In 1972, Sinhala and Buddhism were officially recognized in the Sri Lankan constitution (Shastri 1990). Not until the thirteenth amendment granted national and (limited) official status to Tamil in 1987 were Tamil typists, stenographers, and translators recruited for government services. Eelam nationalists rejected this amendment as insufficient redress for the historical wrongdoings against the Tamil people of Sri Lanka (DeVotta 2004).
19. Historically, Tamil students performed better than Sinhalese students on competitive entrance exams for higher education. Sinhalese nationalists claim this was due to Tamils' historical access to English-medium schools.
20. Rejecting the LTTE's label of "Muslim Tamil," most Tamil-speaking Muslims in Sri Lanka self-identify as "Moors." The ancestors of Moors include Arabic-speaking traders who arrived between the eighth and the fifteenth century and Indians from Tamil Nadu and Kerala who settled as indentured workers during the British colonial period. Among Tamils, Moors have a unique matrilocal and matrilineal kinship system (McGilvray 2001, 2008).
21. Most upcountry Tamils shunned the LTTE and joined the Ceylon Indian Congress, Ceylon Workers Congress, Freedom Party, or United National Front to work within the parliamentary system to address their grievances.

22. According to BBC Tamil reporter Swaminathan Natarajan (2012), smugglers often "charge between $25,000 (£16,000) and $50,000 (£33,000)" to undertake the voyage by boat to Australia and Canada. Setting off from India or Thailand, refugees are often far from home when they first board wooden fishing trawlers and other rickety boats, despite assurances that they will be transferred to bigger ships once at sea, which rarely happens.
23. Tithes were a percentage of the grain harvest given to landowners (*seigneurs*) as a levy on agricultural products.
24. The British seized Jesuit lands in 1760 before the Pope officially disbanded the Jesuit order in 1773.
25. English elites and Orthodox Jews settling in Montréal in the eighteenth and early nineteenth centuries were the first to self-segregate and establish their own schools, colleges, hospitals, places of worship, libraries, and banks.
26. In 2006 there were 611,850 common law unions and 1,156,930 legal marriages in Québec (Statistics Canada 2006a).
27. To address issues of racism and exclusion, the Canadian government made the following concessions: it established an investigative committee on race relations, included the term "multiculturalism" in the Charter of Rights and Freedoms, created the Multiculturalism Act in 1988, and established the Department of Multiculturalism and Citizenship in 1989.
28. A previous law, Bill 63, passed in 1969 by the *Union nationale* government, only required that children attending English-medium schools have working knowledge of French.
29. Cultural and nonprofit organizations are exempt from the law mandating that public signage be written in French.
30. After a series of amendments, Bill 101 now allows children whose siblings or parents have previously attended an English-medium elementary or secondary school anywhere in Canada, either public or private, to attend English-medium public schools. In 2002, Bill 104 closed a loophole allowing children who had briefly attended private English-medium schools to enter the English-medium public school system (Oakes and Warren 2007). In 2006, more than 80 percent of immigrants or minorities who speak languages other than English or French as their home languages attended French-medium schools. There also has been a notable increase in the percentage of immigrant students enrolled in French-medium colleges or *Collège d'enseignement général et professionnel* (CEGEP), rising from 54 to 64.7 percent from 2001 to 2006, whereas the rate of immigrant students attending French-medium universities stayed the same at around 50 percent (Paillé 2007).
31. According to the 2006 census, 80.1 percent of Québécois identify French as their first language and 95 percent as either their first, second, or third language. The census also states that Montréal is 66 percent francophone, 12 percent anglophone, and 22 percent allophone (Statistics Canada 2006c, 2007).

32. According to most linguists, joual evolved out of prolonged linguistic and cultural contact between the descendants of seventeenth-century French settlers in Canada (who spoke a variety of French, or langue d'oil, similar to those spoken in seventeenth-century northwestern France) and English settlers living in Canada and America (who spoke a northeastern variety of American English) (Bouchard 2008; Oakes and Warren 2007).
33. In the following extract of Tremblay's play, *Les belles-soeurs*, notice the spelling of "toé" rather than "toi," the use of the lexical anglicism "tv" rather than "télé," and the nonstandard morphosyntactic structures, "j'vas" rather than "je vais," and "c'tu" but not "est-ce que c'est": "Ah! J'te dis, j'vas avoir une vraie belle chambre! Pour le salon, j'ai un set complet avec le stirio, la tv, le tapis de nylon synthétique, les cadres... Ah! Les vrais beaux cadres! T'sais, là, les cadres chinois avec du velours... C'tu assez beau, hein? Depuis le temps que j'en veux! Pis tiens-toé ben ma p'tite fille, j'vas avoir des plats en verre soufflé!" (Tremblay 1972:22).
34. Recent studies argue that television and radio news journalists in Québec speak in a style of Québécois French that is phonetically comparable to International French (Lesage 1991). Also, contemporary television sitcoms employ fewer stigmatized sounds and colloquial expressions than they did in previous decades (Arts 2005; Canada News Wire 2006). Even Tremblay writes less frequently in joual, a trend described as his "dés-oralisation" (Vercier 1988).
35. Purists criticize the Internet's use of a phonetic orthography based on a spoken nonstandard Québécois French, singling out as particularly problematic words such as *c* = *c'est* (it is)*; passke* = *parce que* (because)*; ya* = *il y a* (there is)*; yen* = *il y en* (there [are] some)*; chu(e)* = *je suis* (I am) (Caouette 2003).
36. According to one survey, 76.8 percent of Québécois would prefer school instruction in "International French" to improve their literacy skills (Paquot 2001). An anonymous contributor to a Trois-Rivières newspaper makes the following argument, translated from French into English: "First, our very beautiful language is still deteriorating. Young people nowadays are actually less capable of properly speaking and writing. How many of them write by replicating and without modifying the structure of words that they hear spoken orally? Too many individuals, to use the expression, 'don't know how to write.' Mistakes in syntax, spelling, agreement . . . all of these are included. Troubling statistics collected by the *La Presse* newspaper worry many people. Only 43 percent of public school students and 65 percent of private school students can pass spelling exams" (Opinion 2008).
37. In 2006, the mayor of Québec City, Andrée Boucher, instituted a policy requiring applicants for government jobs to pass a written French exam. Rejected applicants to the police force were shocked to learn that their linguistic competences in nonstandard Québécois French were not sufficient for this profession (Allard 2006).
38. "Visible minority" is the term used in Canada to refer to nonwhite "people of color."

39. Only English-medium universities and CEGEPs (pre-universities and community colleges), but not French institutions, permit students to submit assignments in either English or French. This facilitates the transition of students from French- to English-medium schooling.
40. In Québec, 40 percent of immigrant visas are reserved for French speakers. To acquire points, other applicants must demonstrate their "ability to integrate and adapt to Québec culture," by demonstrating French proficiency, previous visits and ties with Québec, and prior knowledge of Québécois culture.

CHAPTER 3

1. See pages 84–93 for an analysis of the original transcription.
2. E. Valentine Daniel (1996) analyzes the trauma of remembering acts of war and torture in Sri Lanka through a Peircean semiotic lens and argues that these memories impact the ethnographic interview by preventing the events' assimilation to a discursive framework. Oral historian Henry Greenspan further argues that "trauma" is too "specific to be foundational" in that it "does not subsume all of the anguish that survivors have known" (Greenspan 2015:143).
3. See Haugen's (1953) classic study of intergenerational language shift in a Norwegian-American community.
4. Variationist sociolinguistics uses statistical and categorical methods to investigate nonrandom variation at all levels of language. This method focuses on explaining the interrelationship of synchronic and diachronic change.
5. In this transcript, standard Québécois French is unmarked and nonstandard Québécois French is underlined.
6. The film *1999*, directed by Lenin M. Sivam (2009), explores the racism faced by Tamil youth gangs in Toronto.
7. In France, laws passed in 2004 banned the display of religious symbols in schools and again in 2010, the niqab and burqa in public. In Québec, provincial-wide debates about what constitutes "reasonable accommodations" for religious and ethnic minorities led the PQ to propose a legislation known as the "Charter of Values" that would curtail the public display of religious symbols. The election of the PLQ in 2014 effectively defeated this bill.
8. This intercultural policy differs from Prime Minister Pierre Trudeau's multicultural policy, established in 1971, which advocates for a pluralistic system in which no one culture—English or French—dominates. The Canadian Charter of Rights and Freedoms officially recognized this policy in 1982. The Bouchard-Taylor Commission sought to frame the discussion of cultural diversity around "the need to perpetuate the French-language culture" (Bouchard and Taylor 2008:117). The discussion did not include aboriginal groups, with whom the Québec government instead negotiates with on a nation-to-nation basis (Bouchard 2012).

9. In this transcript, standard Québécois French is the unmarked form and International French is in italics.
10. In this transcript, standard Québécois French is the unmarked form, International French is in italics, and nonstandard Québécois French is underlined.
11. Tamil Brahmins are comprised of two groups: majority Aiyars, who worship both Siva and Vishnu, and minority Iyengars, who worship Vishnu exclusively. Among the Iyengars, the northern Vadagalai sect uses Sanskrit texts and the southern Tengalai sect favors Tamil texts for worship (Fuller and Narasimhan 2014:6).
12. Joseph Chandrakanthan (2007) writes eloquently of the challenges facing interpreters working with terminally ill Sri Lankan patients in hospitals in Toronto.
13. The Protestant School Board of Greater Montréal introduced French immersion public schools in 1968 to assist students in becoming functionally bilingual in both French and English (Schauber et al. 1995).
14. In Montréal there are separate French- and English-medium hospital systems.
15. Interview 2/19/05.
16. Interview 1/22/05.
17. See E. Keane (2007) for a discussion of Tamil intonation.
18. Cohabitating in Pondicherry's *ville blanche* or white town, Europeans, métis (mixed-race people), and topas (Catholics of unverifiable European ancestry) proclaimed allegiance to the Catholic Church and gained French citizenship on the basis of their social class and wealth. From its inception, the French East India Company offered French nationality to natives who deposited enough capital into the company's treasury or who met the residency requirement of living at least four months in a French territory. Wealthy Tamils from Pondicherry also benefited from the colony's fluid notions of race and citizenship as interracial marriages became the norm. Although the topas temporarily lost French citizenship after the French Revolution, they regained this status several years later.
19. Some teachers and hospital staff in Montréal notoriously refuse to speak with their patients in a language other than the official institutional language, even if they are fully conversant in the patient's preferred language.
20. Interview 5/18/05.
21. In this transcript, standard Québécois French is unmarked, Parisian French is in italics, Tamil is in boldface, and nonstandard Québécois French is underlined.
22. Interview 4/19/05.
23. In this transcript, standard Québécois French is unmarked, English is in boldface, and nonstandard Québécois French is underlined.
24. According to Tran et al. (2005), 80 percent of Tamils claim that at least half of their friends are of Tamil ancestry.
25. In 2008 Pauline Marois, then leader of the *Parti québécois*, unsuccessfully sought to modify Bill 101 to require that immigrant youth also attend French-medium CEGEPs.

CHAPTER 4

1. Barbara Kirshenblatt-Gimblett (2004, 2006) discusses how UNESCO makes arbitrary distinctions between material and immaterial, living and nonliving, and permanent and impermanent aspects of human culture. UNESCO has redefined "intangible heritage" as a type of embodied knowledge or skill: "The 'intangible cultural heritage' means the practices, representations, expressions, knowledge, skills—as well as the instruments, objects, artefacts and cultural spaces associated therewith—that communities, groups and, in some cases, individuals recognize as part of their cultural heritage . . . The 'intangible cultural heritage'...is manifested inter alia in the following domains: (a) oral traditions and expressions, including language as a vehicle of the intangible cultural heritage; (b) performing arts; (c) social practices, rituals and festive events; (d) knowledge and practices concerning nature and the universe; (e) traditional craftsmanship" (UNESCO n.d.). In the same document, UNESCO also refers to "intangible heritage" as a "fragile living treasure."
2. See Jakobson (1990 [1942]) for a discussion of markedness relations in phonological acquisition.
3. When Sir William Jones published his Indo-European proof of Sanskrit in 1786, he created a hybrid style by adopting the Vedic phonetic order and yet using Italian vowels and consonants to transliterate Indian words. Sir Francis Whyte Ellis, who later published the Dravidian language family proof in 1816, did the same. Although he emulated the *Tolkappiyam*'s phonetic order, he also borrowed heavily from categories influencing Beschi's grammatical analysis, despite this dictionary being ordered according to the Latin alphabet.
4. Dupuis' name is spelled as Dupuy in this reprinted dictionary.
5. Heeding a directive issued by the Council of Europe in 1977, France recognized the importance of heritage language instruction for facilitating immigrants' social integration and acquisition of French. Yet in a comparative study of Canadian and French heritage language schools conducted by Nathalie Auger (2007), she found teachers and administrators of the French ELCO (*Enseignement des langues et cultures d'origine*) to be relatively lacking in how they incorporate the values of "multiculturalism" in their pedagogy and curriculum. The ELCO serves immigrants from Algeria, Croatia, Spain, Italy, Morocco, Portugal, Serbia, Tunisia, and Turkey, but not India or Sri Lanka.
6. Some public schools in Manitoba, Saskatchewan, and Alberta offer 50-percent instruction in a heritage language, including German, Ukrainian, Polish, Arabic, Hebrew, Yiddish, and Mandarin.
7. Réginald Fleury, PELO director at the CSDM, notes that under half of newly enrolled preschool children in heritage language classes are Tamil and Hindi speakers.
8. These articles include Association Canadienne d'Éducation (1991), Azzam (1986), Bhullar (1988), Cummins (1983), Fleury (1999), Globensky and Azzam (1987), McAndrew and Gress-Azzam (1987). Park and Sarkar (2007) also discuss

the influence of parental attitudes and community organizations on Korean heritage language instruction in Montréal.

9. To protect the anonymity of children who wanted to participate in the discussion yet whose parents did not sign the permission form, I do not include their responses in my analysis.
10. Sandhi rules explain phonological changes accompanying the agglutination of morphemes in literary Tamil.
11. The Heritage Language Program (*Programme des langues ethniques*, PLE) funds community-based schools.
12. I use her actual name because it is published on the temple's website.
13. This book of hymns is part of the sacred anthology of Tamil Shaiva Siddhanta.
14. When I checked this website again on June 7, 2008, the page had been deactivated.
15. Krishnan uses upper- and lowercase letters and different letter combinations to distinguish between phonemes that sound allophonic to English speakers. For example, he uses lowercase "l" for the sound [l] in "late," "L" for the sound [ɭ] in "play" (rather than "l"), and "zh" for the sound [ɻ] in "Tamil" (rather than "ḻ"). He also writes long vowels in duplicate; for example, long "a" is <aa> (rather than "ā").

CHAPTER 5

1. Webb Keane (2003) defines "semiotic ideology" as the basic assumptions of "what signs are and how they function in the world" (419). Much of his work on semiotic ideologies in the context of Protestant conversion in Sumba investigates, for example, folk beliefs about the role of intentions in meaning-making, beliefs about different kinds of human and nonhuman agents, and beliefs about materiality and immateriality (i.e. the spiritual) (see also W. Keane 2007). He credits the study of language ideologies, based on Peircean semiotics, for inspiring this concept.
2. Ūr should not be confused with the German prefix *ur-*, referring to original or primitive forms.
3. Rather than translating jāti as "caste," Daniel (1984) argues that jāti is more analogous to the concept of "genus" in the sense that it classifies human beings, plants, animals, and inorganic materials.
4. I want to thank the late Bernard Bate for bringing to my attention how the suburban layout of the region of Jaffna differs from most South Indian villages.
5. There are approximately 200,000 Sri Lankan Tamil refugees living in India, 200,000 to 300,000 in Canada, 180,000 in Great Britain, 60,000 in Germany, 40,000 in Australia, 47,000 in Switzerland, 40,000 to 50,000 in France, 20,000 in the Netherlands, 25,000 in the United States, 10,000 in Norway, 7,000 in Denmark, 3,000 in New Zealand, and 2,000 in Sweden (International Crisis Group 2010).
6. These schools also offer classes in Vietnamese, Laotian, Créole, Mandarin, and Arabic.

7. In Tamil Nadu, petty shops (and tailor and construction materials stores), especially those run as cooperatives, are the most sustainable enterprises in poor rural and urban India, according to a recent study conducted by Microsoft Research India, because of their locally appropriate costs and clear market values (Challenges of Sustainability n.d.).
8. This table was created based on my observations in Côte-des-Neiges in summer 2008.
9. This observation is confirmed by informal research in Paris and conversations with Jean-Luc Chevillard, a Tamil linguist and historian at the Université de Paris, who made similar observations of street signs in Pondicherry, India.
10. The letter for "j" is a hybrid script between "k" and "c" that I have never before seen. I would like to thank Jean-Luc Chevillard for pointing this out.
11. There are no available statistics on Sri Lankan Tamil Muslim and Protestant populations in Canada.
12. Among Tamil Catholics, Karaiyars are the most dominant and upwardly mobile jāti (McDowell 1996). Karaiyar Tamils are originally from the coastal regions of northern Sri Lanka where they used to work as fishermen. Recently, many have moved to cities, where urban Karaiyars pursue lower-middle-class professions such as teaching, government service, trade, and factory labor. Other prominent Tamil Catholic jātis are Colombo Chettiars and Parathavar Bharathas (Sivathamby 2005).
13. In Toronto, where Indian Tamils and Sri Lankan Tamils are more numerous, there is a congregational-style Ganesha temple where Vaishnavites and Saivites of both Indian and Sri Lankan heritage worship (Coward 2000).
14. *Kāvaṭi* (kavady) worship of Lord Murukan is a Saivite tradition in India and Sri Lanka where devotees fast and carry on their shoulders a semicircular structure decorated with flowers, ferns, lime, sacred ashes, peacock plumes, brass vessels of milk, and the *vel* (Lord Murukan's spear), from a river or pond to the temple sanctum (Gopal 2013).

CHAPTER 6

1. Thiranagama (2011) emphasizes the point that, well into the twentieth century, middle-class Sri Lankan Tamils, but not Muslims, celebrated the virtues of "chosen migration," which refers to the act of voluntarily leaving the marginal and overpopulated lands of rural Jaffna to seek profitable work in Colombo or elsewhere in Southeast Asia and Africa.
2. Shiv Sena is a Hindu nationalist organization that also promotes Marathi language rights in Mumbai.
3. Deepavali or Diwali, also described as the Festival of Lights, celebrates the victory of light over darkness. Many Hindus view Deepavali as the day that Rama returned to his kingdom with Sita and Lakshmana after fourteen years in exile.

4. See the appendix for the drama's original verses written and performed in colloquial Tamil.
5. Lava and Kusa are the twin sons of Rama and Sita.
6. Kannadasan (1927–1981), a celebrated Tamil poet, writer, and devotee of Krishna, wrote song lyrics for Tamil films that emphasized philosophical themes.
7. Krishna, Venkateswara, and Rama are all incarnations of the Hindu god, Vishnu.
8. Kushboo is a South Indian movie actress who created a controversy with her comments about premarital sex in 2005.
9. Vairamuthu is a Tamil poet and lyricist who collaborated with the award-winning Tamil composer, A.R. Rahman.
10. Sanath Jayasuriya and Marvan Atappattu are cricket players who played on the Sri Lankan team that defeated India in 1997. Muttiah Muralitharan is an Indian player of Tamil heritage.
11. *Madisaar Maami* is the name of a Tamil film that was briefly censored for negatively portraying Brahmins.
12. Rama Pillai, who claimed to have invented herbal fuel, was found to have falsified the ingredients in 2000.
13. Vikram is a popular Tamil movie actor who also appears in Bollywood movies.
14. Ram Rajyam refers to Lord Rama's peaceful and just rule over Ayodhya after his rescue of Sita.
15. The Chief Minister of Tamil Nadu from 1991 to 1996, 2002 to 2006, and 2011 to the present, Jayalalithaa is commonly referred to as Amma ("mother").
16. Rambha and Urvashi are Apsaras, who are nymphs known for their beauty and dancing and who live in heaven.
17. These are the names of holy places and the estates of minor gods.
18. Police killed Ayodhyakuppam Veermani, the leader of a fisherman's gang in Chennai, in August 2003.
19. Ramanuja was a Tamil Brahmin, Hindu philosopher, and pre-eminent teacher of Sri Vaishnavism.
20. At the Tamil Studies Conference in Toronto in 2010, my conversation with a master's student studying Tamil religion at the Université de Montréal confirmed that the 2007 pilgrimage was similar in size and organization to the 2005 pilgrimage.

GLOSSARY OF FOREIGN WORDS

accommodements raisonnables (*French*) adjustments in the legislative system to ensure fair treatment for minorities

ākama cattiram (*Tamil*) ritual prescriptions for building Hindu temples followed by Vaishnavites and Saivites

ammā (*Tamil*) mother

Ancien Régime (*French*) monarchic and aristocratic political system of early modern France of the fifteenth through the eighteenth century

appā (*Tamil*) father

bhakti (*Tamil*) devotional tradition in Hinduism

bharatanatyam (*Tamil*) classical South Indian dance

bindi (*Hindi*) decorative dot placed on the forehead usually on the third eye

cabane à sucre (*French*) maple sugar shack

ceṉtamiḻ (*Tamiḻ*) pure Tamil

cēttu (*Tamil*) bridge

Chettiar (*Tamil*) a mercantile caste of South India

cittar (*Tamil*) Saivite saints

classe d'accueil (*French*) welcome class for immigrant children to learn French

comptoir (*French*) branch

conta ūr (*Tamil*) ancestral village

coureurs des bois (*French*) French Canadian woodsmen

Cypahi or sipahy (*French*) **or sipahi** (*Turkish*) Indian cavalry serving in French colonial armies in India

Dalit (*Hindi*) a diverse caste group formerly known as Untouchables

Damila (*Prakrit*) term used in fifth and sixth centuries B.C.E. Sri Lanka to refer to a Tamil person

dépanneur (*French*) corner convenience store

dupatta (*Hindi*) shawl

Durkai (*Tamil*) Hindu goddess and primary incarnation of *shakti*, or cosmic energy
église (*French*) church
eḷututtamiḻ (*Tamil*) written Tamil
habitants (*French*) French settlers in New France (Canada)
jāti (*Hindi*) clans, tribes, caste subgroups, religions and other communities in South Asia that are sometimes reflected in a person's surname
joual (*French*) nonstandard French spoken in Québec historically associated with Montréal's working class
kaṅkani (*Tamil*) system in which middlemen recruit migrant laborers, usually from the same caste group
Karaiyar (*Tamil*) seafaring and warrior caste in Tamil Nadu and Sri Lanka
kāvaṭi (kavady) (*Tamil*) flattened pole with heavy loads of brass vessels with milk and other substances on either end carried in a procession to show devotion to Murukan
kōpuram (*Tamil*) ornate monumental tower at the entrance of a temple in South India
koṭun tamiḻ (*Tamil*) crooked or corrupted Tamil
kuṭumi (*Tamil*) lock of hair
kuṅkumam (*Tamil*) vermillion powder that Hindus place on their third eye and married women place on the middle parting of their hair
langues d'origine (*French*) heritage language
Mahabharata (*Sanskrit*) epic of the Iron Age war between the Kaurava and Pandava princes of India
makan (*Tamil*) son
Māvērer Nāl (*Tamil*) Martyr's Day honoring fallen Liberation Tigers of Tamil Eelam (LTTE) soldiers in Sri Lanka's civil war
mēṭai tamiḻ (*Tamil*) staged or oratorical Tamil
Murukan (*Tamil*) also known as Karthikeya; a Hindu god of war popular among Tamils
mutuvāy (*Tamil*) ancient wisdom associated with Sangam writers
pandit (*Sanskrit*) scholar or teacher usually skilled in a classical language like Sanskrit or Tamil
pañca (*Tamil*) cloth used as men's bottom garment
parāṭṭā (*Tamil*) unleavened fried flatbread
paruppu (*Tamil*) lentil soup
pāṭṭi (*Tamil*) grandmother
paṭṭi manṛam (*Tamil*) debate
pāvāṭai (*Tamil*) embroidered skirt
pāyasam (*Tamil*) vermicelli milk pudding
pēccu tamiḻ (*Tamil*) spoken Tamil
puja (*Sanskrit*) Hindu prayer ritual
pure laine (*French*) pure wool; refers to people of exclusively French Canadian ancestry

pushpaka vimana (*Sanskrit*) mythical flying palace
quartier (*French*) a residential neighborhood or commercial district of a city
Québécois de souche (*French*) old stock Quebecer; a person of French Canadian ancestry
rāsam (*Tamil*) pepper soup
salwar kameez (*Hindi*) tunic and trousers worn by women
sambar (*Tamil*) lentil soup made with tamarind
sandhi (*Sanskrit*) phonological processes that occur at morpheme or word boundaries
Sangam (*Tamil*) ancient assemblies of Tamil poets and scholars
sannyasi (*Sanskrit*) a Hindu ascetic who renounces the world
seigneurie (*French*) narrow strips of land measuring between 5 and 15 km located near a river system in New France often owned by clergy and military officers; peasants who worked these lands owed tithes to landlords
Shaiva Siddhanta (*Sanskrit*) **or Caiva Cittāntam** (*Tamil*) a form of tantric Saivism, based on Agamic scriptures written in Sanskrit and Tamil; a ritual worship of Siva especially popular in Sri Lanka
Siva (*Sanskrit*) Hindu god primarily worshipped in Saivism; Ganesha and Murukan are his children
tambura (*Tamil*) stringed musical instrument that is plucked
Tamiḻttāy (*Tamil*) goddess of the Tamil language
tāymoḻi (*Tamil*) mother tongue
ūr (*Tamil*) town or village
Vaishnava (*Sanskrit*) branch of Hinduism focused on the veneration of the god Vishnu and his ten incarnations, including Rama
vaṭai (*Tamil*) donut-shaped fritters made with lentils
vel (*Tamil*) Murukan's spear which represents wisdom and intellect
Vellālar (*Tamil*) aristocratic agricultural, landowning caste in historical Tamil Nadu, Kerala, and Sri Lanka that enjoyed privileged relations with kings; the dominant caste in Sri Lanka
ūrmakkal (*Tamil*) people of the village; usually only the dominant castes

REFERENCES

Abu-Laban, Yasmeen, and Christina Gabriel. 2002. Selling Diversity: Immigration, Multiculturalism, Employment Equity, and Globalisation. Peterborough, Ontario: Broadview Press.

Agha, Asif. 2005a. Introduction: Semiosis across Encounters. Journal of Linguistic Anthropology 15(1): 1–5.

Agha, Asif. 2005b. Voicing, Footing, Enregisterment. Journal of Linguistic Anthropology 15(1): 38–59.

Allard, Marc. 2006. Haro sur les fautes de français: La mairesse souhaite imposer des examens avant l'embauche des policiers et des fonctionnaires. Le Soleil, July 29: 6.

Anderson, Benedict. 1983. Imagined Communities: Reflections on the Origins and Spread of Nationalism. London: Verso.

Annamalai, E. 1979. Movement for Linguistic Purism: The Case of Tamil. *In* Language Movements in India. E. Annamalai, ed., pp. 35–59. Mysore: Central Institute of Indian Languages.

Annamalai, E. 2007. The Challenge of Spoken Language to Creative Writers in Modern Tamil. *In* History and Imagination: Tamil Culture in the Global Context. R. Cheran, D. Ambalavanar, and C. Kanaganayak, eds., pp. 63–75. Toronto: TSAR Publications.

Annamalai, E. 2011. Social Dimensions of Modern Tamil. Chennai: Cre-A.

Annamalai, E., and S. B. Steever. 1998. Modern Tamil. *In* Dravidian Languages. Sanford B. Steever, ed., pp. 100–128. London: Routledge.

Appadurai, Arjun. 1996. Modernity at Large: Cultural Dimensions of Globalization. Minneapolis: University of Minnesota Press.

Arasaratnam, Sinnapah. 1994. Sri Lanka's Tamils: Under Colonial Rule. *In* The Sri Lankan Tamils: Ethnicity and Identity. Chelvadurai Manogaran and Bryan Pfaffenberger, eds., pp. 28–53. Boulder: Westview Press.

Archdiocese of Pondicherry and Cuddalore. n.d. The Archdiocese. http://www.pondicherryarchdiocese.org/archdiocese.php?link_id=8, accessed April 1, 2014.

Arputhanathan, J. I. 1955. Census of India 1951 Anantapur and Kurnool Districts: Village-Wise Mother-Tongue Data for Border Taluks. S. o. C. Operations, Superintendent Government Press Madras.

Arts. 2005. La qualité du français dans les médias est acceptable. Le Droit, August 3: 27.

Arudpragasam, A. R. 1996. The Traditional Homeland of the Tamils. Kotte, Sri Lanka: Kanal Publications.

Assisi, Francis. n.d. Indian Diaspora: Where Bharat Mata Lives in Their Souls. http://www.indolink.com/displayArticleS.php?id=040705095703, accessed July 9, 2014.

Association Canadienne d'Éducation. 1991, Les programmes d'enseignement des langues d'origine dans les Commissions Scolaires Canadiennes. Montréal.

Auger, Nathalie. 2007. Enseignement des langues d'origines et apprentissage du français: Vers une pédagogie d'inclusion. Le Français aujourd'hui 158: 76–83.

Axel, Brian. 2004. The Context of Diaspora. Cultural Anthropology 19(1): 26–60.

Azzam, Simone. 1986. Le programme d'enseignement des langues d'origine de la C.E.C.M. Montréal: La Commission des Écoles Catholiques de Montréal.

Baker, Catherine. 2015. The Frames We Use: Narratives, Ethnicity, and the Problem of Multiple Identities in Post-Conflict Oral Histories (Bosnia-Nerzegovina). *In* Beyond Testimony and Trauma: Oral History in the Aftermath of Mass Violence. Steven High, ed., pp. 285–331. Vancouver: UBC Press.

Bakhtin, Mikhail M. 1981. [1975] Discourse in the Novel. *In* The Dialogic Imagination. M. Holquist, ed., pp. 259–275. Austin: University of Texas Press.

Barnett, Marguerite Ross. 1976. The Politics of Cultural Nationalism in South India. Princeton, NJ: Princeton University Press.

Bass, Daniel. 2013. Everyday Ethnicity in Sri Lanka: Up-country Tamil Identity Politics. New York: Routledge.

Basso, Keith. 1996. Wisdom Sits in Places: Landscape and Language among the Western Apache. Santa Fe: University of New Mexico Press.

Bate, Bernard. 2009. Tamil Oratory and the Dravidian Aesthetic: Democratic Practice in South India. New York: Columbia University Press.

Bauman, Richard, and Charles L. Briggs. 2003. Voices of Modernity: Language Ideologies and the Politics of Inequality. Cambridge: Cambridge University Press.

BBC News. 2014. Australia Asylum: Minister in Sri Lanka amid Row. BBC News, July 9. http://www.bbc.com/news/world-asia-28223598, accessed July 9, 2014.

Bean, Susan. 1974. Linguistic Variation and the Caste System in South Asia. Indian Linguistics 35: 277–293.

Becker, Jo. 2006. Funding the "Final War": LTTE Intimidation and Extortion in the Tamil Diaspora. Human Rights Watch 18(1C).

Belzil, Suzanne. 2006. Le programme de formation en espagnol, langue tierce et ses incidences sur les pratiques pedagogiques. TINKUK 3: 67–74.

Berman, Marshall. 1982. All That Is Solid Melts into Air: The Experience of Modernity. New York: Penguin.

Bhullar, Devinder Kaur. 1988. Principles of Second Language Instruction, Manitoba Heritage Review 4(1): 10.

Blanchette, Josée. 2005. C'est la vie!–En remontant la Côte des Neiges: Mon quartier, ce n'est pas un quartier, c'est une terre d'accueil. Le Devoir, January 7: B8.

Bloch, Jules. 1910. Castes et dialectes en Tamoul. Memoires de la Société de Linguistique 16: 1–30.

Blommaert, Jan. 2007. Sociolinguistic Scales. Intercultural Pragmatics 4(1): 1–19.

Blommaert, Jan. 2008. Grassroots Literacy: Writing, Identity and Voice in Central Africa. New York: Routledge.

Blommaert, Jan. 2010. The Sociolinguistics of Globalization. Cambridge: Cambridge University Press.

Blommaert, Jan, J. Collins, and S. Slembrouck. 2005. Spaces of Multilingualism. Language and Communication 25(3): 197–216.

Bose, Sumantra. 1994. States, Nations, and Sovereignty: Sri Lanka, India, and the Tamil Eelam Movement. New Delhi: Sage Publications.

Bouchard, Chantal. 2008. Obsessed with Language: A Sociolinguistic History of Quebec. Toronto: Guernica.

Bouchard, Gérard. 2012. Interculturalism: A View from Quebec. Toronto: University of Toronto Press.

Bouchard, Gérard, and Charles Taylor. 2008. Building the Future: A Time for Reconciliation. Gouvernement du Québec: Québec City.

Boudreau, Annette, and Chantal White. 2004. Turning the Tide in Acadian Nova Scotia: How Heritage Tourism Is Changing Language Practices and Representations of Language. Canadian Journal of Linguistics 49(3–4): 327–351.

Briggs, Charles, and Richard Bauman. 1992. Genre, Intertextuality, and Social Power. Journal of Linguistic Anthropology 2(2): 131–172.

Bright, William. 1960. A Study of Dialect and Caste in Mysore. Indian Linguistics 21: 140–144.

Bright, William. 1966. Language, Social Stratification, and Cognitive Orientation. Sociological Inquiry 36(2): 313–318.

Bright, William. 1968. Social Dialect and Semantic Structure in South Asia. *In* Structure and Change in Indian Society. Milton Singer and Bernard Cohn, eds., pp. 455–460. Chicago: Aldine Press.

Bright, William, and A. K. Ramanujam. 1972. Sociolinguistic Variation and Language Change. *In* Proceedings of the Ninth International Conference of Linguists. John Pride and Janet Holmes, eds., pp. 1107–1113. The Hague: Mouton.

Britto, Francis. 1986. Diglossia: A Study of the Theory with Application to Tamil. Washington, DC: Georgetown University Press.

Bucholtz, Mary, and Kira Hall. 2005. Identity and Interaction: A Sociocultural Linguistic Approach. Discourse Studies 7(4–5): 585–614.

Cajolet-Laganière, Hélène, and Pierre Martel. 2005. Le dictionnaire du français standard en usage au Québec: Un projet scientifique d'envergure. Le Devoir, January 26, B5.

Canada News Wire. 2006. Le français à la télévision québécoise. Canada News Wire, January 11: 14, 26. Montréal, Québec: Archives nationales du Québec.

Canadian Education Association. 1991. Heritage Language Programs in Canadian School Boards. Toronto: Canadian Education Association.

Canadian Tamil Congress. n.d. CTC Mission and Objectives. http://www.canadiantamilcongress.ca/ctc-mission-objectives/, accessed on July 28, 2014.

Caouette, Marie. 2003. Les ados parlent-lls français? Les jeunes bousculent les règles établie. Le Soleil, October 4: D1.

Carens, Joseph H. 1995. Liberalism, Justice, and Political Community: Theoretical Perspectives on Quebec's Liberal Nationalism. *In* Is Quebec Nationalism Just? Perspectives from Anglophone Canada. Joseph H. Carens, ed., pp. 3–19. Montréal: Mc Gill-Queen's University Press.

Cauchy, Clairandrée. 2003. De "Parc-Ex" à "Little Hindustan." Le Devoir, December 23: A1.

CBC. 2006a. Canada Adds Tamil Tigers to List of Terrorist Groups. http://www.cbc.ca/news/canada/canada-adds-tamil-tigers-to-list-of-terrorist-groups-1.603477, accessed April 10, 2006.

CBC. 2006b. Police Pore over Tamil Papers Seized in Raid.

CBC Digital Archive. n.d. Quebec Referendum Reaction. http://www.cbc.ca/archives/categories/politics/federal-politics/separation-anxiety-the-1995-quebec-referendum/money-and-the- ethnic-vote.html, accessed June 7, 2012.

CECM. 1998. Study Program Elementary Tamil Heritage Language Level 1. Montréal: CECM.

Challenges of Sustainability. n.d. Challenges of Sustainability. http://64.233.167.104/search?q=cache:Q22N1uJg9mgJ:research.microsoft.com/toyama/talks/2005%252005%252004%2520Challenges%2520of%2520Sustainability.ppt+Tamil+petty+shop&hl=en&ct= clnk&cd=16&gl=us&client=firefox-a, accessed May 19, 2008.

Chamberland, Martin. 1998. Un pooja pour Duchesneau. La Presse, October 11: A7.

Chandrakanthan, Joseph A. 2007. When Two Cultures Collide at the Bedside: Religio-Cultural Value Conflicts and Medico-Ethical Decision-Making among the Tamil Community in Canada. *In* History and Imagination: Tamil Culture in the Global Context. Rudhramoorthy Cheran, Darshan Ambalavanar, and Chelva Kanaganayakam, eds., pp. 138–149. Toronto: TSAR Publications.

Charusheela, S. 2007. The Diaspora at Home. Cultural Dynamics 19(2–3): 279–299.

Chatterjee, Partha. 1993. The Nation and Its Fragments: Colonial and Postcolonial Histories. Princeton, NJ: Princeton University Press.

Cheran, Rudhramoorthy. 2000. Changing Formations: Tamil Nationalism and National Liberation in Sri Lanka and the Diaspora. Ph.D. Dissertation. York University.

Cheran, Rudhramoorthy. 2007. Citizens of Many Worlds: Theorizing Tamil DiasporiCity. *In* History and Imagination: Tamil Culture in the Global Context. Rudhramoorthy Cheran, Darshan Ambalavanar, and Chelva Kanaganayakam, eds., pp. 150–168. Toronto: TSAR Publications.

Citizenship and Immigration Canada. n.d. Refugee Claims in Canada–Who Can Apply. http://www.cic.gc.ca/english/refugees/inside/apply-who.asp, accessed May 29, 2012.

Colpron, Suzanne. 1988. La GRC saisit des faux titres de voyages: Deux Sri Lankais sont arrêtés [à Montréal]. La Presse, June 5: A1.

Comaroff, Jean, and John Comaroff. 1993. Introduction. *In* Modernity and Its Malcontents: Ritual and Power in Postcolonial Africa. J. Comaroff and J. Comaroff, eds., pp. xi–xxxvii. Chicago: University of Chicago Press.

Commission scolaire de Montréal. n.d. New Developments in Heritage Languages in Quebec. Languages Without Borders.

Coon Come, Matthew. 1995. Des partenaires consentants: Les cris de la Baie James, la sécession du Québec et le Canada. *In* Pour l'amour de ce pays. C. Good, ed., pp. 105–122. Toronto: Penguin Books.

Corbeil, Jean-Claude. 2005. Un cas de révisionnisme linguistique: Les linguistes l'inventent pas la norme, ils ne peuvent que tenter de la décrire. Le Devoir, January 14: A9.

Côte, Émilie. 2004. Quatre jeunes blessés dans une bagarre. La Presse, September 20: A9.

Courtemanche, Gil. 2008. Parler le Créole Québécois? Le Devoir, March 15: B2.

Coward, Harold. 2000. Hinduism in Canada. *In* The South Asian Religious Diaspora in Britain, Canada, and the United States. H. Coward, ed., pp. 151–172. Albany: SUNY Press.

Crapanzano, Vincent. 1996. "Self"-Centering Narratives. *In* Natural Histories of Discourse. Michael Silverstein, ed., pp. 106–127. Chicago: University of Chicago Press.

Cummins, Jim. 1983. Heritage Language Education: A Literature Review. Toronto: Ontario Ministry of Education.

Cummins, Jim. 1992. Heritage Language Teaching in Canadian Schools. Journal of Curriculum Studies 24(3): 281–286.

Daniel, E. Valentine. 1984. Fluid Signs: Being a Person the Tamil Way. Berkeley: University of California Press.

Daniel, E. Valentine. 1996. Charred Lullabies: Chapters in an Anthropology of Violence. Princeton, NJ: Princeton University Press.

Daniel, E. Valentine, and Yuvaraj Thangaraj. 1995. Forms, Formations, and Transformations of the Sri Lankan Tamil Refugee. *In* E. Valentine Daniel and John C. Knudsen (eds.), Mistrusting Refugees. Berkeley: University of California Press.

Das, Sonia. 2008. Between Convergence and Divergence: Reformatting Linguistic Purisms in the Montreal Tamil Diasporas. Journal of Linguistic Anthropology 18(1): 1–23.

Das, Sonia. 2011. Rewriting the Past and Reimagining the Future: The Social Life of a Tamil Heritage Language Industry. American Ethnologist 38(4): 774–789.

Das, Sonia. 2015. Une division sociale du travail linguistique: Enseigner le Tamoul comme langue d'origine à Montréal, Québec. Anthropologie et Sociétés 39(2): 153–172.

Daveluy, Michelle, and Jenanne Ferguson. 2009. Scripted Urbanity in the Canadian North. Journal of Linguistic Anthropology 19(1): 78–100.

David, Kenneth. 1977. Hierarchy and Equivalence in Jaffna, North Sri Lanka: Normative Codes as Mediator. *In* The New Wind. Kenneth David, ed., pp. 179–226. The Hague: Mouton de Gruyter.

Davis, Christina P. 2014. Speaking Conflict: Ideological Barriers to Bilingual Policy Implementation in Civil War Sri Lanka. Anthropology & Education Quarterly 46(2): 95–112.

Denis, Serge. 2008. Le Français est-il en danger au Québec? La Tribune (Sherbrooke), March 15:28.

Desbiens, Jean-Paul. 1960. Les insolences du Frère Untel. Montréal: Les Éditions de L'Homme Itée.

Deschênes, Gaston. 2012. La devise "Je me souviens." Encyclopédie de L'Agora. http://agora.qc.ca/documents/quebec_-_etat--la_devise_je_me_souviens_par_gaston_deschenes, accessed on August 5, 2014.

Devaneyan, N. 1966. The Primary Classical Language of the World. Madras: Nesamani Publishing House.

de Villers, Marie-Éva. 2005. Comparaison avec Le Monde pour établir la norme réelle du français québécois: Les mots et expressions propres au devoir. Le Devoir, January 5: A7.

DeVotta, Neil. 2004. Blowback: Linguistic Nationalism, Institutional Decay, and Ethnic Conflict in Sri Lanka. Stanford: Stanford University Press.

Dick, Hilary Parsons. 2010. Imagined Lives and Modernist Chronotopes in Mexican Nonmigrant Discourse. American Ethnologist 37(2): 275–290.

Dickey, Sara. 1993. The Politics of Adulation: Cinema and the Production of Politicians in South India. Journal of Asian Studies 52(2): 340–372.

Dickinson, John, and Brian Young. 2000. A Short History of Quebec. Second edition. Montréal: McGill-Queen's University Press.

Dirks, Nicholas B. 2001. Castes of Mind: Colonialism and the Making of Modern India. Princeton, NJ: Princeton University Press.

Duchêne, Alexandre. 2008. Ideologies across Nations: The Construction of Linguistic Minorities at the United Nations. Berlin: Walter de Gruyter.

Dugas, Sylvie. 2003. L'intégration des minorités est longue et difficile. La Presse, March 3: D1.

Dumas, Denis. 1987. Nos façons de parler. Sillery, Québec: Presses de l'Université du Québec.

Durham, Earl. 1839 [2000]. Report of the Affairs of British North America. London: The House of Commons. Reproduced in Documents in Quebec History Marianopolis College. Electronic document, http://faculty.marianopolis.edu/c.belanger/quebechistory/docs/durham/index.htm, accessed on June 21, 2008.

Dutrisac, Robert. 2008. Curzi ne veut pas entendre parler d'une langue standard québécoise. Le Devoir, March 3: A5.

Eagleton, Terry. 1991. Ideology: An Introduction. London: Verso.

Eisenlohr, Patrick. 2006. Little India: Diaspora, Time, and Ethnolinguistic Belonging in Hindu Mauritius. Berkeley: University of California Press.

Eisenstein, Elizabeth. 1983. The Printing Revolution in Early Modern Europe. Cambridge: Cambridge University Press.

Errington, Joseph. 2001. Colonial Linguistics. Annual Review of Anthropology 30: 19–39.

Fader, Ayala. 2009. Mitzvah Girls: Bringing Up the Next Generation of Hasidic Jews in Brooklyn. Princeton, NJ: Princeton University Press.

Faudree, Paja. 2013. Singing for the Dead: The Politics of Indigenous Revival in Mexico. Durham, NC: Duke University Press.

Ferguson, Charles. 1959. Diglossia. Word 15: 325–340.

Fishman, Joshua. 1965. Who Speaks What Language to Whom and When? La Linguistique 2: 67–88.

Fleury, Bergman. 1999. 1978–1999: Le PELO de la CECM à la CSDM intégration et plurilinguisme: Une contribution à l'ouverture sur le monde. Montréal: Commission Scolaire de Montréal.

Frekko, Susan. 2009. Signs of Respect: Neighborhood, Public, and Language in Barcelona. Journal of Linguistic Anthropology 19(2): 227–245.

Friedman, P. Kerim, and Sonia Das. 2013. Scaling Linguistic Diversity: Language Standardization as a Scale-Making Project. http://www.aaanet.org/meetings/program/upload/2013-AAA-Annual-Meeting-Program.pdf, accessed August 3, 2014.

Friedrich, Paul. 1991. Polytropy. *In* Beyond Metaphor: The Theory of Tropes in Anthropology. James Fernandez, ed., pp. 17–55. Stanford: Stanford University Press.

Fuglerud, Øivind. 1999. Life on the Outside: The Tamil Diaspora and Long-Distance Nationalism. London: Pluto Press.

Fuller, Christopher J., and Haripriya Narasimhan. 2008. From Landlords to Software Engineers: Migration and Urbanization among Tamil Brahmans. Comparative Studies in Society and History 50: 170–196.

Fuller, Christopher J., and Haripriya Narasimhan. 2014. Tamil Brahmans: The Making of a Middle-Class Caste. Chicago and London: University of Chicago Press.

Gade, Daniel W. 2003. Language, Identity, and the Scriptorial Landscape in Québec and Catalonia. Geographical Review 93(4): 429–448.

Gair, James, and S. Suseendirarajah. 1998. Some Aspects of the Jaffna Tamil Verbal System. *In* Studies in South Asian Linguistics: Sinhala and Other South Asian

Languages. James Gair and Barbara Lust, eds., pp. 170–181. New York: Oxford University Press.

Gal, Susan. 2005. Language Ideologies Compared: Metaphors of Public/Private. Journal of Linguistic Anthropology 15(1): 23–37.

Gal, Susan. 2012. Sociolinguistic Regimes and the Management of "Diversity." *In* Language in Late Capitalism: Pride and Profit. A. Duchêne and M. Heller, eds., pp. 22–42. New York: Routledge.

Gamage, Amarasena. 2008. Attempt to Make Madhu Church a "National Basilica" on False Pretexts (Originally the Pattini Devale of Sinhalese Buddhists). http://www.lankaweb.com/news/items02/190802-2.html, accessed on April 9, 2008.

Gaur, Albertine. 1968. Father Beschi and His Grammar of High-Tamil. The British Museum Quarterly 32(3–4): 103–108.

Gilroy, Paul. 1993. The Black Atlantic: Modernity and Double Consciousness. Cambridge, MA: Harvard University Press.

Girard, Mario. 2007. Hérouxville cause tout un emoi: Les "immigrants" de Hérouxville. La Presse, January 28: A4.

Globensky, Guy, and Simone Azzam. 1987. C.E.C.M. Description du rendement scolaire des élèves inscrits au PELO. Montréal: Commission des Écoles Catholiques de Montréal.

Goel, Bhim, and S. K. Saini. 1972. Mother Tongue and Equality of Opportunity in Education. New Delhi: National Council of Educational Research and Training.

Gopal, Krishan. 2000. Nationalism in Sri Lanka: Genesis and Evolution. Delhi: Kalinga Publications.

Gopal, N. D. 2013. Music, Trance and Dance in the Thaipusam Kavady Festival: Reflections of a Select Group of South Africans. Journal of Sociology and Social Anthropology 4(1–2): 159–166.

Grillo, Ralph D. 1989. Dominant Languages: Language and Hierarchy in Britain and France. Cambridge: Cambridge University Press.

Gumperz, John. 1982. Conversational Code-Switching. *In* Discourse Strategies. John Gumperz, ed., pp. 59–99. Cambridge: Cambridge University Press.

Guyane. 1819. "Extrait d'une lettre écrite de Fr Louis Sénégal en date du 12 Avril 1819 à Son Excellence, le Ministre de la Marine, par M. Mahé, Capitaine de Vaisseau." Introduction d'Indiens à la Guiane française. 1818–1822. Aix-en-Provence, France: Archives nationales d'outre-mer.

Guyane. 1862. "Procès-verbaux de la Commission instituée par décision du Gouverneur en date du 28 Janvier 1862, à l'effet de procéder a une enquête sur l'état moral et sanitaire des immigrants indiens introduite dans la colonie par le navire Le Parmentier." Convoi du Parmentier. Partie de Pondichéry 25 mars 1861 arrivé à Cayenne 9 juillet 1861. Aix-en-Provence, France: Archives nationales d'outre-mer.

Habermas, Jürgen. 1981. Modernity versus Postmodernity. Translated by Seyla Ben-Habib. New German Critique 22: 3–14.

Hamel, Marcel-Pierre. 1948. Le rapport de Durham: Présenté, traduit et annoté par Marcel-Pierre Hamel. Montréal: Société Historique de Montréal.

Hamelin, Jean, and Jean Provencher. 1997. Brève histoire du Québec. Montréal: Boréal.

Handler, Richard. 1988. Nationalism and the Politics of Culture in Quebec. Madison: University of Wisconsin Press.

Haque, Eve. 2012. Multiculturalism within a Bilingual Framework: Language, Race, and Belonging in Canada. Toronto: University of Toronto Press.

Harvey, David. 1990. The Condition of Postmodernity: An Enquiry into the Origins of Cultural Change. Cambridge, MA: Blackwell Publishers.

Hastings, Adi, and Paul Manning. 2004. Introduction: Acts of Alterity. Language and Communication 24(4): 291–311.

Haugen, Einar. 1953. The Bilingual's Dilemma. *In* The Norwegian Language in America. Vol. 1. Einar Haugen, ed., pp. 1–16. Philadelphia: University of Pennsylvania Press.

Haviland, Charles. 2013. Dream Over for Boat People Back in Sri Lanka. BBC News, http://www.bbc.com/news/world-asia-23047162 accessed on July 9, 2014.

Heller, Monica. 1988. Strategic Ambiguity: Codeswitching in the Management of Conflict. *In* Codeswitching: Anthropological and Sociolinguistic Perspectives. Monica Heller, ed., pp. 77–96. Berlin: Mouton de Gruyter.

Heller, Monica. 2011. Paths to Post-Nationalism: A Critical Ethnography of Language and Identity. Oxford: Oxford University Press.

Heller, Monica, and Alexandre Duchêne. 2012. Pride and Profit: Changing Discourses of Language, Capital and Nation-State. *In* Language in Late Capitalism: Pride and Profit. Alexandre Duchêne and Monica Heller, eds., pp. 1–21. New York: Routledge.

Helly, Denise. 1996. Le Québec face à la pluralité culturelle, 1977–1994: Un bilan documentaire des politiques. Sainte-Foy, Québec: Institut Québécois de Recherche sur la Culture.

Helly, Denise. 2001. Appartenir au Québec: Citoyenneté, nation et société civile: Enquête à Montréal. Sainte-Foy, Québec: Editions de l'IQRC.

High, Steven. 2014. Oral History at the Crossroads: Sharing Life Stories of Survival and Displacement. Vancouver: UBC Press.

High, Steven. 2015. Introduction. *In* Beyond Testimony and Trauma: Oral History in the Aftermath of Mass Violence. Steven High, ed., pp. 3–28. Vancouver: UBC Press.

Hill, Jane H., and Bruce Mannheim. 1992. Language and World View. Annual Review of Anthropology 21: 381–406.

Ho, Engseng. 2006. The Graces of Tarim: Genealogy and Mobility across the Indian Ocean. Berkeley: University of California Press.

Hymes, Dell. 1977. Qualitative/Quantitative Research Methodologies in Education: A Linguistic Perspective. Anthropology and Education Quarterly 8(3): 165–176.

Immigration, Diversité et Inclusion Québec. n.d. French and English Language Knowledge for Candidates from the Regular Skilled Worker. http://www.immigration-quebec.gouv.qc.ca/en/immigrate-settle/permanent-workers/

official-immigration-application/requirements-programs/language-knowledge.html, accessed on July 29, 2014.

Inbanathan, Anand. 1997. Migration and Adaptation: Tamils in Delhi. Delhi: Kalinga Publications.

Inde. 1831. Rapport du Ministère de la Marine et des Colonies, 26 avril 1831, re: Proposition de souscrire à exemplaires d'un dictionnaire français-malabar. Dictionnaire français-malabar. Aix-en-Provence, France: Archives nationales d'outre-mer.

Inde. 1855. "Spécimen de typographie et de fonderie envoyé à l'exposition universelle de Paris année 1855, par l'imprimerie des missionaries apostoliques de Pondichéry-Indes Orientale." Circulaire adressée aux colonies et relative à une souscription à des ouvrages en langue tamoule edités par l'imprimerie de la Mission catholique en Inde. 1863–1865. Aix-en-Provence, France: Archives nationales d'outre-mer.

Inde. 1863. "Envoie du catalogue des ouvrages en langue tamoule édités par l'Imprimerie de la Mission," Letter from Governor to Minister of the Marine and Colonies, Pondichéry, 18 fevrier 1863. Circulaire adressée aux colonies et relative à une souscription à des ouvrages en langue tamoule edités par l'imprimerie de la Mission catholique en Inde. 1863–1865. Aix-en-Provence, France: Archives nationales d'outre-mer.

Inde. n.d. "Catalogue des livres de l'imprimerie de la Maison des Missions étrangères à Pondichéry." Circulaire adressée aux colonies et relative à une souscription à des ouvrages en langue tamoule edités par l'imprimerie de la Mission catholique en Inde. 1863–1865. Aix-en-Provence, France: Archives nationales d'outre-mer.

Indra, Doreen. 1980. Changes in Canadian Immigration Patterns over the Past Decade with Special Reference to Asia. *In* Visible Minorities and Multiculturalism: Asians in Canada. Victor Ujimoto and G. Hirabayashi, eds. Toronto: Butterworth and Co.

Inoue, Miyako. 2004a. Introduction: Temporality and Historicity in and through Linguistic Ideology. Journal of Linguistic Anthropology 14(1): 1–5.

Inoue, Miyako. 2004b. What Does Language Remember? Indexical Inversion and the Naturalized History of Japanese Women. Journal of Linguistic Anthropology 14(1): 39–56.

International Crisis Group. 2010. The Sri Lankan Tamil Diaspora after the LTTE. Asia Report 186: 1–34.

Irvine, Judith T. 1989. When Talk Isn't Cheap: Language and Political Economy. American Ethnologist 16(2): 248–267.

Irvine, Judith T. 2004. Say When: Temporalities in Language Ideology. Journal of Linguistic Anthropology 14(1): 99–109.

Irvine, Judith T. 1996. Shadow Conversations: The Indeterminacy of Participant Roles. *In* Natural Histories of Discourse. Michael Silverstein and Greg Urban, eds., pp. 131–159. Chicago: University of Chicago Press.

Irvine, Judith T., and Susan Gal. 2000. Language Ideology and Linguistic Differentiation. *In* Regimes of Language: Ideologies, Polities, and Identities. Paul V. Kroskrity, ed., pp. 35–84. Santa Fe, NM: School of American Research Press.

ISCA. 2015. L'empreinte. 1001 Vies. Radio Canada. http://ici.radio-canada.ca/tele/1001-VIES/2015/episodes/352157/empreinte-roy-dupuis, accessed on August 13, 2015.

Ishimatsu, Ginette. 1999. The Making of Tamil Shaiva Siddhānta. Contributions to Indian Sociology 33(3): 571–579.

Jackson, Jean, and María Clemencia Ramírez. 2009. Traditional, Transnational, and Cosmopolitan: The Colombian Yanacona Look to the Past and to the Future. American Ethnologist 36(3): 521–544.

Jakobson, Roman. 1990 [1942]. The Sound Laws of Child Language. *In* On Language. Linda R. Waugh, ed., pp. 294–304. Cambridge, MA: Harvard University Press.

Jobin, Jean-Louis. 1987. Le vocabulaire de deux générations de Québécois: Différences temporelles (1966 et 1981) et régionales (Montréal et Québec). Québec: International Center for Research on Bilingualism.

Kalainathan, R. 2000. Linguistic Heritage of Sri Lankan Tamil. *In* Linguistic Heritage of India and Asia. O. Koul and L. Devaki, eds., pp. 300–304. Mysore: Central Institute of Indian Languages.

Kamatchinathan, A. 1969. The Thirunelveli Tamil Dialect. Annamalai Nagar: Annamalai University Press.

Kanaganayakam, Chelva. 2007. Poetics, Language, and Genre in Contemporary Tamil Literature from Sri Lanka. *In* History and Imagination: Tamil Culture in the Global Context. Rudhramoorthy Cheran, Darshan Ambalavanar, and Chelva Kanaganayakam, eds., pp. 124–137. Toronto: TSAR Publications.

Kandiah, Thiru. 1978. A Standard Language and Socio-Historical Parameters: Sri Lankan Tamil. International Journal of the Sociology of Language 16: 59–76.

Karunakaran, Krishnamoorthy. 1978. Studies in Tamil Sociolinguistics. Annamalai Nagar: Malar Padhippu.

Karunakaran, Krishnamoorthy, and C. Sivashanmugan. 1981. Study of Social Dialects in Tamil. Annamalai Nagar: All Indian Tamil Linguistics Association.

Keane, Elinor. 2007. Distribution and Alignment of F0 Contours in Tamil. Paper presented at the 16th International Congress of Phonetic Sciences Satellite Workshop, Säarbrucken, Germany, August 6–10.

Keane, Webb. 2003. Semiotics and the Social Analysis of Material Things. Language and Communication 23(3–4): 409–425.

Keane, Webb. 2007. Christian Moderns. Berkeley: University of California Press.

Khan, I. H. 2000. Minority Languages and Mother Tongue Teaching in Asia, with Special Reference to India. *In* Linguistic Heritage of India and Asia. Omkar N. Koul and L. Devaki, eds., pp. 7–12. Mysore, Central Institute of Indian Languages.

Kirshenblatt-Gimblett, Barbara. 2004. Intangible Heritage as Metacultural Production. Museum International 56(1–2): 52–65.

Kirshenblatt-Gimblett, Barbara. 2006. World Heritage and Cultural Economies. *In* Museum Frictions: Public Cultures/Global Transformations. Ivan Karp, Corinne

A. Kratz, Lynn Szwaja, and Tomás Ybarra-Frausto, eds., pp. 161–202. Durham, NC: Duke University Press.

Kockelman, Paul. 2006. A Semiotic Ontology of the Commodity. Journal of Linguistic Anthropology 16(1): 75–102.

Krishnan, Ramaiyer A. 2004. Spoken Tamil Grammar Book, vol. 1. Chennai: Giri Trading Agency.

Kroskrity, Paul V., ed. 2000. Regimes of Language: Ideologies, Polities, and Identities. Santa Fe, NM: School of American Research Press.

Kulick, Don, and Bambi B. Schieffelin. 2004. Language Socialization. *In* A Companion to Linguistic Anthropology. Alessandro Duranti, ed., pp. 349–368. Malden, MA: Blackwell.

Labov, William. 1963. The Social Motivation of a Sound Change. Word 19(3): 273–309.

LaDousa, Chaise. 2002. Advertising in the Periphery: Languages and Schools in a North Indian City. Language in Society 31(2): 213–242.

Lalonde, Michèle. 1979. Défense et illustration de la langue québécoise: Suivie de prose & poèmes. Paris: Serghers/Laffont.

Lamarre, Patricia, Julia Paquette, Emmanuel Kahn, and Sophie Ambrosi. 2002. Multilingual Montreal: Listening in on the Language Practices of Young Montrealers. Canadian Ethnic Studies 34(3): 47–75.

Lamarre, Patricia, and Diane Dagenais. 2004. Language Practices of Trilingual Youth in Two Canadian Cities. *In* Trilingualism in Family, School and Community. Charlotte Hoffman and Jehannes Ytsma, eds., pp. 53–74. North York: Multilingual Matters Ltd.

Langlois, Simon, Jean-Paul Baillargeon, Gary Caldwell, Guy Féchet, Madeleine Gauthier, and Jean-Pierre Simard. 1990. La société québécoise en tendances, 1960–1990. Montréal: McGill-Queen University Press.

La Presse. 2004. Huit suspects arrêtés. La Presse, July 22: A11.

Laroche, Marcel. 1997. 15 Ressortissants Sri Lankais apprehendés. La Presse, December 4: A20.

Latour, Bruno. 1993. We Have Never Been Modern. Cambridge, MA: Harvard University Press.

Laurence, Jean-Marie. 1957. L'anglicism, problème social. La Press, June 22.

Lemco, Jonathan. 1992. Quebec's "Distinctive Character" and the Question of Minority Rights. *In* Language Loyalties: A Source Book on the Official English Controversy. James Crawford, ed., pp. 423–444. Chicago: University of Chicago Press.

Lempert, Michael, and Sabina Perrino. 2007. Entextualization and the Ends of Temporality. Language & Communication 27(3): 205–211.

Lesage, René. 1991. Norme et usage: L'Emploi de l'indicatif après bien que et quoique dans la presse québécoise. The French Review 65(1): 15–29.

Létourneau, Jocelyn. 2004. Le Québec, les québécois: Un parcours historique. Montréal: Fides, Musée de la Civilization.

Lévesque, Kathleen. 2001. De la contrainte à la suggestion: L'Office de la langue française abolira sa commission de terminologie. Le Devoir, June 14: A1.

Losonky, M. 1999. Introduction to Wilhelm von Humboldt "On Language." Cambridge: Cambridge University Press.

Makihara, Miki, and Bambi B. Schieffelin, eds. 2007. Consequences of Contact: Language Ideologies and Sociocultural Transformations in Pacific Societies. New York: Oxford University Press.

Manor, James. 2001. Center-State Relations. *In* The Success of India's Democracy. Atul Kohli, ed., pp. 78–102. Cambridge: Cambridge University Press.

Marcil-Gratton, Nicole, and Evelyne Lapierre-Adamcyk. 1983. Sterilization in Quebec. Family Planning Perspectives 15(2): 73–78.

Marmen, Louise, and Jean-Pierre Corbeil. 1999. Languages in Canada 1996 Census: New Canadian Perspectives. Official Languages Support Program. Ottawa: Department of Canadian Heritage.

McAndrew, Marie. 1991. L'Enseignement des langues d'origine à l'école publique en Ontario et Québec (1977–1989): Politiques et enjeux. Montréal: Les publications de la faculté des sciences de l'éducation.

McAndrew, Marie, and Simone Gress-Azzam. 1987. Evaluations des services offerts dans le cadre du PELO et de son impact sur les élèves et sur les écoles. Montréal: Commission des écoles catholiques de Montréal.

McDowell, Christopher. 1996. A Tamil Asylum Diaspora: Sri Lanka Migration, Settlement and Politics in Switzerland. Providence and Oxford: Berghahn Books.

McGilvray, Dennis. 2001. Tamils and Muslim Identities in the East. Colombo: Marga Institute.

McGilvray, Dennis. 2008. Crucible of Conflict: Tamil and Muslim Society on the East Coast of Sri Lanka. Durham, NC, and London: Duke University Press.

McNicoll, Claire. 1993. Montreal: Une société multiculturelle. Paris: Belin.

Meek, Barbra. 2010. We Are Our Language: An Ethnography of Language Revitalization in a Northern Athabaskan Community. Tucson: University of Arizona Press.

Meintel, Deirdre, with Victor Piché, Danielle Juteau, and Sylvie Fortin. 1997. Le Quartier Côte-des-Neiges à Montréal: Les interfaces de la pluriethnicité. Paris: L'Harmattan.

Mendoza-Denton, Norma. 2008. Homegirls: Language and Cultural Practice among Latina Youth Gangs. Malden, MA: Blackwell.

Meney, Lionel. 2004. Parler français comme un vrai québécois? Le Devoir, January 7, 2004.

Meney, Lionel. 2005a. La soirée des Jutra: La francophonie ou la joualophonie? Le Devoir, February 23: A6.

Meney, Lionel. 2005b. La langue de chez nous. Le Soleil, April 6: A17.

Merry, Sally Engle. 2011. Measuring the World: Indicators, Human Rights, and Global Governance. Current Anthropology 52(3): S83–S95.

Milroy, Leslie. 2001. Britain and the United States: Two Nations Divided by the Same Language (and Different Language Ideologies). Journal of Linguistic Anthropology 10(1): 56–89.

Mines, Diane P. 2005. Fierce Gods: Inequality, Ritual, and the Politics of Dignity in a South Indian Village. Bloomington: Indiana University Press.

Ministère de l'Éducation, de Loisir et du Sport du Québec. 2008. Les langues d'origine dans le système scolaire québécois. Présentation aux 21e Entretiens du Centre Jacques-Cartier. http://74.125.155.132/search?q=cache:MvZ35D4ito YJ:www.chereum.umontreal.ca/activites_pdf/JacinthePELO2008.10.30.ppt+pelo+quebec+langues+d%27origine&cd=2&hl=en&ct=clnk&gl=ca&client=firefox-a., accessed November 1, 2009.

Mitra, A. 1956. Census of India, 1951: Village-Wise Mother-Tongue Data for Certain Selected Border Thanas of Midnapur, Malda, West Dinajpur, and Darjeeling Districts, West Bengal. S.O.C. Operations, Office of the Superintendent of Census Operations.

Mougeon, Raymond, and Edouard Beniak. 1994. Présentation. *In* Les origines du français québécois. Raymond Mougeon and Edouard Beniak, eds., pp 1–55. Sainte-Foy: Les Presses de L'Université Laval.

Mousset, Louis-Marie, and Louis-Savinien Dupuy. 1895. Preface. *In* Dictionnaire Tamoul-Français. Louis-Marie Mousset and Louis-Savinien Dupuy, eds., pp. v–xxiii. Pondichéry: Imprimerie de la Mission. (reprinted) Aix-en-Provence, France: Archives nationales d'outre-mer.

Myers, Fred. 2004. Ontologies of the Image and Economies of Exchange. American Ethnologist 31(1): 5–20.

Nadeau, Jean-Benoît, and Julie Barlow. 2007. Le français change. . . .et dérange! Il existe très peu d'écart dans la maîtrise générale d'écrit en langue française entre maintenant et "le bon vieux temps." La Presse, November 8: A25.

Nakassis, Constantine V., and Melanie A. Dean. 2007. Desire, Youth, and Realism in Tamil Cinema. Journal of Linguistic Anthropology 17(1): 77–104.

Natarajan, Swaminathan. 2012. The Hazardous Journeys of Sri Lankan Tamil Refugees. BBC News, April 19. http://www.bbc.com/news/world-asia-16530218/, accessed July 9, 2014.

Nesiah, Devanesan. 2001. Tamil Nationalism. Colombo, Marga Institute.

Oakes, Leigh, and Jane Warren. 2007. Language, Citizenship and Identity in Quebec. Hampshire and New York: Palgrave.

O'Bryan, Kenneth, Jeffrey Reitz, and Olga Kuplowska. 1976. *Non-official Languages: A Study in Canadian Multiculturalism*. Ottawa: Minister Responsible for Multiculturalism.

Olender, Maurice. 1992. The Cycle of the Chosen Peoples: J. G. Herder. *In* The Languages of Paradise: Race, Religion, and Philology in the Nineteenth Century. Translated by Arthur Goldhammer, pp. 37–50. Cambridge, MA: Harvard University Press.

Ondaatje, Anusha. 2005. Tigers Build Houses, Wait for Tsunami Aid. http://www.tamilguardian.com/article.asp?articleid=428, accessed May 30, 2012.

Opinion. 2008. Retour à la dictée. La Nouvelliste (Trois-Rivières), March 12: 9.

Our Lady of Deliverance. n.d. Our Lady of Deliverance. http://www.ourladyofdeliverance.com/en/, accessed August13, 2014.

Paillé, Michel. 2007. Diagnostic démographique de l'état de la francisation au Québec. Rapport à la Commission de consultation sur les pratiques d'accommodements reliés au différences culturels. Montréal, http://www.accommodements.qc.ca/documentation/rapports/rapport-7-paille-michel.pdf.

Pandian, Anand. 2007. Culture, Cultivation, and Civility in the Tamil Country. *In* History and Imagination: Tamil Culture in the Global Context. Rudhramoorthy Cheran, Darshan Ambalavanar, and Chelva Kanaganayakam, eds., pp. 48–62. Toronto: TSAR Publications.

Pandian, J. 1987. Caste, Nationalism and Ethnicity: An Interpretation of Tamil Cultural History and Social Order. Bombay: Popular Prakashan.

Papen, Robert A. 1998. French Canadian Varieties. *In* Language in Canada. John Edwards, ed., pp. 160–176. Cambridge: Cambridge University Press.

Paquot, Annette. 1992. Le français à la dérive: Comment en sommes-nous arrivés jusque là? La Presse, February 12: B3.

Paquot, Annette. 2001. Conception identitaire de la langue et enseignement du français. La Presse, March 14: A17.

Park, Seong Man, and Mela Sarkar. 2007. Parents' Attitudes toward Heritage Language Maintenance for Their Children and Their Efforts to Help Their Children Maintain the Heritage Language: A Case of Korean-Canadian Immigrants. Language, Culture and Curriculum 20(3): 223–235.

Pattanayak, Debi Prasanna. 1981. Multilingualism and Mother-Tongue Education. Delhi: Oxford University Press.

Peebles, Patrick. 1990. Colonization and Ethnic Conflict in the Dry Zone of Sri Lanka. The Journal of Asian Studies 49(1): 30–55.

Peebles, Patrick. 2001. The Plantation Tamils of Ceylon. London: Leicester University Press.

Peirce, Charles S. 1955 [1902]. Logic as Semiotic: The Principles of Phenomenology. *In* Philosophical Writings of Peirce. Justus Buchler, ed., pp. 98–115. New York: Dover Publications.

Pelchat, Martin. 1991. A la suite d'une saisie record, deux Sri- Lankais sont accusés de trafic d'héroïne. La Presse, January 19: A7.

Pfaffenberger, Bryan. 1994. Introduction: The Sri Lankan Tamils. *In* The Sri Lankan Tamils: Ethnicity and Identity. Chelvadurai Manogaran and Bryan Pfaffenberger, eds., pp. 1–27. Boulder: Westview Press.

Piché, Victor. 2002. Immigration, Diversity and Ethnic Relations in Quebec. Canadian Ethnic Studies 34(3): 5–27.

Pillai, M. Shanmugam. 1965. Merger of Literary and Colloquial Tamil. Anthropological Linguistics 7(4): 98–103.

Poirier, Cécile. 2006. Parc Extension: Le renouveau d'un quartier d'intégration à Montréal. Les Cahiers du Gres 6(2): 51–68.

Pollock, Sheldon. 1998. The Cosmopolitan Vernacular. The Journal of Asian Studies 57(1): 6–37.

Pollock, Sheldon. 2006. The Language of the Gods in the World of Men: Sanskrit, Culture, and Power in Premodern India. Berkeley: University of California Press.

Première Chaîne. 2006. Tamil Tigers Extortion. Radio-Canada Radio, March 15.

Rajan, Theva. 1995. Tamil as Official Language: Retrospect and Prospect. Colombo: International Centre for Ethnic Studies.

Rajanayagam, Dagmar-Hellmann. 1994. Tamils and the Meaning of History. *In* The Sri Lankan Tamils: Ethnicity and Identity. Chelvadurai Manogaran and Bryan Pfaffenberger, eds., pp. 54–84. Boulder: Westview Press.

Rajasingham-Senanayake, Darini. 2001. Identity on the Borderline: Multicultural History in a Moment of Danger. Colombo: Marga Institute.

Ramaswamy, Sumathi. 1993. En/gendering Language: The Poetics of Tamil Identity. Comparative Studies in Society and History 35(4): 683–725.

Ramaswamy, Sumathi. 1997. Passions of the Tongue: Language Devotion in Tamil Nadu, 1891–1970. Berkeley: University of California Press.

Ramaswamy, Sumathi. 1998. Language of the People in the World of Gods: Ideologies of Tamil before the Nation. Journal of Asian Studies 57(1): 66–92.

Ramaswamy, Sumathi. 1999. The Demoness, the Maid, the Whore, and the Good Mother: Contesting the National Language in India. International Journal of the Sociology of Language 140: 1–28.

Ramaswamy, Sumathi. 2000. History at Land's End: Lemuria in Tamil Spatial Fables. The Journal of Asian Studies 59(3): 575–602.

Rao, Narasimha. 2000. Mother Tongue Education: Theory and Practice. Mysore: Central Institute of Indian Languages.

Régis, Amélie. 1999. Le petit Sri-Lankais qui a perdu sa mère verra enfin son père. La Presse, July 8: B10.

Renan, Ernest. 1990 [1882]. What Is a Nation? Trans. Martin Thom. *In* Nation and Narration. Homi Bhabha, ed., pp. 8–22. London: Routledge.

Romaine, Suzanne. 2001. Signs of Identity, Signs of Discord: Glottal Goofs and the Green Grocer's Glottal in Debates on Hawaiian Orthography. Journal of Linguistic Anthropology 12(2): 189–224.

Safran, William. 1991. Diasporas in Modern Societies: Myths of Homeland and Return. Diaspora: A Journal of Transnational Studies 1(1): 83–99.

Saiva Mission of Quebec, Canada. n.d. School of Heritage Studies. http://montrealmurugantemple.faithweb.com/custom.html, accessed May 27, 2008.

Salazar, Noel B., and Alan Smart. 2011. Introduction: Anthropological Takes on (Im) Mobility. Identities: Global Studies in Culture and Power. 18: i–ix.

Saletti, Robert. 1998. La langue nationale. Le Devoir, March 21: D6.

Sanctuaire Notre-Dame-de-Lourdes de Rigaud. n.d. Petite histoire du Sanctuaire. http://www.lourdesrigaud.ca/?page_id=10, accessed March 18, 2016.

Sarkar, Mela, and Lise Winer. 2006. Multilingual Codeswitching in Quebec Rap: Poetry, Pragmatics and Performativity. International Journal of Multilingualism 3(3): 173–192.

Sarkar, Mela, Bronwen Low, and Lise Winer. 2007. "Pour connecter avec le peeps": Québequicité and the Quebec Hip-Hop Community. *In* Identity and Second Language Learning: Culture, Inquiry, and Dialogic Activity in Educational Contexts. Miguel Mantero, ed., pp. 351–372. Charlotte, NC: Information Age Publishing.

Schalk, Peter. 1997. Historisation of the Martial Ideology of the Liberation Tigers of Tamil Ealam (LTTE). South Asia 20(2): 35–72.

Schauber, Holli, Pierrette L. Morissette, and Lorraine R. Langlois. 1995. The Second Language Component of Primary French Immersion Programs in Montreal, Quebec, Canada. Bilingual Research Journal 19(3–4): 525–536.

Schieffelin, Bambi B., Kathryn A. Woolard, and Paul V. Kroskrity, eds. 1998. Language Ideologies: Practice and Theory. Oxford: Oxford University Press.

Schiffman, Harold. 1978. Diglossia and Purity/Pollution in Tamil. Contributions to Asian Studies 11: 98–110.

Schiffman, Harold. 1998. Standardization or Restandardization: The Case for Standard "Spoken" Tamil. Language in Society 27(3): 359–385.

Schiffman, Harold. 1999. A Reference Grammar of Spoken Tamil. Cambridge: Cambridge University Press.

Schmitt, Thomas M. 2008. The UNESCO Concept of Safeguarding Cultural Heritage: Its Background and *Marrakchi* Roots. International Journal of Heritage Studies 14(2): 95–111.

Shastri, A. 1990. The Material Basis for Separatism: The Tamil Eelam Movement in Sri Lanka. The Journal of Asian Studies 49(1): 56–77.

Silverstein, Michael. 1979. Language Structure and Linguistic Ideology. *In* The Elements: A Parasession on Linguistic Units and Levels. Paul Clyne, William Hanks, and Carol L. Hofbauer, eds., pp. 193–247. Chicago: Chicago Linguists Society.

Silverstein, Michael. 1985. Language and the Culture of Gender: At the Intersection of Structure, Usage and Ideology. *In* Semiotic Mediation: Sociocultural and Psychological Perspectives. Elizabeth Mertz and Richard Parmentier, eds., pp. 219–259. Orlando, FL: Academic Press.

Silverstein, Michael. 1996. Encountering Language and Languages of Encounter in North American Ethnohistory. Journal of Linguistic Anthropology 6(2): 126–144.

Silverstein, Michael. 2003. Indexical Order and the Dialectics of Sociolinguistic Life. Language and Communication 23: 193–229.

Silverstein, Michael. 2005. Axes of Eval: Token versus Type Interdiscursivity. Journal of Linguistic Anthropology 15(1): 6–22.

Singaravélou, Pierre. 1991. Les Indiens de la Caraïbe. Vol. 3. Paris: Editions L'Harmattan.

Singer, Colin R. 2009. Quebec Immigration Rules: Economic Immigration Stream. Canada's Immigration and Citizenship Bulletin 20(7). http://www.immigration.ca/permres-qc-rules.asp, accessed June 30, 2010.

Sivam, Lenin M., dir. 2009. 1999. 101 min. Toronto: Khatpanalaya Production and Bagavan Productions.

Sivarajah, Ambalavanar. 1996. Politics of Tamil Nationalism in Sri Lanka. New Delhi: South Asian Publishers.

Sivashanmugam, C. 1981. Social Differentiation of Tamil in Coimbatore. Ph.D. Dissertation. Annamalai University.

Sivathamby, Karthigesu. 1995. Understanding Dravidian Movement: Problems and Perspectives. Madras: Kannapa Art Publishers.

Sivathamby, Karthigesu. 2005. Being a Tamil and Sri Lankan. Colombo: Aivakam.

Southworth, Franklin. 1975. Sociolinguistic Research in South India: Achievements and Prospects. *In* Essays on South India. Burton Stein, ed., pp. 181–205. Honolulu: University Press of Hawaii.

Srinivas, M. N. 1952. Religion and Society among the Coorgs of South India. Bombay: Asia Publishing House.

Statistics Canada. 1991a. Communauté Sri Lankaise du Québec.

Statistics Canada. 1991b. Communauté Sud-Asiatique du Québec.

Statistics Canada. 2001. Ethnic Origin (232), Sex (3) and Single and Multiple Responses (33) for Population, for Canada, Provinces, Territories, Census Metropolitan Areas 1 and Census Agglomerations, 2001 census–20% Sample Data.

Statistics Canada. 2006a. Census Families by Number of Children at Home, by Province and Territory (Quebec). http://www40.statcan.ca/l01/cst01/famil50f.htm, accessed March 14, 2008.

Statistics Canada. 2006b. Detailed Mother Tongue (103), Knowledge of Official Languages (5), Age Groups (17A) and Sex (3) for the Population of Canada, Provinces, Territories, Census Divisions and Census Subdivisions, 2006 Census–20% Sample Data Laval. http://www12.statcan.ca/english/census06/data/topics/RetrieveProductTable.cfm?ALEVEL=3&APATH=3&CATNO=&DETAIL=0&DIM=&DS=99&FL=0&FREE=0&GAL=0&GC=99&GK=NA&GRP=1&IPS=&METH=0&ORDER=1&PID=89202&PTYPE=88971&RL=0&S=1&ShowAll=No&StartRow=1&SUB=701&Temporal=2006&Theme=70&VID=0&VNAMEE=&VNAMEF=&GID=773015, accessed May 27, 2008.

Statistics Canada. 2006c. Immigrant Population by Place of Birth, by Census Metropolitan Area (2006 Census). http://www40.statcan.ca/l01/cst01/demo35b.htm, accessed on June 17, 2008.

Statistics Canada. 2007. 2006 Census: Immigration, Citizenship, Language, Mobility and Migration. Daily. http://www.statcan.ca/Daily/English/071204/d071204a.htm, accessed May 27, 2008.

Subramanian, Narendra. 1999. Ethnicity and Populist Mobilization: Political Parties, Citizens and Democracy in South India. Delhi, Oxford University Press.

Sumathy, S. 2001. Militants, Militarism, and the Crisis of (Tamil) Nationalism. Colombo: Marga Institute.

Suseendirarajah, S. 1970. Reflections of Certain Social Differences in Jaffna Tamil. Anthropological Linguistics 12(7): 239–245.

Tamilagam. n.d. Tamilagam. http://www.tamilagam.org, accessed on January 15, 2007.

Tamilnation. 2007. Tamils: A Trans State Nation. http://tamilnation.co/diaspora/index.htm, accessed July 12, 2008.

Tamilnet. 2005. LTTE Invites Poets to Compose Thamileelam National Anthem, Tamilnet. October 27. http://www.tamilnet.com/art.html?catid=13&artid=16192, accessed July 28, 2014.

Tamilnet. 2006. SLA Closes Vavuniya, Uyilankulam, Madhu Checkpoints. http://www.tamilnet.com/art.html?catid=13&artid=19203, accessed on April 9, 2008.

Tamilnet. 2007. Norwegian Tamils Protest against Sri Lankan Rights Violation. http://www.tamilnet.com/art.html?catid=13&artid=23269, accessed October 1, 2007.

Tamilnet. 2008a. A Church in Madu Destroyed, Dreaded Stage of Ethnic Cleansing. http://www.tamilnet.com/art.html?catid=13&artid=25240, accessed April 8, 2008.

Tamilnet. 2008b. LTTE Urges Norway to Take Steps to End Military Assault on Madu Shrine. http://www.tamilnet.com/art.html?catid=13&artid= 25231, accessed April 7, 2008.

Tamilnet. 2008c. "Sinhala Regime Transforming Holy Land into Battlefield": LTTE Political Head. http://www.tamilnet.com/art.html?catid= 13&artid=25196, accessed April 8, 2008.

Tamilnet. 2008d. The Temporal and Spiritual Conquest of Tamils: Mahinda's Book of Dreams. http://www.tamilnet.com/art.html?catid=79 &artid=25197, accessed April 7, 2008.

Tasso, Lily. 1986. Montréal en accueillera la moitié [des réfugiés de la mer recueillis au large de Terre-Neuve]. La Presse, August 13.

Tasso, Lily. 2004. Terrorisme international au Canada. Le Devoir, December 24.

Thiranagama, Sharika. 2010. In Praise of Traitors: Intimacy, Betrayal, and the Sri Lankan Tamil Community. *In* Traitors: Suspicion, Intimacy, and the Ethics of State-Building. Sharika Thiranagama and Tobias Kelly, eds., pp. 127–149. Philadelphia: University of Pennsylvania Press.

Thiranagama, Sharika. 2011. In My Mother's House: Civil War in Sri Lanka. Philadelphia: University ofPennsylvania Press.

Thiru Murugan Temple. n.d. Thiru Murugan Temple, http://montrealmurugantemplefaithweb.com, accessed May 21, 2008.

Thurlow, Crispin, and Adam Jaworski. 2010. Silence Is Golden: Elitism, Linguascaping and "Anti-communication" in Luxury Tourism. *In* Semiotic Landscapes: Language, Image, Space. Adam Jaworski and Crispin Thurlow, eds., pp. 1–19. London: Continuum International Press.

Tran, Kelly, Jennifer Kaddatz, and Paul Allard. 2005. Social Asians in Canada: Unity through Diversity. Canadian Social Trends 11(8): 20–25.

Trautmann, Thomas R. 1997. Aryans and British India. New Delhi: Vistaar Publications.

Trautmann, Thomas R. 2005. The Aryan Debate. Oxford: Oxford University Press.

Trautmann, Thomas R. 2006. Languages and Nations: The Dravidian Proof in Colonial Madras. Berkeley: University of California Press.

Tremblay, Michel. 1972. Les belles-soeurs. Ottawa: Collection Théâtre Canadien, Léméac.

Trottier, Éric. 1998. Montréal et ses quartiers: Deux quartiers "oubliés" en un. La Presse, October 9: B6.

Tsing, Anna. 2000. The Global Situation. Cultural Anthropology 15(3): 327–360.

UNESCO. n.d.a. What Is Intangible Heritage? http://www.unesco.org/culture/ich/index.php?lg=en&pg=00002, accessed March 30, 2011.

UNESCO. n.d.b. Memory of the World Register: Classical Tamil Manuscript Collection of the Dr. U.V.S. Library. http://www.unesco.org/new/en/custom-search/?cx=000136296116563084670%3Ah14j45a1zaw&cof=FORID%3A9&ie=UTF-8&q=Memory+of+the+World+Register%3A+Classical+Tamil+Manuscript+Collection+of+the+Dr.+U.V.S.+Library&hl=en&sa=ok&siteurl=www.unesco.org%2Fnew%2Fen%2Fcommunication-and-information&ref=&ss=17j289j2, accessed June 10, 2009.

Vallières, Pierre. 1968. Nègres blancs d'Amérique. Montréal: TYPO.

Vanikam. 2008. Vanikam. http://www.vanikam.com/about_us.php, accessed on May 19, 2008.

Vecchiato, Sara. 2000. The *Ti/Tu* Interrogative Morpheme in Québec French. Generative Grammar in Geneva 1: 114–163.

Vercier, Bruno. 1988. La "dés-oralisation" dans les romans de Michel Tremblay. Écrivains québécois–dossiers (L'Île), January 1.

Weiner, Myron. 2001. The Struggle for Equality: Caste in Indian Politics. *In* The Success of India's Democracy. Atul Kohli, ed., pp. 193–225. Cambridge: Cambridge University Press.

Westhead, Rick. 2014. Canadian Tamil Congress wins $53,000 Libel Judgment. http://www.thestar.com/news/world/2014/02/20/canadian_tamil_congress_wins_53000_libel_judgment.html, accessed on July 28, 2014.

Whitaker, Mark. 2006. Internet *Counter* Counter-Insurgency: Tamilnet.com and Ethnic Conflict in Sri Lanka. *In* Native on the Net: Indigenous and Diasporic Peoples in the Virtual Age. Kyra Landzelius, ed., pp. New York: Routledge.

White, Chantal. 2014. Broadcasting the Voices of Pluralism in Québec: Language Ideology and Choice in Montreal's Haitian Radioscape. Ph.D. Dissertation, Department of Anthropology, New York University.

Whiteman, Dominic. n.d. LTTE "Tamil Tigers" and Its UK-Wide Network. http://www.sinhale.com/Tamil%20Tigers%20and%20its%20UK%20wide%20 network.htm, accessed October 1, 2007.

Woolard, Kathryn. 1989. Simultaneity and Bivalency as Strategies in Bilingualism. Journal of Linguistic Anthropology 8(1): 3–29.

Woolard, Kathryn. 1998. Introduction: Language Ideology as a Field of Inquiry. *In* Language Ideologies: Practice and Theory. Bambi Schieffelin, Kathryn Woolard, and Paul Kroskrity, eds., pp. 3–30. Oxford: Oxford University Press.

Woolard, Kathryn A. 2004. Is the Past a Foreign Country? Time, Language Origins, and the Nation in Early Modern Spain. Journal of Linguistic Anthropology 14(1): 57–80.

Woolard, Kathryn. 2011. Is There Linguistic Life after High School? Longitudinal Changes in the Bilingual Repertoire in Metropolitan Barcelona. Language in Society 40(5): 671–648.

Woolard, Kathryn, and Bambi B. Schieffelin. 1994. Language Ideology. Annual Review of Anthropology 23: 55–82.

Wortham, Stanton. 2004. From Good Student to Outcast: The Social Emergence of a Classroom Identity. Journal for the Society of Psychological Anthropology. 32(2): 164–187.

Zvelebil, Kamil Veith. 1959a. Dialects of Tamil-I. Archiv Orientalni 27: 272–317.

Zvelebil, Kamil Veith. 1959b. Dialects of Tamil-II. Archiv Orientalni 27: 572–603.

Zvelebil, Kamil Veith. 1960a. Dialects of Tamil-III. Archiv Orientalni 28: 220–224.

Zvelebil, Kamil Veith. 1960b. Dialects of Tamil-IV. Archiv Orientalni 28: 414–456.

Zvelebil, Kamil Veith. 1961. Some Features of Dindigul Tamil. T. P. M. Manivilaimalar. Coimbatore: 424–426.

Zvelebil, Kamil Veith. 1964. Spoken Languages of Tamil Nadu. Archiv Orientalni 32; 237–264.

Zvelebil, Kamil Veith. 1995. Lexicon of Tamil Literature. Handbuch der Orientalistik, zweite Abteilung: Indien, Band 9. Leiden: E. J. Brill.

INDEX

CPSIA information can be obtained
at www.ICGtesting.com
Printed in the USA
BVHW030003151119
563908BV00002B/3/P

9 780190 461782